PRIMA Official Game Guide

Written by:
VG SPORTS
(Bert Ingley, Jon Faulkner, Paul Gleason, Ron Jackson, Bernie Hayes, & Clifton Gilmore)

Prima Games
An Imprint of Random House, Inc.
3000 Lava Ridge Court, Suite 100
Roseville, CA 95661
www.primagames.com

D1314364

The Prima Games logo is a registered trademark of Random House, Inc., registered in the United States and other countries. Primagames.com is a registered trademark of Random House, Inc., registered in the United States. Prima Games is an imprint of Random House, Inc.

Design & Layout: Bryan Neff, Jody Seltzer
Copyedit: Deana Shields
Manufacturing: Stephanie Sanchez & Suzanne Goodwin

This guide would not have been possible without the support of Ari Ratner, Matthew Bialosuknia, Phil Frazier, Jeremy Strauser, Lorraine Honrada, Daniel Davis, Michelle Manahan, Randy Hembrador, Robert Bierman, Carlos Moreira, Brett Harris, Shaun Kiggens, Forrest Tarleton and Jim Stadelman.

Important:
Prima Games has made every effort to determine that the information contained in this book is accurate. However, the publisher makes no warranty, either expressed or implied, as to the accuracy, effectiveness, or completeness of the material in this book; nor does the publisher assume liability for damages, either incidental or consequential, that may result from using the information in this book. The publisher cannot provide any additional information or support regarding gameplay, hints and strategies, or problems with hardware or software. Such questions should be directed to the support numbers provided by the game and/or device manufacturers as set forth in their documentation. Some game tricks require precise timing and may require repeated attempts before the desired result is achieved.

ISBN: 978-0-307-46744-7
Library of Congress Catalog Card Number: 2010932110
Printed in the United States of America

08 09 10 11 MM 10 9 8 7 6 5 4 3 2 1

CONTENTS

HOW TO USE THIS GUIDE

Our guide will show you the fundamentals of playing the game all the way through creating advanced schemes to dominate the competition. Here's how we have organized all of the information in this guide for easy reference:

Chapter 1: New Features

explains all of the exciting new features that have been added to *Madden NFL 11* this season like GameFlow, Catch Tuning, Locomotion and Assignment AI.

Chapter 2: Offensive Strategy

will help you learn to have a successful running game and master the skills you need to have a devastating aerial attack.

Chapter 3: Defensive Strategy

will teach you the foundation of building a lock down defense. We'll teach you all the defensive options at your disposal, plus teach you how to shut down the run and unleash killer blitzes.

Chapter 4: Advanced Strategies

is about taking your game to the next level. Learn how to attack different types of coverages as well as put together blitz schemes to get after the quarterback.

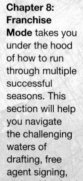

Chapter 5: Making Defensive Adjustments

helps you learn various defensive schemes to knock the stuffing out of any offense. From defending the outside run to the flats and screens, this chapter has you covered.

Chapter 6: Team Strategy

is an in-depth break down of all 32 NFL Teams. This section has complete offensive and defensive scouting reports, playbook breakdowns, and easy to read depth charts.

Chapter 7: Playbook Breakdown

takes a hard look at six offensive playbooks with seven plays each. Balanced, Pass Balanced, Run Balanced, Run Heavy, West Coast and Run N Gun.

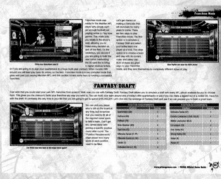

Chapter 8: Franchise Mode

takes you under the hood of how to run through multiple successful seasons. This section will help you navigate the challenging waters of drafting, free agent signing, and making trades so that you can build the next NFL dynasty.

Chapter 9: Roster Attributes

gives you the top players at every position along with their key ratings. This is an invaluable resource for players that like to use the Fantasy Draft feature of Franchise Mode.

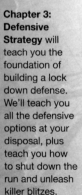

NEW FEATURES

Simpler. Quicker. Deeper. These three words are the focal point of everything that is new and improved in *Madden NFL 11*. EA SPORTS continues on its quest to make the *Madden NFL* series the most realistic football gaming experience ever. Pro-Tak™ returns, but with the addition of new Locomotion changes, it's even better than ever. Let's dive right in and take a look at what's been added to *Madden NFL 11*.

GameFlow and Game Planning

Rate that play high

In sitting down with various NFL advisors, including John Madden himself, the EA SPORTS team was challenged to take a closer look at the way they present play calling to the user. The result was one of the biggest changes in the many years of the *Madden NFL* football franchise, with the introduction of GameFlow and Game Planning. The days of scrolling through over 300 plays to find that one play you need for any given situation are over.

With GameFlow, plays are sent to you over your headset from your coordinator, just like on Sundays. Now you don't have to spend as much time looking through your playbook, and you can spend more time playing the game. You can always come up to the line and pull a Peyton Manning by making line adjustments and audibles with your Strategy Pad. You can use GameFlow for the entire game, or at anytime you can choose to pull from your entire playbook. With the use of GameFlow, the time it takes to play a game has

been cut almost in half, giving gamers the ability to enjoy more games in the same period of time.

The key behind GameFlow is Game Planning. Game Planning allows you to script your best plays for any given situation in the game. Each team in *Madden NFL 11* has a team-specific Game Plan that best utilizes that team's best players and strengths. Before any game, you can change your team's Game Plan to better fit the style that you want to play.

You have 15 play slots available for each situation. For each play in any situation, you can adjust the weighting of the play from one-half to five stars. The higher you rate a play, the more often that play will be called in the game. Make sure that your favorite money plays have a five-star rating.

GameFlow and Game Planning carry over to the defensive side of the ball as well. Plays will be called in over your headset to match up against the personnel and formation that the offense is coming out in.

One of the best parts of GameFlow and Game Planning is that you can take your Game Plan into Franchise, Superstar, Online, Madden Ultimate Team, and Play Now modes. This allows you to speed up the game in every way you play. We will cover more details about GameFlow and Game Planning later in the guide.

Catch Tuning

In *Madden NFL 11* there has been much focus put into making the game look and feel as real as possible. This year the franchise has made huge improvements in the passing game with Catch Tuning. In implementing Catch Tuning the *Madden NFL* developers were able to change every aspect of how a receiver interacts with his surroundings— everything from the way the receiver is bumped at the line by a defender to how he dives to catch a touchdown pass. Let's jump into Catch Tuning and break it down so you can see how it affects the way you play *Madden NFL 11*.

Receiver animations have been changed in many different areas to correct a few issues that you may have encountered in years past. The first area that Catch Tuning corrected was sideline and end zone animations. It was always frustrating when you would have a receiver open in the flats, and instead of picking up extra yardage he would toe tap and fall down thinking that he was about to go out of bounds. This issue has been fixed, so now the receiver catches the ball with awareness of where he is on the field and turns it downfield for extra yards.

Another crucial area that was corrected with Catch Tuning relates to curls and other routes that have a receiver come back for the ball. For example, when you need 3 yards for a first down, you would think that throwing a 5-yard curl would do the trick. But last year the receivers would aggressively come back to the ball, which unfortunately would cut the route too short. In *Madden NFL 11*, players still work to get to the ball, but now they are mindful of first down yardage and won't come back too far. Your receiver will now sprint down the field, pin his defender on his back, and hold him off until the ball gets there, to ensure that you get the yardage you need. You will also notice this come into play on screen passes.

These are only a few areas where Catch Tuning has made a huge impact in creating one of the best football games of all time. Now get out on the field and utilize your aerial attack with confidence, knowing that your receivers are going to hold up to whatever you throw at them.

Fitzgerald to the corner

Listen up, here's the play

Locomotion

Now that we have covered how receivers catch the ball, let's talk about a new feature called Locomotion. Locomotion was created in this year's game to give the players a more realistic and lifelike feel when running on the field. This new feature affects three key areas: acceleration, momentum, and direction change.

In the spin cycle

Acceleration has always been an overlooked rating when it came to the *Madden NFL* series. Gamers typically just looked a player's speed, and pretty much ignored acceleration as a rating. This has all changed with the introduction of Locomotion. Now players with high acceleration ratings will be noticeably faster from the line of scrimmage than players with low acceleration ratings. Players with high acceleration will be capable of hitting a hole in the line or beating a defender for a quick hit much better this year. Overall speed will come into play once the players are up to speed and sprinting down the field, but that quick burst may be all you need to get open against a defender.

The next two critical components of the new Locomotion system are momentum and direction change. With Locomotion, a player's ability to cut or spin in different directions at full speed is a thing of the past. A player's agility now determines how much speed he loses when he cuts, spins, and jukes on the field. Trying to make hard cuts while running at full speed can cause a player to stumble or possibly even trip and fall. On the other hand, while not sprinting a player can cut in any direction with little affect on his forward momentum.

With Locomotion, a player's moves on the field look and feel more realistic. Now you will be able to feel the difference between controlling a big heavy lineman and controlling a quick, agile running back coming out of the backfield.

EA SPORTS added a new setting called **auto-sprint** to help players get used to the new Locomotion system. With auto-sprint enabled, you don't have to hold down the Sprint button for your user-controlled player to sprint. The in-game AI will cause your player to sprint based on need. If you are working quick cuts through the line, your player won't sprint (a common error made by new players). Once you break into the open field, your player will accelerate to full speed.

Assignment AI

The *Madden NFL* series has almost always been a predominantly passing game, but that may all change with the introduction of the Assignment AI. The run blocking in this year's game has been completely reworked to bring you realistic blocking schemes based on real life run-blocking rules. Double-team blocks, scrapping to the second level, and back blocks on counters and Power O plays are all represented in the game. With the new run-blocking AI you can have an effective, if not dominating, run game to go along with your passing attack.

All of the blocking rules in *Madden NFL 11* have been rewritten to match the rules that teams use in the NFL. These new rules can be seen in many different areas on the field. We will provide a detailed look at Assignment AI in the "Running Controls" of the guide, but let's give you a quick look right now.

The first rule you will notice is double-teaming. Offensive linemen double-team defensive tackles on most inside run plays, like HB Dive, to create a bigger hole for the running back to run through. This run-blocking rule ensures that the defensive tackle doesn't stop your running back for a loss (unless you are facing an elite tackle who has a high block shedding rating).

Assignment AI rules don't just help out with runs up the middle. On Toss or Stretch plays you will notice an entirely new set of blocking rules that will help your running back bounce the ball to the outside and take the ball to the house. Outside run plays are all about how the offensive tackle and the tight end work together to seal the end of the defensive line. With these new run-blocking rules in effect, go out and pound the ball!

Sproles turning it up the field

Double-team engaged

EA SPORTS

MADDEN NFL 11

OFFENSIVE STRATEGY

Contents

RUNNING CONTROLS

Juke

Xbox 360: ⓡ in the direction you want to go

Playstation 3: ⓡ in the direction you want to go

Turner makes a quick cutback inside

The running moves this season are really sick. If you learn to use these moves correctly your rushing attack will be very hard to defend against. The juke is a great move for making a quick change of direction once the defender has committed to his angle. The good thing about this move is that you won't lose any speed when you apply this move. The key is timing and making sure you hit the juke at the right time. When this is done correctly you can gain another 5 yards on the ground or more. Remember that when you make one juke you need to gain 5 yards.

Spin

Xbox 360: ⓑ

Playstation 3: ●

Turner makes a spin move inside

The spin move is back and better than ever before. This is another great way to change direction while running to abuse a defender who is overly aggressive when attempting to tackle you. This move is great when you have a blocker up front and you see a cutback lane to hit. When timed correctly, the spin sometimes allows you to break tackles.

The rule for the juke applies here: If you make a spin move you have to obtain 5 yards. Your goal is to get downfield. That tap dancing will get you in bad down and distance. If you make a move, always push for no less than 5 extra yards.

Stiff Arm

Xbox 360: ⓐ

Playstation 3: ✕

A.P. is guilty as charged for strong-arm assault

The stiff arm is a no-nonsense move that when applied can take the defender out of the play completely. The problem with this move is that you lose momentum. The positive thing is that if no other defender is near or you have a lead blocker you will get an excellent gain.

Highlight Stick

Xbox 360: ⓡ

Playstation 3: ⓡ

A.P. blows up the defender

The highlight stick is a great quick move, and it's based on the player's ability. If the player is a power back he will run through the defender. If he's a finesse player he will slip past the defender. When you have a player like Adrian Peterson you get a combo of both. In this case, A.P. blew the defender up with no problem. The timing of this move can make or break a big play for you. You will slow down a bit, but not as much as if you stiff arm the defender.

Cover Up

Xbox 360: ⓡⓑ

Playstation 3: ⓡ1

A.P. has a low carry to protect that rock

When you're in close quarters and about to get hit you need to get in the habit of covering up the ball. A player like A.P. fumbles often. The CPU will make an attempt to strip the ball if you're stood up by other defenders. Make sure you secure the ball because a fumble can be a game changer.

Hard Cut

Xbox 360: ⓛ in the direction you want to go

Playstation 3: ⓛ in the direction you want to go

About to break ankles

This is one of the best additions to the game. You can now use both analog sticks in the running game, and the left analog stick allows you to make hard cuts and change direction.

Ouch—he could go all the way

You need to master the left analog stick because it can help you break off long runs.

High Step

Xbox 360: ⓡ

Playstation 3: ⓡ

Looking to cut back inside

The back juke has been replaced with the high knees. This allows the runner to chop in place and make another move away from the defender. This move is done when you hit down on the right analog stick.

PASSING CONTROLS

Learning the passing controls is essential if you plan on having a potent passing attack. Those who have played *Madden NFL* over the years will find themselves right at home as nothing has changed in *Madden NFL 11*. Those new to the game will want to read through this section to learn the ins and outs.

Bullet and Lob Passes

Two types of passes can be thrown in *Madden NFL:* bullet and lob passes. A bullet pass has the quarterback throwing a low fast pass to the intended receiver.

A hard bullet pass is thrown to the open receiver

This type of pass is generally thrown on short to intermediate routes, although it can be used on deep routes as well. To throw a bullet pass, press the receiver's pass icon button and hold it until the quarterback throws the ball.

The QB puts a lot of air on the ball

The other type of pass is a lob pass. This is generally thrown deep when trying to get some air on the ball so that the intended receiver can have time to chase it down. The bullet pass is harder to user catch than a lob pass. The bullet pass is also harder for the defense to pick off than the lob pass.

Pass Receiver Icons

Each receiver icon is a different color

When a receiver is open and you want to throw to him, press the button that corresponds to that receiver. Don't drop too far back; if you do, the pass icons will disappear. You will then be on your own to determine what the receivers' pass icons are. This was done so players would not drop the quarterback so far back.

Pass Lead

Xbox 360: ❶ in any direction   Playstation 3: ❶ in any direction

Learning to use pass lead can make a big difference when throwing the ball, especially when throwing into tight spots. You can lead the intended receiver by pressing one of four directions on the left thumbstick. Which direction is pressed determines the type of pass thrown. When you press up on the left thumbstick, the quarterback will throw a high pass to the intended receiver. When you press down on the left thumbstick, the quarterback will throw a low pass to the intended receiver.

Brees leads the receiver inside

When you press right or left on the left thumbstick, the quarterback will throw an inside or outside pass to the intended receiver.

Pump Fake

Many top players use the pump fake to draw the safeties away from where they want to throw the ball to.

The pump fake freezes a few defenders

For instance, say you pump fake to the right; the quarterback will act like he is going to throw the ball. If you're lucky, the safeties will bite and go towards the pump fake direction. If this happens, you should have more space to the left to complete the pass.

Sprint

The QB sprints out looking for an open receiver

The Sprint button can still be used when in control of the quarterback. It is useful when trying to avoid the blitz, rolling out, or just looking to take off and run with the quarterback for positive yardage on the ground. As your quarterback is about to be tackled, make sure to use the Slide button to get him down to the ground to avoid fumbling or being injured.

Throw Away

Use the Throw Away button when no receiver is open down the field, rather than trying to force the pass into tight coverage.

The QB throws the ball out of bounds to avoid the sack

Another reason to use the Throw Away button would be to avoid being sacked. Make sure when using the Throw Away button that you do it when the quarterback is outside the pocket; otherwise you will be flagged for intentional grounding.

Taking Control of the Quarterback

When you're controlling the quarterback, while he's dropping back to pass you can't move him until he takes his last initial step. For instance, on shorter passes, he takes a three-step drop.

The pocket forms as the QB drops back

After his third step, you can take control of him. On deeper throws, the quarterback takes a seven-step drop; thus you cannot take control of him until after his seventh step. If you want to take control sooner but want to run deep passing plays, try calling short pass plays and then hot routing the receivers on streaks and fades. That way you can take control of him earlier while still running deeper passing routes.

9

OFFENSIVE PRE-SNAP CONTROLS

In this year's game, the offensive pre-snap controls have been redefined with the new addition of the **Strategy Pad**. Both veterans and newcomers should read this section to get up to speed quickly in *Madden NFL 11*.

Audibles

How many times have you played an opponent and been faced with an offensive or defensive scheme that spells certain disaster for you? You immediately audible out of your play, only to find that the default audibles for that particular playbook are all but useless to help you counter what your opponent is doing. This has happened to us all at one point or another.

Usually when this occurs you're forced to call a timeout, go with your original play call, or audible to a play that you've probably never used before. Each scenario will most likely have a negative effect on your team. In times like these, having a good audible system can save you many moments of frustration.

The word "audible," in football terms, simply means to change the play that was called in the huddle to a different one once at the line of scrimmage. Both the offense and defense can use audibles as a way to adjust to a specific situation that may present itself during a game.

There are two types of audibles in *Madden NFL 11*. There are five that you choose (user-set audibles), and there is another set with four predetermined plays set for each formation (pre-set audibles), generally consisting of a quick pass, a run, a deep pass, and a play action pass.

Steps to Execute Pre-Set Audibles

Scroll through to call an audible

1. Press the Audible button.
2. To select pre-set audibles, press left or right on the Strategy Pad or left thumbstick. Once the pre-set play you want is highlighted, press Ⓐ (Xbox 360) or ✕ (PS3) to select the play.

Steps to Execute User-Set Audibles

There are five audibles to choose from

1. Press the Audible button.
2. Press ✕ (Xbox 360) or ● (PS3) button.
3. Press the letter or symbol for the play that you want to audible to.

Hot Routes

Use hot routes to beat the defensive coverage

Steps to Execute Hot Routes

1. Press the Strategy Pad in any direction.
2. Press the Strategy Pad up to access hot routes.
3. Press the pass icon of the receiver you want to hot route.
4. Execute the command given in the following sections for the specific route you want.

Streak

The split end is sent on a streak

To execute: After you've accessed hot routes and selected the receiver, press the Strategy Pad up to hot route the receiver on a streak.

The streak hot route sends the selected receiver on a straight line down the field. It's best used when the receiver is matched up with a slower defensive back in one-on-one coverage. Once the receiver gets a few steps on the defensive back, throw the ball.

Curl

Curl routes work against man and zone coverage

To execute: After you've accessed hot routes and selected the receiver, press the Strategy Pad down to send the receiver on a curl.

The curl hot route sends the selected receiver up the field about 8 yards; then he curls back towards the quarterback. Use it when the defense is playing normal man coverage or soft zone coverage. Just as the receiver curls back, throw a high pass to him. Watch for defenders dropping back in buzz zones.

Out Right

Outs work against soft zone coverage

To execute: After you've accessed hot routes and selected the receiver, press the Strategy Pad right to hot route the receiver on an out or in to the right.

This hot route sends the selected receiver on a 5-yard out or 5-yard in depending on what side the receiver is lined up on. The out route works best when the defense plays soft zone. Once the receiver makes his cut toward the sideline, make the throw. Don't be late on the throw or it may be picked off. The in route works best when the defense plays man coverage. Once the receiver breaks over the middle, make the throw. Make sure the receiver has underneath position on the defender before making the throw.

Out Left

If the receiver lines up on the right, he will run an in route

To execute: After you've accessed hot routes and selected the receiver, press the Strategy Pad left to hot route the receiver on an out or in to the left.

The out left hot route sends the selected receiver on a 5-yard out or 5-yard in depending on what side the receiver is lined up on. Use the out route when the defense plays soft zone. Make the throw when the receiver makes his cut toward the sideline; don't be late or it could be picked off. Go for the in route when the defense plays man coverage. Once the receiver breaks over the middle, make the throw, but before you do make sure the receiver has underneath position on the defender.

Fade

Fade routes work best against zone coverage

To execute: After you've accessed hot routes and selected the receiver, press the right thumbstick up to hot route the receiver on a fade.

The hot routed receiver takes a few steps upfield, then heads towards the sideline before finally breaking straight up the field. This is best used against defenses that are in zone coverage. Look for the receiver once he breaks down the field. If you take control of the receiver as the ball is coming down, you can jump high for the ball if you time it right.

Drag

Drags work well against man coverage

To execute: After you've accessed hot routes and selected the receiver, press the right thumbstick down to send the receiver on a drag.

This hot route sends the selected receiver on a drag or shallow cross over the short middle of the field. His drag route can be changed to a flat route if the hot routed receiver is sent in motion to the opposite side of the field. It is best used for defenses that are in bump-n-run man coverage. Once the receiver breaks the jam, he often gets inside position on the defender. Once he does, make the throw. This hot route is also effective against zone coverage, and it's even more effective if another receiver runs a deep route above the drag route at the same time.

Slant Right

Use the slant to beat the blitz

To execute: After you've accessed hot routes and selected the receiver, press the right thumbstick right to hot route the receiver on a slant right or left depending on what side of the field he is lined up on.

On a slant, the hot routed receiver heads straight up the field about 2 yards and then takes a sharp cut at approximately a 45-degree angle towards the middle of the field. Use this hot route when the defense calls bump-n-run man coverage and a blitz is called. Wait for the receiver to break the jam at the line of scrimmage. Once he does, throw a hard bullet pass if the receiver has inside position.

Slant Left

If the receiver lines up on the left side, he runs a slant out

To execute: After you've accessed hot routes and selected the receiver, press the right thumbstick left to hot route the receiver on a slant right or left depending on what side of the field he is lined up on.

This hot route sends the selected receiver straight up the field about 2 yards. He then takes a sharp cut at an angle towards the middle of the field. It's best to use this hot route when the defense calls bump-n-run man coverage and a blitz. Wait for the receiver to break the jam at the line of scrimmage and then throw a hard bullet pass if the receiver has inside position.

Pass-Block Left/Right

Leave extra pass blockers in to pass-block

To execute: After you've accessed hot routes and selected the player, press Ⓛ or Ⓡ (Xbox 360) or L2 or R2 (PS3) to hot route the running back, tight end, or receiver to pass-block left or right depending on what side of the field he is lined up on.

Using this hot route leaves the running back, a tight end, or even a receiver in to pass-block. Try this when the defense calls a blitz and you don't think your offensive linemen can block all the blitzing defenders. If done right, this is an effective counter for inside blitz schemes.

Motion

Top offensive players use motion for a few different reasons, such as being able to tell if man or zone coverage is called. If the defender follows the receiver in motion, then it is man coverage. If the defender doesn't follow the receiver then it's zone coverage. However, there are ways for the defender to make it look like zone coverage when it's really man coverage. Also, an astute player on defense might put one defender in man coverage on a receiver whom he thinks you will send in motion. This makes it look like a man coverage defense has been called, when actually it is zone coverage.

Motion is also used to give the formation a different look. For instance, say you come out in the Gun Spread. You then motion the left slot receiver to the right. You now have a Gun Trips formation.

Finally, top players like to use motion to add an extra run blocker. For example, say an inside run play has been called, where the play is designed to have the halfback run between the center and right guard; the offense will motion the flanker to the left. Once the flanker gets near the right guard, they will snap the ball. The flanker now becomes an extra inside blocker. This is mainly done only if zone coverage is called.

Motion a receiver to see if man or zone coverage is called

To execute: Select the receiver you want to put in motion, then press left or right on the left thumbstick to send the receiver in motion.

Play Art

Use the play art to view the passing routes. This is very effective when you are playing online if you forget what your pass routes are after you call the play. You can also use it to view run-blocking assignments if you are not sure who the run blockers are supposed to block.

To execute: Press the Show Play Art button.

Slide Protection

Slide protection returns to *Madden NFL 11*. Here is a quick overview of how it works: Pressing the Slide Protection button allows you to adjust your pass protection schemes on the fly. Slide protection was put in the game to help counter the blitz in the passing game, but it can be used in the run game also. It may not always be effective, but in some run plays it can help create running lanes for the ball carrier. Four protection adjustments can be made.

Slide Protection Out

This aggressively blocks the defensive linemen

Strengths:

- When the defensive line is spread out, slide protection out puts the offensive linemen in a better position to counter them.
- It's good to use when the defense is showing blitz from the outside, because the offensive line protects out.

Weaknesses:

- With the offensive linemen sliding out, the quarterback is more susceptible to being sacked from the inside pass rush.
- If the defense overloads the middle of the offensive line, the offensive linemen won't be in position to block the inside pressure.

Slide Protection In

If pinch out or pinch in is used, the pass-blocking assignments don't change

Strengths:

- If the defensive linemen are pinched in, slide protection in puts the offensive linemen in a better position to block them.

- If the defense overloads the middle of the offensive line with multiple defenders, the offensive linemen are in better position to block all the pass rushers because they slide protect towards the middle.

Weaknesses:

- The quarterback is at greater risk of being sacked from the outside pass rush because the offensive linemen are blocking towards the inside.
- If the defense overloads the outside on both sides to blitz, the offensive linemen won't be able to block all the pass rushers.

Slide Protection Right

Slide protection can also be used in the run game

Strengths:

- If the defense overloads the right side of the offensive line, slide protection right puts the offensive line in a better position to counter the overloaded right side.
- When rolling the quarterback out to the left, it helps keep the backside pass rush off of him because the offensive slide protects to the right side.

Weaknesses:

- The quarterback is not protected from the left side of the defensive line if the defense brings the blitz.
- If the defense puts multiple defenders on the left side of the offensive line, do not use slide protection right because the offensive linemen won't be able to block all the pass rushers coming from the overloaded side.

Slide Protection Left

Use slide protection to pick up different blitz schemes

Strengths:

- If the defense overloads the left side of the offensive line, slide protection left puts the offensive line in a better position to counter the overloaded left side.
- When rolling the quarterback out to the right, it helps keep the backside pass rush off of him because the offensive slide protects to the left side.

Weaknesses:

- The quarterback is not protected from the right side of the defensive line if the defense brings the blitz.
- If the defense puts multiple defenders on the right side of the offensive line, do not use slide protection left; the offensive linemen won't be able to block all the pass rushers coming from the overloaded side.

ASSIGNMENT AI—THE RUNNING GAME

The EA SPORTS team has worked extra hard this season to improve offensive line play and the running game. You will see more double teams to help the offensive linemen seal defensive linemen off to create holes. Next, you will see the offensive linemen push to the second level to help seal off the linebackers. The days of hitting speed burst and of undisciplined running are over.

Inside Zone Plays

The key to running Inside Zone plays effectively is reading the defensive tackle. If you are up against a solid defensive tackle, Inside Zone plays allow you to co-op block that player. Based on his reaction, you will know where to go with the ball. The Inside Zone gives you three basic options: You can either bang, bend, or bounce the ball. If the defensive tackle slices inside you will bounce to the open gap. If the defensive tackle charges upfield, you bang the ball inside the B gap. If the defensive tackle comes upfield to the outside, you bend inside towards the A gap.

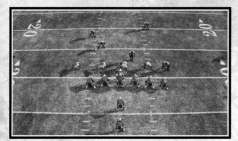

An Inside Zone running play out of the I-Form Pro

Even a back as good as Adrian Peterson struggled a bit until he mastered zone running concepts. Just look at him now! Zone running requires you to read and then react. The other component to being successful is having patience when you use zone concepts. The next part of your zone running education is to understand uncovered and covered concepts: When an offensive lineman has no one over him he's uncovered. When he has a defensive lineman in front of him he is covered. So what does this all mean? If the player is uncovered he will double-team with another offensive lineman to the play side. If the guard is uncovered he will co-op block with the tackle. Once the defensive tackle is forced backward, a linebacker has to commit to the gap. When that happens, one of the offensive linemen will slide off the double-team block and pick up the backer.

The offensive guard is uncovered

Here's a screenshot of the uncovered offensive guard. He will co-op block with the lineman next to him. This play is set up to take Haynesworth out of the play. He's too good of a player to have anyone block him one-on-one.

Haynesworth is being doubled at the line of scrimmage

Haynesworth slants inside, so this tells us we need to bend the run to the nearest open gap. The tackle came off of Haynesworth and is now pressing to the second level to get the linebacker.

Johnson bends the run inside

You've got a great seal at the line. Once you see the hole you have to hit it and get downfield before it closes.

Johnson hits the hole

Haynesworth is sealed off pretty well, so now you can break it downfield to get those necessary yards.

Johnson is about to open up

You should have a pretty good idea now of how effective zone blocking can be once you make the right reads. Even in close quarters, backs who are elusive can be hard to tackle. All you have to do is work the dual stick control and watch the magic.

Johnson works the bounce theory

Now we run the play again, and this time some heat is coming with it. Haynesworth is coming upfield so we have to bounce to the next hole. We can't bang because the other defenders are taking that area away from us. So we have to bounce the play outside.

See ya!

You have nothing but open space now. Even though this play is by default an inside run, you can attack the flank quite easily if the defense overcommits bodies inside. Be careful and read the flow of the linebackers. In this season's game the linebackers react to plays much better than before.

Johnson is cutting outside and reading his blocks

All gaps inside are filled, but you have a back who can outrun any defender. Even if you have a slower back you still can get good yards if you read the blocks correctly.

Iso Run Plays

An Iso run play from the I-Form Normal

The Iso is another play that concentrates on double-teaming the defensive tackle. This is more of a midline play that slams inside the A gap. Your reads and running rules are the same as they were for the Inside Zone. You have to read the reaction of the tackle. Once the defensive tackle makes his move you will either bend, bang, or bounce the play. Once you get used to the reads, you will be able to attack at will on the ground. The Iso attacks the inside bubble of the defense. In *Madden NFL 11*, you don't typically see five-man defensive fronts. This means there will be gaps in the line.

So you want to hit the inside bubble between the center and the guard. If the defensive tackle shades either offensive lineman you will know where to go with the ball pre-snap. If he shades the center you can expose the bubble behind the guard. If you see that the defensive tackle shades the guards, then you know you will work inside and run behind the center. This concept goes hand-in-hand with the uncovered lineman theory as well.

Pre-snap, Haynesworth is shading over the guard

In this example our opponent has had enough of players being uncovered and has made sure that every offensive lineman is covered on this go around. The bubble we will attack pre-snap is inside the guard and towards the center. We still need to make our post-snap read to tell us which of the three Bs (bounce, bang, or bend) we need to use.

Haynesworth stunts outside

This read tells us that we have to bang this run into the bubble we saw pre-snap. Now you begin to see why it's important to make those pre-snap reads. This can help us understand where we need to go with the ball. Then if the line uses a stunt we can still stay with our basic running rules and get positive yards on the ground.

We get a good seal, which allows Johnson to bang the A gap

Now that we have a nice seal on the defensive tackle it's time to get those shoulders squared up and get positive yards. You have no time to do any dancing in the backfield. You can see that Fletcher is coming through the A gap. We need to make our read, trust our read, and react to what we see.

Johnson follows his lead blocker downfield

When you make the right reads you will find that this season's game is a joy to play. The running game should be a big part of your offensive attack this season. Using plays like this will help you move the ball more effectively. The key is understanding the outline of the rushing attack and how to use the correct play for each situation. Now you have two plays that can isolate a dominant player to take him out of the mix. By reading his reaction, you can generate good yards on the ground.

Johnson is off to the races

Once all of your blocks are picked up you can get huge yards on the ground. Now let's take a look at this same play after the defense has made an adjustment.

Johnson works the bounce read

We come back with the same play, but this time the defense uses a run blitz to slow our rushing attack down. You can see that we have an inside hole to bend to. But there are two linebackers filling this hole. You have a co-op block on Haynesworth and you also have a decent seal on the defensive end by the tight end. Now you only have the outside linebacker to contend with. This is a good time to bounce the ball outside.

Johnson makes a hard cut outside

It's good to wait for your blocks to set before you bounce the ball out.

A highlight reel run for Chris Johnson

Our read opens up an opportunity to get some big gains on the ground. Backs like C.J. make running the ball fun this season.

Power O Plays

The Power O play from the I-Form Normal

The Power O is one of the most used plays in the NFL. This season, with the improvements to the offensive line blocking, you can really take advantage of the blocking assignments. The key to this play is to force a double team on the tackle and have the guard on the back side fold around and pull. As he pulls, he will fire up the A gap while the center down-blocks the defender that the backside guard was supposed to block. You must allow the pulling guard to get around the center and be your lead blocker. If any defenders come upfield he will block them first. If no one gets inside, the guard will go downfield and pave the way for a big gain.

The guard is pulling around the down block by the center

Here is a great shot of how this play works. You see that the center is down-blocking on the defensive tackle. Next, you see that the guard is folding behind the center and hugging the rump of the center. If anyone gets free he will block and not pull. If no one shows he will fire through the A gap. This is a very important point. If a heavy blitz comes upfield, the job of the pulling guard is to stop any leakage inside. If there isn't anyone leaking inside he will be free to lead-block through the hole. The idea of the co-op block is to create an opening for the pulling guard and fullback to lead-block through. This is a play you have to let develop. If you read pressure, square up and get what you can. If you have no inside holes, you have to bounce this play outside.

Johnson hits the hole

This is when you have to make your read to bang or bounce. If you have the guard clean and the fullback free, you should bang the ball inside. If the guard gets picked up you have to bounce the ball outside and stay with your fullback. This is one of the better inside power running plays in the game. This is also a play you won't use every down, so your opponent can't adjust to stop you. If you catch the defense in the wrong play call, you can overwhelm them with blockers at the point of attack.

Once you get your blocks picked up you just have to square up and grind out those yards. One problem to watch out for is that Johnson is so fast he can easily outrun the blockers. You have to get in the habit of making sure you stay with your line. If you outrun them you may get a defender coming off his block to make a play on you.

Johnson is showing why he is an All-Pro runner

Because you have numbers you can get downfield and have a lineman to run with you to pick up any defender that may get free. You will want to get plenty of reps under your belt with this play so you learn to make the correct reads. The Power O allows you to maximize the abilities of teams with elite guards.

Johnson works the bend

We have three reads again (bend, bang, and bounce). In this example, we show Johnson bending his run. This is when you cut the ball all the way back across the line to get to the inside gap.

The guard breaks off his pull assignment

Remember when we talked about defenders leaking into the backfield? This screenshot shows you what we are talking about. The guard filled the lane that the linebacker got through. He is picked up now, but you have to bend the run inside to make the play work.

The linebacker overpursued and allowed a cutback

We are able to cut back against the grain and take advantage of this nice seal block.

Where did he go?

When you're elusive like Johnson you can make plays like this all day long.

Stretch Plays

A Stretch play from the I-Form Normal

The Stretch has been a good play for a long time, but now with the addition of the Assignment AI you can really do damage with this play. The Stretch is basically an outside zone run. You will zone in on the outside defender as your read. This can be the defensive end on even fronts or the outside linebacker on odd fronts. Whoever is hanging on the edge of the line will be your read. We use the same running rules as before, but there is a difference when running the outside/stretch play: If the edge defender slants in you bounce the ball outside. If the edge defender comes upfield or takes an outside rush you bang it inside.

The entire offensive line reach-blocks on this play. This is when they all take a six-inch step towards the play side. They seal defenders off from getting inside, while at the same time preventing them from getting out quickly. You only have to lock on the edge defender for your read, because he will tell you where you should go with the ball.

A look at the edge defender

Here is a screenshot of the player we use to make our read. This is an even front, but the linebacker is sitting on the edge. You have to read his reaction to tell you where you should go with the ball.

The edge defender shoots upfield

Now that we see that the edge defender is coming upfield we can bounce the ball outside. He has been sealed off and you have a lead blocker. Normally, when you see the defender come upfield like this, you are supposed to cut it up inside. The problem is that you have a defender sitting in that gap. So you have to bounce the ball outside. Things don't always go to plan so you have to keep an eye on the whole field. Making the right read will prevent you from getting negative yards. If a defender is sitting in your gap, you have to move your focus to the next gap. You can see that if the linebacker wasn't there, the cut inside would have been sweet.

Johnson on the loose with blockers downfield

By making the right reads and showing patience you can get some nice yards with a lead block or two.

Johnson makes reads downfield

To be great at running you have to learn to set up your blocks downfield. Once you make your read at the hike you should then focus on the next level. This is what people call "ball carrier vision." You can recreate this in *Madden NFL 11* even though you're playing a video game. As soon as you make your first cut, start scanning downfield to set the next defender up. Once the edge defender showed his face, we knew he would be blocked, and this told us to run inside of him. Next we saw the linebacker in the hole, so we looked towards the outside. The next read should be the secondary.

Allowing the wideout to seal off two defenders

To help set your blocks up, you need to run at the defender to help the wideout get in position to make the block. Once you see the seal then you cut outside and draw the other defender in. This idea will take time to get used to, but once you do you will see that you will get bigger gains.

Getting the extra 5–10 yards

When you make solid downfield reads you will see your yards per carry increase. This move alone helps us get 10 more yards on the ground. Get in the habit of labbing your downfield reads in practice mode. You never know when you need that extra yard to win the game or get that critical first down.

Here is the bend by the running back

In this shot you see the defender is coming upfield and slanting inside a bit. This tells us to cut back inside and use the bend attack. A quick tap to the inside on the right thumbstick will set things up for you.

We have a great seal, which allows us to bend the ball

Since all of the defensive linemen are sealed off, you have a lane inside to cut back into open space.

COVERAGE BASICS

In this section of the guide, we take a look at all five defensive coverage types in the game. We break down the strengths and weaknesses of each one. Be sure to read this section if you are unfamiliar with them; that way, once you get in the game, you will have a better idea of how to read and attack them.

Cover 0

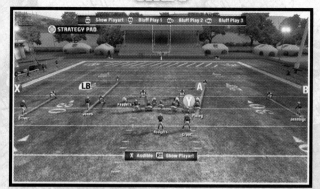

Four defenders are in man coverage

Teams that are aggressive and like to blitz play a lot of Cover 0 defenses. This type of coverage has no safety playing deep. Generally, there are six or seven pass rushers rushing the quarterback while the rest of the defense plays man coverage.

The nickelback is coming off the edge hard at the QB

Other Cover 0 defenses have safeties doubling up on the outside receivers. Even though these are technically Cover 0, they aren't as aggressive since there are no defenders blitzing the quarterback.

The Cover 0 defense brings a lot of heat on the quarterback. Many of the Cover 0 defenses are designed to bring inside pressure, which is the quickest way to get to the quarterback.

It's a high-risk, high-reward coverage scheme, meaning that sometimes the offense might get a big play and sometimes the defense might get a big play. The defense requires fast cornerbacks who can cover the outside receivers in one-on-one coverage. If your team doesn't have fast cornerbacks, consider running coverage schemes such as Cover 2 and Cover 3. Be sure to call bump-n-run or delayed bump-n-run man coverage so that the receivers are slower to get into their pass routes.

Cover 1

The free safety plays the deep middle

In a Cover 1 pass defense, one of the safeties drops to the deep middle of the field as the ball is snapped and plays zone coverage. He is responsible for guarding the deep middle and for providing assistance to the corners on deep sideline routes.

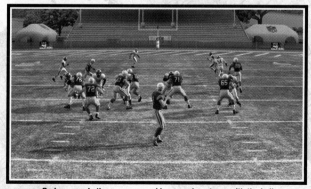

Rodgers reads the coverage and knows where to go with the ball

The majority of the time the FS acts as the center fielder unless he is involved in double coverage on the left side. The cornerbacks and the other safety play man-to-man coverage.

With man-to-man all around, this technique provides tight coverage with help to the deep middle. The SS can cheat up, giving this play strong run support to his side. Usually one of the linebackers is free to blitz, creating a four- to five-man rush. There is very little underneath help, so crossing routes and pick routes can be very effective against this scheme. If the deep safety bites on play action there is a good chance for a deep gain.

Cover 2

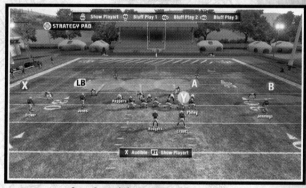

Cover 2 zone is just one kind of Cover 2 defense

In a Cover 2 pass defense, both safeties drop deep as the ball is snapped and play zone coverage. They can provide assistance to the corners on deep sideline routes or clog the middle against the post.

This coverage scheme is strong against the short passing game because it allows for up to five underneath zones if desired. The CB can move up and jam the receivers at the line, disrupting the timing of the play. The short flats areas can be pretty well locked down as well.

Both safeties split out wide to cover the deep halves of the field

This scheme can be vulnerable against fades and deep middle routes. A post corner route can also cause trouble for this scheme. Strong-side run support is weaker than in the Cover 1 because the SS must play the pass first. You need to have a strong defensive line that can get pressure on the QB.

Cover 3

The defensive backs play a three-deep shell

In a Cover 3 pass defense, three defensive backs drop deep as the ball is snapped and play zone coverage. This can be both corners and one of the safeties or both safeties with one corner.

Three men in deep zones help cover the entire width of the field. You can get good strong-side run support if the SS is not involved in the three-deep coverage.

The QB stares down the pass coverage

Flood routes to either side can be difficult to defend with this scheme. If the defense attacks with four players vertically, you can get outmanned at the point of attack. Flats attacks to the side with the CB in deep coverage and in routes over the middle are effective against this scheme.

Cover 4

The Dollar Normal—Cover 4 provides excellent deep coverage

In a Cover 4 pass defense (also known as Quarters), all four defensive backs drop deep with the instruction to let no one get behind them. Also known as a four across, this defense blankets the entire deep part of the field.

This defense provides excellent deep coverage. Against two-wide-receiver sets, the safeties can provide double coverage on the deep routes. The corners can jam at the line knowing they have help from the safeties over the top.

The defensive backs play four-deep coverage

The flats areas to either side are vulnerable in this scheme. Safeties can be fooled by play action, causing a breakdown deep. Sending multiple receivers to one side can nullify the benefits of the over-the-top double coverage.

COMMON PASSING CONCEPTS

So what is a passing concept? Think of a football field as a flat, two-dimensional plane. You attack a defense horizontally or vertically along a line on this plane. Try imagining there are five horizontal lines and three vertical lines on the field. Now, in between some of those lines there are defenders, and other lines are vacated. Offensive coordinators will create passing concepts with the idea of putting receivers in the spaces where no defenders are located. In this section of the guide, we showcase many different passing concepts that you will find in *Madden NFL 11*. Some are very common, while others are found only in specific playbooks.

Types of Passing Concepts

There are four basic types of passing concepts in the game:

- **Horizontal** passing concepts horizontally stretch the defensive coverage.
- **Vertical** passing concepts vertically stretch the defensive coverage.
- **Horizontal/vertical** passing concepts are a combination of horizontal and vertical passing concepts.
- The **objective receiver** concept is when a specific receiver is isolated against a single defender.

Choosing a Passing Concept to Run

- A good passing concept has individual routes that attack man and zone. This may not always be possible, but at least make this a point of focus.

- Look for plays that integrate anti-man coverage concepts within a zone-stretching framework (such as with mesh or option routes).
- Run plays that put man combinations to one side and zone combinations to the other. Many of the best NFL and college teams do this quite effectively.
- Find passing concepts that beat bump-n-run man coverage. We cannot stress this enough. In the book a vast quantity of the passing concepts we show are designed to beat bump-n-run man coverage. If the passing concept beats bump-n-run man coverage, then it also will beat normal man coverage in most cases.

Horizontal Passing Concepts

Curls Attack

The Curls Attack (a.k.a. All Curls) is a horizontal stretch passing concept with five potential passing lanes stretching four underneath zones. Cover 2 zone with five underneath zones is difficult to throw this passing concept against, but against Cover 3 and Cover 4, this play is money. This particular concept can be found in most Bunch formations. The receiver who gets open the most consistently is the outside receiver on the bunch side, who runs his curl route to

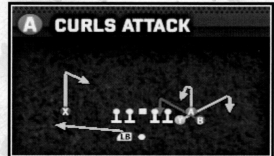

the short middle of the field. The only pass route that is not a curl belongs to the running back, who runs a flat route to the back side. If you look closely, you will notice a curl-flat route combo between the running back and backside receiver.

Curl Flat

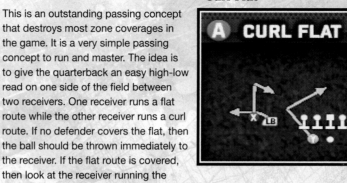

This is an outstanding passing concept that destroys most zone coverages in the game. It is a very simple passing concept to run and master. The idea is to give the quarterback an easy high-low read on one side of the field between two receivers. One receiver runs a flat route while the other receiver runs a curl route. If no defender covers the flat, then the ball should be thrown immediately to the receiver. If the flat route is covered, then look at the receiver running the curl route. He will usually be open if the flat is covered.

Double Slant

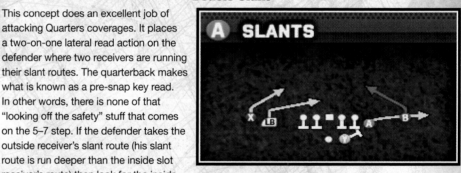

This concept does an excellent job of attacking Quarters coverages. It places a two-on-one lateral read action on the defender where two receivers are running their slant routes. The quarterback makes what is known as a pre-snap key read. In other words, there is none of that "looking off the safety" stuff that comes on the 5–7 step. If the defender takes the outside receiver's slant route (his slant route is run deeper than the inside slot receiver's route) then look for the inside receiver's slant route. If the defender takes the inside receiver's slant route, then look for the outside receiver's slant route. The concept is effective against other pass coverages as well.

Drive

The Drive concept is designed to do the same things as the Follow concept. The key difference is that the two pass routes are switched. The outside receiver runs the shallow cross while the inside receiver runs the in route. Much like the Follow concept, the idea is to high-low the defender playing over the short middle of the field. If the defender takes the high route, then the low route is open. Conversely, if the defender takes the low route, the high route will be open. This concept can be run against both man and zone coverage with great success.

Follow

Another high-low passing concept that attacks zone coverage is the Follow. This passing concept has two receivers running separate routes at different depths over the middle of the field. The inside receiver runs a shallow cross or drag route, and the outside receiver on the same side runs a 10-yard in route. The design of this passing concept is to high-low the middle linebacker. If he drops back to defend the in route, then the underneath route run by the inside receiver will be open. If he takes away the inside receiver's route, then the in route will be open. In *Madden NFL 11*, the middle linebacker will almost always cover the high route, leaving the underneath route open. The only time he won't is if the receiver running the underneath route has been spotlighted or is manually covered by a human controlling the middle linebacker. Another reason the underneath route may not be open is the presence of a defender who is spying the quarterback.

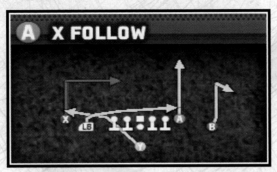

Inside Cross

The Inside Cross, also known as the Double Cross concept, is an excellent passing concept that attacks man coverage by having two receivers cross each other. The two receivers will cross each other at some point over the short middle of the field. At this point they will cause a rub between the two defenders covering them. The rub action often leaves one if not both receivers open because the defenders run into each other. Find the open receiver and throw him the ball. There are different personnel and formation variations of the Inside Cross. For instance, you may have the slot receiver and the tight end running the Inside Cross concept. Or you may have a slot receiver and running back running the Inside Cross concept. Regardless of which receivers run it, just know it's a very effective passing concept against man coverage.

Levels

Levels is another high-low passing concept that is used to attack zone coverage by attacking a defender at two different levels on the field. One receiver will run a deeper in route while the other receiver runs a short in route. As the receivers run their routes, they force the isolated defender to cover the high receiver or the low receiver. As with all of these high-low concepts, the defender will most likely cover the deeper receiver, leaving the shallower receiver open.

Mesh

The Mesh passing concept is a flexible scheme designed to beat both man and zone coverage. It has two receivers running across the field from opposite sides and crossing within inches of each other a few yards past the line of scrimmage. Once the two receivers have meshed, they look to settle in an open area vs. zone coverage or keep running to the sideline vs. man coverage. Many of the Mesh concepts have a running back running a wheel route out of the backfield. He is another solid option to look for if neither of the mesh receivers is open underneath.

Shallow Cross

The Shallow Cross concept has one receiver running an in route while another receiver on the other side of the field runs a shallow cross. At some point they will cross each other over the middle, but at different depths. The design of this concept is to give the quarterback a high-low read. The defender the QB keys on is the linebacker dropping back in a hook zone over the middle. Just as with the Drive and Follow passing concepts, the linebacker will generally take the deep route; in this case, it's the in route. This allows the receiver running the shallow cross to get open underneath. This passing concept also works well against man coverage as both receivers will potentially be open.

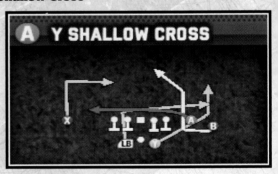

Shoot

The Shoot passing concept has been around for while; many of the West Coast Offenses utilize it as one of their primary means of moving the ball through the air. The route combination is simple: The outside receiver runs a slant while the inside receiver runs to the flat (shoot). Read the flat receiver first; if he is open throw him the ball. If not, work your way to the slant route. Try making a key read by picking out a defender you think is going to cover the flat or slant. For instance, say the defense comes out in the Nickel Normal. On offense, we come out in the Singleback Double Flex. The Shoot passing concept is being run to the left side. The nickelback is lined up across from the slot receiver. He is the key defender we are reading. If he covers the flat, we then throw to the slot. If he drops back in coverage, we then look for the throw to the flat. Of course, we still need to make sure no other defender covers the flat before making the throw.

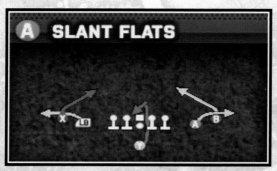

Spacing

One of our favorite passing schemes is the Spacing concept. This concept has multiple receivers running the same horizontal routes, but each is spaced out across the field. The idea of this concept is to have more receivers than the defense has defenders covering the underneath zones. Don't expect to pick up a ton of yardage, but it will help move the chains and increase your pass completion percentage. This is an excellent passing concept to run down near the goal line as it consistently gets the ball in the end zone for a score.

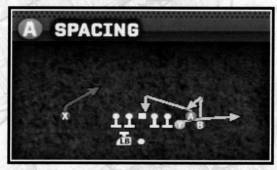

Spot

The Spot concept is designed to beat man coverage but also is effective against zone coverage. The receiver to look for first is the one running a flat route. If he is open, the ball should be thrown to him right away. If not, work your way to the receiver who is running the spot route. The route combination between them has the potential to cause a natural pick. If man coverage is called, look to throw to the spot receiver before he sets in position. If zone coverage is called, wait for the receiver to spot up before making the throw.

Stick

By nature, the Stick concept is designed to be a very high percentage pass play. It is a half-field read that attacks the defensive under-coverage with horizontal bracketing. The passing clock is quick, which both attacks the perimeter with speed and aids in protection. The Stick concept is also an all-purpose play, meaning it works well vs. all types of coverages. The play's primary receiver is not the receiver running the stick, but the receiver running the flat. If the flat is open the ball should be thrown to him first. If the flat route is covered, then work your way back to the stick route, which should be open underneath against most zone coverages in the game. If man coverage is called with a blitz, look to throw to the receiver running the flat first. If the opening is not there, look to throw to the backside receiver running the slant.

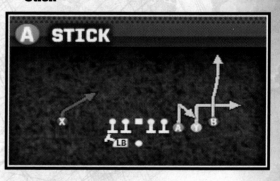

Texas

The Texas passing concept is used extensively with teams that run the West Coast Offense. It was made famous by the Green Bay Packers and Mike Holmgren. A running back runs an angle route while another receiver, generally the TE, runs his route over the top. The idea behind this concept is to create a two-on-one isolation on the defender dropping back in a hook zone in the area of the field in which those receivers run their routes. The defender will look

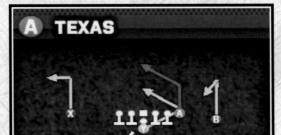

to cover the receiver running the over-the-top route, leaving the angle route run by the running back open for a quick bullet pass underneath. Expect to pick up 5–7 yards a pop. The only way to stop this concept if zone coverage is called is for the human playing on defense to either spotlight or manually cover the running back running the angle route.

Vertical Passing Concepts

Four Verticals

This passing concept stretches the defense vertically by sending four receivers deep. It does an excellent job of attacking Cover 2 and Cover 3 coverages because the receivers outnumber the deep defender four to two (Cover 2) or four to three (Cover 3). Against Cover 2, the safeties tend to cover the inside receivers running streaks because the outside receivers are slow to get into their routes since they are jammed at the line of

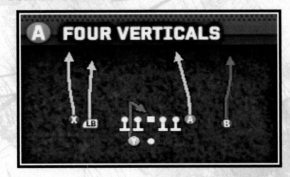

scrimmage. When making the pass to the outside receivers, try pass-leading them towards the sideline for best results. If Cover 3 coverage is called, look for the receiver down the seams. Watch to see where the safety plays the deep middle.

Seattle

Seattle is another vertical stretch concept that sends four receivers deep. Much like the Four Verticals concept, the idea behind it is to outnumber Cover 2 and Cover 3 coverages by sending more receivers vertically than the defense can cover. In a Bunch formation the outside receiver on the bunch side runs a wheel. The inside slot receiver runs a seam. The inside receiver on the bunch side runs a deep crossing route. He is the concept's primary receiver. The backside receiver

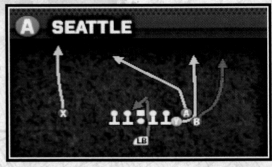

runs a go route, clearing out the safety on his side for the receiver running the crossing route to get open. The halfback runs a check-down curl route out of the backfield. Look for him if nothing opens up deep.

Stick N Nod

The Stick N Nod is a variation of the Stick concept. It has the receiver acting like he is going to run the stick route before breaking down the seam. Many NFL teams use this pass concept to get the tight end open down the middle of the field. As you might guess, this concept is very effective against Cover 2 zone coverage because not only is a receiver running down the seam, but both outside receivers run go routes down the sideline. With three receivers

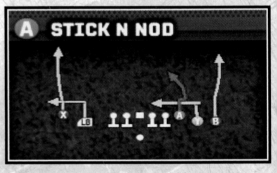

running vertical routes, the two safeties are outnumbered. If Cover 3 coverage is called, the receiver running the seam is open, but the passing window is small. The ball must be thrown between the underneath and deep coverage. The better option would be to throw to the receiver running the pivot route underneath as the seam route will lift the coverage.

Stick Post

Here is yet another variation of the Stick concept that many NFL teams run. This one is called the Stick Post. Like the other Stick concepts, this is designed to beat three- and four-deep zone coverage. The outside receiver runs a post while the inside receiver, who is lined up on the same side, runs the stick route. The post route lifts the coverage over the top of the stick route. Just as the stick receiver turns around, he will be open for a bullet pass. This concept works best against

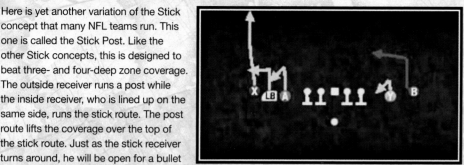

Cover 3 and Cover 4 defenses. It doesn't work as well against Cover 2 zone coverage because the outside receiver gets jammed. This throws the timing off between him and the stick receiver.

Wheel Out

Another popular passing concept used to beat zone coverage is the Wheel Out. You may not see this play's name in a lot of playbooks, but you will see the passing concept if you look closely at the play diagrams. The outside receiver runs a post while the inside receiver on the same side runs a wheel route. If Cover 2 zone is called, the outside receiver running the post will be open. If Cover 3 coverage is called, the inside receiver running the wheel route will be

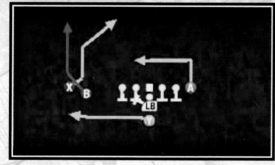

open. If man coverage is called, throw the ball before the slot receiver goes down the sideline.

Wheel Dig

This concept is pretty much the same as the Wheel Out; the only difference is the outside receiver runs a dig route instead of a post route. The results are the same; the outside cornerback steps inside a few yards to cover the dig route. At this point the ball needs to be thrown to the receiver running the wheel route. When making the throw, watch for a defender dropping back in a buzz zone because he will be in position to defend the wheel unless you wait longer for the receiver to get down the field. This will give the outside cornerback time to recover and the wheel won't be as open. Look for plays named WR In—these plays have this passing concept.

Horizontal/Vertical Passing Concepts

Bench

Bench is another version of the Smash concept that features a high-low read. One receiver will run a quick out towards the bench while the other receiver on the same side runs a corner route. Look for the high read first. If he is covered, look for the low read. This concept is effective against both man and zone coverage. Generally, against Cover 2 and Cover 3 zone coverage, the receiver running the corner route will be open. Watch for defenders dropping back

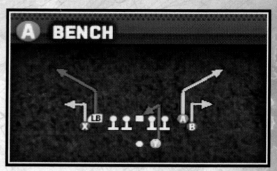

in buzz zones, also known as curl/flat zones. If Cover 4 coverage is called, look for the receiver running the out route. If man coverage is called, both may be open. If a blitz is called, look to throw the quick out route.

Curl Flat Corner

Another popular variation of the Flood concept that is used to beat zone coverage is the Curl Flat Corner. This passing concept has three receivers running different routes at different depths. The play-side cornerback is forced deep to cover the corner route if Cover 3 coverage is called. This leaves the flat defender isolated in a two-on-one situation between the flat and curl receivers. If the flat route is covered, then look for the curl route.

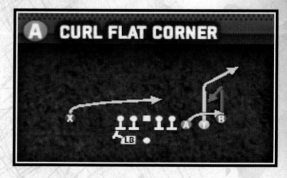

On the other hand, if the curl route is covered look to throw to the flat. The backside receiver runs a crossing route and is another option to look for if man coverage is called.

Flood

In the game are several different flood concepts that vertically stretch the defense when zone coverage is called. One of the more common floods has one receiver running a flat, another running a 10-yard out, and the third receiver running a streak. The primary receiver is the one running the 10-yard out. Against Cover 3 coverages, the flat defender will defend the flat receiver, while the cornerback will drop back to cover the receiver running the streak. This leaves a hole in the coverage between those two defenders for the receiver running the out route to get open. The only way his route would be defended is if a third defender drops back in the curl/flat area.

Hitch Seam

This is one of the more common passing concepts in the game, but we still want to mention it. If Cover 2 or Cover 4 coverage is called, this concept is rather effective. The outside receivers run hitch routes while the inside receivers run seam routes. If Cover 2 is called, the seam routes will be open. If Cover 4 is called, the hitch routes will be open.

Naked Bootleg

A great way to attack Cover 2 man coverage is the Naked Bootleg concept. The naked bootleg action refers to the fact that no offensive lineman pulls to the back side to pass-block for the quarterback, who is bootlegging. Look for the fullback in the flat, or look for one of the receivers running the crossing routes—at least one of them should be open. As always, use the run game to set up the play action to maximize the overall effectiveness of the naked bootleg concept.

Objective Receiver Passing Concepts

Deep Cross

There is one play in *Madden NFL 11* specifically called Deep Cross. It can be found only in the Falcons playbook. However, there are other plays such as the Strong Flood that the Deep Cross concept can be run with. The idea of this passing concept is for the receiver to work one-on-one against man as he comes over the deep middle. By clearing out the over-the-top coverage, this passing concept has big-play potential behind it. The Gun Y-Trips—

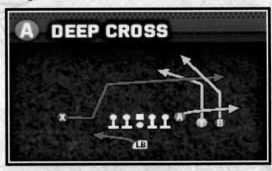

Strong Flood is a good example of how this concept can be created with just one hot route. The slot receiver, who by default runs an out route, can be hot routed on a streak. Now you have two receivers that run deep routes. Their two routes will clear the pass coverage out for the split end, who is running the deep crossing route. The Deep Cross works against any type of man coverage in the game.

Delayed Route

Delayed Route concepts are very effective against bend-but-don't-break coverages. With the defenders dropping back to cover receivers who are running normal pass routes, the receiver running the delayed route will have plenty of open space once he releases. Plays that have the tight end running a delayed end seam route are a perfect example of how effective delay routes are in *Madden NFL 11*. The only downside is if the defense calls a blitz from the delay receiver's side; he won't go out because he will stay in to pass-block. Be sure to not focus in on the receiver running the delay route, because he may not go out if a blitz is called, and the end result may be you being sacked. If zone coverage is called, you may want to hot route the slot receiver on a drag. His route will be open because the split end's deep crossing route will open his route underneath.

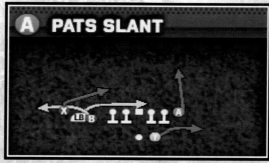

Pivot Clearout

This is another passing concept where you won't find any play that is actually called Pivot Clearout. But plenty of plays in the game have receivers running pivot routes (look at the play diagram for an example of what a pivot route is). What we like to do against man coverage is have the slot receivers run pivot routes and then hot route the outside receivers on streaks. This isolates them in one-on-one coverage. Once the receivers pivot and head towards the sidelines, they generally gain separation from the men covering them. As soon as we see this, we throw a hard bullet pass to one of them.

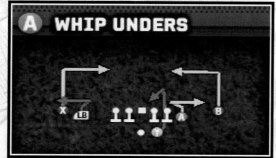

Smash

The high-low read Smash concept attacks Cover 2's biggest weakness: the deep outside halves of the field near both sidelines. The Smash concept has a two-route combination: a corner route (high) and a hitch route (low). If the cornerback (flat defender) sits on the receiver running the low read, then the receiver running the high read will be open. Conversely, if the cornerback sinks back on the receiver running the high read, then the low-read receiver will be open. Not only does this concept work well against Cover 2 zone coverage, it also is effective against Cover 3 and Cover 4 coverages. Watch for defenders dropping back in buzz zones, as they do a good job of defending corner routes.

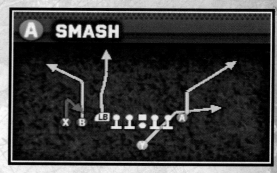

WR Screen

Pretty much every playbook in the game has some type of WR Screen. These plays are very effective at beating most zone coverage and can be effective at beating man coverage as long as the defender covering the receiver running the screen is blocked. They are even more effective when the defense puts eight or nine defenders in the box, since there are not as many defenders playing on the perimeter to defend the pass. When running WR Screen plays against zone coverage, we like to hot route receivers on the opposite side of the field on drag routes. We do this to provide extra blocking once the receiver makes the catch. For instance, say we come out in the Gun Doubles On—FL Screen. There are three offensive linemen pulling out to block for the screen, but we can add two more blockers by hot routing the slot and split end on drag routes. Once the FL makes the catch, these two receivers become extra blockers.

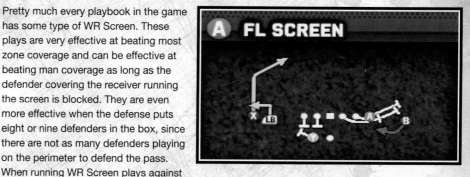

PLAY ACTION PASSING

We have talked about balance being one of the fundamental principles of offense. One of the surest ways to balance the offensive attack is to coordinate the running game with the play action pass (PA).

Texans quarterback Matt Schaub is feeling the pressure

The quarterback hands off to the halfback

Andre Johnson breaks over the middle on his dig route

It used to be that when calling a PA play, it was almost a guaranteed sack if the defense called some type of blitz. Over the last few years, EA Tiburon has worked very hard at getting PA pass plays to actually work and be an effective part of the offensive play-calling strategy for *Madden NFL*. With all the formations in the game, there shouldn't be a problem finding a few good PA plays to beat any type of defense that is called.

Developing a strong rushing attack forces the defense to focus on stopping the run. When this is the case, the play action pass can be highly effective because it draws the defenders in and does not allow them to drop into their coverage assignments quickly. Thus, the play fake opens up the intermediate passing game.

Last season, many players flocked to using play action plays when lining up under center to counter all the inside pressure that was being generated. In *Madden NFL 11*, many of these same under-center play action plays are just as effective.

Advantages of Using Play Action

- Play action attacks a defense with a great run-stopping MLB.
- It offsets the effectiveness of blitzing defenders.
- The pass rush can be compromised and slowed.
- It gets quick passing lanes open to the TE or any underneath pass route.
- It attacks man-to-man corners by making them take a step up because of the run threat.
- Specific defenders can be isolated if they are prone to being fooled or commit to the run before accounting for their coverage responsibility.
- Defensive caution due to a successful play action game can add to the effectiveness of the running game.

Key Elements of Play Action

- The PA play must appear as close to the basic running play as possible.
- Line blocking, at least at the point of attack, must simulate run blocking.
- The running backs must run the same courses as they do on the run play, and must deliberately hold the fake through the line of scrimmage.
- The defender being attacked must be pinpointed. He could be the inside linebacker, outside linebacker, weak safety, strong safety, or cornerback. The design of the play should be directed at a specific defender.
- The more successful and often used running play is the logical action from which to run play action.

Two Play Action Plays to Run

I-Form Twins Flex—PA TE Leak

The I-Form Twins Flex—PA TE Leak has the tight end as the play's primary receiver. He runs a corner route and is very effective against man coverage.

I-Form Pro—PA Boot

This play action play gets the quarterback rolling out to the play side. The play's primary receiver is the flanker running a deep hitch. Instead of him running a hitch route, we like to hot route him on a streak.

The quarterback bootlegs to the left

There are two types of play action. Play action pass plays are driven off of the inside running game. These are pretty straightforward plays.

I-Form Twins Flex—PA TE Leak

I-Form Pro—PA Boot

The quarterback fakes the handoff to the halfback

Bootleg action is driven off of the outside running game. It makes use of misdirection. The bootleg name comes from the quarterback often hiding the ball from the defense by his thigh to make the run look more convincing.

Here are two examples of play action plays in *Madden NFL 11*.

The split end is open as he comes across the deep middle

The fullback runs a flat route and should be your second read if the tight end is not open deep. The third option is the flanker, who is lined up in the slot. Look for him as he comes across the deep middle of the field.

Matt Schaub throws a bullet pass to his tight end

The two receivers we look to throw to when running this play are the tight end running the flat and the split end running the crossing route over the middle. One of them usually gets open.

SCREEN PLAYS

In the past few seasons of the game, screens have been one of the best ways to attack a blitzing defense and get them back on their heels. This play has always been a very high percentage pass play and a very effective way to deal with the blitz. The one problem that we have had in *Madden NFL* is how hard it is to really use the screen in the game. It is almost impossible to run a screen against the computer because the defense always sends a defender out to cover the screen. We don't really worry about this too much.

Brees throws a dart past a jumping defender

The screen is designed to beat the blitz. So if the computer blitzes, the screen will work. But we'll have the most success running the screen against a human opponent. We can read tendencies and adjust our attack to use the screen. Doing this provides some very helpful advantages for our offense.

Benefits of Using the Screen

- The screen is great against the blitz because it gives the offense big-play potential.
- It's a low-risk pass play that works against most zone coverages.
- It slows down the pass rush.
- It keeps the defense guessing.
- It gives the QB more time to throw on other passing plays.

- It forces a human opponent to set up or call plays to defend the screen, allowing you to call other plays to take advantage of schemes that otherwise might not work as well.

These benefits will be achieved by using a multiple screen passing attack. The HB Screen and WR Screen together will allow us to handle any possible blitz or heavy pass rush attack by the defense.

Types of Screens

There are a few different types of screen plays. We are going to break down a couple of them to give you a better idea of how they work.

WR Screen

The FL Screen is one of the best plays in the game

One the most widely used WR Screen plays found in *Madden NFL 11* is the Gun Doubles—FL Screen. This play has the flanker setting up for the screen. The tight end, right tackle, right guard, and running back all go out to the flanker's side to set up blocking in front of him.

The flanker gets some nice blocking down the field

As long as the flat defender or man covering the flanker is blocked, this play has potential to pick up big-time yardage.

Slot Screen

The Patriots playbook has the Slot Screen

One of the best screen plays in the game is the Slot Screen. To find this play, look in the Patriots or Broncos playbook. The left tackle and left guard set up the blocking out in front for the slot receiver. One thing that has changed in this year's game is that you can't sprint back as soon the quarterback gets the ball out of the Gun formation.

The Slot Screen is tough to defend

For this reason, if an inside blitz is called, you may not have time to sprint, and instead you must throw the ball while the quarterback is dropping back on his own. Once the slot receiver makes the catch, look to see how the blocking shapes up and then move down the field accordingly.

HB Slip Screen

The most common screen in the game

The HB Slip Screen is an extension of the outside run game. The three interior linemen pull to the right to set up the blocking. While they are blocking, the halfback pauses for a split second and then follows the interior linemen out.

The blocking is set up for a big play

Once the blocking is set up, throw a hard bullet pass. Don't take control of the halfback until he starts heading down the field. Follow your blocks and look to pick up positive yardage.

PA FB Screen

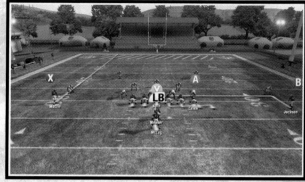

This unique screen is found only in the Eagles and Rams playbooks

Only two playbooks in the game have a fullback screen—the Eagles and Rams playbooks. The formation is the I-Form Normal. The name of the play is PA FB Screen.

Kolb fires the ball to his fullback

As you might expect, this play has the quarterback faking a handoff to the halfback while the fullback goes out to set up the screen. The right guard and right tackle provide the blocking. Once the fullback makes the catch, follow their blocks.

MADDEN NFL 11
DEFENSIVE STRATEGY

Contents

DEFENSIVE CONTROLS

Welcome to *Madden NFL 11,* where the mechanics of the defensive controls have been overhauled. The adjustment to the new controls should put all players on an even playing field from the technical aspect. What you do from there is what will rank you in the *Madden NFL* masses.

To give you a jump-start on everyone who does not have this guide, we will take a detailed look at all of the game's controls and how to activate them. If you expect to be a solid defensive player you need to use every tool in the bag to slow down the offense. Without further ado, let's look at the defensive controls for *Madden NFL 11.*

Pre-Snap Controls

Audibles

A defense is only as good as the play that's called. Audibles let us switch into a better play based on what we're seeing from the offense. To access the defensive audibles, press the Audible button and then left or right on the left thumbstick or D-pad for any of the four preset audibles. You can also select one of your custom audibles by pressing the Audible button a second time to access those play calls.

Defensive Line Adjustments

This is where the changes to the defensive controls come into play. Changing the way the defensive line sets up prior to the snap affects how the line reacts after the snap. The new Strategy Pad controls access this. Please read the "Defensive Line Audibles" section for more detail.

Linebacker Adjustments

Use the linebacker audibles to change the way the linebackers line up before the snap. Changing the linebackers' position on the field affects blitz and coverage angles after the snap. For more information, please read the "Linebacker Audibles" section.

Coverage Adjustments

Coverage audibles affect the way our defensive backs and even some linebackers cover the field once the play starts. For more information, please read the "Coverage Audibles" section.

Individual Defensive Hot Routes

Whenever we need to change the defensive assignment for a specific player on the defense we use the individual hot routes. Please read the "Defensive Playmaker" section.

Player Assignment Cam

Use the player assignment cam to see the assignment of the selected player without exposing all your defensive assignments.

Pump Up the Crowd

Use the pump up the crowd control to get your fans involved and charge up the home stadium atmosphere.

Play Art Cam

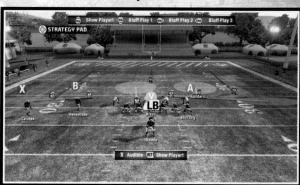

By pressing the button to show the play art, you can see the icons of each receiver on the field as well as the defensive assignments for every defender on the field.

Switch Player

There's more than one way to switch players in *Madden NFL 11.* You can cycle through the players by pressing either Switch Player button, or you can go back and forth by pressing the button opposite the one originally pushed. You can also switch players by holding down one of the Switch Player buttons and pressing up, down, left, or right on the left thumbstick or D-pad.

Post-Snap Controls

Defensive Line Moves

When in control of a defensive lineman use the right thumbstick to add pressure on the quarterback. The right thumbstick allows you to navigate around, away from, or through the offensive linemen.

Hands Up/Bat Ball

Defensive linemen never give up on a play, so if you can't reach the quarterback use the Hands Up/Bat Ball button to knock down the pass at the line of scrimmage.

Tackle/Dive

Use the Dive button to make a leaping tackle on a ball carrier. This type of tackle can create a big hit or save the defense from giving up a big gain.

Hit Stick

This is one of the best tackle options in the game, but it is also a high-risk option. To activate the hit stick, push up on the right stick for a crushing blow or down on the right stick to cut the ball carrier's legs out from under him.

Sprint

The Sprint button gives the defender you're in control of a little boost in speed. This helps you accelerate faster to chase down a ball carrier.

Strafe

Use the Strafe button to get your defender in perfect position to make a solid tackle or the best play on a ball in the air. This button squares your defender to the line of scrimmage.

Strip Ball

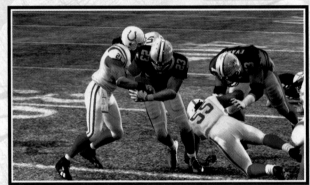

When you close in on a ball carrier try using the Strip Ball button to pry the ball loose from his arms. This is most effective when you initiate the tackle on the side of the ball. The flaw in trying to strip the ball is that you are less worried about the tackle, which can lead to the ball carrier breaking the tackle.

Catch/Intercept

The Catch button allows you to go up and aggressively go for the interception. Follow the play and get into perfect position to make the play on the ball. Using the Strafe button can increase your chances as well.

Swat

Sometimes the best way to defend the pass is to swat the ball down. Use the Swat button to break up passes when you are not in perfect position to intercept the ball. The more you practice this technique the better your pass defense will be.

DEFENSIVE LINE AUDIBLES

Football is a game that is won and lost in the trenches. Of course, the spotlight is on the players in the more visible skill positions, but without the linemen up front, nothing will work.

Our first area of preparation needs to be the defensive line. In *Madden NFL* we can dominate the game by perfecting the use of the line audibles and line shifts that are in the game. These shifts will let us get better position to stop the run or help us add more pressure on our way to the opposing quarterback. If we can dominate the line of scrimmage it will make it that much easier to win the game.

Pinch Defensive Line

Strengths

- Pinching the defensive line protects against the inside run by placing defensive linemen over both guards or both guards and the center.
- It creates pressure over top of the center.
- It creates overloads in the A and B gaps and can lead to clean hits on the opposing quarterback.

Weaknesses

- This adjustment relies on the offense to run inside, leaving the outside exposed.
- Defensive ends can't set contain on the quarterback or backs because of their alignment.
- It relies on smaller outside linebackers to support the outside run or add pressure. This takes them out of coverage and can hurt the defense.

Spread Defensive Line

Strengths

- Spreading the defensive line puts the line in position to prevent runs to the edge.
- The defensive ends have a great chance of preventing quarterbacks from rolling out to pass.
- It gives the faster defensive ends a chance to use their athleticism to beat offensive tackles and sack the quarterback.

Weaknesses

- With so much concern about protecting the edge, we give up the ability to play the inside run well.
- It's vulnerable to the QB sneak from any Shotgun set as well as spread Singleback sets.
- It eliminates the effectiveness of slower defensive ends. The spread alignment benefits speed rushers.

Shift Right

Strengths

- This is a strong-side shift that allows us to chip the tight end if he releases for a pass as well as aggressively pursue strong-side runs.
- It creates premium blitz opportunities because of overloads.
- This shift plays strong-side runs and quarterback rollouts well. It also works wells against the inside run.

Weaknesses

- The strong-side shift leaves weak-side runs more attractive to the offense.
- It cannot contain quarterback rollout passes to the weak side.
- It allows the weak-side defensive end to get double-teamed and makes weak-side pressure extremely hard.

Shift Left

Strengths

- This weak-side shift allows us to play counter runs and weak-side runs better.
- It creates premium blitz opportunities because of overloads.
- It works well against the inside run.

Weaknesses

- The weak-side shift leaves strong-side runs more attractive to the offense.
- It cannot contain quarterback rollout passes to the strong side.
- It allows the strong-side defensive end to get double-teamed by the tight end and right tackle.

Crash Right

Crashing the defensive line to the right makes the line step to the strong side after the snap. This attacks any runs to the strong side or play action QB rollouts.

Crash Left

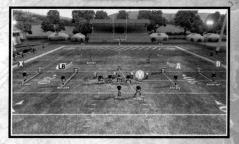

Crashing the defensive line to the left makes the line step to the weak side after the snap. This attacks any runs to the weak side or play action QB rollouts.

Crash In

When the offense is running up the gut, use the inside crash stunt to shut down the inside run game.

Crash Out

Use the crash outside stunt to counter outside runs or to force the defensive end to loop around the offensive tackles.

LINEBACKER AUDIBLES

The second line of the defense is the linebacker unit. In competitive *Madden NFL* play, this is the most important defensive grouping on the field. All of the high-pressure blitz packages revolve around the placement or alignment of the linebackers. We want to maximize the performance from our linebackers so we will use almost every linebacker adjustment throughout the course of a game. If we mix our linebacker shifts with the multiple defensive line shifts we will have success against both the run and pass.

Pinch Linebackers In

Strengths

- Pinching the linebackers in provides great protection vs. the inside run.
- The scariest heat in *Madden NFL* is always through the A gap; pinching the linebackers in puts us in position to enjoy some of this success.
- Often this alignment forces the offense to change their blocking scheme, making this a perfect option to give a false look.

Weaknesses

- We can get beaten easily on outside running plays, like tosses or sweeps.
- It makes the HB Screen a potential big play every time.
- It cannot cover Bunch, Spread, or Trips receiver packages.

Spread Linebackers Out

Strengths

- Having the linebackers spread out puts them in great position to defend any outside run plays.
- The mobile quarterback is becoming a serious threat again, and this alignment limits the effectiveness of that offensive scheme.
- When the linebackers are spread out wide we have a better chance of reaching the quarterback with a wide blitz.
- It allows us to remain in our defense against balanced Shotgun or Spread formations.

Weaknesses

- It puts the success of defending the inside runs solely on the middle linebacker.
- It makes it possible for the offense to throw quick routes to the tight ends when inside of our outside linebackers.

Shift Linebackers Right

Strengths

- Shifting the linebackers right is effective vs. Bunch receiver sets on the strong side.
- It puts our strong-side linebacker in position to blow up strong-side tosses or sweeps in the backfield.
- It plays the HB Screen and inside run to the strong side well.

Weaknesses

- It makes the defense vulnerable to weak-side run or toss plays.
- It gives the offense the freedom to run naked bootlegs.
- It makes the weak side responsible for setting the backside edge.

Shift Linebackers Left

Strengths

- Shifting the linebackers left is effective vs. Bunch receiver sets to the weak side.
- It gives the weak-side linebacker a better blitz angle to the quarterback.
- It plays the HB Screen and inside run to the weak side well.

Weaknesses

- It makes the defense vulnerable to strong-side run or toss plays.
- It gives the offense the freedom to run roll out passing plays to the strong side.
- It puts the strong-side linebacker in a bad position to defend a pass or run to his side.

All Linebackers Blitz

Press the D-pad to the right and then press down on the right thumbstick.

Have all linebackers blitz when you want to sell out against the run or you just want to send more defenders than the offense has blocking for. High risk, high reward.

Strong Outside Linebacker Blitz

Press the D-pad to the right and then press right on the right thumbstick.

Any time you want to send pressure from the strong side or add a faster defender off of the edge, call for a strong outside linebacker blitz.

Weak Outside Linebacker Blitz

Press the D-pad to the right and then press left on the right thumbstick.

Any time you want to send pressure from the quarterback's blind side or add a faster defender off of the edge, blitz the weak outside linebacker.

All Linebackers in Hook Zones

Press the D-pad to the right and then press down on the right thumbstick.

If you're facing an opponent that has problems vs. Cover 2, show man and then audible into the all hook zones. This is great in the goal area with multiple receivers on the field.

COVERAGE AUDIBLES

The passing game is the most popular style of offense in football right now. Many of the rules currently in place are designed to make it easier to pass the ball. The more passing, the faster the pace of the game and the more exciting the game feels. When playing defense we want to make the offense struggle, stall, and fail. *Madden NFL 11* gives us coverage audibles to help deal with the potent offensive passing attacks that we will face in the game. Let's take a closer look at the pros and cons of the available coverage audibles.

Press Coverage

Press the D-pad up and then press down on the D-pad.

Strengths

- Press coverage is the perfect counter to the West Coast Offense or any timing-based offense. Pressing the receivers disrupts the design of the offensive play.
- It can make the opposing quarterback feel rushed or anxious as he waits for routes to get open.
- It forces the offense to call routes with automotion or Bunch receiver sets.

Weaknesses

- If the defensive back misses the jam on the receiver we could give up a big pass gain.
- It requires the cornerback to jam the receiver but also to break free if the offense is running the ball.
- It's hard to use when the offense puts the receiver in motion.

Back Off Coverage

Press the D-pad up and then press up on the D-pad again.

Strengths

- By backing the defensive backs up we put our defense in better position to defend the deep ball.
- It allows the defensive backs to break on passes in the air at full speed.
- It allows us to keep our cornerbacks from getting sealed by run-blocking receivers because of better pursuit angles.

Weaknesses

- It leaves WR Screen passes and many other short routes uncontested.
- It plays the run after the line of scrimmage.
- It also moves the linebackers back and can leave the inside run wide open.

Man Align

Press the D-pad up and then press right on the D-pad.

Strengths

- Man align puts our man defenders directly over top of who they are covering.
- It's normally used on a lot of enhanced blitz setups because it freezes the defense.
- It's more efficient than manually moving defenders into position.

Weaknesses

- It shows the offense that we are in man-to-man coverage.
- When using it to prevent defenders from constantly adjusting, it can have us out of position when in zone.

Show Blitz

Press the D-pad up and then press left on the D-pad.

Strengths

- This crowds the line of scrimmage and makes it easier to play the run.
- Additional defenders around the line of scrimmage can lead to easy sacks.
- It rattles some quarterbacks into making quick throws into perfect zone defense.

Weaknesses

- It leaves deep go routes open at the hike.
- It doesn't layer the defense, and if one tackle is broken it can give up a touchdown.

Zones to the Middle

Press the D-pad up and then press down on the right thumbstick.

Strengths

- This adjustment defends the seam routes well.
- It also defends post routes well.

Weaknesses

- It leaves sideline routes open.
- It keeps the safeties closer to the hash marks so they can't get over to play streaks or corner routes effectively.

Zones to the Sideline

Press the D-pad up and then press up on the right thumbstick.

Strengths

- The zones to the sideline adjustment plays outside breaking routes well.
- It works well for us in the red zone area when teams are looking to run fades and bunch route combos that go to the sideline.

Weaknesses

- It does not play deep post or seam routes well.
- It can be beaten quickly with slant routes.
- It vacates zone defenders in the middle of the field and can leave open QB draws.

Zones to the Right

Press the D-pad up and then press right on the right thumbstick.

Strengths

- The coverage cheats to the offense's right side. This is normally the strong side of the formation for right-handed quarterbacks.
- It protects against intermediate and deep outside breaking routes.

Weaknesses

- The left side of the field is vulnerable to passes.

Zones to the Left

Press the D-pad up and then press left on the right thumbstick.

Strengths

- The coverage cheats to the offense's left side. This is normally the weak side of the formation for right-handed quarterbacks.
- It protects against intermediate and deep outside breaking routes.

Weaknesses

- The right side of the field is vulnerable to passes.

DEFENSIVE PLAYMAKER

One of the most useful tools for anyone trying to defend an opponent in *Madden NFL* is the defensive playmaker. This can truly be considered the MVP of the defensive controls. Having the ability to manually alter any player assignment on defense is the way EA SPORTS gives each user the ability to have a completely unique defense.

With the standard shifts and controls there is a limited number of looks a defense can present to the offense. Our defensive playmaker lets us combine the shifts and basic controls into some of the more potent and aggressive defensive schemes in *Madden NFL*. This is put on display when spectators watch any live MLG/ EA SPORTS Madden Challenge event. These events showcase the best *Madden NFL* competitors in the world, and the one thing that they all rely on is the ability to alter and adjust coverages and assignments on the fly.

On a smaller level, when at home, with friends, or online, these adjustments allow you to disguise your actual play call and make the offensive player think about counters based on every player you have touched.

In the past, this function has been overused, and EA SPORTS has introduced defensive adjustments through the D-pad this year; it looks like this will limit some of the excessive adjustment abuse that players have been guilty of. Let's take a look at the individual defensive hot routes.

To call a defensive hot route, press the D-pad to access the Strategy Pad once you have the player you want to adjust selected. To make playmaker adjustments press down on the D-pad and then select one of the four options associated with the D-pad or one of the four associated with the right thumbstick.

Hook Zone (Yellow Circle)

Press the D-pad down and then press up on the D-pad.

This hot route puts the selected defender into a hook zone. This works well against curl routes and short routes in the defender's area.

Curl to Flat (Purple Circle)

Press the D-pad down, and then press right on the D-pad.

This hot route puts the selected defender into a curl to flat zone. This is a good option for defending flat, hook, and out routes.

Blitz (Red Arrow)

Press the D-pad down, then press the D-pad down once more.

This hot route assigns the selected defender to blitz. This also eliminates any preset blitz angle and makes the controlled defender blitz straight down.

Flat Zone (Blue Circle)

Press the D-pad down and then press the D-pad to the left.

This hot route assigns the selected defender to guard the flat. This is a good option for defending quick outs, slant outs, swing routes, and the quarterback if he rolls out to the flat.

Deep Zone (Dark Blue Circle)

Press the D-pad down and then press up on the right thumbstick.

Using this hot route assignment puts the selected defender into a deep zone in his area. This is a good option if you notice your opponent sending the same receiver on streak or fade routes.

QB Contain (Horizontal Red Arrow)

Press the D-pad down and then press right on the right thumbstick.

This hot route option puts the selected defender into QB contain. The defender will try to prevent the quarterback from getting outside of the pocket.

Man Coverage (Gray Line)

Press the D-pad down and then press down on the right thumbstick; you must then select which offensive player to cover.

This hot route option puts our selected defender in man coverage on the offensive player we select. This is good option to add a double team or to assign coverage on an uncovered player.

QB Spy (Orange Circle)

Press the D-pad down and then press left on the right thumbstick.

This hot route assigns our selected defender to mirror the quarterback's movements. This also protects us when an offensive player rolls out and plans to throw back across the shallow areas of the field.

DEFENSIVE COVERAGES

There are five standard coverage shells in football, and with those five, coaches have come up with numerous ways of combining them or creating their own unique looks. No matter what the coach likes to call it, it will fit into one of the five coverage shells: Cover 1, Cover 2, Cover 3, Cover 4, or Cover 0. Each has a unique set of qualities and a design to attack the offense. Let's take a detailed look at each coverage scheme and its strengths and weaknesses.

Cover 1

When a coach calls for a Cover 1 defense, he is sending the defense on the field with one defender responsible for playing deep coverage. The majority of the time, this will be the free safety playing the deep middle of the field. This is typically a man-to-man defense underneath.

Strengths

- Cover 1 is very flexible vs. the pass.
- It is often used with pressure and brings as many as eight defenders in on the blitz.
- When using the strong safety in robber coverage we get short middle and deep middle coverage.

Weaknesses

- The free safety is responsible for any deep pass.
- It takes the free safety out of run support because of pass responsibilities.
- Double sideline routes can nullify the deep safety.

Cover 2

The Cover 2 is the most popular defensive coverage because of all the success that the Tampa Bay Bucs enjoyed from it in their years of producing dominating defenses. This coverage scheme is also well known because of the success the Indianapolis Colts have had with it.

The coverage calls for the safeties to split the field into halves and provide coverage over the top of the cornerbacks, who are typically in man coverage. The Cover 2 scheme that Tampa Bay and the Indianapolis Colts have made famous is the Tampa 2, which has both corners in flat zones and the middle linebacker dropping into zone over the shallow middle of the field.

Strengths

- The defense is designed to prevent the big play by keeping everything in front of the corners and safeties.
- It allows corners to gamble and go for interceptions because safeties cover.
- Cover 2 is solid against the run.

Weaknesses

- The offense can pick on the corner by sending two shallow routes his direction.
- If the offense sends a receiver down the sideline they can control the middle of the field.

Cover 3

The Cover 3 defensive shell is probably the most used in *Madden NFL* games. This defensive coverage has the most zone blitz play calls in *Madden NFL 11* and is easily the most confusing for offenses to figure out because of the many variations that are in the game.

The Cover 3 defense normally has one cornerback added in deep coverage, with one of the safeties rotating his zone to the sideline and the other to the middle of the field. When the defense is running a 46 or 4–4 set, the free safety will drop to the deep middle while the cornerbacks drop to their deep zones, creating a three-deep look.

Strengths

- Cover 3 provides shut-down defense if the offense doesn't have time to wait for routes to open.
- It has the protection of a Cover 2 defense but with a defensive back covering the deep middle zone.
- It has numerous blitz packages, including the infamous zone blitz.
- It plays the run well.
- It can be run with two safeties and a corner or two corners and a safety.

Weaknesses

- Passes to the flat can be wide open.
- It breaks down if there is no pressure.
- It can be beaten with level routes to the sideline.
- Tight ends can control the middle safety's movement and weaken coverage.

Cover 4

The Cover 4 defense is also known as a true bend-but-don't-break defense. This is the only defensive coverage shell that everyone agrees is a passive defense. Normally the coach will call Cover 4 when the game is approaching halftime and the opposing offense is attempting a Hail Mary pass. This defense doesn't care about anything short and is designed to prevent the deep pass. The Cover 4 defense calls for both cornerbacks and safeties, or some combination of four defensive backs, to cover the deep quarter zones.

Strengths

- Cover 4 protects the defense from getting beaten deep.
- If the offense is using three receivers we will double-team one receiver.
- It forces the offense to settle for short gains.

Weaknesses

- It leaves all short routes open and uncontested.
- It does not work well vs. the run.
- It can let the opposing team get in a passing rhythm because of lax coverage.

Cover 0

Cover 0 is exactly what it sounds like: There are no defenders responsible for playing deep coverage. Some coaches believe that Cover 0 means all man coverage, and others believe that Cover 0 just means there is no deep protection at all. For the purpose of this article, we are equating Cover 0 with no deep coverage. In the past, Cover 0 was primarily a blitz-only coverage. With the heavy use of hybrid-style defenses, the Cover 0 can be a great asset to confuse the offense and get easy hits on the opposing quarterback.

Strengths

- Cover 0 is aggressive coverage because no defenders are responsible for deep zones.
- It can look like man coverage but still be zone.
- It challenges all short routes and defends intermediate routes well.

Weaknesses

- There's no deep help, and it leaves the deep pass open.
- It can be destroyed by a poised pocket passer.
- Combo routes easily beat it.

DEFENSIVE FORMATIONS

There is only one way to win a football game, and that is to prevent the other team from scoring more points than our team. Some people think this means we have to score a bunch of points, but all it really says is that the defense will determine the outcome of every game. Before we get into more details about playing defense, let's take a look at the different formation sets in *Madden NFL 11*.

4-3 Defense

The most common defense in football is the 4–3. This defense uses four defensive linemen and three linebackers. The big bodies up front make this a defense built on beating the man in front of you. This is the front that players feel the most comfortable with when trying to stop the run. When you have a dominant player on the line, especially at a tackle position, this defense can wreak havoc on an offense. Normally, inside pressure from the 4–3 will result in the offense needing to use double-teams in the interior of the line. If the offense has to start double-teaming any of our down linemen, they're at a disadvantage because one of our extra linemen will come free, and the linebacker that plays behind him may as well. This defense is perfect against the Spread formation because of the width of the outside linebackers and their ability to roll up and cover the flats or drop off into hook or curl zones.

3-4 Defense

The 3–4 defense has become the standard defensive formation and playbook for many *Madden NFL* competitors. There used to be only a handful of teams that ran the 3–4, but with offenses having so much success, the 3–4 has charged back because of the way the defenders are aligned prior to the snap. Just looking at the personnel shows that the defense is in better position to make a play vs. passing sets. Only having three down linemen on the field may put a lot of pressure on our linemen to hold their ground, but the benefit of adding another linebacker in place of a lineman makes up for the loss in size with speed.

You always want to put your best players on the field, and with the 3–4, you have a better opportunity to match up against the offense when passing, while keeping enough speed on the field to stretch out any runs that the offense attempts. The perfect time to use the 3–4 is when starting a drive in any compressed area situation. By having four linebackers spread across the field, we will make the offense second-guess the use of any timing or quick-pass routes. A base 3–4 call will effectively eliminate the slant and crossing routes. If the offense tries to take advantage of our three down linemen by running inside, then we have two athletic linebackers who will be able to stuff the run and shift between the tackles to create pressure based on alignment. The 3–4 also has many variations, which allows you to create a unique pressure scheme when playing *Madden NFL 11*.

4-4 Split

The 4–4 Split defense is an attacking defense that is primarily used to stop the run. There is no way we can have eight men near the line of scrimmage and allow the offense to have any success running the ball. When playing the run, the defense is designed to (at the very least) create a wall at the line of scrimmage and prevent the running back from having any success inside. The defensive line is responsible for crashing the line down and letting the linebackers play over top to make the tackle if the back tries to break outside.

This defense is also great against the pass because of the spacing of our defenders and the many different packages we can put together when attacking the offense. The base defense of a 4–4 front is the Cover 3. We will have the corners and safety drop out in deep thirds and have the four underneath backers handle any of the short to medium passing routes. We do not want to use this defense as a pure coverage defense. Our strength in this front is to handle the short to medium passing game. If we don't get pressure then we will be open for big-play opportunities. Look for this defense in the Titans defensive playbook.

4-6 Defense

One of the most heralded defenses in all of football, the 46 defense, is a 4–3 but with the strong safety up near the line of scrimmage. When it was first used, it created matchup problems for the offense because they didn't know who to block. This defense is much like the 4–4 in that it is geared to stop the run. The other side of the 46 is that it really wants to get to the opponent's quarterback and, in the process, tackle anyone who has the ball.

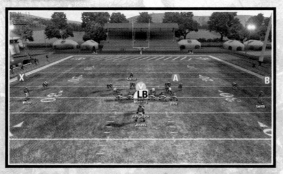

With any high-pressure defense, we're giving the offense the opportunity to have a big play. However, if we do our job, the offense will get negative yardage more often than not. One of the things we have to keep in mind when running the 46 defense is that it is not the best defense for the quick-pass game. As a rule of thumb, we want to use this defense against opponents who like to throw the ball downfield or at least take five-step drops. If we run the 46 vs. the quick-pass game, even if we have success we're risking giving up a game-changing play.

Nickel Defense

The Nickel defense is one of your standard defenses to counter the pass. It uses four down linemen, two linebackers, and five defensive backs. This is what you constantly hear described as a passing down defense. Most of the time, the defense will run some sort of Nickel on third and fourth down. We can keep a respectable run defense on the field by having four down linemen, but we also defend the pass because we have an extra defensive back on the field.

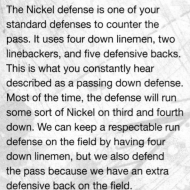

When running plays from the Nickel formation it is easy to establish a solid pass and run defense. The basic setup vs. the run would be to manually play the nickelback and roam him inside but behind the linebackers. By moving the nickelback inside, we have created a 4–3 look and can treat the offense as if we were in the 4–3.

Dime Defense

When we face an opponent who is going to abandon the run or throw the ball close to 70 percent of the time, then it's time to bring out the Dime defense. For years, teams have used the Dime as a base pass defense, because it's fairly simple to teach and is basically a prevent-the-pass defense. This defense typically uses four down linemen, one linebacker, and six defensive backs.

The Dime is a great defense for countering a pocket-passing quarterback. If we see that our opponent is not going to threaten us with a lot of scrambling or running out of their passing formations, then we want to go to this.

Dollar Defense

The Dollar formation incorporates a three-man line, two linebackers, and six defensive backs. This defense uses line stunts and multiple defensive backs in blitz schemes to throw the quarterback off and make him hesitate in throwing the ball. If blitzing is your thing, the Dollar is the equivalent of the zone blitz, because almost every play brings pressure. Don't worry, though; if you want to play a bend-but-don't-break defense, the Dollar has a few pure drop-back and QB contain zones for you.

Quarter Defense

The Quarter defense uses a three-man line, one linebacker, and seven defensive backs. This defense is the perfect counter to an opponent who likes to come out with five wide receivers and then run no huddle on us. The speed that we have on the field is a positive and negative for us when running the Quarter defense. With so many defensive backs on the field, if the offense has one running back on the field they can audible down and start pounding the ball between the tackles. This is a pass-only defense, so be very cautious if you try to use it to defend the run.

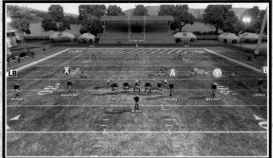

DEFENSIVE FRONTS AND GAP ASSIGNMENTS

From a coaching perspective, alignment is the single most important aspect of having a successful defense. If your players are not in the right position to execute the design of the play, then we have to rely on pure athleticism to save the play. At no point does a coach want to rely solely on ability to determine the success of the play call. If our players are fundamentally sound and always in the right spot, the defensive play call will put them in position to be successful while showcasing their ability.

The differences in defensive fronts change the responsibilities or gap assignments of the defensive linemen and linebackers. As a defense, we can dominate the offense even before the snap by getting our alignments correct. The offensive line numbering will never change; there will be eight possible gaps on the offensive line, four to the right of the center and four to the left of the center. By changing the number of defenders we have on the line, we can effectively change how the offense will call its protection.

So how does this relate to *Madden NFL 11*? The better the understanding you have of the foundations of a defense, the easier it will be for you to make adjustments and create your own pressure schemes.

Let's take a look into the most common fronts and gap responsibilities that you will come across in *Madden NFL 11*. Some of this may seem complicated, but it will give you a general idea of your responsibility for any player you use, instead of just running around on defense.

Three-Man Front

The 3–4 defense is the most common three-man front

As you take a look at the image, you will see the basic responsibilities that you need to keep in mind when playing a base three-man front. Any time you are using a three-man front and you get confused or forget an assignment, these base assignments will keep your defensive play call intact.

Gap Rules

- Defensive ends are responsible for two gaps. When in control of a defensive end, you have to control the gap to either shoulder of the offensive tackle.
- The nose tackle is responsible for both A gaps (the gaps at the shoulders of the center).
- Outside linebackers are responsible for the C gap or the gap between the tackle and the tight end. When the offense is passing, we play our assigned pass responsibility.
- Inside linebackers are responsible for the B gaps, the gaps between the guards and tackles. When the offense passes the ball, we play our assigned pass responsibility.

The weak-side inside linebacker shoots through the B gap and chases down the back

When you know your position assignments it doesn't matter what the offense does, because you will know where to go with the defender you're in control of. Playing real techniques will make your overall defense tougher to move the ball against, and make the offense rely on real schemes instead of gimmick play.

Four-Man Front

The image shows the basic responsibilities that you need to keep in mind when playing a base four-man front. Just like before, these base assignments will keep your defensive play call intact and prevent you from being worried about the play call if you forget the play art somehow.

The 4–3 is the most common four-man front

Gap Rules

- Defensive ends are responsible for the C gap or the tackle/tight end gap and should crash down to the B gap. When facing the pass we have pass rush or contain responsibility.
- The weak-side defensive tackle is responsible for controlling the weak-side A gap.
- The strong-side defensive tackle is responsible for the strong-side B gap (the gap between the guard and tackle).
- Outside linebackers are responsible for B gap and should attack the run from the inside out. When facing the pass we play our assignment.
- The middle linebacker is responsible for the strong-side A gap and will play the run inside out. When facing the pass we play our assignment.

The strong-side linebacker shoots through the B gap and stops the run in the backfield

Defense is designed to be similar to math and science—you input the numbers and come out with an expected result. As long as we know our assignments and are in position, we will enjoy success defending any offensive style out there.

Contents

PRE-SNAP DEFENSIVE COVERAGE READS

It's well-documented that Colts quarterback Peyton Manning spends a good amount of time watching game film each week to prepare for his upcoming opponents. Part of his film study is to get an idea of the types of coverages his opponent likes to call. In *Madden NFL 11*, you can simulate film study by looking at defensive coverage alignments before the snap. Often, these alignments are direct tip-offs to the pass coverage your opponent is calling on defense. We are going show some of the tip-offs you can use to gain the upper hand on your opponent.

Use Motion

The most common technique for pre-reading the defense is to motion a receiver from one side to another. If the defender lined up across from the receiver follows him, then you know it's man coverage. This is known as man lock coverage.

The left cornerback follows the flanker

If the defender lined up across from the receiver doesn't follow him, then it's zone coverage.

There are exceptions to this rule. For instance, say the right outside linebacker is covering a slot receiver in man coverage. The defense comes out in the Nickel Normal—2 Man Under and the offense comes out in the Gun Dice Slot. The flanker is sent in motion to the left. The left cornerback will follow the receiver as soon he goes in motion. By the time the flanker receiver gets to the other side of the field, the right inside defensive tackle covers him. That's because the cornerback is not locked in man coverage. Instead they are just playing man coverage. Remember this: Man lock coverage means the defender will follow the receiver; man coverage means the defender will release the receivers. The offensive and defensive formations called will determine if man lock is used or not. Also, linebackers

and safeties never play man lock coverage, only cornerbacks. The only way this doesn't hold true is if individual defensive assignments are used, either on the field or in the Coaching Options menu. For instance, say your opponent puts the free safety in man coverage on the split end while on the field. If the split end is motioned to the other side, the free safety will follow him all the way across the field in man coverage.

Making Pre-Snap Reads with Formations

There are many offensive formations in the game in which you can tell if man or zone coverage is called by just looking at how defenders line up.

The right cornerback is lined up almost directly across from the tight end

The offense comes out in the Singleback Bunch. The defense comes out Dime Normal—2 Man Under. There are three defenders lined up across from the three receivers bunched up on the right side. This is a clear indication that man coverage is called.

Not all the defenders are lined up directly across from the receivers

This time the Dime Normal—Cover 3 coverage is called. Notice that the right cornerback lines up across from the split end and there are four defenders lined up over the three bunch receivers. Also, not all the defenders are lined up across from the receivers. This tells us zone coverage is called. Keep an eye on the left cornerback—he may line up farther outside of the flanker.

We suggest going into practice mode or finding a buddy online to practice making pre-snap reads of the defense with your favorite playbook, and using multiple formations to get an idea if man or zone coverage is being called. Look at how the defenders are lined up, then watch instant replays to check whether you were correct.

Watch the Defensive Backs

Most quarterbacks are told to locate the safeties before the snap to get an idea of the coverage shell that is being called. In *Madden NFL 11*, you do the same thing. We will take it one step further by also reading the outside cornerbacks. Here are a few examples of how we like to read the coverage shell.

Cover 0

If Cover 0 is called, watch the safeties. If neither is playing deep or in the middle, chances are it's Cover 0 coverage. If this coverage is called, you can bet there is a blitz coming after you.

Cover 2

If the safeties stay at even depth and the cornerbacks are in press coverage, you can bet it's Cover 2 coverage. You may need to use motion to tell if it's Cover 2 man or zone coverage.

Cover 4

Watch the safeties first. If they play at even depth, then it's Cover 2 or Cover 4. Next watch the corners—if one or both move, then it's Cover 4.

No safety aligns deep

Two safeties align deep

Two safeties align deep

Cover 1

If one safety rotates to the middle of the field while the other safety comes up, then it's either Cover 1 or Cover 3. To tell if man coverage is called, watch the outside corners. If they don't move, then it's Cover 1 man coverage. Of course you can always use motion to tell. Keep in mind that the safety playing the deep middle may not roll that much towards the deep middle.

Cover 3

It's pretty easy to tell if Cover 3 coverage is called. Watch the safeties first. If one rotates to the deep middle while the other one comes up, then it's Cover 1 or Cover 3. Next, watch the corners. If one or both of them move, then it's Cover 3.

One safety aligns deep

One safety aligns deep

BEATING BUMP-N-RUN MAN COVERAGE

One of the first things you will want to do after picking up your latest copy of *Madden NFL* is find bump-n-run man beaters. Bump-n-run man coverage can be a nuisance in your offensive game plan, but it can be beaten with good play calling.

The RCB jams the SE at the line of scrimmage

Many of the enhanced blitz schemes have man coverage behind them. Most players who run these blitz schemes call bump-n-run man coverage. Even if they run Cover 2 man, you can bet they will use bump-n-run to try to disrupt your passing game. We are going to show several common bump-n-run man beaters that have been tried and tested over the years.

Motion

Motion has long been used as a way to beat bump-n-run man coverage. There are all kinds of ways in *Madden NFL* to use motion to beat this coverage. Let's look at a few different ways that we like to use motion to get receivers off the line of scrimmage without being jammed.

Gun Snugs Flip—Stick

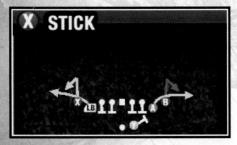

Our first example of how we like to beat bump-n-run man coverage with motion comes out of the Gun Snugs Flip. The play called is Stick. On the right, the inside receiver runs a flat route while the outside receiver runs a stick route. We are going to use motion to get them both off the line of scrimmage without being jammed.

The outside receiver is hot routed on a slant route

We make one pre-snap adjustment: to hot route the outside receiver on a slant out. We take control of the inside receiver and motion him to the left.

The inside receiver takes one step inside

After he takes just one step, snap the ball. Once the ball is snapped, he will run behind the outside receiver and towards the flat. Notice the switch between the left cornerback and left inside defensive back.

The left cornerback now covers the inside receiver running the flat, while the left inside defensive back covers the

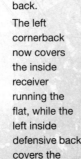

The flat receiver is tightly covered

outside receiver on the slant route. Because the two defenders switch, they don't jam the receivers.

The QB throws a high bullet pass to the open receiver

The flat receiver may or may not be open. In this case, he is not, so we look towards the receiver running the slant out. We see that he is open and throw him a high bullet pass. The catch is made about 10 yards down the field. Once the receiver has the ball in his hands, we take control of him and head down the field for positive yardage.

Gun Empty Y-Flex—Curl Flats

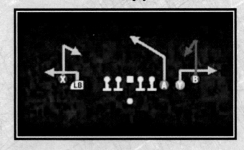

This next use of motion to beat bump-n-run man coverage has been in the game for some time. This play is not always going to pick up a ton of yardage, unless the receiver breaks the tackle. The norm is 4–5 yards a pop, but there is potential for more. The play we come out in is the Gun Empty Y-Flex—Curl Flats. Notice that the left inside receiver is running a flat route to the left. If we were to snap the ball, he wouldn't be jammed at the line of scrimmage. However, he wouldn't have much room to work with once the catch is made.

The SE is now pass-blocking

To give him some extra room, we like to hot route the outside receiver on the same side to pass-block. We do this to make sure the defender covering the outside receiver is nowhere near the slot receiver when we make the throw.

The left slot receiver has been motioned inside

We then motion to the inside receiver so that he lines up next to the left tackle. The defensive back covering him is about 4 yards away. Once the ball is snapped, the inside slot receiver won't be jammed. As a matter of fact, he gets some separation from his man.

The QB delivers a perfect throw to his open receiver

The outside receiver brings the right cornerback inside, effectively taking him out of the play so he can't make a tackle. Once the slot receiver gets past the right cornerback, we want to throw him the ball. For this example, we throw a hard bullet pass to the left.

Once the catch is made, we take control of the receiver and head down the field. The faster the receiver, the better the chance of picking up more yardage.

The catch is made about 4 yards past the line of scrimmage

Gun Normal Flex Wk—Patriots Corner

One last way to beat bump-n-run man coverage with motion is to run plays with automotion. We come out in the Gun Normal Flex Wk—Patriots Corner. This play has the split end sent in automotion. He runs a corner route. Many of the automotion plays are designed so that when the ball is snapped, the receiver sent in automotion gets behind another receiver.

Neither receiver is jammed at the line of scrimmage

This allows both receivers to get off the line of scrimmage without being jammed. The split end gets cleanly off the line of scrimmage.

The QB throws a laser to the SE as he gets inside position

Before he goes towards the corner, throw him a hard bullet pass. The catch is made for an 8-yard pickup.

Delay Routes

Gun Trips TE—Deep Fork

Delayed routes are effective not only against zone coverage, but also against man coverage and bump-n-run man coverage.

Any time a receiver runs a delayed route, he won't be jammed at the line of scrimmage. Of course, since he delays his route, it actually takes him a little longer to go out than if he were actually jammed at the line of scrimmage. However, once the receiver does go out, he is usually open. A good example of a delayed pass route is the flat route ran by the tight end. The Gun Trips TE—Deep Fork out of the Patriots playbook has the tight end running a delayed flat route to the right.

The TE stays in to pass-block

Once the ball is snapped, the tight end looks to pass-block first. After about two seconds, he runs his delayed flat route. Notice that he doesn't get jammed at the line of scrimmage.

The tight end goes out on his delayed flat route

Don't wait too long to throw him the ball, as his man may close in on him quickly. When throwing the pass, we want to lead the tight end so that the defender covering him can make a play on the ball.

The QB spots the TE open and throws him the ball

In this case, we throw a hard bullet pass to the right. The tight end makes the catch and picks up 5 yards. Regarding delayed pass routes; if a defender is blitzing on the same side as the receiver who is running the delayed pass route, then that receiver will not go out on his route. Instead, he will stay in to pass-block. Receivers running delayed routes cannot be sent in motion.

The HB is wide open in the flat

Finally, if the running back is running a delayed route out of the backfield, he obviously cannot be jammed. He also might get wide open, as the defender who is covering him may end up blitzing, thinking that the running back is pass-blocking. If this happens, look for the running back; he should be able to pick up a good chunk of yardage.

Quick Tips for Beating Bump-n-Run Man Coverage

- When labbing your playbook, look for routes that are uncommon. There are some routes in the game that very few plays have. Some of these routes can beat bump-n-run man coverage without having to do anything outside of snapping the ball.

- If you are practicing by yourself, put one controller on offense and one on defense. Call bump-n-run man coverage and run your plays. Try different formations and plays to see what happens. Also use hot routes, because some of them can be used in conjunction with other routes to get receivers off the line of scrimmage. Be creative with them and you will find some nice bump-n-run man beaters.

- There are some defenses in the game called Man Press. If you are labbing individual pass routes with outside receivers, you can call these defenses without having to use two controllers since the cornerbacks jam the outside receivers.

- Find a buddy and lab together online. That's probably the most efficient way to lab bump-n-run plays.

- Some teams have plays where receivers are stacked, such as the Saints' Gun Split Offset. These plays, although hard to find, are natural bump-n-run man beaters.

- Receivers with high press release ratings get off the line of scrimmage quicker than those with low press release ratings.

BEATING COVER 2

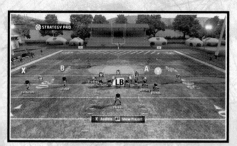

The defense comes out in a Cover 2

The Cover 2 zone is one of the most used zones in the game. This pass defensive coverage is used in two ways. The main purpose of the Cover 2 is to have both safeties split the field in half. This allows the corners to have help behind them. The middle is defended with hook zones sitting down and defending any underneath routes. The defensive backs sit in the flats, and the defensive line runs a stunt to try to generate pressure up front. The idea behind this defense is that having your corners press up on the outside wideouts disturbs the timing of the quarterback. The defensive line generates a pass rush, and when the quarterback looks to pass, you have the whole field accounted for. This is a great defense against players who like to quick-pass and throw short- to medium-depth routes. You have different kinds of Cover 2 as well. You have the Tampa 2 and Cover 2 sink zones. The Tampa 2 or Buc was the version Tony Dungy used when he was coaching. He had his middle linebacker drop to the deep middle because people began to attack the deep middle of the field against his Cover 2s. So dropping the Mike linebacker in the middle took away the deep middle attack.

Man version of Cover 2 with spy

This is another version of the Cover 2 where you have man coverage underneath with a spy in the middle of the field. You also have a version of this defense where you can have the defensive ends in contain. This is good for players who like to roll out with the quarterback. The defensive ends only rush when they see that the quarterback is moving.

How to attack Cover 2 defense

There are many ways you can attack Cover 2. When you're playing an opponent who uses a Cover 2 zone, there are many areas open. You can work the fade outside, the deep middle, the seam, corner-post routes, and spread formations against Cover 2 zone. Let's look at attacking the middle and the use of fades.

The Cover 2 shell read

You make your coverage reads by reading the safeties. When you read the safeties, they will show what shell is over the defense.

The flanker attacks the gap between the corner and strong safety

The fade allows you to get past the press coverage and attack the gap between the corner and the safety. You can see that gap clearly here. Then if the strong safety moves over too much to help out, the tight end is working the seam with his fade route as well.

Nice catch by the flanker

You can see that the strong safety is put in conflict here. When you have pressure in the seam and outside it can make for a long day in regards to pass coverage. The key is that they have to get to you before you can flood the zone. The fade route releases well and allows you to attack the gaps in the coverage.

Using post and corner routes to attack Cover 2

Post and corner routes can tear up the Cover 2 zone coverage pretty well. Let's take a look at how these routes work against man Cover 2.

Double moves to beat man coverage

Any route that allows you to make a double move will help you beat man coverage. This is especially true if your receivers have speed. In this play, you have the post route and the corner route working to press the Cover 2 shell of the safeties.

Attacking the middle of the field

Shockey got leverage on his defender and fell right in the hole of the secondary.

Route Combos for Attacking Cover 2 Zone

- Four verticals
- Curl-flat
- Streak-wheel
- Streak-post

Routes and Route Combos for Attacking Cover 2 Man

- Crossing
- Dig
- Mesh
- Slot out

BEATING COVER 3

Cover 3 is called the true zone

This zone coverage drops three players back deep. Then you will have two players in the flats, and the rest play the middle of the field. Most of your zone blitzes have Cover 3 shells behind them. The strong safety, in most cases, drops down to play the flat or the hook route. When you read three men dropping back, you know you have Cover 3 out there. The strength of the Cover 3 is that the defense has total zone coverage on the field. The problem with Cover 3 is that it doesn't offer much flexibility. You can attack this coverage with curl-flat combos, flood routes, four verticals, and delay routes. You can also attack well with compressed or spread sets. The middle of the field is open most of the time because the inside defenders usually flare out and defend the flats. Cover 3 is often confused with Cover 1, since many players see the free safety or strong safety drop back and this triggers a read of Cover 3. Let's look at how to attack this coverage.

Cover 3 man

Certain playbooks have a man version of this coverage. This is a good prevent defense to use. Most players sit on the middle safety and roam the field with him. The defense now has a man on every man and also has three safeties back deep.

Curl-flat attack

When you attack with a curl-flat combo you need to attack the weak side of the defense. In Cover 3 the strong safety or the free safety will drop down in coverage underneath. Whatever side that safety drops down on is the strong side. In order for the curl-flat to work, you have to attack the weak side. This passing combo almost always works, but it works better against the weak side of the coverage. When you want to use this combo, try to get a play that has the curl-flat on both sides. That way you will be covered when attacking this coverage shell.

Pulling the flat defender

What makes this play tick is the receiver pulling the flat defender outside with his route. The flat defender breaks on the flat; the outside corner's job is defending the deep outside. This leaves a gap between the cornerback and the flat defender. The curl will be wide open, and in football this would be called "sitting in the hole of the zone." When you make your read, look at the alley defender to see what you should do with the ball. If you see a defender flare, you attack the curl. If you see that a defender sits or runs with the wideout, you hit the flat.

The alley defender broke on the flat route

You can see the wide-open gap once the flat defender has flared out. Notice that the outside defensive back is drifting back to defend his deep part of the third of his zone coverage. The curl-flat route combo opens up a nice gap.

The gap is clearly visible

When you see the defender flare out, throw the ball to the curl wideout. Don't get in the habit of waiting for him to sit. You have to get the ball moving when you see the flare and see the cornerback drop back in his deep third.

Four verticals attack

Now we will attack with four verticals and an underneath route combo.

The FS shows the Cover 3 shell

The four vertical routes force the coverage back. What you're looking for here is the seam.

Take your pick

You have the TE and the slot wideout open. Once the FS commits, you simply hit the open guy.

Routes and Route Combos for Attacking Cover 3

- Three and four verticals
- Stick
- Curl-flats
- Floods
- Delay routes

The Cover 4 defense is often called "prevent" defense

In Cover 4 coverage, the defense drops four men back in deep coverage. This is the coverage of choice when you want to take anything away deep. The shell will show four defenders dropping back and everyone else playing underneath. The key to defeating this shell is attacking it underneath and attacking with floods. When you get your playmaker in open space, you can work your way down the field underneath. When you run floods, you can outnumber the defenders that are playing their deep quarter coverage across the field. This is coverage you will see before the end of the half or at the end of the game. If this is the case, you can work underneath and get out of bounds to conserve time on the clock. This will force them to adjust from this shell to something else. You've probably heard the saying, "The prevent prevents you from winning the game." We will show you how this coverage can be exploited to get into scoring position.

Cover 4 with man combo coverage underneath

You will see an adjustment at times where someone will call a Cover 4 deep shell with man and zone underneath. This can cause confusion, so you need to lab any and all coverages. Then when you see these adjustments you can attack

them accordingly. You can still use crossing routes and such to get open, but the problem is the Cover 4 shell sitting behind the man and zone underneath.

Crossing routes and the use of the HB

You've heard the saying, "Take what the defense is giving you." This is what you need to do. Find plays that drive the secondary back and allow you to attack underneath. You need to find a play where you have the HB in the passing game, crossing routes, and someone pressing the secondary back.

The HB out of the backfield

Having receivers attack downfield forces the secondary to go back and defend the deep options. This allows you to attack underneath and make a play. When you get the ball to the playmakers in space, beautiful things can happen. We will focus on the dig and the C route of the halfback.

Attacking with the dig route underneath

The split end has a great gap inside the defensive coverage because the seam vertical route is forcing the coverage back. This allows us to get a sizable gain and more if we can get one-on-one with a defender. Why drive the ball into four deep when you have all of this open space to exploit?

Great catch made by Jennings

There's no one within 10 yards of him. When you attack a defense like this, they think you won't or can't have the patience to work the underneath stuff all the way the down the field. If they miss one open-field tackle, it can be much more of a gain than they think.

The HB in the passing attack

When the coverage drops back, it allows the halfback to work the underneath. If you have a

talented halfback, you can generate some nice gains underneath to get down the field. The mind-set of your opponent is that no one will have the patience to dink and dunk the ball downfield. However, you will have the correct mind-set and take what they give you.

The halfback secures the catch

Now you don't see anyone near this player, and you have room to get downfield. Screen plays are also great in situations like this. You will see why in the next shot.

Plenty of room to get YAC

With the defenders dropping deep to defend the deeper routes, the halfback now has downfield blockers.

Routes and Route Combos for Attacking Cover 4

- Drags
- Curl-flat
- Screens
- Flats

BEATING ALL-COVERAGE

Only one man rushes the quarterback

As a last resort, your opponents may drop all of their men back in deep coverage. This is something that plenty of players do when they can't stop your passing attack. However, we know this is something you don't see in real football. This technique is also used when a player has the lead and wants to burn time off the clock while their opponent has to wait for people to get open. Here are some tips on how to tear all-coverage apart and force opponents to defend you the way they should. All-coverage is usually set up by having the best defensive tackle on the team blitz while everybody else drops into coverage.

Crossing routes

Crossing routes allow you to find holes in this coverage. We have learned how to beat every single shell. Look down the field to make your read, and then attack the underlying coverage. We will treat this like a prevent defense. Remember that you have no pass rush, so stay calm and look for gaps in the coverage. Also, put your better wideouts in the slot to help you get open faster. You will have your best man against possibly a lineman or weaker defensive back. The coverage is dropping back to defend the deeper routes. The crossing routes help you in many ways (digs, ins,

drags, and post routes). They also allow you to get picks and rubs when defensive linemen drop back, along with the defensive backs. In this screenshot, you can see a pick or two being created with this theory.

Routes come open

As you can see, your men are becoming open. When you see a window, you must hit it quickly, because if they're sitting on a defender deep they will be waiting to jump your pass. As soon as you see a window, you must hit that wideout. Then run hurry-up with a quick snap to prevent your opponent from dropping all of the men in coverage again.

The post route is open because of a pick or rub

Hit the slot working the middle after coming off his pick from another wideout going downfield. You can also playmaker guys back and forth to wait for someone to get open. You can do this because you have little to no pass rush.

Using a mobile QB's legs to get yards

Another way to beat all-coverage is by running with your mobile quarterback. When you drop back and don't see any contain defenders or a spy, take off with your quarterback.

Aaron Rodgers shows why he's a double threat

Since everyone is defending downfield, you're able to get some nice yards because of the lack of a pass rush. Make sure you always play with a QB who has some sort of mobility, so if your routes are covered you can take off and force the defense to take away linemen from pass coverage to QB contain coverage.

HB Draw

Draw plays are one of our favorite ways to work all-coverage. The defense drops back because

they read high heat from the offensive line. When they drop back, this opens up rushing lanes and allows you to get yards on the ground to force them to keep some linemen at the line to protect against the rushing attack.

Open rushing lanes for the HB

As you can see, the action by the line and the QB totally sells the pass to allow you to run.

Off to the races

Now you have downfield blockers to help you get more yards.

Methods for Attacking All-Coverage

- Drag routes
- Delay routes
- Running with mobile QBs
- Running the HB Draw

WILDCAT OFFENSE

The Wildcat offense made its appearance in *Madden NFL 10* after the Dolphins used it so successfully the season before. EA SPORTS has made some changes to the game play with this set so that it cannot be exploited. You can't audible into or out of this set. Nor can you use formation audibles within the Wildcat. Hot routes are disabled as well. You've got to make good play calls, because once you make a call, you are stuck with it. Let's look at two of our favorite Wildcat plays from the Dolphins playbook.

Wildcat Trips Over—Power

Dolphins playbook: Wildcat Trips Over formation

The Fins turned the NFL world upside down and put the Wildcat on the map with Ronnie Brown's multi-touchdown game against the Patriots in 2008. Once the Fins had success with this package, other teams began doing the same. The purpose behind the Wildcat is to get your most athletic player the ball with 10 men blocking for him up front. By using the option and jet motion you keep the defense in constant conflict. When the Fins use Brown and Williams in this package, you have two excellent runners who threaten to take any running attempt to the house. Now people have gotten smart when defending the Wildcat. They blitz everyone because no one fears a halfback being a passing threat. When you have mobile QBs you can now add another dimension to this scheme.

Using the option in the Wildcat

In this play, we will use the zone read concept. We will read the defensive end. If he pushes upfield, take the Wildcat QB and run the ball up the middle. If the defensive end slants inside, you should hand the ball off to the HB in jet motion.

If you miss your read, use the option

In some cases you may miss your read. The defensive end showed he was coming upfield but slants inside. You can work the option in this case. You have to stay in pitch relation with the jet halfback. This will allow you to draw the defenders in so you can now pitch the ball to the jet halfback. This is why the option is such a pain in the neck to defend. If your first read is shut down, you still have ways to keep the play going.

Pitching the ball to jet halfback

Here you can see why the Wildcat is so hard to stop. Not only do you have to contain the Wildcat QB, but now you have to contain the jet motion with the option as well. The key is making the read off the inverted defender and making him commit. In this example, the Wildcat QB has been hit, yet you still have time to pitch the ball. Please note that this play was drawn up to work just like this. This is a basic direct snap to the Wildcat QB to run the power or hand off to the jet halfback. What we did was use all of our tools. We simply turned this play into a speed option with the power option if the inside running lanes are open.

Attacking the perimeter

Now the jet halfback has nothing but room to work with to get a sizable gain on the ground.

Wildcat Trips Over—PA Jet Sweep

Wildcat Trips Over—PA Jet Sweep

The Wildcat Trips Over has a package where you can add your backup quarterback in as your Wildcat QB. This is a huge advantage if you have a mobile quarterback on the bench who can pass well. Most people you face will send the house when you come out in a Wildcat formation. The main reason is that there is no threat of passing in most cases with people who use the Wildcat. Now you add Pat White and magic happens. You just turned the Wildcat into a triple threat right before their eyes.

The defense bites on play action

You see that the defense is selling out to defend the run. This play looks just like the other play. This is why play action passing is the best passing attack you can use when you have a solid running game behind it. Once you show you can pass they will respect your Wildcat run plays.

Overcommitting to the run leaves the jet halfback wide open

Your first read is the jet halfback and then the dig across the middle. The jet halfback will be open 90 percent of the time.

Can you say wide open?

In this instance we make an easy catch for a nice gain, and now the defense has trouble on they're hands. If you can attack multiple areas of the field from the Wildcat offense, you put the defense in all kinds of difficulty.

BLITZING 101

The Holy Grail to most players on defense is finding quick blitz schemes to bring pressure on the quarterback. If you want to disrupt your opponent's passing attack, bringing the heat is the best way to achieve this.

The ROLB comes off the edge untouched

In *Madden NFL 11*, there are a few different blitz concepts for bringing the pressure on the opposing quarterback. In this section, we go into great detail to cover those concepts so that you get a better understanding of how they work in this year's game.

Rushing the Passer

A successful defensive package depends upon its ability to rush the passer as well as its ability to cover. Our goal on defense is to disrupt and destroy the intention of the offensive player. That is our focus here.

The QB is about to be sacked

The object is to sack the quarterback. We do not advocate being cautious when going after the quarterback. We are not concerned with screens or draws. We are concerned with getting to the quarterback. We can funnel screens and draws back to the inside and prevent a big play. The quarterback is the primary focus.

The LB gets in the QB's face

Sometimes the defense may not come away with a sack, but getting in the quarterback's face on a consistent basis can play a large role in the outcome of the game.

Attacking the Blocking Scheme

Players on offense always wonder how it is that many of the blitzes we send work. It is simple; it is all about recognizing what it is that we are attacking. Here we are referring to the offensive line blocking scheme. There are ways to block the inside blitz in *Madden NFL 11,* such as using slide protection, but most players on offense don't take the time to use it. Blitzing against the default protection schemes is successful when one offensive lineman has to account for more than one defender.

The LE drops back in zone coverage

Zone blitzes are very effective against this blocking scheme because they allow the defense to put a defender in the face of the designated hot receiver. Second, with defensive linemen dropping into coverage, and linebackers and secondary personnel pass rushing, it causes a great deal of confusion for the offensive linemen and their assignments.

The O-line is confused by the zone blitz concept

Picture it this way. You are an offensive lineman and you are assigned to block the man directly in front of you. Another defender lines up in that area.

There are three blockers trying to block one pass rusher

You still block the man in front of you. But on the snap, that man steps forward as if he is going to pass rush. The other defender blows by you, and then the guy you were supposed to block drops out into coverage. This is the type of blocking scheme that we will be attacking.

Stick Skills and Block Shedding

Not everybody is the greatest player in the world on the sticks, but we all need to practice because sometimes a game will come down to just that: who's better on the stick. Sometimes the best player on the stick doesn't win. But the point here is to practice it as often as you can.

The RE sheds the LT out of the way

Also be sure you work on shedding blocks with the linebackers and defensive linemen. Check your players' shed block ratings as well as the best type of moves that each player has (power or finesse) to determine which moves to use in dealing with blocks.

The RE has a clean shot at putting pressure on the QB

Shedding blocks works a lot better this year. When playing a linebacker, we wait to see which blocker is coming after us. Before he goes into his animation, we use a power or finesse move. If your backer has a high shed block rating, he will be off that block in no time and ready to make the play on the running back.

The Five Key Objectives of a Blitzing Defense

Sacking the quarterback is a defender's goal when blitzing, but it does not mean failure if the quarterback is not sacked.

1. Sack the quarterback.
2. Pressure the quarterback into throwing incomplete passes.
3. Force turnovers—either interceptions or fumbles.
4. Make the quarterback throw shorter passes in long yardage situations.
5. Dictate the tempo of the game.

The RILB shoots right through the A gap

Being able to generate instant heat makes the quarterback uncomfortable in the pocket, causing him to throw more quickly than he normally wants to.

The CB jumps up and picks the pass off

The quarterback is more likely to throw errant passes that can lead to interceptions. Even if the quarterback makes the correct read, avoids the heat, and gets the pass off, his throws will be considerably short of the first down marker.

The QB is sacked by the blitzing linebacker

Disadvantages of Blitzing

There are some disadvantages of blitzing.

The CB has no extra help to cover his man

1. Unless the defense is zone blitzing, it requires man-to-man coverage. Often defensive backs will be left in one-on-one coverage with no safety help deep.

2. It increases the chance for the offense to score on a big play if the offensive line and backs are able to pick up the blitz and give the quarterback time to scan the field to find the open receiver for a scoring strike.

3. Athletic quarterbacks who can get out of the pocket can break containment and scramble for huge chunks of yardage.

4. Defenders wear out faster if they are continually sent on a blitz.

Types of Blitz Schemes

Inside Blitz

The inside blitz is the most wanted blitz concept in the *Madden NFL* community. These blitz schemes are known as nanos or enhanced blitzes.

The LB shoots through the B gap and goes after the QB

Nano blitzes get their name because they take such a short time to bring A and B gap pressure. The A gap is between the center and guards on both sides of the ball. The B gap is between guards and tackles on both sides of the ball. By creating A and B gap pressure, you can really throw off the quarterback's ability to step up in the box.

The QB cannot step up in the pocket to make the throw

To set up most inside blitz schemes, you must manually move at least one defender around. Some players see this as cheating because they consider it taking advantage of the AI. We disagree. Most of these blitz schemes are based on sound overload and blitz disguise principles. In addition, the offense has many tools they can use to block incoming pass rushers, so if they don't pick up the heat, it's on them. Inside blitz schemes can be set up with either man or zone coverage behind them.

No safeties are playing the deep zones

A good portion of the inside man coverage blitz schemes have either Cover 0 or Cover 1 shells. Most of the inside zone coverage blitz schemes have Cover 3 behind them, although you will find a few Cover 2 ones.

Overload Blitz

Another often-used blitz technique is to overload one side of the offensive line with multiple pass rushers.

An overloaded blitz has been set up on the right side of the offensive line

By sending more defenders in on a blitz than the offensive line can block, the offense is often overwhelmed and can't handle all the pass rushers from the overloaded side.

The LOLB comes hard after the QB

On the other side, there are multiple defenders either playing man or dropping in zone coverage. In *Madden NFL 11*, a good number of the overload blitz schemes have zone coverage behind them, but there are a few man overload blitz schemes as well.

Delay Blitz

Another blitz scheme that is often implemented is the delay blitz concept. This works by having a defender delay his pass rush, hoping that the offensive linemen get preoccupied with the other pass rushers so you can sneak in and get pressure.

The LILB is sent in on a delayed blitz

Once the defender who is pass rushing on a delay blitz sees the linemen commit, he will rush the quarterback. In *Madden NFL 11*, there are a few stock delayed blitz schemes, but by manually controlling a defender you can create your own delay blitzes.

The LILB waits a second, then rushes the QB

As soon as you see the offensive linemen blocking the pass rushers, manually rush the defender you are in control of. The defender can already be blitzing by the play's default design or he can be a player assigned to drop back in pass coverage. Sometimes you will get blocked and other times you will get a free shot at the quarterback.

Fake Blitzes

There are a few zone defenses where defensive linemen act like they are going to rush the quarterback and then drop back in pass coverage, such as Nickel Normal—Nickel Fire.

The LE acts like he is going to rush the QB

These are also known as zone blitz schemes. In *Madden NFL 11*, there are a few defenses where the linebackers will actually fake blitz by the design of the play. However, you can also achieve this by manually taking control of a defender playing zone coverage before the snap.

As soon as the ball is snapped, manually blitz the defender you are in control of. Once an offensive lineman tries to block him, drop him back into coverage by either clicking to a new player or manually dropping back yourself. This often gets an offensive lineman out of position so that he cannot block another defender rushing the quarterback.

The LE drops back in a buzz zone after he fakes pass-rushing the QB

Key Blitz

The SS is in man coverage on the RB

This blitz scheme occurs when man coverage is called. The defender looks to see if his man (usually a running back or tight end) stays in to pass-block. If he does, then the defender will blitz the quarterback.

The RB stays in to pass-block, so the SS rushes the QB

A good example of this occurs when the strong safety covers the running back. If the running back stays in to pass-block, we manually rush the strong safety to add extra pressure.

Outside Blitz

A common practice among players to prevent their opponent from rolling out the quarterback is to set up outside blitz schemes.

The LCB looks like he is playing pass coverage before the snap

Usually these blitzes have the outside cornerbacks blitzing, or a combination of an outside/inside defensive back along with a linebacker or two inside defensive backs.

Once the ball is snapped, the LCB is sent in on a corner blitz

For instance, one side may have a defensive back blitzing, while on the other side, a linebacker blitzes. Just like inside blitz schemes, there is a man or zone coverage shell behind it.

Zone Blitz

The zone blitz principle relies on confusing the offensive linemen by making them believe that the defensive ends and defensive tackles will rush the passer.

The NT drops back in a hook zone

By using a zone blitz, the defense throws off the blocking assignments of the offensive line by switching the responsibilities of a defensive lineman with those of a linebacker or defensive back. Zone blitz schemes generally have either Cover 2 or Cover 3 coverage behind them. Cover 3 is the one most used in *Madden NFL 11* when calling zone blitz concepts.

Quick Blitz Tips

- Blitzing is used not only to put pressure on the quarterback, but also to stop the run. For example, some of the same defenses that are set up to bring inside heat can be used to stop inside run plays. Look for defenders with high shed block ratings (85 or better). Those are the ones you should look to blitz with when setting up your blitz schemes. If they get blocked, they have a better chance of shedding the block than defenders with lower shed block ratings.

- For best results, put your fastest defensive personnel out on the field when blitzing the quarterback. The more speed the defender has, the quicker he will get to the quarterback.

- Test blitz packages in actual game modes. A blitz that works in practice mode may not always work the same way in regular game mode. Once you feel your blitz schemes will work, try them in a real game situation.

- Put one controller on your team and the other controller on the other. Once on the field, set up the defense and then run the play to see if it works. If it does, then you know you can run it against a human opponent online or offline.

- Learn to manually blitz a defender if he is playing zone or man coverage. We like to call these defenders flex defenders.

- Hot route defenders to blitz to create different blitz schemes in *Madden NFL 11*.

- Use defensive line shifts and linebacker shifts to create blitz schemes.

- Manually move defenders in different places to generate different types of pressure.

- Test your blitz schemes against different types of slide protection and pass-blocking schemes. What works against one type of slide protection may not always work against others.

- Use instant replay to see how your blitz schemes work or even how the CPU schemes work.

- Use man align to keep the blitzing defenders in the right position.

- Simplify the number of manual adjustments made to set up the blitz. For instance, don't try to flip the defense, hot route five defenders, and then call a line shift just to set up one blitz scheme. There just isn't enough time in this year's game to make that many adjustments. Try to keep blitz schemes to 2–3 pre-snap adjustments at most for best results.

- No matter how great your blitz scheme is, don't think for a minute that it will always work, especially when playing a human. Unlike the CPU, a human opponent will make adjustments if he or she is knowledgeable of the game and pass protection schemes.

3-4 BLITZ SCHEMES

3-4 Normal—Pinch

One of the simplest inside blitz schemes to set up from the 3–4 Normal is the Pinch. This defense requires no pre-snap adjustments. Six pass rushers are sent in after the quarterback: the three defensive linemen, the right outside linebacker, the right inside linebacker, and the left outside linebacker.

The right inside linebacker shoots through the A gap

The inside pressure comes from the right inside linebacker, who shoots through the A gap between the left guard and center. A few adjustments that can be made are to call bump-n-run man coverage and hot route the right end to blitz straight down. Again, those adjustments are entirely up to you. If you want to flip the defense to get inside pressure from the left inside linebacker, go ahead, as he will shoot between the center and right guard to get after the quarterback. If you are looking to bring outside pressure instead of inside pressure, manually move the right inside linebacker up near the left guard.

This creates an overload to the left side of the offensive line, allowing the right outside linebacker to put pressure on the quarterback. If the offense comes out in a two-back set, consider taking control of the defender covering the fullback. If the fullback stays in to pass-block, manually blitz the defender you are in control of. This will put the numbers back in your favor.

The quarterback has very little time to find the open receiver

3-4 Rush—Weak Blitz 3

The 3–4 Rush is a new defense that has been added to *Madden NFL 11*. One of the blitz schemes we like to create is an overload blitz out of the Weak Blitz 3. This defense features five pass rushers rushing the quarterback while six defenders drop back in pass coverage. Three defenders drop back in hook zones (the free safety, left inside linebacker, and left defensive end).

The offensive line is confused about where the pressure is coming from

The three remaining defenders drop back in three-deep coverage; these are the right cornerback, strong safety, and left cornerback. The default design of the blitz is to create pressure from the left side of the offensive line by overloading it. Notice that the right outside linebacker lines up on the line of scrimmage in a three-point stance just outside of the left tackle. If no adjustments are made, he generally is the defender who gets pressure on the quarterback. We like to manually fake blitz the left inside linebacker to make sure the right guard or right tackle doesn't try to slide over to block the right outside linebacker.

The QB doesn't even see the ROLB coming hard from his blind side

Once we see one of those two offensive linemen try to block the left inside linebacker, we drop him back in coverage. Make sure you have the left inside linebacker about 5 yards off the line of scrimmage before the snap. That way, once the ball is snapped, he can take a few steps forward and then drop back into coverage. The weakness of this defense is that the flats are left wide open.

3-4 Solid—Trio Sky Zone

Overload blitz schemes are very simple to set up in the game, which makes them ideal for those who are not very fast on the controls. The 3–4 Solid— Trio Sky Zone creates an overload to the right side of the offensive line by sending the left inside and left outside linebackers on a blitz. The pass coverage is Cover 3, with the right cornerback, free safety, and left cornerback dropping back in deep coverage.

The RILB fakes the blitz to confuse the protection schemes

The right outside linebacker plays a curl/flat zone, while the right inside linebacker and strong safety drop back in hook zones. Without making any pre-snap adjustments, the left inside linebacker is the defender that gets pressure on the quarterback by shooting through the B gap. Keep in mind that this depends on the formation the offense comes out in. To help ensure that we get some pressure, we like to take control of the right inside linebacker and hot route him to blitz. Much as with the 3–4 Rush—Weak Blitz 3, we have no intention of actually blitzing him.

No offensive lineman blocks the LOLB as he comes hard off the edge

Instead, we manually fake blitz him to prevent the left tackle from sliding inside to block either the left inside linebacker or the left outside linebacker. If the offense comes out in a Spread formation, make sure to use man align so the linebackers will come back inside and line up like they are supposed to. The biggest weak spot in the pass coverage is the flats, where no defenders are playing. If the offense does throw to the left flat, the right outside linebacker will be able to close in quickly since he plays the curl/flat zone.

3-4 Over—Sting Pinch Zone

A very popular inside blitz concept out of the 3-4 Over is the Sting Pinch Zone. Top players used it in *Madden NFL 10*, and it is just as effective in *Madden NFL 11*. This defense does require a few steps, but nothing that most can't handle. As far as the pass coverages go, the right cornerback and left cornerback drop back in two-deep zone coverage. The free safety and strong safety play hook zones along with the right inside linebacker. Six defenders rush the quarterback: the three defensive linemen, the right outside linebacker, the right inside linebacker, and left outside linebacker. To set up the defense, we need to use man align if the offense comes out in a Spread formation.

The RILB shoots through the A gap

If you are playing online, look to see what personnel your opponent is using. That way you know if you need to use man align or not. The next step is to take control of the nose tackle and hot route him to blitz, so that his blitz angle shoots straight down at the center. At this point, we could go as is and hope to get pressure on the quarterback. Making one last adjustment, however, increases our chances of success: Move the right inside linebacker behind the nose tackle to finish things off.

The pressure is quick with this defensive setup

Once the ball is snapped, the right outside linebacker shoots between the center and right guard. The pass coverage is solid underneath with three defenders playing hook zones; it's the deep coverage that we need to be worried about. If the blitz is picked up, there is big-play potential for the offense.

3-4 Stack—SS Snake 3 Stay

Another simple overload setup to put pressure on the quarterback is provided by the 3-4 Stack—SS Snake 3 Stay. This version gets pressure by overloading the right side of the offensive line and showing a fake blitz. We like how it is only a five-man pass rush and that the pass coverage itself is solid. The only real weakness is the short middle of the field where only one defender drops back in a hook zone.

The RT blocks the SS as he comes in on the blitz

The right outside linebacker and left inside linebacker both drop back in buzz zones, while the right cornerback, free safety, and left cornerback drop back in three-deep coverage. To set this defense up, all we need to do is show the fake blitz. This will bring the strong safety down near the line of scrimmage. This creates the overload by having the left outside linebacker and strong safety blitz off the edge of the right side of the offensive line.

The LOLB is free to put pressure on the QB

Once the ball is snapped, the strong safety engages the right tackle, allowing the left outside linebacker to get pressure on the quarterback. If you'd rather have the free safety down in the box, no problem—just flip the defense. The right outside linebacker will get the pressure on the quarterback while the free safety engages the left tackle.

3-4 Solid—CB Dogs Blitz

The 3-4 Solid—CB Dogs Blitz is an excellent blitz to call when your opponent likes to roll the quarterback out to one side or the other. As the play name suggests, the pressure comes from the corners, who blitz from the outside. The pass coverage has the two outside linebackers dropping back in buzz zones while the inside linebackers play hook zones. The two safeties drop back in two-deep coverage. Some players like to hot route the two defensive ends into flat coverage so that if their opponent tries to throw to the flats the area is covered.

The QB rolls to the left side of the field

Another option that players may choose is to hot route both defensive ends into QB contain. This makes it even more difficult for the opposing quarterback to roll out of the pocket. The only downside of this defense is that if the quarterback stays in the pocket, he will have time to look deep down the field where the pass coverage is not as strong.

The RCB is in perfect position to make the tackle

If a vertical stretch play is called, there is a good chance for a big play, so that is something you must consider when running this defense. Of course, the advantage of running this defense is that it doesn't require any pre-snap adjustments to work.

NICKEL 1-5-5 AND NICKEL 1-5-5 PROWL BLITZ SCHEMES

Nickel 1-5-5—Inside Zone Blitz

With the addition of the Strategy Pad this year, you won't be able to make as many defensive pre-snap adjustments as in years past. Finding simple blitz setups that don't require many steps is the optimal way to go. A good example of a quick blitz setup out of the Nickel 1–5–5 is the Inside Zone Blitz.

The ROLB shows blitz, getting the LT to block him

The pass coverage has three defenders playing deep coverage, while three other defenders drop in hook zones underneath. This leaves five pass rushers to go after the quarterback. Over the years, the Nickel 1–5–5—Inside Zone Blitz has been used by top players to bring inside pressure on the quarterback. One of the simpler ways to set it up is to hot route the outside linebackers to blitz, while making sure the middle linebacker stays behind the center. While this setup does add an extra pass rusher, the downside is it leaves one fewer defender to drop in zone coverage.

A more efficient way to set it up is to hot route the ROLB to blitz but not actually blitz him. Instead, let him act like he is blitzing so that the left tackle reacts to blocking him. Once the left tackle commits to blocking him, drop him back in a hook zone coverage. The middle linebacker still gets pressure by shooting through the A gap between

The middle linebacker shoots through the open gap to apply pressure

the center and left guard. Keep in mind that you can flip the defense and get the same pressure. This time, however, you need to fake blitz the left outside linebacker.

Nickel 1-5-5—DT Blitz

One of our favorite Cover 0 defenses out of the Nickel 1–5–5 to get inside pressure on the quarterback is the DT Blitz. This blitz scheme is really simple to set up because it doesn't require any pre-snap adjustments for it to work. The only pre-snap adjustment we suggest making is to call bump-n-run man coverage to slow down the receivers so that the middle linebacker has time to get pressure on the quarterback.

The offensive line is overwhelmed by the number of pass rushers

We like to key blitz with the defender covering the running back if the offense comes out in a one-back formation. For instance, say the strong safety covers the running back. We would bring him up near the line of scrimmage. Once the ball is snapped, we wait to see if the running back goes out. If the running back stays in to pass-block, we would rush the quarterback. If the running back were to go out on a pass route, we would click off the safety so that he goes to cover his man.

The QB is unable to step up in the pocket, and the MLB closes in on him

As with most blitz schemes, you can flip the Nickel 1–5–5—DT Blitz to get the same type of pressure, but this time, rather than the middle linebacker shooting through the A gap between the center and left guard, the middle linebacker shoots through the A gap between the center and right guard. Since there is no deep coverage, it's imperative that the blitz gets to the quarterback; otherwise, there is a chance that the offense will end up getting a big play.

Nickel 1-5-5—FS Zone Blitz

Another Nickel 1–5–5 zone blitz that gives the same type of pressure as the Inside Zone Blitz is the FS Zone Blitz. This defense sends six pass rushers, including the free safety. The cornerbacks

drop back in two-deep pass coverage. The strong safety, left outside linebacker, and nickelback drop back in hook zones.

The pass coverage is solid with five defenders covering the field

To get this defense to work, we need to hot route the left outside linebacker by pressing any direction on the Strategy Pad, then right on the Strategy Pad, and then right on the right stick. We need to be in control of the free safety while we are doing this since we don't want to tip off our opponent. Once the ball is snapped, we don't want to blitz the free safety; instead, we drop over the deep middle or drop him in a hook zone—it's up to you.

The QB is about to be sacked and knocked down to the ground

The middle linebacker will shoot through the A gap between the center and left guard. Once through the gap, he will get a clear shot at sacking the quarterback. As far as the pass coverage goes, we still have five defenders dropping back. The biggest weakness of the pass coverage is that the flats are left uncovered. It's best to run this defense when the offense needs more than 7 yards to pick up the first down.

59

www.primagames.com | PRIMA Official Game Guide

Nickel 1-5-5 Prowl—Cover 3

The first Nickel 1–5–5 Prowl blitz setup we want to show is the Cover 3. To set this defense up, we like to hot route the right and left outside linebackers to blitz. Keep in mind that if you do this, the flats are not covered. Next, we take control of the free safety and hot route him to blitz. We then bring him up near the line of scrimmage so that his blitz angle is shooting between the center and right guard.

The FS shows blitz but is about to drop back in pass coverage

Notice that at this point, we have a six-man pass rush and five defenders dropping back in hook zones. Since we hot routed the free safety on a blitz, the deep middle of the field is vacant and left open. Hopefully, the pressure will get to the quarterback fast enough to mask the lack of the deep middle coverage. Something we can do to at least make it less open is to shade two cornerbacks to the inside so that deep coverage assignments go more towards the middle, although there may not be time to do this. Once the ball is snapped, the nose tackle and right inside linebacker will force the center and right guard to block them both.

The FS keeps his on eye on the receiver coming over the middle

The left tackle and right tackle will be occupied by the outside linebackers. The free safety will shoot through the A gap and go straight after the quarterback. Something you may want to do if you have time before the ball is snapped is to hot route the outside linebackers into QB contain. It won't have much of an effect on the blitz, but it gives you the added benefit of preventing the quarterback from rolling out.

Nickel 1-5-5 Prowl—Zone Blitz 2

The Nickel 1–1–5 Prowl has a few good overload blitz schemes that are well worth checking out. One of the overload blitz schemes we like to run is the Zone Blitz 2. This zone blitz has the cornerbacks dropping back in two-deep coverage. The free safety, strong safety, and left inside linebacker drop back in hook zones. The right outside linebacker plays QB spy.

To create an overload on the left side of the offensive line, we need to hot route the right outside linebacker to blitz. We also want to call bump-n-run coverage so that the nickelback lines up closer to the line of scrimmage. Once the ball is snapped, the left tackle looks to block the right outside linebacker. The nickelback will come from

The FS is ready to get himself a sack

his position and put pressure on the quarterback. Another version that is similar to the other set is to take control of the right inside linebacker and move him inside so that he lines up between the center and left guard. Be sure to re–hot route him to blitz, so that his blitz angle shoots between the center and left guard.

No offensive lineman picks up the blitzing FS

Next, hot route the left outside linebacker to blitz. You could also move the nickelback closer to the right outside linebacker if time permits. Once the ball is snapped, there will be an overload to the left side of the offensive line. This allows the nickelback a clear path at the quarterback. The pass coverage is pretty good, but the flats are not covered.

Nickel 1-5-5 Prowl—OLB Fire

We have shown two Nickel 1–5–5 Prowl zone blitz plays; now we want to focus on two-man blitz schemes that bring inside pressure. This man blitz scheme is simple to set up since it requires moving just one defender. Notice that the free safety is playing the deep middle zone.

The nickelback is lined up close to the line of scrimmage

We will change his deep zone coverage assignment. The only player we need to move and blitz for this scheme to work is the free safety: hot route him to blitz and then move him down the box. Make sure his blitz angle is shooting between the center and right guard. If you want, go ahead and call bump-n-run man coverage. Once the ball is snapped, the center and right guard will block the nose tackle and right inside linebacker. This creates a gap for the free safety to shoot through and go straight after the quarterback.

The LT can't block both pass rushers on his side of the field

Something else you could do is hot route the outside linebackers to blitz before the snap. This may help open up a bigger hole for the free safety. Also, the free safety is not the one who always gets in; it may be one of the other blitzing linebackers. One last thing—don't forget to use man align as soon as the defense breaks the huddle to make sure the defenders are properly aligned.

46 Normal—Inside Blitz

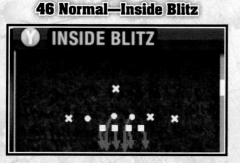

The 46 Normal—Inside Blitz has always been one of the better Cover 0 defenses to use to bring A gap heat on the quarterback. It is usually just a matter of a shift or two, moving or hot routing a defender. The 46 Inside Blitz has the middle linebacker and left outside linebacker shooting through the A and B gaps, giving the defense a six-man pass rush to get after the quarterback.

Two inside linebackers are set in the A gaps

Five defenders play man coverage. To set this version of the 46 Normal—Inside Blitz, all we need to do is hot route the weak-side defensive tackle to blitz. His blitz angle will now be shooting down at the center. This blitz scheme has the middle linebacker and left outside linebacker attacking the A gaps. Once the ball is snapped, the center blocks the weak-side defensive tackle while the right guard blocks the strong-side defensive tackle. This allows the left outside linebacker to get a clean shot at the quarterback.

To get the right outside linebacker to put pressure on the quarterback, simply flip the defense. Instead of hot routing the weak-side defensive tackle to blitz, hot route the strong-side defensive tackle to blitz. The right outside linebacker will now shoot through the A gap between the center and right

The LOLB shoots through the right A gap and gets pressure

guard and put pressure on the quarterback. Don't forget to call bump-n-run man coverage to slow down the outside receivers.

46 Normal—Rush Outside

Now that we have shown an inside blitz, it's time to show an outside blitz from the 46 Normal. The play we use is the Rush Outside. This defense sends the right outside linebacker and strong safety on a blitz from both sides of the offensive line. The free safety plays the deep middle. Only four defenders are in man coverage, leaving one receiver left uncovered if all five should go out.

The defense overloads the right side of the O-line

We use the same setup as the 46 Normal—Inside Blitz: We hot route the weak-side defensive tackle. At this point, we don't need to make any

more pre-snap adjustments. Notice that the strong safety's blitz angle is shooting inward. The problem is, he may get caught up as he rushes the quarterback. To ensure that he doesn't, we hot route him to blitz. His blitz angle now shoots straight down rather than inward. If our opponent slide protects to the inside, the strong safety will have clean shots at the quarterback. Even if there's no slide protect, the strong safety will still put pressure on the quarterback.

The SS comes in unblocked

The downside to this blitz is that one receiver is left uncovered. For that reason, it's best to run this defense when the offense comes out in base formations such as I-Form Pro or Strong Pro. Bump-n-run man coverage may also be applied to keep the receivers from getting off the line of scrimmage too quickly.

46 Normal—Zone Blitz

A zone blitz concept we like to run from the 46 Normal that provides A gap pressure is the 46 Normal—Zone Blitz. By default, this defense sends five defenders (strong-side defensive tackle, three linebackers, strong safety) after the quarterback. While those defenders are rushing the quarterback, three defensive linemen (right end, weak-side defensive tackle, left end) all drop back in pass coverage.

The FS is in position to put some heat on the QB

This type of blitz can cause some confusion for players not paying attention. To set the defense up, we need to flip the defense at the Play Call screen and make sure we freeze the defense so that the defenders align properly. Next, we need to make sure we are in control of the free safety. Notice that our opponent is playing the deep middle zone. The coverage type is Cover 3. We are going to change that coverage to Cover 2. We do this by hot routing the free safety to blitz. We then need to move him up near the line of scrimmage so that he lines up across from the center.

A big gap is created inside for the FS to shoot through

We also hot route the strong-side defensive tackle to blitz. Once the ball is snapped, the free safety will shoot through the A gap and go after the quarterback. If you don't have time to hot route the strong-side defensive tackle, that's fine. Instead of the free safety applying pressure, it will come from one of the linebackers blitzing.

46 Bear—Safety Fire

The 46 Bear—Safety Fire is quite simple to set up, as we only need to make two pre-snap adjustments. First, we hot route the free safety to blitz. This straightens his blitz angle. Next, we move him between the center and right guard. Once the ball is snapped, the free safety will engage the center.

The SDT is about to earn his paycheck for the day

The strong-side defensive tackle won't be blocked and will have a clear path to the quarterback. As far as the pass coverages go, all the receivers are covered, making it one of the better inside blitz setups in the 46 Bear. Here is another setup that only requires one adjustment: Take control of the free safety and don't blitz him. Instead, just move him up behind the strong-side defensive tackle. He should line up about a yard from behind the center. Once the ball is snapped, the right end will force the left guard to block him, while the weak-side defensive tackle will force the center to block him.

The free safety will shoot through the A gap between center and left guard. He then will put pressure on the quarterback. As good as these two blitz schemes are from the 46 Bear—Safety Fire, you must mix in other defenses from the 46 Bear

The FS closes in quickly as he shoots through the gap

to keep your opponent guessing. For instance, since this is a man defense, try calling the 2 Man Under. Set the defense up the same way; that way your opponent thinks blitz, when really it's just a four-man pass rush coming after him.

46 Bear—Weak 2 Deep

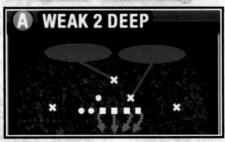

By default, 46 Bear—Weak 2 Deep has only four men pass rushing. The good news is you can get instant pressure with this defense with just these four. The bad news is it does require you to be fast on the controls. Flip the defense at the Play Call screen. Next, pinch the defensive line. When you do this, you should see all kinds of shuffling going on between the defensive linemen and linebackers. The right end should be standing up once everyone sets. Take control of each defensive lineman and hot route them all to blitz.

The one defensive lineman you don't have to hot route is the weak-side defensive tackle, since his pass rush angle is already shooting straight down. Once the ball is snapped, the left tackle and left guard will look to block the right end and strong-side defensive tackle.

The left side of the O-line is overloaded with defenders

The WDT shoots through the B gap and puts instant pressure on the QB

This allows the weak-side defensive tackle to shoot through the B gap between the left tackle and left guard. He now has a clean path after the quarterback. If the quarterback tries to roll out, the linebacker should be in position to make the sack or force a bad pass. Notice how the receivers are just getting off the line of scrimmage as the weak-side defensive tackle closes in on the quarterback. Having a fast defensive lineman at the weak-side defensive tackle position is important to maximize this blitz. If you don't have a fast defensive tackle, sub a fast defensive end in at weak-side defensive tackle.

46 Bear—Outside Blitz

This is a good blitz out of the 46 Bear to generate pressure from the right side of the offensive line. The pressure is generated by overloading that sideline with extra pass rushers. The downside of this blitz is that the pass coverage is extremely weak over the short middle of the field.

The ROLB is in a two-point stance and is ready to put pressure on the QB

To strengthen the pass coverage over the short middle of the field, the first thing we do is spread the linebackers. This really doesn't spread the linebackers out that much, but it does move the right outside linebacker farther out wide, and the left outside linebacker moves up on the line of scrimmage in a three-point stance. There are now five defenders in a three-point stance on the line of scrimmage, giving the look of a five-man front. If you are following along in practice mode, you will notice that the right outside linebacker's blitz angle does not change. The downside of this blitz is that the short middle of the field is left wide open since the middle linebacker and strong safety play curl/flat zones.

No offensive player picks up the blitzing ROLB

To help deal with this lack of coverage, we take control of the free safety and move him up so he lines up closer to the center and about 5 yards from the line of scrimmage. Once the ball is snapped, the left outside linebacker will force the right tackle to block him, allowing the right outside linebacker to put pressure on the quarterback.

4-4 SPLIT BLITZ SCHEMES

4-4 Split—LB Fire

The LB pass-rushes hard as he shoots the A gap

The first 4-4 Split blitz scheme we want to show is the LB Fire. This defense sends six pass rushers after the quarterback while having the other five play man coverage. To set the defense up, we take control of the right inside linebacker and hot route him to blitz. Next, we stay in control of the right inside linebacker and move him in front of the center.

The QB surveys the defense before he snaps the ball

We then switch to the free safety and move him across from the slot receiver if one is on the field. We also call bump-n-run man coverage. Finally, we switch to the defender covering the running back. If the running back goes out, we then go cover him. If the running back stays in to pass-block, we can drop back in pass coverage or rush the quarterback. Once the ball is snapped, the center blocks the right inside linebacker. This allows the left inside linebacker to shoot through the A gap between the center and right guard.

Hopefully the left inside linebacker gets to the quarterback before the receivers can get off the line of scrimmage after they are jammed. This is one of the simpler 4-4 defenses you will find as far as setting up the blitz. Just like any other Cover 0 man blitz scheme, it's a high-risk, high-reward scheme. This means that you may get burned, but you may get a sack or cause a turnover. Use this blitz scheme with caution.

4-4 Split—Crash Gold

There are few good 4-4 man blitz schemes that can be set up without much player movement. One of those defenses is the 4-4 Split—Crash Gold. This 4-4 man blitz defense sends six pass rushers after the quarterback, while the other five defenders play man coverage.

The inside LBs are lined up near the line of scrimmage

To set this defense up, we hot route the left outside linebacker to blitz. We then take control of the left outside linebacker and move him between the center and left guard. His blitz angle is now shooting towards the left guard. We need to make sure the left inside linebacker stays behind the strong-side defensive tackle. His blitz angle shoots between the center and right guard. Once the ball is snapped, the center looks to block the left outside linebacker.

The LILB applies the pressure on the QB

This allows the left inside linebacker to have a clear blitz angle shooting between the center and right guard. Mix this defense with other 4-4 Split defenses, but with the same look. Make sure you move the left outside linebacker between the center and left guard to give it the same look.

4-4 Split—Crash 3

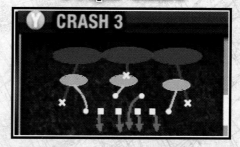

Here is a 4-4 Split zone blitz scheme that we like to throw in from time to time that brings A gap heat from the left inside linebacker. The 4-4 Split defense we use is the Crash 3. Notice that the left inside linebacker shoots through the A gap between the center and right guard. If we were to run this defense as is, he would get blocked by the center. To prevent the left inside linebacker from getting blocked, we need to bring another defender in on the blitz.

The line is overloaded by the number of blitzing defenders

The defender we like to use is the free safety. Because we hot route the free safety to blitz, we shade the two cornerbacks inside so that they play more towards the middle of the field. We are now playing a Cover 2 shell. We take control of the free safety and move him down in the box so that he lines up between the center and left guard. His blitz angle is shooting between the center and left guard. Once the ball is snapped, the center goes towards the free safety to block him.

The QB doesn't have much time in the pocket—the pressure is coming

This allows the left inside linebacker to shoot through the A gap between the center and right guard without being blocked. He then has a clear path after the quarterback. Overall, this is a good inside zone blitz out of the 4-4 Split that brings pressure on the quarterback while providing solid pass coverage. The only drawback is that the flats are not covered.

4-3 BLITZ SCHEMES

4-3 Normal—OLB Fire Man

The 4–3 Normal—OLB Fire Man is another defense where there is no safety help deep. This is known as Cover 0 coverage. Many of the man blitz defenses in *Madden NFL 11* have this coverage scheme. The 4–3 Normal—OLB Fire Man sends multiple pass rushers at the quarterback. This defense is designed to bring pressure from the outside from both outside linebackers. However, the quickest way to bring pressure on the quarterback is right up the gut. To set the defense up to bring A gap pressure, we need to first pinch the defensive line and linebackers. Notice that the offense comes out in the Strong I Pro.

The blitz scheme is set up to bring some heat on the QB

The free safety is covering the fullback. The fullback is pass-blocking to the right side. Instead of having him cover the fullback, we are going to send him in on a blitz. We prefer to run this blitz when our opponent comes out in a two-back set. Once the ball is snapped, both outside linebackers will blitz. The left outside linebacker is picked up by the right guard. However, the right outside linebacker is not blocked, and he shoots through the open gap to go straight at the quarterback. When you're running this blitz, if your opponent leaves the fullback in to pass-block,

The ROLB shoots right through the open gap

consider taking control of the defender covering him. Watch to see if the fullback stays in to block or not. If he does, blitz the free safety to bring extra pressure on the quarterback.

4-3 Over—Smoke Mid Zone

The 4–3 Over—Smoke Mid Zone is still as effective in *Madden NFL 11* as it was last season. We are going to add an extra wrinkle to it to knock our opponent's passing offense into shambles. Notice that we have flipped the defense. You can tell this by looking at the right end, who is dropping back in a hook zone. The free safety and left outside linebacker also drop back in hook zones. The right cornerback, strong safety, and left cornerback play three-deep zone. Get in the habit of using the man align coverage audible. To set this defense up, we take control of the strong-side defensive tackle and hot route him to blitz. His blitz angle now shoots straight at the center.

The final step we make is to hot route the right end to blitz. We are not going to actually blitz him, but we need to make sure the left tackle at least thinks we are. Once the ball is snapped, we manually drop the right end back. You may want to hold the Strafe button down pre-snap, so he doesn't rush, and then drop him back.

This blitz is designed to create instant inside pressure

The RE draws the LT out towards him

This should hold the left tackle long enough so that the right outside linebacker shoots through the A gap to apply pressure on the quarterback. You may need to move the right outside linebacker so he is stacked behind the weak-side defensive tackle; otherwise, if he moves on his own, he may mess up the blitz.

4-3 Over—Fire Zone 2

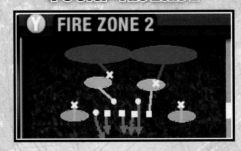

The second 4–3 Over blitz scheme we show is the Fire Zone 2. This 4–3 Over defense also brings pressure from the right outside linebacker, but instead of having man coverage behind it, we now have zone coverage. Both the right outside linebacker and left outside linebacker blitz. The left end drops back in a hook zone. The coverage is Cover 2 with two safeties splitting out wide and the two cornerbacks playing the flats.

The defense awaits the snap of the ball to unleash pressure on the QB

To set the defense up, we spread the linebackers out. Next, we re-blitz them so that their blitz angles shoot straight down. Finally, we take control of the left outside linebacker and move him so that he lines up across from the center. We also make sure he lines up 5–7 yards from the center. While in control of the left outside linebacker, we allow him to blitz. As soon as the center looks to block the left outside linebacker, we drop him back over the middle. The left tackle and left guard will block the right end and weak-side defensive tackle. With the center now occupied with trying to block the left outside linebacker, there is only one offensive lineman who can block the right outside linebacker, and that's the RT.

The QB doesn't see he is about to be sacked from his blind side

The problem for the right tackle is that he has to slide all the way across. If the right outside linebacker is fast enough, the right tackle won't be able to do that. Make sure you have your fastest linebacker coming off the edge from the right outside linebacker spot. You may need to package or sub him in. In any case, this is a good zone defense to bring pressure on the QB without giving up much coverage. Also keep in mind, the left outside linebacker can be dropped not only over the short middle, but also over the deep middle if you feel the need to drop him that far back.

4-3 Over—Fire Man

Of the three 4-3 formations in the game, we think that the 4-3 Over is the best when it comes to setting up heat on the QB. We want to look at a simple defense from the 4-3 Over that can be set up to bring outside pressure from the ROLB. The name of the defense is the Fire Man. This defense sends six pass rushers after the QB. The other five defenders play man coverage. To set this defense up, we only need to make one adjustment, and that's to show the fake blitz.

The QB looks to see where the blitz is coming from

The fake blitz coverage audible brings both safeties down in the box. Once the ball is snapped, the right end forces the left tackle to block him. This allows the right outside linebacker a clear path at the quarterback, providing a back is not left in to pass-block to the left side of the offensive line. The same can be done with the left outside linebacker by flipping the defense. He now will get the pressure because the right tackle will look to block the left end.

No offensive linemen pick up the blitzing ROLB

Another way to set this defense up is to hot route the weak-side defensive tackle. This changes up offensive line pass-blocking assignments. The center now will block the weak-side defensive tackle, the right guard will block the strong-side defensive tackle, and the right tackle will block the left end. This allows the left outside linebacker to get pressure on the quarterback.

4-3 Under—Edge Sting

The 4-3 Under—Edge Sting sends six defenders rushing the quarterback. The remaining five defenders play man coverage. There is no safety playing deep coverage, meaning this is a Cover 0 defense. The right outside linebacker is lined up behind the weak-side defensive tackle.

This man defense brings A gap pressure from the ROLB

His blitz assignment has him blitzing between the center and guard. The left outside linebacker is lined up outside of the right tackle. If there is a tight end on the field, he lines up across from him. His blitz angle has him rushing the quarterback from the outside. The way we like to enhance the 4-3 Under—Edge Sting is to re-blitz the weak-side defensive tackle. The only pre-snap adjustment we may make is to take control of the left outside linebacker and move him in front of the right guard.

The QB should have left the FB in to pass-block

We also hot route him to blitz. We wanted to show this blitz because of how the right outside linebacker rushes the quarterback. Instead of rushing the quarterback at any angle, he takes a slightly different rush angle. With all offensive linemen committed to blocking the other pass rushers, the right outside linebacker has a huge hole to blitz the quarterback. The quarterback doesn't have time find the open receiver and the result is a sack. Don't forget to call bump-n-run man coverage to slow the outside receivers down so it takes them more time to get out on their pass routes.

4-3 Under—Str Snake 3 Deep

A zone blitz concept we want to show out of the 4-3 Under is called Str Snake 3 Deep. This zone blitz sends the strong safety on a blitz, along with middle linebacker, for a total of four pass rushers. The left end plays QB contain. The right end drops back in a buzz zone, while the right and left outside linebackers drop in hook zones. The free safety and the right and left cornerbacks play three-deep coverage.

The SS is up near the line of scrimmage

We like to set this defense up by shifting the defensive line to the left. Next, we take control of the right end and hot route him to blitz. Once the ball is snapped, the right guard and right tackle look to block outward toward the left end and strong safety. The strong-side defensive tackle will engage the center. With the center, right guard, and right tackle blocking three of our pass rushers, there is a huge gap for our middle linebacker to shoot through.

The LOLB finds a big gap to blitz through

You might want to try flipping the defense for a different look. This time, shift the defensive line to the right. Next, hot route the left end to blitz. This setup tends to be a little more effective by allowing not only the middle linebacker to get pressure on the quarterback, but other defenders as well.

NICKEL BLITZ PACKAGES

The Nickel formation has silently taken over the *Madden NFL* competitive community because of how versatile the defense is. Many teams can now run an entire scheme from all of the formations that make up the modern-day Nickel. Each year, *Madden NFL* tunes the game so that it becomes harder for the advanced tournament players to create high-pressure blitz plays, and every year the elite tournament players find a way to adjust the players and allowed hot route options to create that perfect competitive blitz.

Nickel 2–4–5—FS Slant 3

As we look into the blitz, we start off by exploring a technique that was popular in the competitive arena a few years back: line looping.

Here is the pre-snap alignment

We set this defense by calling for press coverage and then re-blitzing the free safety. After blitzing the free safety, bring him down to the line of scrimmage and place him directly above the left tackle. We then click on the left outside linebacker. He is aligned on the right side of the screen and is assigned in a hook zone. Re-blitz him and then you are all set.

By bringing the free safety down and stacking him above the left tackle, we give our right outside linebacker an opportunity to stunt behind the safety and get a clean rushing lane to the quarterback. The

The linebacker loops around and has a clear shot at the quarterback

pressure is quick and unexpected. The quarterback normally takes a sack because of the delayed rush on this blitz. We also benefit from solid zone coverage behind our blitzing defenders.

Nickel 2–4–5—Ray Smoke

Having a solid blitz package is what elevates a player from average to top-notch. The elite players in *Madden NFL* all have two things in common: They have great command of the control pad or thumbstick, and all have an insane blitz package. Make sure to spend time in practice mode learning blitzes that have similar setups as well as similar coverages. A successful blitz package will bring pressure from the same area of the field but from different fronts.

Manually control the right outside linebacker

The Nickel 2–4–5 Ray Smoke is an easy play to set up, but with the new Strategy Pad you will need time in practice mode to get familiar with the button controls. This blitz brings good pressure through the A gap. We set the defense by first calling for press coverage. We then select the left outside linebacker, aligned on the right side of the screen, and assign him to blitz. A key thing to remember when making hot route adjustments is that the first adjustment, no matter what, will be three movements. It is easiest to click on your blitz defender and press down on the Strategy Pad three times; everything that follows will require only two movements.

We get two defenders in on the sack

This blitz works because once the offense starts the play, we let our manually controlled defender approach the line of scrimmage but then pull him back to cover his previously assigned zone. This minor adjustment freezes the right tackle and doesn't allow him to peel back to help block our A gap pressure. In the end, our defense is rewarded with a sack on the play.

Nickel 3–3–5—Prowl Bear Blitz

When you prepare a defensive game plan, you have to account for every possibility the offense can throw at you. A good offense is not going to allow us to get comfortable on defense and just keep sending insane blitzes at them all game without making some sort of adjustment. To add to this fact, *Madden NFL 11* makes

it more advantageous for the offense to just quick-hike our defense if we are making manual adjustments to attack them. We will try to counter this by heading to the Nickel 3–3–5 and the Prowl Bear Blitz.

No setup required

Most times, it requires a few manual adjustments to make a defensive play call ready for in-game action. It is rare that we can find a play that allows us to call on it without needing to make any adjustments. The Nickel 3–3–5 Prowl Bear Blitz is exactly this type of play. With all of the anxiety of trying to make sure you have the right hot route adjustments or the defender aligned correctly, it's a relief to have a play that doesn't require us to do anything. This is going to help us in the long run, as an offense won't be able to change the tempo of the game against us and try to quick-hike our defense to create open spots.

We've got amazing pressure considering we didn't have to make any adjustments

The offense ran the ball on this play, from a Gun formation, and the pressure from the defense was so good that we stopped the play in the backfield. If we want to speed up the defense to get in their Prowl look, all we need to do is call for press coverage.

Nickel 3-3-5—Prowl Blitz

A PROWL BLITZ

Before moving to another formation, we want to focus in on another blitz from the Nickel 3–3–5. To be considered a top-notch defense, you must be able to attack the same areas but from different spots. We can also attack different areas from our same initial setups, but the theory is the same: Show the offense multiple fronts but still get the same pressure. If we can become consistent doing this, then our opponent on offense will start to feel like we are setting up pressure no matter what we do. At the point where we have a nervous offense, we have completely won the game because they are a play or two away from making fatal mistakes.

Here comes the pain

We set up this defensive play quickly and easily. The free safety is assigned to blitz—all we do is bring him down to the line of scrimmage and place him over top of the left guard. Back him up just a yard or two yards away and then click off of him. We suggest manually controlling the strong safety and using him to protect the middle of the field.

This play is very useful because the pressure that we generate can come from multiple areas of the offensive line. This falls in line with our theory of same setup but different pressure. Our opponents are at a loss because they see us set the defense up the same way, but it keeps reaching them through different gaps.

Another quarterback sack from a solid defensive play

Nickel Psycho—DT Blitz

X DT BLITZ

One of the most popular defenses in *Madden NFL* football last season was the Nickel 1–5–5 formation. This formation has been the downfall of many high-powered offenses in *Madden NFL* over the last two seasons. The one downfall of this set is that it is not in a lot of playbooks. The other negative is that because it is limited to a few playbooks, our opponents can easily go to practice mode after facing us and pretty much get an exact look at what we were doing. Well, things have changed in *Madden NFL 11,* and the Packers now have a 1–5–5 look that is called the Nickel Psycho.

We have solid coverage and pressure coming

We have chosen to run the Nickel Psycho—DT Blitz. This is a man coverage blitz that allows us to play aggressive coverage on the outside while our linebackers and linemen work to get to the quarterback. Our setup for the play is quick and will make sure that we always have an opportunity to set our blitz up, regardless of what the offense does. We game plan for our defense to have plays that can still generate pressure for when our opponent goes to a quick-hike tempo.

Our middle linebacker reaches the quarterback

We set the Nickel Psycho—DT Blitz up by pinching our linebackers. You have the option of calling press coverage if you feel it's needed, but we suggest using the standard coverage because the corners have a better chance of not letting a receiver run free for an easy downfield bomb. We reached the quarterback with our middle linebacker and prevented him from making a throw to any hot receiver on the play.

Nickel Psycho—FS Zone Blitz

A FS ZONE BLITZ

We are very pleased with the pressure that we have been able to apply on the offense when running plays from the Nickel Psycho. This formation will make the Packers defensive playbook as popular as the those of the Jets, Ravens, Patriots, and Titans. A dominant defensive formation is all that some players need as

motivation to drop a common book and move on to the next one. We are pretty sure that the Packers playbook will be one of the most used this season. We have chosen the Nickel Psycho—FS Zone Blitz to display how easy it is to continuously get pressure on the opposing team's quarterback.

Line the safety up over the right guard

For years, coaches have used the safety to add pressure on the offense's running game and also to add him as an extra player to blitz with. We have seen how successful the safety blitz can be in *Madden NFL 11,* and we feel it is a perfect option for us to add into our blitz scheme. Before we can drop the safety down on the line of scrimmage, we have to make sure we're comfortable with the coverage we have around the field. The Nickel Psycho—FS Zone Blitz has both cornerbacks in deep half coverage and three underneath hook zones. We are very comfortable using our safety in the blitz game with this type of coverage behind him.

The middle linebacker is the first to reach the quarterback

All we do to set the play up is stack the safety over the right guard. Once the play starts, we have four of our defenders fighting to get to the quarterback first. The beauty of this play is that the same setup can get pressure from different gaps.

EA SPORTS
MADDEN NFL 11
MAKING DEFENSIVE ADJUSTMENTS

Contents

DEFENDING THE INSIDE RUN

To play this season's game well you need to know how to control or shut down the run game. There is nothing worse than facing opponents who pound you up the middle all game long and not being able to stop them. This type of attack is the worst because it exposes you for play action passing as well as running to the perimeter. The main key is to overload the inside gaps and use a seven- or eight-man front. The 4–3 is a great defense to use, and we will look at using three different types to help you contain the inside attack. You want to take away the offensive line's ability to double when linemen are uncovered. If you have excellent interior linemen they can overtake a weaker guard or tackle to make a play. The other point is to free up your talented linebackers. The linebackers flow to the ball well. Just find certain defenses that can get them in clean. Slanting at the line or stunting works well too. Let's take a look at inside run defense 101.

4-3 Normal—Weak Slant 3

4–3 Normal—Weak Slant 3

This is a great play because of the stunt at the line by the defensive line. You also have the Mike and Sam linebackers coming with pressure. This play works well against play action and weak-side attacks. When you pick a defense you need to have one that can handle many situations. Don't fall in love with a defense for each type of play. You will face hurry-up and other situations. You need a base defense to handle your needs. This one fits the bill against inside zones, dives, the iso, and any attack in the middle.

The inside and outside gaps are contained

You see that the inside and outside gaps are accounted for. You just want to stuff the middle and make it hard for them to cut the ball outside. You have backside help because the defensive line is stunting away from the strong side.

The play is stuffed for zero yards

This play was blown up before it could even get going. This is a great play to have in your audibles, so that when a person is pounding the middle you can contain it. You can also squeeze the defensive line to close it off better and force the offense to go outside, which you have covered anyway.

4-3 Over—Smoke Mid Zone

4–3 Over—Smoke Mid Zone

This is another Cover 3 zone blitz. This play will handle all inside running plays and cover you for play action passing as well. All you have to do is pinch your linebackers, which gives you pressure inside to take away any inside rushing attack. You also have a defensive line stunt.

The Mike and Sam backers come free

The stunt allows the linebackers to get free. If you have a stud at the defensive line this can be a problem from the hike. The key is that you want to get the guy inside cleanly and take away cutbacks or cuts outside. You have a gap open, but by the time the back gets the ball it will be filled.

Blown up in the backfield

The player is taken down for a loss on the ground because this zone-based blitz contained the play.

4-3 Under—Mike Fire

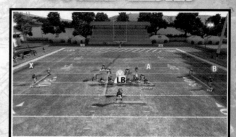

4–3 Under—Mike Fire

This is a Cover 1 man defense that sends the MLB inside to take away the inside gap. If you have an outstanding MLB you can blow the play up quickly.

The cut outside is taken away

The MLB has filled the A gap.

A big loss on this play

Now the offense has been hit for a loss.

DEFENDING THE OUTSIDE RUN

The best defense to use for an outside attack is the 3–4 or any odd front, because your alignment is already set for the outside attack. The outside linebackers are uncovered, and their main rule is to contain the outside. In some cases you need to use outside blitzing schemes to contain the edge and turn the play back inside. The defensive line in the 3–4 is used to draw a double team and plug the middle. We will look at three ways to contain the outside rushing attack and at the same time protect you against play action passing and running up the middle. The key to defense is to take away what they're good at and what they want to do. You need base defenses that handle many situations, because with the changes to the pre-snap adjustments you don't have the time you had before to make adjustments. Let's take a look at the 3–4 and the use of odd fronts to contain the outside rushing attack. These defenses work well against counters, outside zones, stretches, tosses, and pitches.

3–4 Normal—Strike Spy 2

3–4 Normal—Strike Spy 2

This is a great base defense that takes away the play action pass as well as the outside rushing attack. This combo defense plays well against the stretch, toss, pitch, and counter. The key is that you have to spread your linebackers out pre-snap. Don't worry about your opponents cutting the ball back inside. This is what you want them to do. You want to take them out of what they like to do and force them to do something else. You have your defensive line there with two linebackers behind them.

Gaps are filled and the weak-side counterattack is stuffed

This is what you want out of your defense. You have taken away the outside and the inside angles. This forces the player to go outside.

The OLB came off the block and stopped the play

Spreading the linebackers out allowed your OLB to work the outside edge to get free and turn this play back inside for a loss. It was a loss because you took away the inside cutback.

3–4 Even—Weak Blitz 3

3–4 Even—Weak Blitz 3

This is a Cover 3 zone blitz that sends pressure outside and also protects you from the pass. The better run defenses are zone-based, because they keep your defenders facing the play. When you use man-based defenses the defenders will run with their assignments and have their backs to the play. Zone-blitzing schemes allow you to get pressure and keep the play in front of you.

You will face people who use twin and trip sets. The key is to use zone to keep the players in front of you. The OLB faked like he was defending the slot receiver and came off clean inside on the outside running play.

Hit for a loss

This great play resulted in a loss in the backfield. We were in position to eat up play action as well.

Nickel 3-3-5—Prowl Cover 3

Nickel 3-3-5—Prowl Cover 3

The Nickel 3–3–5 can be used as a run stopper when you're playing someone who likes to audible down to other sets or who runs well from passing sets. If your opponents like to run counters or weak-side attacks you can blow them up quickly.

Many will run counters against three-man fronts. The key here is that you plugged those holes and you see how all of the defenders are facing the play. If this had been man coverage they would have gotten a large gain.

The running back is hit as he gets the ball

This play worked so well the defender hit the running back as he got the handoff. Keep in mind that you have a second delay before the back gets the ball. This is an adjustment in the AI this season. You can use this to your advantage. That delay allows you to get men free and at times allows you to blow plays up in the backfield. Just shift your blitzers to the side they want to run on and stunt the line in the other direction in case they want to flip the play and sit on the safety.

DEFENDING FLATS AND SCREENS

In *Madden NFL 10*, the flats and screens were two of the hardest types of plays to defend. In *Madden NFL 11*, they can still be difficult but are not impossible to defend. We are going to show a few defensive schemes that do a good job of covering them.

Defending the Flats

How many times online last year would you see your opponent come out in a Gun Tight formation and call a flat play? On defense, you called what you thought was the proper Cover 3 defense to defend this formation, only to fail. As soon as the QB received the snap, your opponent would roll him out and throw on the run to the receiver running the flat. The defender covering the flat couldn't get out quick enough, leaving the receiver open. In this year's game you can't roll the quarterback out as quickly because the computer controls him for the first few steps. This gives the defender time to cover the flat and the receiver.

3-4 Normal—Cover 2

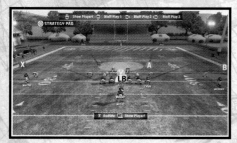

The two inside linebackers drop back in hook zones

The 3–4 Normal—Cover 2 is one of our favorite red zone defenses to call because it does a superb job of defending all areas of the field. We also like to use it when our opponents like to throw to the flats. Notice how the outside cornerbacks play the flat zone areas.

The quarterback throws to the halfback in the flat

Normally the cornerbacks would jam the outside receiver, but in this year's game, they won't if they see a receiver running a flat route.

The left cornerback breaks towards the halfback as he is about to make the catch

This puts them in position immediately to defend any receiver running a flat route in their area of the field. This holds true for any Cover 2 zone defense in the game.

Nickel 3-3-5—Cover 3

The RCB, FS, and LCB play three-deep coverage

A Cover 3 defense we like to run to defend the flats is the Nickel 3–3–5—Cover 3. This play does an excellent job; the nickelback and left outside linebacker cover the flat while the strong safety and right outside linebacker drop back in buzz zones.

The LOLB goes to cover the receiver in the flat

The downside of this defense is that the short middle of the field has only the middle linebacker defender dropping back in a hook zone.

There is very little chance of the receiver making the catch

If your opponent attacks the short middle of the field with multiple receivers, the QB is going to find at least one of them open. Be sure to adjust accordingly to the type of player you are up against.

Defending Screens

Screen plays to wide receivers were another type of play that many players on defense found difficult to defend. In this year's game, they are covered better thanks to the defenders fighting through blocks that are being thrown.

Dollar Normal—DE Contain

The safeties play two-deep coverage

A defense that defends WR screens like the Gun Doubles On—FL Screen is the DE Contain. This man coverage defense is effective because it puts the left cornerback in man coverage on the flanker. We call bump-n-run man coverage.

The screen is set up for the flanker to pick up yardage

Once the ball is snapped, notice that the tight end is one of the blockers who goes out to set up the blocking for the flanker. The defender who covers the tight end follows him outside. Often he ends up being blocked by one of the offensive linemen.

The left cornerback steps in front of the flanker to knock the pass away

However, the left cornerback is not blocked and is in position to tackle the flanker or possibly pick the pass off. To add another defender in the mix, we might hot route the left end, who by default is in QB contain, into the flat. This ensures that at least one of the defenders can make a tackle on the flanker as soon as the catch is made.

DEFENDING SLANTS AND CROSSING ROUTES

Two of the more common passing routes that players use to beat defensive coverages are slants and crossing routes. Let's look at a few options for shutting these routes down.

Defending Slants

3–4 Under—Cover 2 Sink

Five defenders drop in underneath coverage

Several plays in each team's playbook have slant-type plays in them. Throw in the fact that your opponent can hot route any receiver on a slant, and it makes them that much more dangerous. One of the defenses we use to shut them down is the Cover 2 Sink. The more defenders that drop back in hook zones, the better the chance of defending slants since there are fewer voids in the zone.

The right inside linebacker drops back in a hook zone

This defense drops five defenders in hook zones, making it very hard for any receiver running a slant to get open. The great thing about this coverage is that it requires no adjustments.

The quarterback tries to thread a bullet pass to the split end

Of course, the downside of this defense is that if the offense calls a vertical stretch play, there is potential for a big pickup deep downfield. If you want to add another defender into a hook zone, you can always hot route the right inside linebacker, who is blitzing by default.

3–4 Normal—2 Man Under

Cornerbacks are locked in man coverage

Man coverage defenses don't do a good job defending slants because the receivers get inside position. The only chance you really have to defend slants if you call man coverage is to call bump-n-run man coverage with a blitz behind it and hope one of the defenders can get to the receiver before the receiver breaks the jam and the quarterback can throw the ball. We come out in a man defense such as 3–4 Normal—2 Man Under.

The split end is jammed at the line of scrimmage by the right cornerback

Notice that all the linebackers are in man coverage except the right inside linebacker. We globally hot route the linebackers in hook zones. We then call bump-n-run coverage. Notice that the cornerbacks are in man coverage. Your opponent will think man coverage if you use motion, and then think man coverage can be beaten with a slant.

The inside linebacker is sitting, waiting to pick the pass off

Once the ball is snapped, the right cornerback jams the split end. Once he breaks, he runs his slant route. The right outside and inside linebackers drop into his area, taking away any chance of the quarterback completing a pass to him.

Defending Crossing Routes

Dollar Normal—Cover 3

Three defenders drop in hook zones

Crossing routes have always been pretty useful in *Madden NFL* against man coverage. As with slants, the only chance to defend them when playing man coverage is to bring pressure. You can't just sit back in 2 Man Under and hope to stop the crossing routes. If our opponent tends to run a lot of crossing routes, we play zone coverage, hoping the QB will make a mistake and throw an interception.

The QB tries to throw the ball to the receiver running the crossing route

A zone defense that does a good job covering crossing routes is Dollar Normal—Cover 3. This defense puts three defenders in hook zones. With these three defenders dropping back in the area of the crossing route, it makes for a small window for the quarterback to complete the pass.

The defender drops in front and swats the pass down

The downside of this defense is that the pressure comes from the defensive line. You can manually create pressure by controlling a defensive end and using a few pass-rush moves to get to the quarterback quicker.

DEFENDING STREAKS, CORNER ROUTES, AND POST ROUTES

We have already shown you how to cover some of the more common short and intermediate passing routes. Now we look at how to defend some of the deep passing routes found in *Madden NFL 11*.

Defending Streaks

Against the streak route, 2 Man Under defenses are solid

Most top players defend the streak down the sidelines by calling 2 Man Under coverage. This puts the safeties covering the deep halves of the field while five defenders play man coverage underneath.

The QB throws to the flanker down the right sideline

To ensure that the safeties are in position to cover streaks, we have them play zones to the sidelines by pressing the Strategy Pad in any direction, then pressing up on the Strategy Pad, and then pressing up with the right thumbstick.

The defenders get in front of the receiver and swat the ball down

This puts their deep coverage assignments closer to the sidelines. Even if the receivers beat the man coverage being played on them, the safeties will be in position to defend the pass.

Fade routes are defended much like streak routes—by simply calling 2 Man Under coverage. Cover 3 and Cover 4 defenses with defenders dropping back in buzz zones work best at defending fades when calling zone coverage defenses.

Seam routes are run by slot receivers, tight ends, and, in some cases, running backs. Whatever you do, don't play zone to the sidelines. Instead, leave the safeties to play their normal two-deep coverage. As far as zone coverage goes, a Cover 3 with defenders playing buzz zones, such Nickel 3–3–5—Cover 3, is a good defense to call. Dollar Normal—Cover 4 is also a good choice when defending streaks since there is four-deep coverage, along with the inside defensive backs playing buzz zones.

Defending Corner Routes

Four defenders drop back in deep zone coverage

The best way to defend corner routes (outside of manually defending them) is to call a defense where defenders drop back in a curl/flats zone (purple zone). Every defensive playbook has plays designed with them, plus you can always hot route a defender or defenders into zones if you choose to.

The ROLB drops back in a buzz zone

For example, the 3–4 Normal—Drop Zone has outside linebackers dropping back in the curl/flat zones on both sides of the field. Playing over the top of the outside linebackers are the four defensive backs (RCB, FS, SS, LCB). The two inside linebackers drop back in hook zones.

The RCB steps in front and is about to pick the pass off

This type of pass coverage makes it very hard for the offense to complete any corner routes.

The outside linebackers will drop back, forcing the quarterback to wait to throw the ball to the receiver running the corner route. At some point, the outside linebackers will stop dropping. But don't worry, the outside corners will still be in position to either knock down or pick off the pass. This coverage makes it very hard for the receiver to make the catch. One thing to note—if a receiver runs a short curl route, the outside linebacker will come up to cover him. This means that he won't drop as far back in his zone coverage.

Defending Post Routes

Two defenders play robber coverage over the middle

The post is another route that can be difficult to defend unless the proper coverage is called. Cover 1 with robber coverage is the most effective man coverage defense to call for defending post routes.

A good example would be Dime Normal—Cover 1. The free safety plays the deep middle while the linebacker plays a hook zone underneath. The rest of the defense plays man coverage, except for the defensive linemen, who rush the quarterback. As far as zone coverages are concerned, Cover 3 and Cover 4 are the ones to call.

The linebacker drops back in his zone while looking at the QB

Cover 3 drops a deep safety over the top while one or more defenders play hook zones underneath. For the quarterback to complete the pass, he has to throw between the hook zone defenders and the deep safety. As you can imagine, the passing window is not very big, making it difficult to complete the pass, but not impossible. There are route combos in the game that expose Cover 3 coverage and allow the receiver running the post to get open by forcing him to drop farther over the deep middle.

The linebacker jumps up to knock the pass down

Cover 4 coverage does a good job because the safeties play quarter deep zones. They are both in position to make a play on the ball if a receiver runs a post in their area.

DEFENDING TRIPS FORMATIONS

The passing game has completely taken over how football is being played. With all of the rules favoring high-flying offense, we have to really buckle down when playing defense. The one aspect of the professional passing game that has made its way down to the virtual gridiron is the use of Trips and Bunch formations. These three-receiver groupings have made it extremely difficult to defend the pass when the offense uses them.

The MLG/EA SPORTS Madden Challenge saw a few of the final eight championship-qualifying competitors use these formations as they dominated opponents throughout the tournament season and even in the championship finals, which were held in Miami during Super Bowl week. We will take a look at three ways to attack this formation and give you a chance at slowing down this offensive set while establishing your unique scheme for defending it.

Dime Normal—Cover 1 Press

Pre-snap look against the Gun Trips Bunch formation

Normally, using man-to-man defense vs. a Trips or Bunch formation will open the defense up to getting beaten by crossing routes and quick mesh routes. The theory when using this defensive coverage is to shift the middle linebacker to the right to help defend against any inside breaking route, while the cornerbacks play man on the receivers who release towards them.

We use our middle linebacker to chip the inside-breaking receiver and then drop back to play the seam. We will control the weak-side inside cornerback and delay any drag, slant, or crossing route.

Manually control the inside cornerback to defend the crossing receiver

The defender prepares to swat the pass out of the air

If we take away the initial read and prevent the expected quickly open route, the QB will be left with options that play to our strength. He attempts a pass into double coverage here and has it swatted down.

4-3 Normal—Cover 3

Pre-snap look of the Cover 3

The Cover 3 defense is a great option to run against Trips formations because of the shallow hook and flat zones. Trips are primarily used to make the quarterback's read easy and let him get rid of the ball quickly. When we run a Cover 3 defense this forces the QB to hold onto the ball and wait for a receiver to get open between our zone drops.

We manually control the FS and guard the hash mark

The one thing to keep in mind when defending any Trips formation is to be aware of the offense's need to send a receiver to the middle of the field. By controlling the FS we can eliminate that option on this play.

The corner breaks up the pass and almost gets the interception

All we ask for from the defense is to prevent the offense from taking advantage of their trips receiver grouping. The Cover 3 has given us the opportunity to get our hands on the ball for a possible turnover.

Nickel Strong—CB Dogs Zone

Now it's time to bring the pain

There is no way we're going to go through an entire section without looking at a way to defend the Trips or Bunch set by throwing a blitz at it. We will let the Nickel Strong—CB Dogs Blitz do the honors.

The cornerbacks are coming in full tilt from both sides

No opponent we face will use the Trips or Bunch formation to attack the defense quickly; many players get in this type of set and start to look for plays with deep, developing routes. If we notice our opponent is looking for the deep pass when in Trips, heat is a perfect counter.

The linebacker is in perfect position and makes the interception

Because of the speed of our blitz and the zone coverage behind it, the quarterback has to make a rushed throw, which turns into an interception. One thing that we love about the CB Dogs Zone is that the defenders in hook zones bump the receivers who run in front of them. This throws the timing off and helps lead to turnovers.

These base plays can be used with different playbooks and formations. The concepts are the same and should give you a nice starting point to build your defensive scheme for Trips and Bunch formations.

DEFENDING SPREAD FORMATIONS

A lot of people who play *Madden NFL* simply run the ball because that is what they believe the game of football revolves around. Then there are those who will game plan a game with nothing but down-the-field throws in it. The player that we are most concerned about here is the second. The player who wants to throw the ball on every down is the one most likely to be using the Spread offense.

The Spread offense is designed to stretch our defense horizontally and take advantage of the passing lanes the defense opens up when trying to adjust to the alignment of the receivers. This is a great concept in actual real life football, but in *Madden NFL,* we as a defense need to take advantage of the fundamentals of the style of offense. For one, this style of play requires a great quarterback with the ability to make quick reads and throws. In the virtual world, with a little bit of pressure or confusion we can eliminate the effectiveness of this scheme's design. Here are some plays with a good design for attacking the Spread offense.

Dollar Normal—Max Sting 3

Dial up a zone blitz

The first way we want to attack the Spread offense is with a zone blitz. The Dollar Normal—Max Sting 3 gives us a high-pressure blitz that can confuse our opponent and force a throw before the second and third reads become available. Whatever we can do to make the quarterback hold onto the ball just a second longer will benefit us in the long run.

To force the quarterback into making a rushed throw, we used press coverage and called for the zones to play the middle of the field. This minor adjustment forces all the routes to be contested at the line of scrimmage and delays the quarterback's downfield reads.

The cornerbacks are bringing pressure

Great hands by the safety

The coverage adjustments that we made prior to the snap also put our safety in better position to defend any seam or post routes. The rushed throw by the quarterback results in an interception for our defense.

Nickel 1-5-5—Sam Snake

The Nickel 1–5–5 can give the most experienced quarterback problems

After confusing the offense with a zone blitz, it's only right to follow that up with a solid man blitz. The Sam Snake is a Cover 1 defense that brings the strong-side linebacker in on a blitz. This can be a great play call because the alignment of the linebackers makes any one of them a potential blitz defender.

A linebacker disrupts the timing of the receiver's route

Another key ingredient in playing good defense against the Spread offense is to slow down the receivers by playing press coverage on them. The benefit of this defensive play call is that the linebackers will bump the receivers as they try to run their routes.

The blitzing defender sacks the quarterback

By using a man blitz defensive play call we challenged every pass route the offense had on the play and used the speed of our defender to reach the quarterback for a sack. We can generally get pressure from the middle or outside when running the Nickel 1–5–5 vs. the Spread offense.

3-4 Normal—Cover 2

Cover 2 always works well vs. the Spread

If the blitz or man coverage doesn't make you feel comfortable, the 3–4 Normal—Cover 2 zone is a perfect option for you. This defense is aligned so that it will make any route questionable. Another great thing about this play call is that it works perfectly against the most potent offensive play in the Spread offense, the slants.

Looks can be deceiving

Even when the offense thinks they have an opening against our defense, the Cover 2 can make a solid read turn into a bad decision.

The linebacker quickly snags the pass out of the air

The quarterback made the perfect read, as the receiver cut inside and just past the defender covering him—the only problem is we had another linebacker in zone and he intercepted the ball on the play. We can expect success when using plays like this vs. the Spread offense.

DEFENDING DOUBLE TE FORMATIONS

One of the toughest offensive sets to deal with in *Madden NFL* is the double tight end set (or Twin TE set). In the hands of an experienced user, this set can be used as both a powerful running set and a three-receiver pass set. As the defense, we cannot afford the offense attacking us with a set that could keep us off-balance. Players may think that any under-center formation is a waste of time and not that intimidating; however, if an opponent can run and pass the ball effectively out of the same formation, while maintaining good protection, then that means we're in for a long day.

The best way to attack a double tight end formation is to make sure we are aligned correctly. Alignment prevents the offense from making a pre-snap read as to the weak spots in our defense, and also makes them play us simply or reveal if what we're doing is making them uncomfortable.

4-3 Under—Slant Crash Left

Proper alignment will give us a chance for success every play

Our main concern when facing the double tight end is being able to stop the run. If a team has two good tight ends and they are on the field at the same time, they can overpower our linebackers or corners if they run-block. We have to eliminate the run from this formation so that the offense becomes one-dimensional.

When defending against the Twin TE, we often control the outside defender, normally a corner or safety, and use him to play any outside breaking pass or set contain on any run and force the play back inside.

The cornerback runs up to set the edge

The linebacker makes the back pay for cutting back

By setting the edge with our defensive back, we forced the play back inside and let our linebackers stop the back behind the line of scrimmage. Alignment is key in making sure we are in position to make a play on the ball. All we need to do is play fundamental football after the snap to make sure the plan is executed.

4-3 Under—Spy 3 Blitz

A pre-snap look at the 4–3 Under—Spy 3 Blitz assignments

Alignment is so much of a factor when defending against a double tight end formation that we'd like to take another look at its benefits. This time we will use the 4–3 Under—Spy 3 Blitz as a point of reference.

The defensive end is still in position to contain anything that comes his way

Aligning our defense properly is important because it allows us to establish gap control, and it prevents the offense from moving about as they wish. By using the under defensive front, our weak-side defensive end is still in position to contain anything the offense sends his way.

Meet you at the quarterback

The offense ran a play action bootleg. After the QB faked the ball to the running back and turned to pass the ball, our defensive end was in the quarterback's face and came away with the sack. If our defensive end had been inside of the tackle we would not have come away with a sack and probably would have given up big yards.

Nickel Strong—NB Blitz

No matter what the formation is we can be successful

The Nickel Strong—NB Blitz is another play that we can use when defending against the double tight end attack and still keep our fundamental alignment. We may be in a completely different formation, but a simple line shift to spread our line keeps our weak-side defensive end with outside leverage.

The defensive end allows the corner to come free

By shifting to spread our defensive line, we force the offensive tackle to account for our defensive end. We're bringing the nickelback in on a blitz, and with the offensive tackle preoccupied, the corner gets a free run at the quarterback.

The quarterback didn't have a chance vs. the blitz

Our cornerback reaches the quarterback almost immediately after he takes his drop. Our method of attack when dealing with the Twin TE formations has given us opportunities to sack the quarterback and shut down the run, simply by making sure our defense is aligned correctly. Sometimes the most effective tactics are the simplest.

DEFENDING THE EMPTY FORMATION

Even the best defensive game plan and blitz package can be tested when the offense decides to go five-wide or "empty" on us. This style of offense may seem easy to attack because of the lack of blocking, but if a quarterback knows how to make quality pre-snap reads of our defense then we could be in for a long day trying to slow this aggressive offense down. The one thing we know about this offensive style is that it is based on timing and quick reads. As a defense, if there is any chance for us to have success, we need to disrupt the receivers as they try to run their pass routes. Having the personnel to run bump-n-run pass coverage is a key to having consistent success vs. the five-wide or Empty set.

Dime Flat—DB Dogs

Stay aggressive against Empty sets

Opponents who tend to use Empty passing formations often use teams that maximize their ability to strike the defense quickly and for big yards. One of the plays that we know we have to prepare for when facing a five-wide receiver set is the flanker screen. We can expect that if they come out in five-wide, we will see an FL Screen. We plan to defend this aggressively with a man blitz, using the Dime Flat—DB Dogs blitz.

The defensive end and dimeback are blitzing the quarterback

One thing that we will drive into our opponent's head when they come out in five-wide is that we will send a relentless attack at them. The disadvantage that the offense has when running a flanker screen is they will have linemen pulling to add blocking. We will get clean shots on the quarterback because of this.

Pressure equals bad decisions

By bringing the blitz against a pass-only option set, we're able to pressure the quarterback into almost throwing an interception. Our cornerback drops the ball but could have easily taken this errant pass in for a touchdown. Step one of our attack: pressure everything.

Dollar Normal—Strike Spy 2

Adding some zone can help ease the pressure of an aggressive attack

If the thought of constant pressure turns your stomach, then we can add a little zone to the mix when facing the five-wide-receiver sets. The Dollar Normal—Strike Spy 2 is a solid Cover 2 blitz defense that adds some insurance that someone will be in the area if we can't sack the quarterback or if we miss the jam on a receiver.

Our zone defenders sit on the crossing routes and react once the ball is in the air

One thing we like about running a Cover 2 blitz against an Empty set is the fact that it protects us from getting beaten by crossing routes. Just as we know the offense will attack us with a screen, we also know they will send crossing routes at our coverage to try to get natural pick plays. With a few of our defenders in zone, we can rest assured that we don't have to worry about getting picked off by a receiver.

The cornerback swats the ball out of the air

This play shows that even when we don't get extreme pressure on the quarterback, we can still come away with a victory on the defensive side of the ball.

Dime Normal—Quarters Man

Cover 4 protects us from Empty set deep passes

The Quarters Man is a Cover 4 defense that lets us handle the Empty sets when they plan to attack with multiple downfield routes. Even though this defense does not bring the pressure we like, it is a solid end-of-the-half or late-in-the-game defense.

Everyone is accounted for

When running this defense, consider manually controlling one of the inside defenders to prevent any receiver from being able to work the middle of the field against us.

The QB hurry forces a bobbled throw

If the quarterback can't find an open receiver, we can get pressure from our defensive line. Normally, the pressure that the defensive line gets yields interceptions for our defensive backs. This time, our coverage yields a quarterback hurry and a terrible throw.

MADDEN NFL 11

TEAM STRATEGY

Contents

SAN FRANCISCO 49ERS

OFFENSIVE SCOUTING REPORT

The 49ers offense may not resemble what it was in the late '80s, but it should be markedly improved from last season. The draft offered an opportunity for the team to address its biggest need at the offensive line. They spent both first round picks on offensive linemen—Anthony Davis and Mike Iupati—to aid in the protection of the first pick in the 2005 draft, quarterback Alex Smith. Both linemen are instant starters and should provide what Smith may have needed—a little more time in the pocket to make a smart throw. The receiving corps is led by TE Vernon Davis and WR Michael Crabtree, with Davis doing his best work deep down the middle, utilizing his size and speed, while Crabtree provides agility and sure-handedness on slant routes. We can't talk about the 49ers offense without discussing its best offensive player, RB Frank Gore. The first and second hits rarely take Gore to the ground. He's relentless in his running style yet shifty enough to make guys miss and then take it 80 yards to pay dirt with breakout speed. Success for the 49ers relies on the offensive line.

DEFENSIVE SCOUTING REPORT

The 49ers defense is led by inside linebacker Patrick Willis, who bears the highest overall ranking of any linebacker. Willis provides tenacity and toughness, which is reinforced by head coach Mike Singletary, who's a motivational wizard. In his first three seasons, Willis led the league in tackles twice and finished second once. There is no one better with his speed, awareness, and sure tackling in the open field. Even feigning a blitz creates a sense of panic for opposing offenses. The 3–4 defense scheme plays right into the strengths of the 49ers. The big guys up front (Isaac Sopoaga, Aubrayo Franklin, and Justin Smith) hold up the line, so the linebackers can get the glory. The secondary, led by CB Nate Clements, does a fine job of keeping the ball in front of them and not allowing the big play, while safety Dashon Goldson seems happy to meet the opposition at full speed. The 49ers gave up the fourth fewest points in the NFL last year.

TEAM RATING

79
Overall

KEY ADDITIONS

QB	David Carr
WR	Ted Ginn Jr.
LB	Travis LaBoy
CB	Karl Paymah
OT	Anthony Davis
OG	Mike Iupati

KEY DEPARTURES

WR	Arnaz Battle
QB	Shaun Hill
CB	Marcus Hudson
T	Tony Pashos
ILB	Jeff Ulbrich

RATINGS BY POSITION

Position	Rating
Quarterbacks	77
Halfbacks	93
Fullbacks	77
Wide Receivers	75
Tight Ends	96
Tackles	81
Guards	82
Centers	84
Defensive Ends	80
Defensive Tackles	90
Outside Linebackers	79
Middle Linebackers	99
Cornerbacks	83
Free Safeties	80
Strong Safeties	80
Kickers	82
Punters	94

DEPTH CHART

POS	OVR	FIRST NAME	LAST NAME
C	84	Eric	Heitmann
C	70	Cody	Wallace
CB	84	Nate	Clements
CB	81	Shawntae	Spencer
CB	73	Tarell	Brown
CB	64	Karl	Paymah
CB	72	William	James
DT	90	Aubrayo	Franklin
DT	60	Khalif	Mitchell
FB	77	Moran	Norris
FS	80	Dashon	Goldson
FS	60	Curtis	Taylor
HB	93	Frank	Gore
HB	71	Glen	Coffee
HB	68	Michael	Robinson
HB	67	Anthony	Dixon
K	82	Joe	Nedney
LE	71	Isaac	Sopoaga
LE	68	Kentwan	Balmer
LE	66	Ricky	Jean-Francois
LG	83	Mike	Iupati
LG	78	David	Baas
LOLB	79	Manny	Lawson
LOLB	64	Travis	LaBoy
LT	87	Joe	Staley
LT	76	Barry	Sims
MLB	99	Patrick	Willis
MLB	84	Takeo	Spikes
MLB	67	Scott	McKillop
MLB	67	Matt	Wilhelm
P	94	Andy	Lee
QB	77	Alex	Smith
QB	65	David	Carr
QB	65	Nate	Davis
RE	89	Justin	Smith
RE	71	Ray	McDonald
RG	81	Adam	Snyder
RG	79	Chilo	Rachal
ROLB	78	Parys	Haralson
ROLB	75	Ahmad	Brooks
RT	75	Anthony	Davis
RT	58	Alex	Boone
SS	80	Michael	Lewis
SS	71	Taylor	Mays
SS	64	Reggie	Smith
TE	96	Vernon	Davis
TE	66	Delanie	Walker
TE	63	Nate	Byham
WR	83	Michael	Crabtree
WR	74	Josh	Morgan
WR	69	Jason	Hill
WR	71	Brandon	Jones
WR	70	Ted	Ginn Jr.

OFFENSIVE STRENGTH CHART

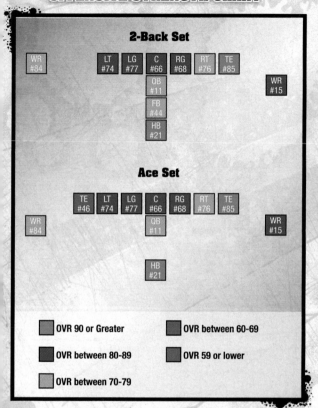

2-Back Set

WR #84	LT #74	LG #77	C #66	RG #68	RT #76	TE #85
			QB #11			WR #15
			FB #44			
			HB #21			

Ace Set

	TE #46	LT #74	LG #77	C #66	RG #68	RT #76	TE #85
WR #84			QB #11			WR #15
			HB #21			

- OVR 90 or Greater
- OVR between 80-89
- OVR between 70-79
- OVR between 60-69
- OVR 59 or lower

Key Player Substitutions

Position: WR

Substitution: Ted Ginn Jr.

When: Situational

Advantage: Ted Ginn has the speed to run past most cornerbacks in the NFL. Whenever you need to add some speed to your wide receiver corps, throw Ginn in.

#21 Frank Gore
Halfback (HB)

Overall	93
Speed	93
Agility	92
Stiff Arm	87
Carrying	80

#15 Michael Crabtree
Wide Receiver (WR)

Overall	83
Speed	88
Catching	88
Release	88
Jumping	92

#85 Vernon Davis
Tight End (TE)

Overall	96
Speed	90
Catching	84
Catch in Traffic	79
Jumping	94

#52 Patrick Willis
Middle Linebacker (MLB)

Overall	99
Speed	90
Awareness	91
Tackle	99
Hit Power	96

#92 Aubrayo Franklin
Defensive Tackle (DT)

Overall	90
Speed	54
Strength	97
Power Moves	88
Block Shedding	96

#94 Justin Smith
Defensive End (RE)

Overall	89
Speed	73
Strength	87
Finesse Moves	64
Power Moves	86

DEFENSIVE STRENGTH CHART

3-4 Defense

	FS #38		SS #32			
CB #36	ROLB #98	MLB #51	MLB #52	LOLB #99	CB #22
	RE #94	DT #92	LE #90		

Dime Defense

	FS #38		SS #32		
CB #36	CB #25	MLB #52	CB #41	CB #22
	RE #94	DT #60	DT #92	LE #90	

- OVR 90 or Greater
- OVR between 80-89
- OVR between 70-79
- OVR between 60-69
- OVR 59 or lower

Key Player Substitutions

Position: SS

Substitution: Taylor Mays

When: Nickel and Dime formations

Advantage: With the speed of a running back and the size of a linebacker, Taylor Mays has the speed to cover a lot of field on deep balls. Use Mays only when you are up against fast wide receivers.

Playbook Breakdown

The San Francisco 49ers have one of the best running backs in the game in Frank Gore. Their offensive game plan starts with him, and they also have Michael Crabtree, who is a talented young receiver entering his sophomore year. The best running formation from this playbook is the I-Form Tight. If you like to run a basic offense with a playbook that has a mix of compression and spread formations, this is a good book. Under center you have formations such as Singleback Bunch and Singleback Snugs Flip. From the Gun you have Snugs Flip, Doubles Y-Slot, and 4WR Trey. This gives you a strong mix of plays that you can use from any given formation from this book to attack the defense with. Mixing up your play selection is key. Whether you like to pound on the ground or attack through the air, it all can be done within the 49ers playbook.

OFFENSIVE FORMATIONS

FORMATION	# OF PLAYS
Gun 4WR Trey	9
Gun Doubles	18
Gun Doubles Y-Slot	15
Gun Snugs Flip	9
Gun Spread Flex Wk	12
Gun Y-Trips	15
I-Form Pro	21
I-Form Tight	12
Singleback Ace	21
Singleback Bunch	12
Singleback Doubles	18
Singleback Snugs Flip	12
Singleback Y-Trips	18
Strong Pro	21
Weak Pro	18
Weak Tight Pair	12
Wildcat Niner	3

OFFENSIVE PLAYCOUNTS

PLAY TYPE	# OF PLAYS
Quick Pass	14
Standard Pass	54
Shotgun Pass	45
Play Action Pass	47
Inside Handoff	29
Outside Handoff	21
Pitch	7
Counter	7

I-Form Tight—Angle

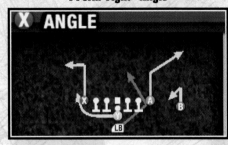

Angle routes have been effective out of the backfield for many years in *Madden NFL*. A West Coast team such as the 49ers likes to set up the run by passing the ball with short passes. Angle allows you to do just that.

The QB snaps the ball and scans the field

With this play, your first two reads should the halfback and the fullback coming out of the backfield. You should see Frank Gore come open on just about any defense. If the defense has him covered, look for the fullback going to the left side of the field. You also have to keep an eye out for Michael Crabtree—the short curl that he runs is a quick read.

The QB passes the ball to the running back

Frank Gore makes the catch and turns down the field to pick up some good yards. Once you get the defense worrying about the HB, you want to involve either fullback Moran Norris or wide receiver Michael Crabtree.

I-Form Tight—Power 0

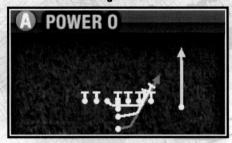

One of the staple run plays the 49ers like to run out of I-Form Tight is Power 0. This play involves left guard Mike Iupati pulling with fullback Moran Norris as lead blocker. With this play, we are going to bring the flanker, Michael Crabtree, in motion to provide additional blocking.

Follow the FB through the hole

Once the flanker is behind the line of scrimmage, snap the ball. Once the ball is snapped, quarterback Alex Smith hands the ball off to running back Frank Gore. This is when you want to follow your blockers inside, or if you see that they've sealed the edge you can bounce it outside.

Picking up more than a first down

Frank Gore sees a hole and takes the run inside behind his blockers to pick up a good gain. With this play, you can keep the defense guessing about which side you're going to run the ball to by flipping the play and sending the flanker in motion. Be sure to mix this in with play action passes.

I-Form Tight—PA Boot

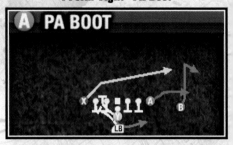

A good play action play that works with any of the runs from the I-Form Tight is the PA Boot. This play is a fake handoff to running back Frank Gore that allows the quarterback to roll out to the right with two options over the middle of the field.

Rolling out to get a good passing lane

Alex Smith fakes the handoff to Gore and scans the field. Once you roll out to the right, you should look over the middle of the field. Tight end Delanie Walker is running a 5-yard crossing route and Vernon Davis is running a delay route to the flat. Your last read for this play is to keep an eye out for Michael Crabtree on the comeback route.

Davis makes a great catch in the flats

We complete a pass to Vernon Davis in the flat, who makes a grab and has plenty of room to run for positive yards. Another thing to consider for maximum protection is to motion the flanker behind the line of scrimmage. This provides us with more pass-blocking and gives the defense the same look as if we were running the ball.

I-Form Tight—PA Power O

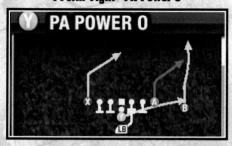

Another good play action play from the I-Form Tight formation is the PA Power O. This play involves the quarterback faking the ball off to the running back while the fullback sneaks out into the flat. The other receivers run a corner route, a post route, and a streak.

Selling the fake on play action

Once you snap the ball, it's a fake handoff to the running back. As you scan the field, look over to the middle and flat area. Fullback Moran Norris should be your primary read; if he isn't open, look down the field to TE Vernon Davis or Delanie Walker.

Hitting the FB with room to run

The flanker's streak route is designed to pull the coverage deep; this is what opens up the underneath corner route and the flat route. The quarterback completes the pass to the fullback in the flat. If you see the corner playing the flat, then you can pass the ball deep to Michael Crabtree on the streak or Vernon Davis. As your last read, you have Delanie Walker on the deep post route.

I-Form Tight—HB Blast

HB Blast is a run play designed to run the ball between left tackle Joe Staley and left guard Mike Iupati with fullback Moran Norris leading the way. A good aspect of this play is that it allows you to choose whether you want to take it up inside or (if you see your blocker seal the edge) take it outside.

Look to hit the A or B gap

With this play, we like to motion the flanker from the left to the right side of the field to provide extra blocking. Also consider flipping the play and running it to the opposite side with the same setup. The quarterback hands the ball off to running back Frank Gore, and he follows his blockers.

Let the blockers set before you make your move

Our blockers seal the edge and Frank Gore sees daylight and bounces it outside to pick up a 15-yard gain. With this play, always look to see which side of the formation has the most defenders. This will help you to decide which side to run the ball on.

I-Form Tight—HB Lead Toss

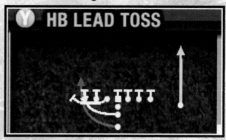

The HB Lead Toss is a strong way to get running back Frank Gore outside. It's the perfect run to use when you have the defense off-balance. After mixing up your play calling with plays such as Power O, HB Blast, PA Boot, and PA Power O you should go to this play. Just like with all the other runs from this formation, we are going to bring the flanker in motion from the right side of the field to provide additional blocking.

Sealing the defensive line

The QB tosses the ball to Gore. We are going to follow left guard Iupati, who is pulling, and our fullback, Moran Norris. Look for when to cut back inside, or bounce it outside if the blocks are sealed.

Turning it up the field

The defenders are picked up and there is plenty of room for Gore to run downfield to pick up some good yards. The key thing to remember is to always mix up which side you're going to run the ball from, with this play or any of the runs in this formation.

I-Form Tight—Z Slant

Z Slant is a pass play that has flanker Michael Crabtree as the primary read on the play. You also have tight end Vernon Davis, who runs a flat route. This provides you with two quick reads on the right side of the field. You also have Delanie Walker on a short curl route on the left that can be used as another quick read.

Avoiding the rush with a quick pass

We begin with motioning wide receiver Michael Crabtree. When you bring him in motion, let him take just a quick step. By doing this you gain separation from the defender and you can tell right away whether it's man or zone. The focus here should be on the slant route and the flat; these are two quick reads in the same area.

Hitting Crabtree on the run for a 5-yard gain

The pass is complete to Crabtree for an easy 5-yard gain. Don't forget to keep an eye on the flat route that Vernon Davis is running—one of the two routes is almost always open vs. either man or zone coverage.

CHICAGO BEARS

OFFENSIVE SCOUTING REPORT

The Bears offense has to rally around the abilities of Jay Cutler. Although he led the league in interceptions last year, he managed to also throw his career high in touchdowns. The traditional run-first offense of the Bears is making the shift to a pass-oriented attack. Cutler has a big arm with a high throw power rating and pretty good legs, allowing him to scramble out of the pocket if needed to make the play. Matt Forte is a solid workhorse as the primary HB. He holds onto the football well, has good acceleration to hit holes quickly, and has plenty of stamina. When Forte does need a rest or to change pace slightly, mix in the newly acquired Chester Taylor, who is a bit more elusive on third down situations. Speed burners Devin Hester and Johnny Knox complement Cutler's big arm for the deep threat, while Devin Aromashodu acts as the outlet WR. Don't forget that TE Greg Olsen has great hands and can be used for a quick dump pass if the offensive line collapses.

DEFENSIVE SCOUTING REPORT

Julius Peppers is now a Bear! This means the Bears have a reputable pass rush simply by having him on the field. The offensive line should be shifted to help stop Peppers from penetrating the line, giving big play opportunities to DT Tommie Harris or openings for a linebacker blitz with Brian Urlacher or Lance Briggs. These same players will provide good run prevention up front to minimize penetration into the backfield, where the Bears secondary is a little lacking. Charles Tillman is the strongest player in the secondary, with the ability to succeed in both zone and man coverage. When it comes to pass defense, however, everything should stem from getting Peppers in on the quarterback and creating pressure so that the Bears can capitalize on offensive mistakes and hurries.

TEAM RATING

77
Overall

KEY ADDITIONS

SS	Chris Harris
CB	Tim Jennings
TE	Brandon Manumaleuna
DE	Julius Peppers
RB	Chester Taylor
FS	Major Wright

KEY DEPARTURES

DE	Alex Brown
DE	Adewale Ogunleye
OT	Orlando Pace
CB	Nathan Vasher
S	Kevin Payne
LB	Jamar Williams

RATINGS BY POSITION

Position	Rating		Position	Rating
Quarterbacks	83		Defensive Tackles	87
Halfbacks	86		Outside Linebackers	82
Fullbacks	56		Middle Linebackers	90
Wide Receivers	76		Cornerbacks	80
Tight Ends	84		Free Safeties	73
Tackles	79		Strong Safeties	81
Guards	78		Kickers	95
Centers	86		Punters	73
Defensive Ends	85			

DEPTH CHART

POS	OVR	FIRST NAME	LAST NAME
C	86	Olin	Kreutz
CB	85	Charles	Tillman
CB	74	Zack	Bowman
CB	70	Danieal	Manning
CB	66	Corey	Graham
DB	68	Tim	Jennings
DT	87	Tommie	Harris
DT	71	Anthony	Adams
DT	68	Marcus	Harrison
DT	65	Jarron	Gilbert
FB	56	Eddie	Williams
FS	73	Al	Afalava
FS	67	Major	Wright
FS	66	Craig	Steltz
G	79	Roberto	Garza
HB	86	Matt	Forte
HB	79	Chester	Taylor
HB	64	Garrett	Wolfe
HB	64	Kahlil	Bell
K	95	Robbie	Gould
LE	74	Mark	Anderson
LE	65	Israel	Idonije
LG	77	Frank	Omiyale
LG	72	Josh	Beekman
LOLB	72	Hunter	Hillenmeyer
LOLB	70	Nick	Roach
LT	82	Chris	Williams
LT	64	Lance	Louis
MLB	90	Brian	Urlacher
MLB	57	Tim	Shaw
P	82	Brad	Maynard
QB	83	Jay	Cutler
QB	66	Dan	LeFevour
QB	64	Caleb	Hanie
RE	95	Julius	Peppers
RE	62	Henry	Melton
ROLB	92	Lance	Briggs
ROLB	73	Pisa	Tinoisamoa
RT	75	Kevin	Shaffer
RT	69	James	Marten
SS	81	Chris	Harris
SS	69	Josh	Bullocks
TE	84	Greg	Olsen
TE	76	Brandon	Manumaleuna
TE	76	Desmond	Clark
WR	78	Devin	Hester
WR	75	Johnny	Knox
WR	74	Earl	Bennett
WR	70	Devin	Aromashodu
WR	66	Rashied	Davis
WR	65	Juaquin	Iglesias

OFFENSIVE STRENGTH CHART

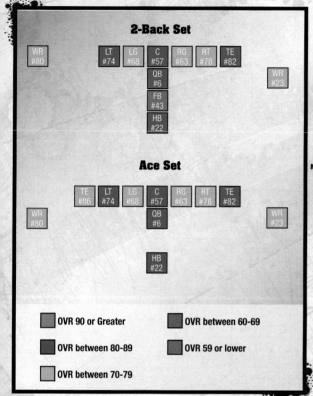

2-Back Set

		LT #74	LG #68	C #57	RG #63	RT #78	TE #82	
WR #80				QB #6				WR #23
				FB #43				
				HB #22				

Ace Set

TE #86	LT #74	LG #68	C #57	RG #63	RT #78	TE #82
WR #80			QB #6			WR #23
			HB #22			

- ■ OVR 90 or Greater
- ■ OVR between 80-89
- ■ OVR between 70-79
- ■ OVR between 60-69
- ■ OVR 59 or lower

Key Player Substitutions

Position: HB

Substitution: Garrett Wolfe

When: Two-back sets

Advantage: Wolfe is a good sub to bring in on two-back sets. He has more speed, agility, and acceleration. Look to get him in the flats.

#6 Jay Cutler
Quarterback (QB)

Overall	83
Throwing Power	97
Short Accuracy	82
Medium Accuracy	79
Deep Accuracy	77

#22 Matt Forte
Halfback (HB)

Overall	86
Speed	89
Agility	87
Stiff Arm	75
Carrying	92

#82 Greg Olsen
Tight End (TE)

Overall	84
Speed	87
Catching	86
Catch in Traffic	84
Jumping	89

#90 Julius Peppers
Defensive End (RE)

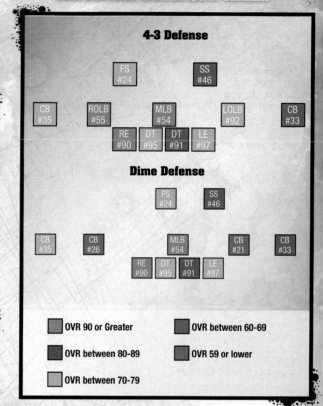

Overall	95
Speed	85
Strength	80
Power Moves	86
Block Shedding	63

#55 Lance Briggs
Linebacker (ROLB)

Overall	92
Speed	78
Awareness	91
Tackle	95
Hit Power	86

#54 Brian Urlacher
Linebacker (MLB)

Overall	90
Speed	84
Strength	76
Awareness	95
Hit Power	89

DEFENSIVE STRENGTH CHART

4-3 Defense

	FS #24		SS #46	
CB #35	ROLB #55	MLB #54	LOLB #92	CB #33
	RE #90	DT #95	DT #91	LE #97

Dime Defense

	FS #24		SS #46	
CB #35	CB #26	MLB #54	CB #21	CB #33
	RE #90	DT #95	DT #91	LE #97

- ■ OVR 90 or Greater
- ■ OVR between 80-89
- ■ OVR between 70-79
- ■ OVR between 60-69
- ■ OVR 59 or lower

Key Player Substitutions

Position: CB

Substitution: Tim Jennings

When: Global

Advantage: Moving Jennings up to the number two spot on the depth charts will give you more speed and better man coverage. This will allow for better coverage against good receivers.

Playbook Breakdown

The Bears aren't the only team that has made major changes to its attack over the years. Since coach Mike Martz is now on board, you can expect more open downfield attacks from this playbook. This playbook uses a lot of spread and takes shots down the field, trying to put the defense in conflict every single play. The key is to get your playmaker lined up in a position with floods and try to free him up. The halfback is often used as a weapon in this system as well. However, if you are a run-first player, don't shy away from this playbook. You have some nice running plays within this open downfield attack. We will provide you with spread attack plays, plays from the Gun, and what we call "close-out" formations for when you can run the ball and secure your win.

OFFENSIVE FORMATIONS

FORMATION	# OF PLAYS
Gun Doubles Wk	15
Gun Empty Trey	9
Gun Snugs Flip	9
Gun Split Offset	9
Gun Spread Y-Flex	12
Gun Y-Trips Wk	12
I-Form Pro	18
I-Form Tight	18
Singleback Ace	18
Singleback Doubles	18
Singleback Spread Flex	12
Singleback Trey Open	12
Singleback Y-Trips Bear	15
Strong Pro	18
Weak Slot	12
Weak Twins Flex	12

OFFENSIVE PLAYCOUNTS

PLAY TYPE	# OF PLAYS
Quick Pass	16
Standard Pass	51
Shotgun Pass	43
Play Action Pass	40
Inside Handoff	28
Outside Handoff	9
Pitch	6
Counter	8

Weak Slot—Curls

This is a great play to work with your spread concept. The key is that you must read your slot wideout. If he's uncovered you must hit him once you hike the ball. If you see a defender slide out on him pre-snap, audible to a running play because the number of defenders in the box is weakened. When running the spread, you want to work the pass to open up your rushing attack. The spread also allows you to read zone or man, and heat. Your reads are the flat, the curl, and then the V route by the FB.

The slot is uncovered—you need to hit him

When you see that the slot is uncovered, you must hit him. You want the defense to account for everyone. If you don't make them accountable they can apply extra coverage on your key playmakers or send extra blitzers.

Getting upfield for YAC

This play kills just about any coverage, and it really hurts heat. You can see it coming in most cases, and this play attacks the areas from which the most pressure is generated.

Weak Slot—Off Tackle

The Off Tackle is one of the best running plays in the game. When you see that the slot wideout is covered, this gives you the green light to pound the ball. You have the right numbers inside to pound the rock. This play is listed in your pre-set formation audibles, so you don't have to waste an audible slot for it. You use spread to open the field and run the ball. When you're under center, you don't want long, developing routes. This play will make your opponents slide the defenders back into the box, and then you will attack via pass again.

A great seal for our runner

Your reads when running this play are to look inside and then outside. Key in on the defensive end. If he slants inside, you bounce it outside. If he comes upfield, you cut it inside. The Off Tackle is one of the few plays that allow you to be a threat inside or outside.

Inside gaps are filled, so bounce outside for yards

Since the defenders plugged the inside and the tackle and fullback are co-op blocking the defensive end, we take the ball outside to get yards.

Weak Slot—Corners

This is a mean play that works well with the other plays we have shown. You have a corner and post route to the right and a C route and a flat combo with the backs as your hot reads. Then you have a C route for the split end. Read the right side to see if you can take a shot downfield. If you read pressure, check down to your backs. If you have time and no one is open, check to your back side with the C route for the split end.

Making deep reads against man coverage

It will only take two seconds to make your read downfield. If you have time, fire the ball downfield. If you don't, you have some excellent check-downs.

Drag those toes inbounds

The SS bit on the post route, which gave us room to hit the SL on the corner route. If the SS had gone with the corner route, we could have driven a pass down the seam to the post route. This play has so many options and meshes well with the other plays that have been shown.

Gun Snugs Flip—WR Stick Nod

This is a new play that was added to the Bears playbook this season. You have a three-way mesh to the right and a two-way mesh to the left. When you read the right, you should read the flat, slant, and then the fade curl. On the left you would read the flat and then the zig route. The flat will clear out for the zig. This is a nice man- or zone-beating play. Also be aware that the flats provide an excellent hot read.

This play opens the field up

The flat routes get open quickly. If there is heat present, you can see that the slant and the flats serve you well when pressure comes. You have time, so wait on the fade curl and the zig route.

Nice catch for our receiver

The flat pulled the alley defender and allowed the zig route to get open. When you're facing zone, the last man to release will be open. Keep that in mind so that when you're up against an opponent who uses a lot of zone coverage, you can beat it effectively.

Gun Snugs Flip—HB Draw

Our rule has always been that when you pick a formation to run plays from, you must be able to run and pass out of it. This will serve you well in tight games. It keeps the people you're playing off-balance and forces them to respect your rushing attack. It will also loosen up the pass defensive coverage you will face. Once you throw a few balls downfield, they will use some sort of zone or deep combo coverage to slow your passing attack. The HB Draw is a great add here to keep your offensive attack fresh.

High hat pushes defenders back

When the offensive line stands up (high hat), the defenders read pass, so they drop back and allow you room to get downfield. Once you see a hole, hit it. The other part that is nice about this formation is that by having a two-by-two look you can get outside on the edge with the running back if the inside gaps are filled. The wideouts can seal and allow you to get outside.

We get a great gain downfield

This is a nice gain, and now you have set the table for the rest of the game.

I-Form Tight—Angle

This is the set to use when you want to close out the game or if you want to get your rushing attack going. You need a passing play from this set to keep them honest and let them know you can still be a threat to pass as well as run. This is a nice combo with your backs. You have the HB on a V route, the FB running a flat route, the TE doing a corner route, the SE on a quick out, and the FL with a curl route. This five-way attack allows you to take advantage of heat, zone, and man coverage. Read your backs first, and then go to the TE, the curl, and the out. If the defender sits on the curl, hit the corner. If the defender sits on the corner, drive the curl.

Pressure is coming up the gut so we check down

When you read pressure, hit your backs. The V route is open since pressure came through the middle.

Keep those chains moving

Now move the chains. You just told the defense to calm down on that heat.

I-Form Tight—Counter Lead

When you lab this game and break it down, you will find that the defenders flow well to the ball when you're running the rock. The best way to slow down that flow is to take advantage of it. The Counter Lead is a quick counter that gets the defenders to move to your initial step and get sealed by a lineman. This allows you to get downfield and hit the open holes that your line will provide. When you use other counters, the defenders will break the play up at times. When you have a playbook that provides you with quick counters, use them because they are great for any situation.

The defense bit on the first step and backfield movement

Since the defenders bit on the first move, the line is now able to seal blocks and allow you to explode into the secondary for extra yardage. Hit the hole and hit it fast before anyone gets off their blocks.

Forte is off to the races

This is a great running play you can mesh with other running plays from the set. This is why the I-Form Tight is such a great close-out formation.

CINCINNATI BENGALS

OFFENSIVE SCOUTING REPORT

Offensively, the Bengals are full of potential. Despite WR Chad Ochocinco's recent decline in real-life productivity, he's still a top-tier wide receiver with the in-game stats to prove it. He retains great speed, good hands, and excellent route-running ability, not to mention that he has more "Old Spice Swagger" than anyone in the game. QB Carson Palmer is still leading the team and provides a solid foundation for the Bengals offense. He's very aware of his surroundings and has great passing ability, being capable of tossing the long ball better than most in the NFL. The unsung hero, however, is RB Cedric Benson. He quietly racked up a thousand-yard season last year as he wore down opposing defensive lines with his strength and persistence. Benson isn't a dynamic back, but he's got everything you need to establish a solid running game behind a decent offensive line.

DEFENSIVE SCOUTING REPORT

The Bengals defense played surprisingly well in 2009 until the loss of DE Antwan Odom. This year, Odom is back and healthy, providing sufficient pass-rush to make QBs aware of his presence. LBs Rey Maualuga and Dhani Jones are a solid foundation for the linebacker squad. Keep Maualuga's eyes on the move to create turnovers and the occasional sack. In the defensive backfield, look to the real standouts of the Bengals defense, CBs Leon Hall and Johnathan Joseph, to create problems for rival wideouts and create turnovers if the quarterback is pressured on the front line. The Bengals aren't the shiniest defense, but they can keep opponents in check when you need them to.

TEAM RATING

86
Overall

KEY ADDITIONS

WR	Antonio Bryant
WR	Matt Jones
CB	Pacman Jones
K	Mike Nugent
S	Gibril Wilson
TE	Jermaine Gresham

KEY DEPARTURES

WR	Laveranues Coles
TE	J.P. Foschi
K	Shayne Graham
FB	Jeremi Johnson
RB	Larry Johnson
DT	Shaun Smith

RATINGS BY POSITION

Position	Rating	Position	Rating
Quarterbacks	87	Defensive Tackles	86
Halfbacks	89	Outside Linebackers	86
Fullbacks	68	Middle Linebackers	82
Wide Receivers	83	Cornerbacks	93
Tight Ends	74	Free Safeties	78
Tackles	84	Strong Safeties	77
Guards	83	Kickers	52
Centers	77	Punters	76
Defensive Ends	83		

DEPTH CHART

POS	OVR	FIRST NAME	LAST NAME
C	77	Kyle	Cook
C	68	Jonathan	Luigs
CB	93	Johnathan	Joseph
CB	92	Leon	Hall
CB	68	Keiwan	Ratliff
CB	67	Morgan	Trent
CB	64	David	Jones
DT	86	Domata	Peko
DT	77	Pat	Sims
DT	77	Tank	Johnson
DT	76	Jonathan	Fanene
FB	68	Fui	Vakapuna
FS	78	Chris	Crocker
FS	73	Gibril	Wilson
HB	89	Cedric	Benson
HB	74	Bernard	Scott
HB	70	Brian	Leonard
K	52	Dave	Rayner
LE	81	Robert	Geathers
LE	67	Frostee	Rucker
LG	77	Nate	Livings
LG	75	Evan	Mathis
LOLB	85	Rey	Maualuga
LOLB	75	Rashad	Jeanty
LT	88	Andrew	Whitworth
LT	79	Anthony	Collins
MLB	82	Dhani	Jones
MLB	66	Abdul	Hodge
P	76	Kevin	Huber
QB	87	Carson	Palmer
QB	60	J.T.	O'Sullivan
QB	53	Jordan	Palmer
RE	85	Antwan	Odom
RE	72	Michael	Johnson
RG	88	Bobbie	Williams
RG	63	Otis	Hudson
ROLB	86	Keith	Rivers
ROLB	72	Brandon	Johnson
RT	79	Andre	Smith
RT	76	Dennis	Roland
SS	77	Chinedum	Ndukwe
SS	77	Roy	Williams
TE	78	Jermaine	Gresham
TE	74	Reggie	Kelly
TE	66	Daniel	Coats
WR	91	Chad	Ochocinco
WR	89	Antonio	Bryant
WR	75	Andre	Caldwell
WR	68	Jordan	Shipley
WR	67	Dezmon	Briscoe
WR	57	Jerome	Simpson

OFFENSIVE STRENGTH CHART

2-Back Set

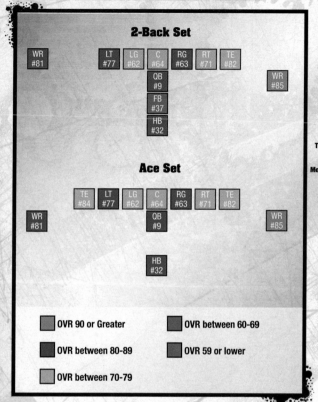

WR #81	LT #77	LG #62	C #64	RG #63	RT #71	TE #82
		QB #9				WR #85
		FB #37				
		HB #32				

Ace Set

TE #84	LT #77	LG #62	C #64	RG #63	RT #71	TE #82
WR #81			QB #9			WR #85
			HB #32			

- OVR 90 or Greater
- OVR between 80-89
- OVR between 70-79
- OVR between 60-69
- OVR 59 or lower

#9 Carson Palmer
Quarterback (QB)

Overall	87
Throwing Power	94
Short Accuracy	89
Medium Accuracy	85
Deep Accuracy	82

#32 Cedric Benson
Halfback (HB)

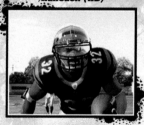

Overall	89
Speed	89
Agility	86
Stiff Arm	90
Carrying	95

#85 Chad Ochocinco
Wide Receiver (WR)

Overall	91
Speed	92
Catching	92
Release	67
Jumping	92

#22 Johnathan Joseph
Cornerback (CB)

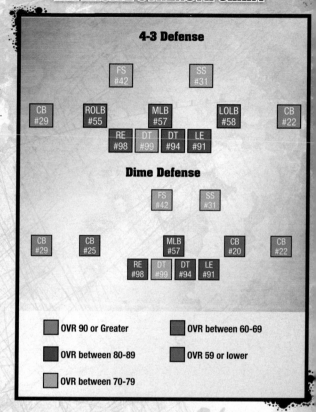

Overall	93
Speed	95
Awareness	87
Man Coverage	95
Zone Coverage	90

#29 Leon Hall
Cornerback (CB)

Overall	92
Speed	88
Awareness	90
Man Coverage	88
Zone Coverage	94

#55 Keith Rivers
Linebacker (ROLB)

Overall	86
Speed	87
Awareness	78
Tackle	89
Hit Power	88

DEFENSIVE STRENGTH CHART

4-3 Defense

	FS #42		SS #31		
CB #29	ROLB #55	MLB #57		LOLB #58	CB #22
	RE #98	DT #99	DT #94	LE #91	

Dime Defense

	FS #42		SS #31		
CB #29	CB #25	MLB #57		CB #20	CB #22
	RE #98	DT #99	DT #94	LE #91	

- OVR 90 or Greater
- OVR between 80-89
- OVR between 70-79
- OVR between 60-69
- OVR 59 or lower

Key Player Substitutions

Position: TE

Substitution: Reggie Kelly

When: Three-wide-receiver sets

Advantage: Reggie Kelly will help keep the defense out of the backfield and give Palmer the time that he needs to deliver a pass to a wide receiver.

Key Player Substitutions

Position: DT

Substitution: Tank Johnson

When: Passing situations

Advantage: Tank Johnson is a faster DT with better finesse moves. Use Johnson in passing situations to try to get more pressure on the quarterback.

The Bengals went from a pass-based offensive team to one that prefers to punch you in the mouth and grind it out. The team went to more of a run-oriented pro style once they upgraded the running back department a season ago. The Bengals have found that establishing a solid running game makes it easier to control the game and take shots with the weapons they have at wideout. The key to this playbook is getting your ground game going, then opening it up with your passing attack. We will show some of the better plays and formations that Cincy has that will make opponents break their sticks after a few quarters of playing you on any level. The key is to use your weapons, stay patient with your rushing attack, and take shots to keep people honest. The Bengals have all of the tools to score plenty of points in any given game. Let's take a look at Cincy's playbook in more detail.

OFFENSIVE FORMATIONS

FORMATION	# OF PLAYS
Gun Bunch TE	9
Gun Double Flex	15
Gun Doubles On	12
Gun Split Slot	15
Gun Wing Trio Wk	12
I-Form Pro	21
I-Form Pro Twins	18
I-Form Tight Pair	12
Singleback Ace	12
Singleback Ace Pair	15
Singleback Bunch	18
Singleback Flex	18
Singleback Trey Open	9
Singleback Y-Trips	15
Strong Pro	18
Weak Pro	15
Wildcat Bengal	3

OFFENSIVE PLAYCOUNTS

PLAY TYPE	# OF PLAYS
Quick Pass	16
Standard Pass	56
Shotgun Pass	41
Play Action Pass	44
Inside Handoff	35
Outside Handoff	9
Pitch	8
Counter	10

Playbook Breakdown

Gun Bunch TE—PA Boot Over

The PA Boot Over is a great flood play to beat man or zone coverage. Hot route your HB on a drag and he will become one of your hot reads. You have four routes working to one side, so your HB will be open in most cases because the coverage will roll over. If not, you have a four-way flood to the right side to fall back on.

Overhead shot of the flood routes

The flood made up of the drag, dig, and post is hard to defend. You have the TE on a flat route to the right side as well. Your key read is the middle. If it's crowded in the middle, dump it off to the HB.

Benson is wide open in the flats

When you have trips, you have to find a way to get the HB to release on the same side as the wideouts to give you a four-way flood to that side. Read the middle from short to deep. Again, if the middle is covered, dump it off to the HB.

Gun Bunch TE—Mesh

The Mesh play is one of the best plays for players who like to press with man coverage and send heat. This is a man-beating play that has plenty of hot reads. You also can get a pick or rub because of the crossing routes. This play also forces your opponent to defend the corner route, which opens things up for you in other areas of the field. You want to read deep, then drop down and read short. See if you can hit the deep corner route. If it's not open then you check down to your crossing routes.

Looking for a pick or rub underneath

If you read pressure, hit the crossing routes or the flats. If you have time, read deep and hit the corner route. This is a Cover 2 shell, so the corner route will be open.

Great sideline catch

When you use compressed sets it puts the defense in conflict. It's hard to defend three wideouts on the same side. The Bunch also allows you to isolate your best weapon for a matchup to your advantage.

Gun Bunch TE—HB Draw

This is the best formation to run the HB Draw from, period! That's because you have a TE on the edge to seal and you have three wideouts to the left. The key is making your read and hitting the first hole. Since you're in a passing set this will catch the defense off-balance. The CPU sells the pass very well, and if you're using Gun Trips, the defense has to respect the possibility of a pass. When the box has fewer than seven defenders in it, consider using this play. You have to remember that with Benson in the backfield you can make magic happen when the defense goes to Dime and Nickel packages. There are six men in the box in this example—time for some pound!

The defense is dropping back in pass coverage

You can see here that the defense bought the pass fake. Look for the nearest hole and hit it. This play can be bounced outside as well.

Lots of open field to work with

This is a nice play to add to your arsenal once your opponent respects your passing attack.

Singleback Bunch—Corner Strike

Singleback Bunch—Weak Flood

Singleback Bunch—Bunch Fade

Singleback Bunch—Quick Pitch

The Corner Strike is a great play that works well against Cover 2 shells. It works well against any coverage. When you're under the center you need quick hitters. This formation provides you with these fast options along with the threat to run the ball. This is typical of the Bengals' attack. They want balance, and the Singleback Bunch provides that. You have three hot reads with the TE, HB, and SL. If you have time, you can look for the corner route attack on both sides.

When you run compressed sets, find plays that have the HB releasing on the same side as your overload. This kind of flood really makes the defense work hard with their adjustments. Your hot reads are the SL, HB, and FL. The TE running the fade route is a great seam route if you read heat or zone. The SE sells the same route as the Corner Strike. That's why this play works well with Corner Strike—it looks the same but attacks a different area altogether.

The Bunch Fade is a great play to isolate the FL. The play eats up most defenses with ease. The key is having time in the pocket to make your reads. This play is set up to attack a single DB. If the DB drops back, you drive the out route to the TE. If the DB sits, use the fade route that the FL is running. If you see that an alley defender flashes over, hit the post route. You have the HB in this play to help with pass protection.

When you pass out of a set you have to run out of it as well to keep your opponent honest. This play is working off of the overload you have on the flank. You also get a pulling guard with a down block by the FL to form a seal. The job of the guard is to hit the first man at the edge. If any defenders line up in the gaps he will not pull. If you get outside you can have up to four blockers on the edge. We like those odds.

Ochocinco gets a step on his defender

You can see that the hot reads are easy to hit. No pressure can get to you before you can hit any of those options. If you have time, look deep and stretch the defense deep.

Our four-way flood overwhelms the defense

The TE's fade route is a great option against zone or pressure. Most people won't cover the TE and you can see that here in this shot.

The DB sits on the out route

This is a shot of the DB read. As you can see, he sat on the out route, releasing the FL to the safety. The post presses and holds the secondary back. Ochocinco is wide open.

Here is the guard pulling to lead the way

Here you see the numbers game and why this formation is great. When you can attack on the ground as well as the air, your opponent is in for a long night.

Great catch by one of the best

Ochocinco secured the catch, and if your stick skills are good, you can get more. The key is first making your short reads and then looking deep when under center. You can't take a loss here.

The TE is using his big body to secure the catch

When you have a team with good TEs, you will love plays like this to get them in open space. TEs are hard to match up with because most DBs are too small and most LBs are too slow to handle them.

Great catch and room to work with

When you make good reads, plays like this make it very hard to defend you. You have plays that are quick hitters. Popping the short routes will force your opponents to play up closer to the line. This play will back them up in a hurry.

And we're out!

You have to read your blocks; don't get in a rush to get outside. Let your line set the blocks, then go get what you can. This play can especially be a backbreaker if you have solid run-blocking wideouts.

BUFFALO BILLS

OFFENSIVE SCOUTING REPORT

The Bills offense has been struggling. Last year, quarterback duties were split between Trent Edwards and Ryan Fitzpatrick, but it appears that Trent Edwards will get the start this season. With Terrell Owens gone, WR Lee Evans is easily their best receiver, and the opposing defenses know this. Look for WR James Hardy and WR Roscoe Parrish to expand their roles as targets with Evans getting all of the defensive attention. With an unsteady air attack, the Bills will have to focus on the run game of Fred Jackson and Marshawn Lynch. Both have play-making abilities, with the slightly faster and more elusive Jackson getting the most touches again this year. Also keep an eye on newly drafted RB C.J. Spiller. Fortunately for the Bills, while the passing game gets polished they have depth, experience, and skill in the backfield.

DEFENSIVE SCOUTING REPORT

The Bills are hoping to change the tide this year on defense by changing to a 3–4 defense. This means they'll have to move some key players around in the positions that they play. Solid players like Chris Kelsay and Aaron Schobel move to outside linebacker positions; both are sure talkers but don't have the fastest feet under them to chase. Look for them to stack the box and create pressure on the quarterback behind a line built around the outside threat and big strength of LE Marcus Stroud. This change may make for a shaky start for the Bills, but with solid talent as the foundation, the move could prove prosperous. The transition will help with the comfort of a formidable backfield of CBs Terrence McGee and Leodis McKelvin, and safety Jairus Byrd. All provide speed and good coverage in the backfield.

TEAM RATING

67
Overall

KEY ADDITIONS

RB	C.J. Spiller
LB	Andra Davis
DE	Dwan Edwards
DT	Marlon Favorite
OT	Cornell Green
WR	Chad Jackson

KEY DEPARTURES

DE	Ryan Denney
LB	Chris Draft
WR	Terrell Owens
WR	Josh Reed
OT	Brad Butler
OT	Jonathan Scott

RATINGS BY POSITION

Position	Rating		Position	Rating
Quarterbacks	70		Defensive Tackles	79
Halfbacks	83		Outside Linebackers	72
Fullbacks	70		Middle Linebackers	86
Wide Receivers	70		Cornerbacks	82
Tight Ends	70		Free Safeties	87
Tackles	74		Strong Safeties	83
Guards	80		Kickers	80
Centers	74		Punters	90
Defensive Ends	81			

DEPTH CHART

POS	OVR	FIRST NAME	LAST NAME
C	74	Geoff	Hangartner
C	65	Christian	Gaddis
CB	83	Terrence	McGee
CB	81	Leodis	McKelvin
CB	68	Drayton	Florence
CB	65	Ashton	Youboty
CB	63	Reggie	Corner
DT	79	Kyle	Williams
DT	63	Torell	Troup
FB	70	Corey	McIntyre
FS	87	Jairus	Byrd
FS	72	George	Wilson
HB	83	Fred	Jackson
HB	81	Marshawn	Lynch
HB	79	C.J.	Spiller
K	80	Rian	Lindell
LE	82	Marcus	Stroud
LE	58	Spencer	Johnson
LG	79	Andy	Levitre
LG	65	Kyle	Calloway
LOLB	67	Chris	Kelsay
LOLB	59	Arthur	Moats
LOLB	58	Chris	Ellis
LT	74	Demetrius	Bell
LT	66	Jamon	Meredith
MLB	86	Paul	Posluszny
MLB	79	Kawika	Mitchell
MLB	78	Andra	Davis
MLB	69	Keith	Ellison
P	90	Brian	Moorman
QB	70	Ryan	Fitzpatrick
QB	70	Trent	Edwards
QB	65	Brian	Brohm
RE	79	Dwan	Edwards
RE	65	John	McCargo
RG	81	Eric	Wood
RG	70	Kirk	Chambers
ROLB	76	Aaron	Schobel
ROLB	60	Aaron	Maybin
RT	73	Cornell	Green
SS	83	Donte	Whitner
SS	80	Bryan	Scott
TE	70	Derek	Schouman
TE	70	Shawn	Nelson
TE	53	Jonathan	Stupar
WR	84	Lee	Evans
WR	64	Roscoe	Parrish
WR	62	Marcus	Easley
WR	61	James	Hardy
WR	59	Steve	Johnson
WR	56	Chad	Jackson

OFFENSIVE STRENGTH CHART

2-Back Set

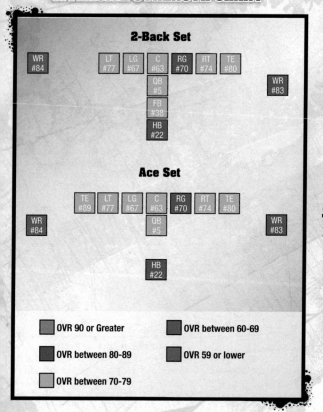

WR #84						
LT #77	LG #67	C #63	RG #70	RT #74	TE #80	
		QB #5				WR #83
		FB #38				
		HB #22				

Ace Set

	TE #89	LT #77	LG #67	C #63	RG #70	RT #74	TE #80
WR #84			QB #5				WR #83
			HB #22				

- ■ OVR 90 or Greater
- ■ OVR between 80-89
- ■ OVR between 70-79
- ■ OVR between 60-69
- ■ OVR 59 or lower

#22 Fred Jackson
Halfback (HB)

Overall	83
Speed	88
Agility	87
Stiff Arm	79
Carrying	83

#83 Lee Evans
Wide Receiver (WR)

Overall	84
Speed	96
Catching	87
Release	75
Jumping	87

#23 Marshawn Lynch
Halfback (HB)

Overall	81
Speed	87
Agility	83
Stiff Arm	94
Carrying	90

#31 Jairus Byrd
Free Safety (FS)

Overall	87
Speed	87
Awareness	72
Tackle	67
Play Recognition	75

#24 Terrence McGee
Cornerback (CB)

Overall	83
Speed	92
Awareness	82
Man Coverage	87
Zone Coverage	91

#51 Paul Posluszny
Linebacker (MLB)

Overall	86
Speed	76
Awareness	85
Tackle	93
Hit Power	84

DEFENSIVE STRENGTH CHART

3-4 Defense

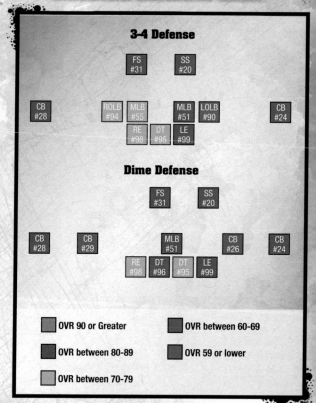

FS #31	SS #20
CB #28	ROLB #94	MLB #55	MLB #51	LOLB #90	CB #24
	RE #98	DT #95	LE #99	

Dime Defense

FS #31	SS #20
CB #28	CB #29	MLB #51	CB #26	CB #24
	RE #98	DT #96	DT #95	LE #99

- ■ OVR 90 or Greater
- ■ OVR between 80-89
- ■ OVR between 70-79
- ■ OVR between 60-69
- ■ OVR 59 or lower

Key Player Substitutions

Position: QB

Substitution: Trent Edwards

When: Global

Advantage: Edwards has better attributes then Ryan Fitzpatrick. Start off with Edwards leading your team on the offensive side of the ball.

Key Player Substitutions

Position: ROLB

Substitution: Aaron Maybin

When: Global

Advantage: Maybin brings much-needed speed to the Bills linebackers. Use his speed to pass-rush the quarterback. Look to rush more and then drop back in zone coverage with Maybin.

Playbook Breakdown

The Buffalo Bills playbook is geared towards running the ball from pro set formations such as I-Form Normal and Strong Normal. In this playbook, we like the three I-Form formations, as each one has strong run plays mixed in with play action and a few standard pass plays. The Weak Tight Twins is a solid formation because it has the two receivers lined up tight on the same side of the field. This makes it very easy to tell if man coverage is called or not. The Bills playbook has two variations of the Wildcat: Wildcat Bills and Wildcat Normal. Each has three run plays worth taking a look at if you like to run the Wildcat. For those who like to call plays from the Gun, the Bills playbook offers five formations. Of those, the Gun Split Slot is the one we like the most. Another formation worth noting is the Singleback Tight Doubles, as it has a few plays to consider checking out.

OFFENSIVE FORMATIONS

FORMATION	# OF PLAYS
Gun 4WR Trey	15
Gun Doubles Wing	15
Gun Split Slot	18
Gun Spread	15
Gun Y-Trips Wk	12
I-Form Pro	18
I-Form Tight	15
I-Form Tight Pair	12
Singleback Ace	15
Singleback Ace Pair Twins	12
Singleback Bunch	12
Singleback Doubles	18
Singleback Tight Doubles	9
Strong Normal	15
Weak Tight Twins	12
Wildcat Bills	3
Wildcat Normal	3

OFFENSIVE PLAYCOUNTS

PLAY TYPE	# OF PLAYS
Quick Pass	14
Standard Pass	36
Shotgun Pass	50
Play Action Pass	42
Outside Handoff	14
Pitch	8
Counter	10
Draw	7

I-Form Pro—Bills Zone Wk

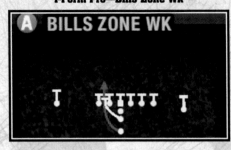

A staple run play that the Bills like to run is the I-Form Pro—Bills Zone Wk. This zone-blocking run play gives running backs Fred Jackson and Marshawn Lynch plenty of inside running room, provided that the offensive line is able to open up holes.

The QB stretches out to hand the ball off to his running back

The play is designed to have fullback Corey McIntyre throw a key block by sealing off any outside defender who comes close. The ball carrier will then look to run up inside between left tackle Demetrius Bell and left guard Andy Levitre. Since this a zone-blocking scheme, there will be double-team blocks thrown by the offensive linemen.

Jackson sees a hole and uses his speed to burst through it

Once the ball carrier gets past the line of scrimmage, use the truck stick or stiff arm to pick up a few tough extra yards. Consider sending the flanker in motion to the left. If zone coverage is called, snap the ball once he gets near the left guard. This will add an extra run blocker into the mix, creating even more running room.

I-Form Pro—PA TE Corner

An I-Form Pro play action play that works with the Bills Zone Wk is the PA TE Corner. Once the ball is snapped, the quarterback fakes the handoff to the running back and then rolls out towards the play side. During his rollout, look down the field to see if the tight end, who is running a corner route, is open.

The QB rolls to the right while looking for his TE to get open

If not, look for the fullback, who runs through the line of scrimmage and then breaks towards the sideline on an out route. The third option to look for is the split end running a crossing route. If man coverage is called, he should be open if he is able to gain some separation from the right cornerback.

The ball is thrown as the TE breaks towards the corner

If zone coverage is called, he may be open if the underneath linebackers bite on the play action. The flanker runs a streak out. His route is designed to lift the coverage over the top of the tight end. However, he may be an option to throw to if no safety plays over the top of him.

I-Form Tight—Power O

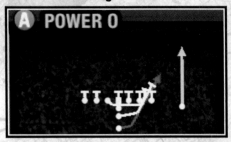

A strong run play that suits what the Bills offensive line is built for is the I-Form Tight—Power O. This play has left guard Andy Levitre pulling to the right side, where he and fullback Corey McIntyre look to clear running lanes for Fred Jackson to run through.

Jackson looks to follow his blocks

Levitre looks first for the fullback's block to cut off of and then heads into the crease, looking to block the first defender that shows up, who generally is the play-side linebacker. Center Geoff Hangartner and right guard Eric Wood down-block, meaning they take the man to the inside of them. They want to use their leverage to get good angles to crush the defensive lineman.

Jackson accelerates through the open hole

McIntyre kicks out, looking to throw a key block on any defender in his area. The running back looks to follow the pulling guard. The running back must hit the hole quickly because it might close up if he hesitates. If nothing is open, look to bounce outside where some positive yardage might be achieved.

I-Form Tight—PA Power O

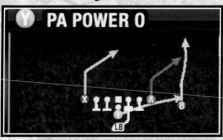

The I-Form Tight—PA Power O works in conjunction with the I-Form Tight—Power O. The key differences are, the left guard doesn't pull and the quarterback doesn't hand off to the running back, but instead play fakes. The play-side tight end, who is running a corner route, is the play's primary receiver. The fullback leaks out into the flat and is the play's check-down receiver if the play-side tight end is not open.

The Bills QB reads the coverage as he rolls out of the pocket

The flanker runs a go route. His route is designed to drive the deep pass coverage deeper so that the play-side tight end can get open once he breaks to the corner. The backside tight end runs a post route and is a good option if Cover 2 coverage is called.

The Dolphins linebacker is not fast enough to swat the pass away

Once the ball is snapped, read the pass coverage. Watch to see if any defenders are dropping in buzz zones. If a defender does drop back in a buzz zone, you will need to pass the ball over the top—the passing window will be smaller than if there were no defender dropping in a buzz zone to the play side.

Strong Normal—HB Off Tackle

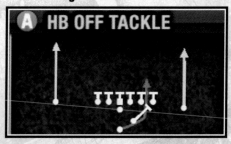

A solid run play to call out of the Strong Normal is the HB Off Tackle. This play is designed to have the lead blocker (fullback) kick out the end man on the line of scrimmage, who is generally the outside linebacker. If the fullback is able to block his man, there should be ample running room to the outside.

The FB throws a key lead block on the LOLB

In *Madden NFL 11*, the fullback may not always block the outside defender; it just depends on what the defensive formation and alignment is. Another key block is the outside receiver on the side that the running back is running to. If the receiver can at least get his hands on the outside cornerback, there will be even more room for the running back to gain positive yardage.

The FL has the LCB locked up, allowing the HB to find extra running room

In *Madden NFL 10*, Off Tackle plays were some of the most used in the game, and we expect they will be again in this year's game, as the offensive blocking as a whole has vastly improved from previous versions.

Strong Normal—Spacing

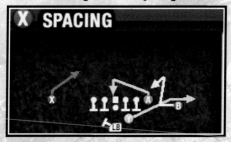

The Bills' passing attack is not one of the stronger ones in the game due to their QBs having lower ratings than average. For this reason, simple low-risk pass plays are the best way to move the ball through the air.

Hardy breaks inward on his slant route

Strong Normal—Spacing is a horizontal stretch pass concept that is a low-risk pass play, allowing the quarterback to throw a short, high-percentage pass that generally picks up positive yardage. Lee Evans, who is lined up in the flanker position, runs a spot route after being sent in automotion. Notice that he is not the play's primary receiver; instead, the play's primary receiver is James Hardy, who is lined up on the left at the split end position. Against man coverage, his slant route is an excellent option to throw to.

The QB throws a hard bullet pass to his TE

If zone coverage is called, his slant route will open up the tight end's spot routes once he sits over the short middle of the field. Evans's spot route may be open, but it depends on if a defender is sent in on a blitz from that side. Against five-under zone coverages, he won't be open.

Gun Split Slot—Cross Weak Flood

Buffalo's offensive line is not very stout when it comes to pass-blocking and giving the quarterback time to throw deep down the field when situations call for it. To give the quarterback the time he needs, we like to call plays from the Gun Split Slot.

The QB spots his primary target over the middle

This formation sits the signal caller 5 yards off the line of scrimmage. Having two running backs flanking him allows us to add extra pass protection if needed. A pass play we like to call from this formation against man coverage is the Cross Weak Flood.

Evans is about to make the catch on the run

This play sends the slot receiver on a crossing route. If man coverage is called, he should get open if he has the acceleration and speed ratings to do so. Once he does gain separation, we throw him a hard bullet while leading him. If thrown on time, this pass has potential to pick up a good chunk of yardage through the air.

DENVER BRONCOS

OFFENSIVE SCOUTING REPORT

Year in, year out, one can always count on the Broncos offensive line to be strong. That doesn't change this year with the continued stellar play from LT Ryan Clady and RT Ryan Harris. Look for both to provide solid protection for any one of their gifted QBs (Brady Quinn, Kyle Orton, and newcomer Tim Tebow). Though the departure of elite WR Brandon Marshall is a major blow to Denver's passing game, look to Eddie Royal to fill the void as much as he can. Royal's speed is his major asset, as it is for rookie Demaryius Thomas, who was drafted with Brandon Marshall's void in mind. Stokley may actually provide some of the best short gains due to his higher ability to catch in traffic, although he has fallen down the depth chart. RB Knowshon Moreno carried the ball nearly 250 times last season, proving he can be a number one back, but he won't have to be. The Broncos will use every horse in their stable, mixing Moreno with other backs, including ex-Eagle Correll Buckhalter, who may be looking to share the spotlight more than he did in Philly. Both backs provide speed, but Moreno can hit the holes much quicker and is a bit more elusive, especially when making use of his good receiving hands. Buckhalter should be used to keep Moreno's legs fresh as stamina could be an issue on long drives.

DEFENSIVE SCOUTING REPORT

The Broncos' recent shift from 4–3 to 3–4 defense marked the end of an era and the beginning of growing pains. Though this is their second year running the 3–4 defense, Josh McDaniels has done everything to make sure that he's got capable players on the line. Having picked up former Chargers NT Jamal Williams, the Broncos immediately upgraded their nose tackle position, despite Williams's age. DE Jarvis Green, highly experienced and versatile, immediately contributes to Denver's D with exceptional pass-rushing ability and sack potential. CB Champ Bailey, though a bit long in the tooth, is still a scary sight across the line for opposing wide receivers. Stick Bailey on the opponent's best wide receiver to help ease the pressure of high-powered offenses. If that's not enough, rely on S Brian Dawkins to help over the top.

TEAM RATING

78
Overall

KEY ADDITIONS

LB	Akin Ayodele
DE	Justin Bannan
DE	Jarvis Green
QB	Brady Quinn
NT	Jamal Williams
QB	Tim Tebow

KEY DEPARTURES

LB	Andra Davis
G	Ben Hamilton
RB	Peyton Hillis
WR	Brandon Marshall
TE	Tony Scheffler
C	Casey Wiegmann

RATINGS BY POSITION

Position	Rating
Quarterbacks	80
Halfbacks	82
Fullbacks	50
Wide Receivers	78
Tight Ends	81
Tackles	92
Guards	80
Centers	67
Defensive Ends	78
Defensive Tackles	87
Outside Linebackers	83
Middle Linebackers	88
Cornerbacks	89
Free Safeties	90
Strong Safeties	74
Kickers	73
Punters	67

DEPTH CHART

POS	OVR	FIRST NAME	LAST NAME
C	67	Seth	Olsen
C	64	J.D.	Walton
CB	95	Champ	Bailey
CB	82	André	Goodman
CB	69	Alphonso	Smith
CB	67	Nate	Jones
CB	67	Perrish	Cox
DB	65	Josh	Barrett
DT	87	Jamal	Williams
DT	76	Ronald	Fields
DT	64	Chris	Baker
FB	50	Spencer	Larsen
FS	90	Brian	Dawkins
FS	74	Darcel	McBath
HB	82	Knowshon	Moreno
HB	78	Correll	Buckhalter
HB	69	J.J.	Arrington
K	73	Matt	Prater
LE	77	Justin	Bannan
LE	77	Ryan	McBean
LG	78	Russ	Hochstein
LG	77	Maurice	Williams
LOLB	72	Robert	Ayers
LOLB	65	Darrell	Reid
LT	98	Ryan	Clady
LT	67	Tyler	Polumbus
MLB	88	D.J.	Williams
MLB	72	Mario	Haggan
MLB	70	Akin	Ayodele
MLB	65	Wesley	Woodyard
P	67	Britton	Colquitt
QB	80	Kyle	Orton
QB	71	Brady	Quinn
QB	70	Tim	Tebow
RE	78	Jarvis	Green
RE	69	Marcus	Thomas
RE	59	Le Kevin	Smith
RG	82	Chris	Kuper
ROLB	93	Elvis	Dumervil
ROLB	66	Jarvis	Moss
RT	85	Ryan	Harris
RT	68	Zane	Beadles
SS	74	Renaldo	Hill
SS	67	David	Bruton
TE	81	Daniel	Graham
TE	67	Richard	Quinn
WR	76	Eddie	Royal
WR	75	Jabar	Gaffney
WR	74	Brandon	Stokley
WR	74	Demaryius	Thomas
WR	70	Brandon	Lloyd
WR	69	Eric	Decker

OFFENSIVE STRENGTH CHART

2-Back Set

WR #88		LT #78	LG #71	C #70	RG #73	RT #74	TE #89		
				QB #8					WR #19
				FB #46					
				HB #27					

Ace Set

	TE #81	LT #78	LG #71	C #70	RG #73	RT #74	TE #89	
WR #88				QB #8				WR #19
				HB #27				

- ■ OVR 90 or Greater
- ■ OVR between 80-89
- ■ OVR between 70-79
- ■ OVR between 60-69
- ■ OVR 59 or lower

#78 Ryan Clady
Offensive Tackle (LT)

Overall	98
Strength	94
Run Blk. Strength	93
Pass Blk. Strength	99
Impact Blocking	95

#27 Knowshon Moreno
Halfback (HB)

Overall	82
Speed	88
Agility	97
Stiff Arm	65
Carrying	72

#8 Kyle Orton
Quarterback (QB)

Overall	80
Throwing Power	80
Short Accuracy	88
Medium Accuracy	84
Deep Accuracy	77

#24 Champ Bailey
Cornerback (CB)

Overall	95
Speed	95
Awareness	95
Man Coverage	94
Zone Coverage	90

#92 Elvis Dumervil
Linebacker (ROLB)

Overall	93
Speed	86
Awareness	88
Tackle	87
Hit Power	77

#20 Brian Dawkins
Free Safety (FS)

Overall	90
Speed	85
Awareness	96
Tackle	73
Hit Power	88

DEFENSIVE STRENGTH CHART

3-4 Defense

		FS #20		SS #23		
CB #21	ROLB #92	MLB #57		MLB #55	LOLB #56	CB #24
	RE #93	DT #76	LE #97			

Dime Defense

		FS #20		SS #23		
CB #21	CB #33	MLB #55		CB #22	CB #24	
	RE #93	DT #91	DT #76	LE #97		

- ■ OVR 90 or Greater
- ■ OVR between 80-89
- ■ OVR between 70-79
- ■ OVR between 60-69
- ■ OVR 59 or lower

Key Player Substitutions

Position: QB

Substitution: Tim Tebow

When: Goal line and short yardage situations

Advantage: Tebow is one of the biggest and strongest quarterbacks in the NFL; bring him in for goal line and fourth and short situations. With his power he should be able to pick up the short yardage that your team needs to score or pick up the first down.

Key Player Substitutions

Position: DT

Substitution: Chris Baker

When: Passing situations

Advantage: With Chris Baker's speed in the middle of the line, along with Dumervil on the same side of the field, offenses will have a hard time double-teaming both players.

Playbook Breakdown

The Broncos are a good offensive team, and when you pick this team's playbook you will have the keys to a pretty potent offense. When looking at a playbook, we like to see what direction the head coach has mapped out for the team. The Broncos playbook has 70 Gun formation plays. That's almost the equivalent of the rest of their pass plays combined. Even though the numbers may paint a picture saying that the Broncos deploy an unbalanced attack, that's not the case. The running game is very much a part of this offense and mixes in well with the many Gun formation passes.

When we have a playbook that shows a lot of Gun formations and can still keep us active in the run game out of those same formations, we know we have a special playbook. With all of that said, we know the real reason some people are looking at the Broncos is rookie quarterback Tim Tebow. You won't be disappointed—he even has a formation developed just for him. We can promise you, because of this formation, the Broncos may have the most-used playbook this year in *Madden NFL 11*.

OFFENSIVE FORMATIONS

FORMATION	# OF PLAYS
Gun Bronco Heavy	9
Gun Bunch Wk	12
Gun Doubles Flex	15
Gun Empty Spread	9
Gun Normal Y-Slot	9
Gun Snugs Flip	9
Gun Split Bronco	9
Gun Trips	12
Gun Wing Trips Wk	18
I-Form TE Flip	15
I-Form Tight	15
I-Form Tight Pair	12
Singleback Ace	15
Singleback Doubles	15
Singleback Flip Trips	12
Singleback Jumbo Z	9
Singleback Trips Open	9
Singleback Y-Trips	12
Weak Tight Pair	12
Wildcat Wild Horse	3

OFFENSIVE PLAYCOUNTS

PLAY TYPE	# OF PLAYS
Quick Pass	11
Standard Pass	35
Shotgun Pass	70
Play Action Pass	41
Inside Handoff	27
Outside Handoff	12
Pitch	10
Counter	4

Gun Bronco Heavy—Bronco QB Power

We're not even going to gradually build up to getting Tim Tebow on the field—we'll get him on the field right away. The Gun Bronco Heavy is a formation built to showcase Tim Tebow's athletic ability and desire to win. If you've seen him play in the college ranks, then you know that he has a nose for the goal line and is determined to get in the end zone.

Tebow feels right at home

The Gun Bronco Heavy formation inserts the third string quarterback in as the starter, so you don't have to manually change your depth chart to get Tebow on the field. When running the QB Power, we have the benefit of getting extra space to read the offensive linemen's blocks because of the depth of our quarterback. This play and this formation are going to be the main reasons why the Broncos will have the most-used playbook in *Madden NFL 11*.

Tebow finds his way to the end zone

As soon as the ball is hiked and the play starts, we quickly scan the offensive line and look for a running lane to get Tebow into the end zone. Tebow is no small guy and has the power to run through a tackle to help us get those critical yards.

Gun Bronco Heavy—PA TE Cross

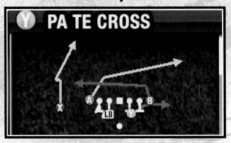

The success that Tim Tebow had in college was heavily related to the threat of him running and passing the ball. When the defense has it in their head that we can run the ball with the quarterback out of this formation, then we can build on that fact and throw in some play action to work the passing game in.

The defense is screaming, "run, run, run!!"

The design of the Gun Bronco Heavy—PA TE Cross includes a jab step forward by the quarterback in an effort to make the defense believe we are running again. We follow the same rules as any other play action pass. When the fake is being given, we need to have our eyes downfield and identifying the coverage.

Passing on the run

Tebow has a 79 speed rating, so we can easily roll him out of the pocket and add a little pressure on the defense. In this play, we were able to roll out to the left side, spot the tight end running the drag, and get the ball downfield to him. Make sure to maximize the ability of your players and the play calls you make. Tebow's athleticism makes our offense more efficient when we get him moving on the edge.

Singleback Flip Trips—Bronco Trail

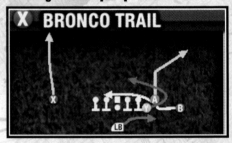

The starting quarterback for the Denver Broncos is Kyle Orton. Orton had his best year as a professional last season and has become a quarterback who can beat you on any throw he makes. We look to the Singleback Flip Trips—Bronco Trail to establish a rhythm for Orton, while also giving him a chance for early success with multiple high percentage routes.

The defense leaves two of our receivers wide open

Plays that use the automotion feature have become the most highly completed pass plays in *Madden NFL 11*. These plays use route combinations that normally break man and zone defense. We benefit from a mesh point between the routes here and have our flanker open right away as he crosses underneath the zone coverage.

Get the ball to the receiver in the clear

The defense may jump to cover the flanker as he blazes through their coverage, and we hope they do. If the defense follows the flanker, we will fit the ball in to the tight slot receiver, who is running the trail route. Our reads when running this play are the flanker, the tight slot on the trail, and then the slot running the corner route. And just in case all of our primary reads are covered, we have a dump-off option to the running back.

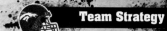

Gun Doubles Flex—PA FL Screen

The Gun Doubles Flex—PA FL Screen out of the Broncos playbook has its own unique twist. This play uses automotion with the receiver who is catching the ball. This presents a way for us to offset bump-n-run man coverage by getting our screen receiver to go in motion prior to the snap and move closer to our slot receiver. This play has "Big Play Potential" written all over it.

We have the screen receiver and a blocker once the ball comes
We pre-read man coverage as our receiver goes in automotion, and as soon as the ball is hiked, our slot receiver releases as if he is running a route downfield. Our flanker settles in and waits for the ball as the quarterback starts his play action fake to the running back. During this time, if we see the corner blitzing from the right side, we can throw a quick pass to our split end on a fade route.

The slot receiver sets a good block
We throw the ball to the flanker, just after the play action fake. Immediately, we turn downfield and benefit from a solid block thrown by our slot receiver. We use this block to turn and explode down the sideline for a touchdown.

Gun Doubles Flex—Slot Post

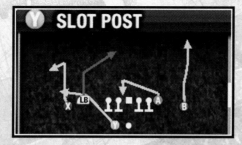

Every quarterback needs to feel comfortable in the pocket and trust the play calls that are being made. The Gun Doubles Flex—Slot Post is a play that will give us the comfort to sit in the pocket, even when there is pressure around us, because it has so many routes that can beat the blitz. Whether we're facing the blitz or regular coverages, we will always have an opportunity to beat the defense with this play call.

We welcome pressure from the defense
As soon as we see blitz from the defense, we immediately start to think about throwing the ball to the tight end running a slant hook or the back running to the left flat. The defense thinks they can outsmart us and have dropped a linebacker in coverage right over the middle. What they don't know is that we've found a weakness in their coverage.

We hit the receiver on a deep pass
The defense does a great job of trying to confuse us and prevent us from going to the common check-down route. However, no defense can stop everything, and because the defense overplayed the slant hook, we spot a void in the middle of the field. We immediately throw the ball to our slot receiver and hit him for a big gain on his post route.

Gun Normal Y-Slot—Bronco Hooks

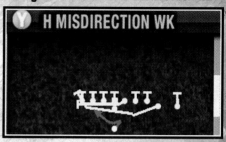

The Broncos offensive line isn't the best of the best in the NFL, so we need to prepare for the blitz and pressure from the defense's front four on any given down. The more efficient the pass play that we call, the more effective it will be. We like the passing play in the Gun Normal Y-Slot formation and feel that the Bronco Hooks is a reliable play that we can incorporate into our passing attack.

Each receiver is open
Even when we know the perfect thing to do, sometimes we go against the grain and throw a ball that shouldn't have been thrown. We look over the field and see that we have numerous receivers open on hook routes. These are perfect options to counter any pressure from the defense.

Feed the rookie the ball
Instead, we make a great throw to the flanker on the streak route in an effort to keep our first round draft pick happy. Demaryius Thomas is a big receiver with great speed and jumping ability. In *Madden NFL 11*, this makes him a valuable option on the Broncos and on any team that drafts him in Franchise mode.

Singleback Jumbo Z—H Misdirection Wk

We have looked at a few passes in the Broncos playbook and don't want to forget about the storied Broncos rushing attack. Knowshon Moreno is a gritty running back, capable of running between the tackles as well as breaking it outside for a nice gain. The Singleback Jumbo Z—H Misdirection Wk is a play call that showcases Moreno's skills as a runner.

What a scary sight for any defense
The Singleback Jumbo Z puts the second string left tackle in at the Z position (pair tight end) and uses him as an additional run blocker or passing option. We like this formation and play call because having an additional lineman on the field can only help the result of any run play we call.

Key blocks spring our running back
Not only do we add an extra offensive lineman to help block on this running play, but the Singleback Jumbo Z—H Misdirection Wk also calls for the right guard to pull and lead our back around the edge with the second string left tackle. We get the benefit of a huge hole opening up for us after we take the handoff. Moreno makes one cut to split the blocking linemen and explodes into the second level of the defense.

CLEVELAND BROWNS

OFFENSIVE SCOUTING REPORT

The Browns are a team in need of an identity and, more importantly, a leader on the offense. Newcomer QB Jake Delhomme was well established as a high-level performer in Carolina, but his decline over recent seasons landed him in Cleveland. In Carolina, Delhomme had star WR Steve Smith to throw to; in Cleveland he'll have to rely on the likes of Chansi Stuckey, Mohamed Massaquoi, and Joshua Cribbs—a young and talented corps, but all potential at the moment. Benjamin Watson at tight end actually provides the most experience at receiving the ball and will make a good outlet for Delhomme. With so many unanswered questions on an offense with so many off-season changes, the only established threat is RB Jerome Harrison's ability to grind out the yardage. He is small, but quick and agile, with a hardy stamina, and he'll be playing behind a proficient line with plenty of run-blocking ability.

DEFENSIVE SCOUTING REPORT

While the Browns offense is full of questions, the defense may be full of surprises. Acquiring Scott Fujita and Chris Gocong adds great depth to the linebacker corps alongside D'Qwell Jackson and Eric Barton. Eric Wright returns to retain his starting position at cornerback, providing much needed stability in the secondary, along with standout Sheldon Brown. The defense's obvious weakness is at the safety position. Watch out for pass-happy teams capable of tossing the long ball. Rely on your line up front, led by Shaun "Big Baby" Rogers to provide pressure and create havoc.

TEAM RATING

70
Overall

KEY ADDITIONS

TE	Benjamin Watson
QB	Jake Delhomme
LB	Scott Fujita
LB	Chris Gocong
RB	Peyton Hillis
CB	Joe Haden

KEY DEPARTURES

QB	Derek Anderson
QB	Brady Quinn
RB	Jamal Lewis
OL	Hank Fraley
TE	Michael Gaines
LB	Kamerion Wimbley

RATINGS BY POSITION

Position	Rating
Quarterbacks	74
Halfbacks	83
Fullbacks	88
Wide Receivers	74
Tight Ends	78
Tackles	84
Guards	84
Centers	87
Defensive Ends	75
Defensive Tackles	93
Outside Linebackers	77
Middle Linebackers	85
Cornerbacks	87
Free Safeties	72
Strong Safeties	69
Kickers	82
Punters	77

DEPTH CHART

POS	OVR	FIRST NAME	LAST NAME
C	87	Alex	Mack
C	69	Eric	Ghiaciuc
CB	87	Sheldon	Brown
CB	86	Eric	Wright
CB	79	Joe	Haden
CB	68	Brandon	McDonald
CB	63	Gerard	Lawson
DT	93	Shaun	Rogers
DT	74	Ahtyba	Rubin
DT	56	Brian	Schaefering
FB	88	Lawrence	Vickers
FB	77	Peyton	Hillis
FS	77	Mike	Adams
FS	72	Abram	Elam
HB	83	Jerome	Harrison
HB	74	Montario	Hardesty
HB	69	James	Davis
HB	65	Chris	Jennings
K	82	Phil	Dawson
LE	75	Kenyon	Coleman
LE	63	C.J.	Mosley
LG	91	Eric	Steinbach
LG	63	Billy	Yates
LOLB	74	Matt	Roth
LOLB	68	David	Veikune
LT	95	Joe	Thomas
MLB	85	D'Qwell	Jackson
MLB	79	Eric	Barton
MLB	76	David	Bowens
MLB	68	Kaluka	Maiava
P	77	Dave	Zastudil
QB	74	Jake	Delhomme
QB	72	Seneca	Wallace
QB	57	Brett	Ratliff
RE	74	Robaire	Smith
RE	56	Clifton	Geathers
RG	76	Floyd	Womack
RG	68	Shawn	Lauvao
ROLB	79	Scott	Fujita
ROLB	73	Jason	Trusnik
ROLB	71	Chris	Gocong
RT	72	Tony	Pashos
RT	71	John	St. Clair
SS	69	Larry	Asante
SS	69	T.J.	Ward
TE	78	Benjamin	Watson
TE	72	Robert	Royal
TE	63	Evan	Moore
WR	78	Josh	Cribbs
WR	75	Mohamed	Massaquoi
WR	68	Chansi	Stuckey
WR	65	Brian	Robiskie
WR	58	Jake	Allen

OFFENSIVE STRENGTH CHART

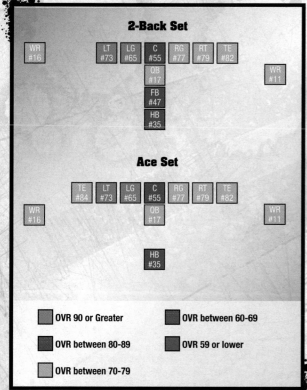

2-Back Set

| WR #16 | | LT #73 | LG #65 | C #55 | RG #77 | RT #79 | TE #82 | |
| QB #17 |
| FB #47 |
| HB #35 |
| | WR #11 |

Ace Set

	TE #84	LT #73	LG #65	C #55	RG #77	RT #79	TE #82
WR #16	QB #17							WR #11
			HB #35

- ■ OVR 90 or Greater
- ■ OVR between 80-89
- ■ OVR between 70-79
- ■ OVR between 60-69
- ■ OVR 59 or lower

Key Player Substitutions

Position: FB

Substitution: Peyton Hillis

When: Passing situations

Advantage: Bring Hillis in on pass-blocking situations to protect Delhomme's backside. You can also slip Hillis out into the flats when needed, and not worry about him dropping the ball.

#73 Joe Thomas
Offensive Tackle (LT)

Overall	95
Strength	91
Run Blk. Strength	87
Pass Blk. Strength	96
Impact Blocking	94

#35 Jerome Harrison
Halfback (HB)

Overall	83
Speed	92
Agility	95
Stiff Arm	55
Carrying	85

#16 Josh Cribbs
Wide Receiver (WR)

Overall	78
Speed	92
Catching	79
Release	73
Jumping	90

#92 Shaun Rogers
Defensive Tackle (DT)

Overall	93
Speed	49
Strength	98
Power Moves	97
Block Shedding	98

#23 Sheldon Brown
Cornerback (CB)

Overall	87
Speed	88
Awareness	88
Man Coverage	87
Zone Coverage	91

#24 Eric Wright
Cornerback (CB)

Overall	86
Speed	89
Awareness	79
Man Coverage	88
Zone Coverage	90

DEFENSIVE STRENGTH CHART

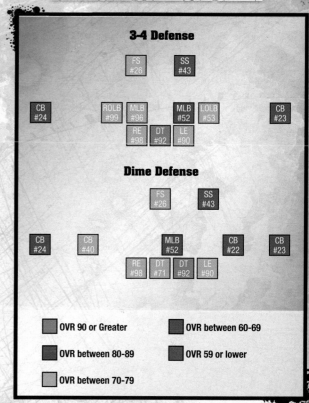

3-4 Defense

	FS #26		SS #43	
CB #24	ROLB #99	MLB #96	MLB #52	LOLB #53	CB #23
	RE #98	DT #92	LE #90	

Dime Defense

	FS #26	SS #43	
CB #24	CB #40	MLB #52	CB #22	CB #23
	RE #98	DT #71	DT #92	LE #90

- ■ OVR 90 or Greater
- ■ OVR between 80-89
- ■ OVR between 70-79
- ■ OVR between 60-69
- ■ OVR 59 or lower

Key Player Substitutions

Position: MLB

Substitution: David Bowens

When: Rushing situations

Advantage: Use Bowens on short yardage situations to clog up the middle gaps. With his strength and power moves Bowens is a hard man to block with just one lineman.

Playbook Breakdown

The Browns are now going to a West Coast Offense. You can expect to see plenty of quick passing with a solid rushing attack at its base. The West Coast Offense, when run correctly, can be a very effective scheme. Don't sleep on this team because they have some nice weapons to work with. You have a great backfield with a fullback that is one of the best in the league. He's a solid runner and catcher from the backfield. Then Harrison is a solid back who can pound and catch well. The offensive line is solid and you have a vet at QB with a nice option coming off the bench in Wallace. You also have the ESPN highlight reel with Cribbs. We will show you how to work these weapons and how to use this West Coast scheme. In addition, we'll explore some of the new sets that have been added.

OFFENSIVE FORMATIONS

FORMATION	# OF PLAYS
Far Pro	12
Flash Split	3
Flash Trio	3
Gun Doubles	15
Gun Empty Y-Flex	9
Gun Snugs Flip	9
Gun Split Offset	12
Gun Spread Wk	12
I-Form Normal	18
I-Form Tight	12
Singleback Ace	15
Singleback Ace Twins	15
Singleback Bunch Base	12
Singleback Flex	15
Singleback Y-Trips	12
Split Pro	9
Strong Pro	15
Strong Twin TE	12
Weak Pro Twins	12

OFFENSIVE PLAYCOUNTS

PLAY TYPE	# OF PLAYS
Quick Pass	16
Standard Pass	41
Shotgun Pass	38
Play Action Pass	48
Inside Handoff	32
Outside Handoff	15
Pitch	7
Counter	7

Flash Trio—Read Option

This newer set showcases one of the most talented players in the league. EA SPORTS really worked on the running game this season, and now you can run the option very well. We will talk about your reads and how to use this set to your advantage as a change-up to your play calling in this breakdown.

Cribbs reads the edge defender

The key to the Read Option is reading the edge defender. If the edge defender slices inside, you keep the ball and run with the QB. If the edge defender comes upfield or slants outside, hand the ball off to the halfback.

The edge defender comes up the field so Harrison gets the handoff

Since the edge defender came up the field, we hand the ball off to the running back. It will take time to get the timing down on your reads. When you do get them down, you will be a weapon to contend with. When you have two weapons like Harrison and Cribbs, they give the defense a major dilemma because you have to contain weapons that can attack inside or outside.

Flash Split—Read Option

This is a Gun two-back formation where you can attack via Wildcat again with your best two weapons. When you have a great play you want to have it in more than one formation. The last one was from a Trips set. This one is very effective because you can have the fullback as a lead blocker. The read player again is the edge defender.

The edge defender slices inside—time to keep the ball

You read the edge defender on the opposite side of the running play because the edge defender is the only one left unblocked. Only this defender has a strong chance to stop the play in the backfield. If he slices in he can hit the back. So we keep the ball and allow Cribbs to get outside and do what he does best. His speed in the open field is sick.

Taking it to the house

You have lead blockers, and the edge defender's overpursuit of the play leaves a gap wide open for you to get good yards on the ground.

Far Pro—Y Post

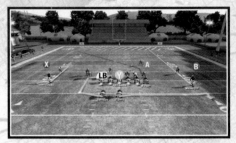

This play is what the West Coast Offense is all about. Your key reads are the backs and the tight end. This play works well against man, zone, and any kind of pressure. Most pressure will come up front. So the backs' routes will punish them for doing so. You read the tight end, the halfback, and then the fullback. If none of them are open, look for the out or the streak.

Pressure with a safety over top

Since you see the safety over the top, look off of him and try to hit your halfback or the fullback. In some cases against man coverage, the defender covering the fullback will get picked by the tight end. When you read that, you have to hit the fullback. If no one was over top of the tight end or sitting in the middle, you hit the tight end. In this case, we will hit the halfback for the bigger gain.

Easy catch for the back

You can hit the back at anytime. You can drive it like a flat, or you can hit him halfway into his route.

Far Pro—HB Seam

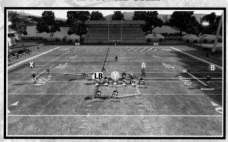

This play is like the Y Post, but now you have the fullback running a C route and the halfback working the seam with a streak. The tight end is doing a quick out. You make the same reads, but this time you read the halfback, then you read the fullback, and the last read will be your tight end. This is a play you use when you're facing an opponent who likes to blitz. Just as with the other play from the Far Pro, you can beat man or zone with this scheme.

The seam is covered with the safety over top, and an alley defender is sitting on the out

You should look for the seam first. If you see that the seam is covered, look to your fullback. Now the fullback can get open via pick because the defender most of the time runs into the tight end trying to get to the fullback.

Great catch by our back

Now the fullback has the ball and the opponents now understand they have to show attention to the backs and the middle of the field. When this happens the outside wideouts get open.

Far Pro—HB Dive

You have to be able to run and pass out of the same formation to keep your opponent off-balance. This is a nice quick handoff inside that can get you 5 yards a clip. When you see that the numbers are right inside or you see some sort of line adjustment, this is a great play to call.

The O-line parts the Red Sea

Once you see a hole you must fire off and get what you can. In most cases, you can have the fullback lead you in the hole. If there's heat or any leaks in the offensive line he will peel off his assignment and hit the first defender. This is why you must fire off in the hole once you see one. You just want to move the chains and keep your down and distance short.

Blocking downfield means more yards

This is what the West Coast Offense is about. You use quick passes to replace your rushing attack. The offense is based on timing and reads. Once the defense's mind is consumed with getting beaten up by the pass, you can run it down their throat. This playbook has some great running plays in every set.

Gun Snugs Flip—Wheel Switch

The Wheel Switch is a play you can use for any situation. You have some nice running plays in this formation to keep them honest. Then you have plays like this one that attack every coverage in the game. Your main reads are the post and the fade. Against most zone coverages, the fade will be open. The secondary drops back to defend the deeper routes and this allows the fade to come open. You also can use the fade as a flat route. Make your read downfield for the post, and if it's covered, look for the fade. You have the flat, quick slant, and the quick out as your hot reads if you see heat.

The safety got caught shifting—hit the post

If you see the safety sitting over top with underneath coverage, check to the fade. Here you see the gap over top. You can throw the post route once the receiver gets inside position on his defender.

Great catch on the post route

The skinny post is a very hard route to defend. If they sit on that route now you can hit the fade and your other routes at will.

Singleback Bunch Base—Browns Go's

This is a nice set you can mix with your other formations. This formation is great because you have the tight end and the fullback in this set. You have your two-back personnel out there and this allows you to audible from this to sets like the I-Form Normal or Tight without losing anything at all. With a good fullback like Vickers, you still have a solid weapon on the field for your passing game. When you're under center you must make quick reads and get the ball out fast. The fade is your main read, you then check to the dig, and your last read is the seam route.

Look at the three-way combo

When it's zone coverage, the fade is open most of the time. If the alley defender sits on the fade you check to the dig and the seam.

Great catch by our receiver

This play will force your opponent to shift the coverage outside. When this adjustment is made you can attack the middle with no problem.

TAMPA BAY BUCCANEERS

OFFENSIVE SCOUTING REPORT

There is no denying that the Buccaneers are a franchise in a rebuilding stage. This can be seen throughout their team and especially in the offense. The young offense only posted three wins last season, but they have the potential to improve now that they have established an identity as a run-first offense with a trio of featured backs. Carnell "Cadillac" Williams should be the workhorse of the group, but Derrick Ward has much better hands when it comes to receiving the ball on dump passes and out of the play action. The receiving corps is young, as is QB Josh Freeman, but a couple of veterans in Reggie Brown and Michael Clayton can allow Freeman to exercise his high throwing power and increasing accuracy. The Bucs did draft a couple of rookies who may be worth subbing in when you need more speed to stretch the defense (Arrelious Benn and Mike Williams). The main target in the Bucs' air attack is TE Kellen Winslow, who proved that he does indeed have what it takes to be successful in the NFL. Look to utilize him often and keep him involved in the offensive scheme.

DEFENSIVE SCOUTING REPORT

The Bucs will have something to prove after posting the worst rushing defense in the league last year. To help fix the issue, they drafted defensive tackles Gerald McCoy and Brian Price with the first two picks in the draft, both of whom should be considered instant starters. If the newcomers can jam the offensive line, it should help put pressure on the quarterback, dampen the run, and allow standout middle linebacker Barrett Ruud to make big plays. As for the Bucs secondary, they finished the year with much better stats with polished play from CBs Ronde Barber and Aqib Talib. If the run defense improves, the secondary will get more opportunities to make plays, including some takeaways by the pair of quality corners.

TEAM RATING

69
Overall

KEY ADDITIONS

WR	Reggie Brown
S	Sean Jones
LB	Jonathan Alston
DT	Gerald McCoy
DT	Brian Price

KEY DEPARTURES

S	Will Allen
WR	Antonio Bryant
DT	Chris Hovan
QB	Byron Leftwich
DE	Jimmy Wilkerson
CB	Torrie Cox

RATINGS BY POSITION

Position	Rating	Position	Rating
Quarterbacks	77	Defensive Tackles	84
Halfbacks	77	Outside Linebackers	75
Fullbacks	78	Middle Linebackers	91
Wide Receivers	70	Cornerbacks	86
Tight Ends	89	Free Safeties	88
Tackles	80	Strong Safeties	77
Guards	83	Kickers	67
Centers	86	Punters	56
Defensive Ends	71		

DEPTH CHART

POS	OVR	FIRST NAME	LAST NAME
C	86	Jeff	Faine
C	66	Jonathan	Compas
CB	87	Aqib	Talib
CB	84	Ronde	Barber
CB	68	Elbert	Mack
CB	66	Myron	Lewis
CB	59	E.J.	Biggers
DT	84	Gerald	McCoy
DT	75	Brian	Price
DT	72	Ryan	Sims
DT	71	Roy	Miller
DT	57	Dre	Moore
FB	78	Earnest	Graham
FB	63	Chris	Pressley
FS	88	Tanard	Jackson
FS	64	Corey	Lynch
HB	77	Carnell	Williams
HB	75	Derrick	Ward
HB	68	Clifton	Smith
K	67	Connor	Barth
LE	68	Tim	Crowder
LE	67	Kyle	Moore
LG	77	Jeremy	Zuttah
LG	60	Marc	Dile
LOLB	79	Geno	Hayes
LOLB	65	Jonathan	Alston
LT	85	Jon	Penn
LT	61	James	Lee
MLB	91	Barrett	Ruud
MLB	63	Niko	Koutouvides
P	56	Brent	Bowden
QB	77	Josh	Freeman
QB	68	Josh	Johnson
QB	58	Jevan	Snead
RE	73	Stylez	White
RG	88	Davin	Joseph
ROLB	75	Angelo	Crowell
ROLB	70	Quincy	Black
RT	74	Jeremy	Trueblood
RT	60	Demar	Dotson
SS	77	Sean	Jones
SS	74	Sabby	Piscitelli
TE	89	Kellen	Winslow
TE	76	Jerramy	Stevens
TE	70	John	Gilmore
WR	73	Arrelious	Benn
WR	71	Maurice	Stovall
WR	70	Reggie	Brown
WR	68	Sammie	Stroughter
WR	67	Michael	Clayton
WR	67	Mike	Williams

OFFENSIVE STRENGTH CHART

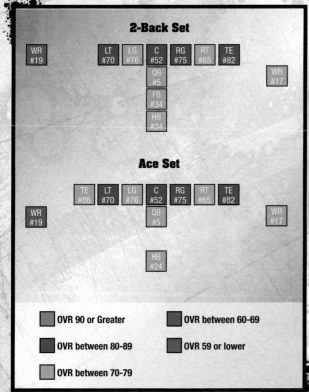

2-Back Set

WR #19		LT #70	LG #76	C #52	RG #75	RT #65	TE #82	
				QB #5				WR #17
				FB #34				
				HB #24				

Ace Set

	TE #86	LT #70	LG #76	C #52	RG #75	RT #65	TE #82	
WR #19				QB #5				WR #17
				HB #24				

- ■ OVR 90 or Greater
- ■ OVR between 80-89
- ■ OVR between 70-79
- ■ OVR between 60-69
- ■ OVR 59 or lower

Key Player Substitutions

Position: WR

Substitution: Mike Williams

When: Running plays

Advantage: Mike Williams doesn't have the best hands out of all the WRs on the Bucs roster, but Williams's good run-blocking skills could help you out even more. Try to run sweep plays to Williams's side.

#82 Kellen Winslow
Tight End (TE)

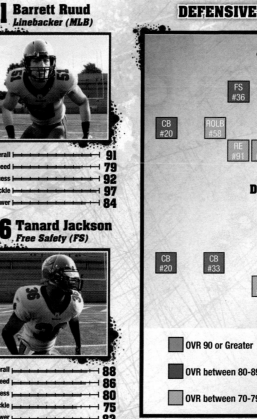

Overall	89
Speed	84
Catching	84
Catch in Traffic	85
Jumping	92

#75 Davin Joseph
Offensive Guard (RG)

Overall	88
Strength	91
Pass Block	85
Run Block	90
Impact Blocking	93

#24 Carnell Williams
Halfback (HB)

Overall	77
Speed	87
Agility	86
Stiff Arm	63
Carrying	83

#51 Barrett Ruud
Linebacker (MLB)

Overall	91
Speed	79
Awareness	92
Tackle	97
Hit Power	84

#36 Tanard Jackson
Free Safety (FS)

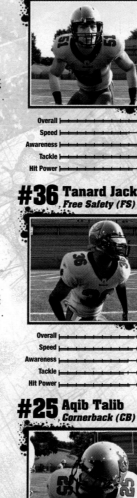

Overall	88
Speed	86
Awareness	80
Tackle	75
Hit Power	82

#25 Aqib Talib
Cornerback (CB)

Overall	87
Speed	88
Awareness	72
Man Coverage	89
Zone Coverage	87

DEFENSIVE STRENGTH CHART

4-3 Defense

	FS #36			SS #26	
CB #20	ROLB #58		MLB #51	LOLB #54	CB #25
		RE #91	DT #92	DT #93	LE #96	

Dime Defense

		FS #36		SS #26		
CB #20	CB #33		MLB #51		CB #23	CB #35
		RE #91	DT #92	DT #93	LE #96	

- ■ OVR 90 or Greater
- ■ OVR between 80-89
- ■ OVR between 70-79
- ■ OVR between 60-69
- ■ OVR 59 or lower

Key Player Substitutions

Position: ROLB

Substitution: Quincy Black

When: Global

Advantage: With better physical attributes, Black can drop back and cover his assignment just as well as any starter in the league. You can also use his speed to increase the pressure from his side of the field.

Playbook Breakdown

The Tampa Bay Buccaneers finished last season with a 3–13 record. Rookie Josh Freeman struggled with interceptions at times, but he did show that he is capable of throwing the ball downfield with his great arm strength. His mobility comes in handy as well. Buccaneers running back Carnell Williams has shown that he still has speed even after a bunch of injuries. The Buccaneers like to use a lot of play action to get their young quarterback outside of the pocket. Their playbook has plenty of formations with play action plays in them. The playbook also has seven Gun formations, including two spread sets and two compression sets. Depending on your offensive style, you can choose to air it out or run the ball. Be sure to mix in play action and work the short passing game with this playbook.

OFFENSIVE FORMATIONS

FORMATION	# OF PLAYS
Gun Bunch	9
Gun Doubles	15
Gun Empty Trey	12
Gun Snugs Flip	9
Gun Split Y-Flex	12
Gun Spread	12
Gun Y-Trips HB Wk	18
I-Form Pro	15
I-Form Tight	12
I-Form Tight Pair	12
Singleback Ace	15
Singleback Ace Pair	12
Singleback Ace Pair Twins	12
Singleback Doubles	15
Singleback Wing Trips	9
Strong Close	9
Strong Pro	15
Weak Pro Twins	12

OFFENSIVE PLAYCOUNTS

PLAY TYPE	# OF PLAYS
Quick Pass	12
Standard Pass	28
Shotgun Pass	62
Play Action Pass	46
Inside Handoff	31
Outside Handoff	14
Pitch	9
Counter	4

Singleback Ace—PA Rollout

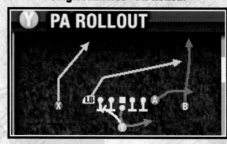

Singleback Ace—PA Rollout is designed to get the QB outside of the pocket. With quarterback Josh Freeman's speed, he can get outside the pocket very easily. The flanker is the primary target on this play; he runs a streak that opens up underneath routes. With tight ends Kellen Winslow and Jerramy Stevens, the Buccaneers have the perfect talent to run this play effectively.

The quarterback rolls outside the pocket

After the snap, take control of the quarterback and roll outside the pocket. You have two targets in front of you, the crossing route and the delay route. With a mobile quarterback such as Josh Freeman, if everything is covered you can take off and run. We spot a target and fire the ball downfield.

The pass is completed to a tight end downfield

Quarterback Josh Freeman completed the pass to tight end Jerramy Stevens—he makes the catch 15 yards downfield. If you see the coverage come down to take away the short pass, this is when you want to fire the deep streak route. Mixing in run plays from this formation helps set up this play action pass.

I-Form Pro—HB Power O

HB Power O is a staple run play that the Buccaneers like to use in their offense. This play has left guard Jeremy Zuttah pulling from the left side of the formation. With fullback Earnest Graham pulling as well, we should have plenty of blockers. Bring the flanker in motion and snap the ball once he is behind the line of scrimmage.

The quarterback hands the ball off

The quarterback hands the ball off to Carnell Williams. We have the flanker as an extra blocker to go along with the pulling left guard and fullback. You have to be patient. You can take this run off the right tackle or up inside.

The running back sees an opening and takes it outside

The running back uses his speed to pick up the first down. Once you have the defense worried about the run, mix in play action pass plays. It's all about reading a defense and calling the correct play. With a quarterback who has speed, like Josh Freeman, play action becomes very effective because you can get outside the pocket.

I-Form Pro—PA TE Corner

After we get a ground game going it's time to mix in the play action passing game. PA TE Corner begins with a fake handoff to the left. Kellen Winslow is the primary target on this play, along with the streak that the flanker runs (which is designed to open up the underneath routes). You also have a crossing route and the fullback coming out of the backfield on a flat route.

The quarterback fakes the handoff to the running back

We suggest taking control of the quarterback and rolling out of the pocket. This gives you the option of taking off and running if your receivers are not open. As you can see, we have two targets open. We can either go for it deep or throw to the shorter route. Quarterback Josh Freeman is locked on target and fires the ball.

The pass is completed to a fullback

Our fullback, Earnest Graham, makes the catch. He has a few yards of space to run in before being tackled for a 5-yard gain. The progression for this play is to look short then deep; if you don't see any of your reads open, you can take off with the quarterback.

I-Form Tight Pair—Curls

I-Form Tight Pair—Curls has two short curls run by the tight ends, two flat routes, and another short route that the split end runs. We like to run this play with pre-snap motion that would suggest we are going to run the ball: We motion the tight end on the outside of the formation. As soon as he takes a step, we snap the ball.

The quarterback sees his target and throws the ball to him

Look for the two short curls right in front of you as your first two reads. With these two short routes in front, it is hard for the defense to sit on both of them. Most of the time, if one is covered the other one is open.

The pass is completed for a short gain

With this play, if you see that both of the tight ends are covered underneath, that's when you want to go to your backs out of the backfield. This is what we call a curl-flat combo.

Singleback Doubles—Curls HB Angle

Singleback Doubles—Curls HB Angle gives you a curl-flat combo with an angle route out of the backfield. The flat route on this play pulls the coverage and opens up the angle route out of the backfield. At the same time, the curl routes open up the field for the flat routes.

The quarterback gets ready to throw the ball

As you can see, we have two reads in one area. The angle route of the running back is very hard to cover, because you can throw it short or, if you have time, let the running back get deeper into his route.

The pass is completed to Carnell Williams

Carnell Williams has room to run and picks up plenty of yards. These routes are very effective at gashing the defense and picking up large chunks of yards at a time. The flat routes in the play can also be used as quick reads if you see them uncovered.

Singleback Wing Trips—PA Boot Rt

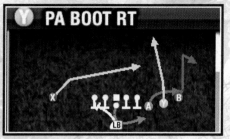

Singleback Wing Trips—PA Boot Rt allows quarterback Josh Freeman to use his speed and get outside the pocket to look downfield for targets. Tight end Kellen Winslow is on a delay route; he stays in to block before going out on his pass route. The slot receiver is on a streak to pull the coverage; you also have the split end on a crossing route.

The quarterback throws the ball to his tight end

After the snap, take control of the quarterback and roll out right. Look for the delay route first and then the crossing route as a second read. Sometimes the defender will drop down on the flat route and leave the slot receiver open.

Kellen Winslow makes the catch

Kellen Winslow uses his speed to gain separation from the defender. When using this play, if you see there is room to take off and run with the quarterback you can do so. With Josh Freeman's speed, it is very hard for a defensive lineman to catch him from behind.

Singleback Wing Trips—Slants

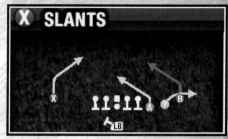

The Slants play from the Singleback Wing Trips formation has three slants going over the middle of the field with one flat route. This play is good to mix with PA Boot Rt, and it is also a quick audible for this formation.

The quarterback scans the field

As you can see, the tight end and the slot receiver are both open. This is because the linebackers have dropped back into coverage. This route combination is very hard for the defense to cover. We have a target, and the quarterback passes the bullet over the middle.

The pass is completed to the tight end

Kellen Winslow makes the catch in the middle for a 5-yard gain. One thing to look out for with this play is that sometimes the defense plays Cover 2. If that is the case, then wait for the slant routes to clear the zones. Another suggestion is to hot route the flanker on the streak if you see the corner playing the flat area.

ARIZONA CARDINALS

OFFENSIVE SCOUTING REPORT

After many successful seasons under newly retired Kurt Warner, Arizona's reins have been handed over to Matt Leinart. This former USC national champion is getting his first real shot since 2007 to prove he can run this talented offense. Leinart's a lefty who can stand in the pocket and deliver strikes when given the time, but his power and accuracy are not as high-powered as Arizona is used to. Fortunately, one of the best players in the league will be on the receiving end of Leinart's throws in WR Larry Fitzgerald. "Fitz," one of last year's *Madden NFL* cover athletes, is a beast in all aspects of getting his hands on the ball and hanging on to it. At the top of his game is the ability to run routes, create space with speed, and make a spectacular catch in traffic. Fitzgerald is a nightmare for defenses and their coordinators. The Cardinals should feel good about their running game, too. Tim Hightower and up-and-comer Beanie Wells run well as a tandem behind a beefy line anchored by Levi Brown and should only improve with newly acquired guard Alan Faneca. Simply put, this offense has a well-balanced attack, and if the line can give Leinart time, their success will continue.

DEFENSIVE SCOUTING REPORT

Adrian Wilson anchors the defense as the longest tenured Cardinal and feared big-hitter. Having the protection of Wilson over the top allows cornerbacks like Dominique Rodgers-Cromartie to make big plays and secure turnovers. Between the two of them, they accounted for 11 interceptions and 4 forced fumbles last year. The addition of LB Joey Porter immediately toughens the linebacking corps of Clark Haggans and Gerald Hayes, although the loss of Karlos Dansby will sting. Porter loves to fly around the field and pressure the quarterback, so look to utilize more blitz packages this season. The speed of the secondary will enable the linebacking unit to take more chances, especially with RE Darnell Dockett rushing the QB. The line for the Cardinals is strongest at the end positions, with Darnell Dockett and outstanding second-year player Calais Campbell. Don't be surprised by this tenacious team.

TEAM RATING

79
Overall

KEY ADDITIONS

QB	Derek Anderson
G	Alan Faneca
K	Jay Feely
OLB	Joey Porter
S	Kerry Rhodes
DT	Dan Williams

KEY DEPARTURES

WR	Anquan Boldin
QB	Kurt Warner
S	Antrel Rolle
OLB	Karlos Dansby
OLB	Bertrand Berry
CB	Bryant McFadden

RATINGS BY POSITION

Quarterbacks	75
Halfbacks	79
Fullbacks	57
Wide Receivers	85
Tight Ends	76
Tackles	77
Guards	86
Centers	72
Defensive Ends	90
Defensive Tackles	76
Outside Linebackers	81
Middle Linebackers	85
Cornerbacks	83
Free Safeties	88
Strong Safeties	96
Kickers	86
Punters	83

DEPTH CHART

POS	OVR	FIRST NAME	LAST NAME
C	72	Lyle	Sendlein
C	65	Ben	Claxton
CB	90	Dominique	Rodgers-Cromartie
CB	75	Greg	Toler
CB	62	Michael	Adams
CB	62	Trumaine	McBride
DT	76	Dan	Williams
DT	72	Bryan	Robinson
DT	68	Gabe	Watson
FB	57	Nehemiah	Broughton
FS	88	Kerry	Rhodes
FS	66	Rashad	Johnson
HB	82	Beanie	Wells
HB	79	Tim	Hightower
HB	69	Jason	Wright
HB	67	LaRod	Stephens-Howling
K	86	Jay	Feely
LE	86	Calais	Campbell
LE	67	Kenny	Iwebema
LG	91	Alan	Faneca
LG	72	Rex	Hadnot
LOLB	75	Clark	Haggans
LOLB	65	Cody	Brown
LT	79	Levi	Brown
MLB	85	Gerald	Hayes
MLB	72	Paris	Lenon
MLB	62	Ali	Highsmith
MLB	61	Monty	Beisel
P	83	Ben	Graham
QB	75	Matt	Leinart
QB	67	Derek	Anderson
QB	62	John	Skelton
RE	94	Darnell	Dockett
RE	65	Alan	Branch
RG	80	Reggie	Wells
RG	76	Deuce	Lutui
RG	66	Herman	Johnson
ROLB	86	Joey	Porter
ROLB	69	Daryl	Washington
ROLB	60	Will	Davis
RT	74	Brandon	Keith
RT	71	Jeremy	Bridges
SS	96	Adrian	Wilson
SS	62	Matt	Ware
TE	76	Anthony	Becht
TE	70	Ben	Patrick
TE	69	Stephen	Spach
WR	97	Larry	Fitzgerald
WR	80	Steve	Breaston
WR	78	Early	Doucet
WR	66	Andre	Roberts
WR	53	Onrea	Jones

OFFENSIVE STRENGTH CHART

2-Back Set

WR #15	LT #75	LG #66	C #63	RG #74	RT #72	TE #84
			QB #7			WR #11
			FB #32			
			HB #34			

Ace Set

	TE #89	LT #75	LG #66	C #63	RG #74	RT #72	TE #84
WR #15			QB #7			WR #11
			HB #34			

- ■ OVR 90 or Greater
- ■ OVR between 80-89
- ■ OVR between 70-79
- ■ OVR between 60-69
- ■ OVR 59 or lower

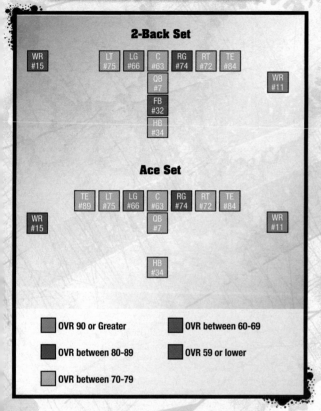

#11 Larry Fitzgerald
Wide Receiver (WR)

Overall	97
Speed	88
Catching	98
Release	94
Jumping	99

#26 Beanie Wells
Halfback (HB)

Overall	82
Speed	89
Agility	85
Stiff Arm	98
Carrying	88

#66 Alan Faneca
Offensive Guard (LG)

Overall	91
Strength	94
Pass Block	82
Run Block	94
Impact Blocking	90

#90 Darnell Dockett
Defensive End (RE)

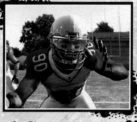

Overall	94
Speed	73
Strength	91
Power Moves	95
Block Shedding	90

#55 Joey Porter
Linebacker (ROLB)

Overall	86
Speed	78
Awareness	92
Tackle	85
Hit Power	95

#29 Dominique Rodgers-Cromartie
Cornerback (CB)

Overall	90
Speed	98
Awareness	75
Man Coverage	96
Zone Coverage	87

DEFENSIVE STRENGTH CHART

3-4 Defense

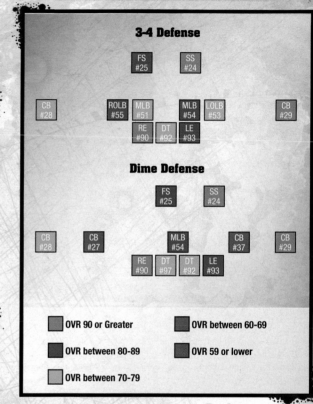

		FS #25		SS #24		
CB #28	ROLB #55	MLB #51		MLB #54	LOLB #53	CB #29
	RE #90	DT #92	LE #93			

Dime Defense

		FS #25		SS #24	
CB #28	CB #27	MLB #54		CB #37	CB #29
	RE #90	DT #97	DT #92	LE #93	

- ■ OVR 90 or Greater
- ■ OVR between 80-89
- ■ OVR between 70-79
- ■ OVR between 60-69
- ■ OVR 59 or lower

Key Player Substitutions

Position: WR

Substitution: Andre Roberts

When: Global

Advantage: Moving Roberts to the number three spot on the roster will add speed to your receiver lineup. With most teams doubling Fitzgerald, look for one-on-one coverage on the outside with Roberts.

Key Player Substitutions

Position: ROLB

Substitution: Daryl Washington

When: Passing situations

Advantage: Bring Washington in when you know your opponent is going to throw the ball. Washington is much better at dropping back and covering guys coming across the middle.

Playbook Breakdown

The Cardinals are known as a passing team, and they have eight Gun formations in their playbook to prove it. With Kurt Warner no longer at the quarterback position, Matt Leinart takes over. The Cardinals have a young playmaking trio consisting of Matt Leinart, Steve Breaston, and star wide receiver Larry Fitzgerald. This trio has the potential to dominate NFL defenses for years to come. With formations such as Gun Bunch Wk, Gun Tight, Gun Y-Trips Open, and Gun Empty Trips, you can attack the defense through the air. With this playbook, you can also run the ball out of formations such as Strong Pro and Strong Twin TE. This allows you to go from attacking the defense through the air to beating them up on the ground. You also have Singleback Bunch Base and Singleback Tight Doubles that you can use as balanced formations to run or to pass out of. By using these under-center formations, you can keep the defense guessing as to whether you are going to run or pass.

OFFENSIVE FORMATIONS

FORMATION	# OF PLAYS
Gun Bunch Wk	12
Gun Doubles Wk	12
Gun Empty Trips	9
Gun Flip Trips	9
Gun Split Offset	12
Gun Spread	12
Gun Tight	9
Gun Y-Trips Open	12
I-Form Pro	15
I-Form Pro Twins	12
Singleback Ace	15
Singleback Ace Pair	12
Singleback Bunch Base	12
Singleback Doubles	15
Singleback Tight Doubles	9
Singleback Y-Trips	15
Strong Pro	15
Strong Twin TE	9
Weak Slot	12

OFFENSIVE PLAYCOUNTS

PLAY TYPE	# OF PLAYS
Quick Pass	20
Standard Pass	38
Shotgun Pass	66
Play Action Pass	38
Outside Handoff	10
Pitch	6
Counter	5
Draw	11

Gun Doubles Wk—Zona Y-Corner

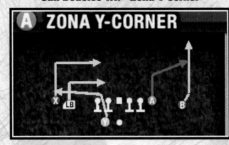

The Cardinals are a passing team, and Gun Doubles Wk—Zona Y-Corner has the tight end as the primary receiver. This play also has the split end and the slot receiver running in routes while the running back is on an out route. The crossing route combination on the left side of the field provides you with quick reads.

Wait for a receiver to get open

Once the ball is snapped, the quarterback scans the field as he sees the crossing routes developing in front of him. Depending on if the defense is playing man or zone, you should see one of the routes come open. In the screenshot, the defense is playing zone and there are two defenders sitting in the area.

Hightower looks for more yards

The QB finds his target, running back Tim Hightower, out of the backfield. Hightower makes the grab and has plenty of room to run before he is brought down. If you see the defense sitting on the running back, throw to the slot receiver as your next read.

Gun Bunch Wk—Mesh

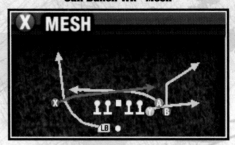

Mesh was a popular play last year in *Madden NFL 10*; the passing concept that you see in this play is used by many teams in the NFL. In this play you have two drag routes that cross each other over the middle of the field. There is a flat route that the receiver next to the right tackle runs and a wheel route out of the backfield.

Watch the crossing receivers draw the defense's attention

The QB scans the field to determine whether he is against man or zone. This is a deadly play; as you can see, you have the crossing routes as well as the flat route and the wheel route out of the backfield open. All of these are quick and easy reads.

The flats are left open

The QB finds his target (running back Tim Hightower) out of the backfield. With this play, most often when the catch is made there is plenty of room to get some good yards after the catch. This is a good play to use in your offense as a base play.

Gun Spread—X Follow

Gun Spread—X Follow has the flanker on a streak route as the primary target. We like the running back's out route and the slot receiver's drag route, which come across the middle of the field.

Leinart gets the ball out quick

As you scan the field with the quarterback, you will notice that the running back and the crossing route get open against most coverages. Matt Leinart sees his target crossing over the middle of the field. Also notice how you have the running back coming open, as well as these two good reads right in front of you.

Try to spin into the open space

The pass is completed to our receiver over the middle of the field for a quick 5-yard gain. Another suggestion is to put the other slot receiver on the right side of the field on a slant route over the middle of the field. Once you do that, you can motion him to give him a running start. This will create a flood over the middle of the field with three targets in one area.

Gun Y-Trips Open—Strong Flood

Strong Flood involves three receivers running flood routes to make the defense think short so the offense can go deep down the field. The great thing about this play is you can tell right away whether the defense is in man or zone by how the defenders line up.

Look to attack the flats

The QB notices that the defense is playing zone and is blitzing off the right side. This allows you to make a quick read to the slot receiver, who runs a flat route. With the streak route that the flanker runs, coverage is pulled deep. This leaves the short route underneath wide open.

Becht fights for yardage

We find our target in the flat area. Tight end Anthony Becht makes the catch, squares his shoulders, and turns downfield for some positive yards. With this play, you can also get creative with the other slot receiver and put him on a slant towards the sideline. Now when you complete the pass to the flat route, the other receiver acts like a blocker so you can pick up more yards.

Gun Empty Trips—Stick Post

In Stick Post, the flanker is the primary receiver in the play; however, we like the two short curls and the out route that the slot receiver on the left runs. The split end is on a streak. His route is designed to push the coverage deep so the short routes can come open underneath.

Look for a receiver to be open on the out routes

The defense is playing zone and you have two defenders sitting on the short curl route run by the inside slot receiver. Matt Leinart sees this and has his eye on his target: second-year wideout Onrea Jones. You can see him coming open as he breaks towards the sideline.

Try to use your receivers for blocks

He makes the catch and turns upfield for some good yards. Remember that you have the two short curls as quick reads if pressure comes. Also, you can bomb the defense on the left with the streak route if you see that the corner is playing the short out route. Another suggestion is to put the flanker on a slant route to the inside.

Gun Spread—WR Screen

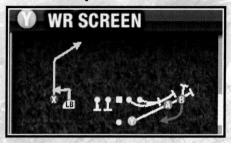

In the Cardinals offense, getting the ball to Larry Fitzgerald is a must if you want to have success in the passing attack. Gun Spread—WR Screen allows you to do just that with a screen to the right side of the formation.

Draw the D-line into the backfield

With this play, wait for your blocks to set up. Just hold onto the ball for a quick second once you snap it. Our blockers are setting up, and Larry Fitzgerald is waiting for the ball. Once you see this it's time to throw the ball to your star wideout.

Follow your big lineman

We complete the pass to him with blockers out in front as we pick up a good gain. With this play, letting your blockers set up is key, as is knowing when to call it. This type of screen play is not that effective vs. man defenses but sure is a zone killer. It's all about calling the right play at the right time. Beat up your opponent with crossing routes until he starts to run zone to defend them. Then pop him with the screen.

Gun Split Offset—Slants Middle

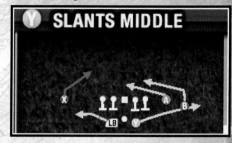

Gun Split Offset—Slants Middle has three receivers running slant routes with two running backs on the flat route out of the backfield. With three receivers flooding the middle of the field, this play kills man defense and is also very effective against zone defense.

Look for the middle of the field first

Matt Leinart spots Larry Fitzgerald with inside position on the defender and fires the ball to him over the middle of the field. Take note of the defender blitzing off of the edge. When you see this, that's when you have the option to throw it to the running back.

Let Fitzgerald go to work

We complete the pass for a 10-yard gain over the middle to Larry Fitzgerald before we are tackled. Another suggestion is to use motion with this play. This tells you if the defense is in man or zone. If they are playing man, that's a good time to throw the ball to the running back out of the backfield. Having two backs in the backfield with speed also helps, or you can audible to this from a four-wide-receiver set to get speed back there.

SAN DIEGO CHARGERS

OFFENSIVE SCOUTING REPORT

You might think that just because legendary running back LaDainian Tomlinson has moved on to greener pastures (literally) it's a whole new ball game for the Chargers. Truth be told, that's not entirely accurate. With the addition of rookie Ryan Mathews, the Chargers can once again rely on fresh legs to complement Philip Rivers's arm. Use Mathews to grind and pound the running game, creating opportunities for the passing game. Darren Sproles will still be worked into the rushing game, but Sproles's main role is as a quality return man. In the passing game, Philip Rivers has long since proved he can lead the team with and without L.T., earning a top passer rating last year behind only Brett Favre and Drew Brees. At his disposal is Vincent Jackson, who can be counted on to create deep threat issues for the opposing team and stretch the field. TE Antonio Gates, one of the most feared tight ends in the league, is a perfect weapon for exploiting the middle, especially when running the post. With VJax's recent emergence as one of the NFL's up-and-coming star wide receivers, a talented running back eager to prove he can fill a huge void, a hall-of-fame-caliber TE in Antonio Gates, and an elite QB in Philip Rivers, it's nothing but business as usual for the San Diego Chargers.

DEFENSIVE SCOUTING REPORT

In 2009, the Chargers were a puzzling team. Though capable of racking up points in a heartbeat, they were just as susceptible to giving up points to high-powered offenses. Their secondary was often the team's Achilles' heel. In an off-season where the Chargers parted ways with several key players on both sides of the ball, the defense saw one of their star cornerbacks, Antonio Cromartie, move on. Luckily, the slow and steady improvement of CB Antoine Cason and CB Quentin Jammer's consistency can ease the pain against most teams. As always, look for ROLB Shawne Merriman and LE Luis Castillo to provide pressure on opposing QBs. Be wary against teams with strong running games, however—the Chargers don't have a strong presence in the middle and can give up major yards to talented backs.

TEAM RATING

85
Overall

KEY ADDITIONS

CB	Donald Strickland
CB	Nathan Vasher
RB	Ryan Mathews

KEY DEPARTURES

CB	Antonio Cromartie
ILB	Tim Dobbins
TE	Brandon Manumaleuna
WR	Kassim Osgood
RB	LaDainian Tomlinson
DT	Jamal Williams

RATINGS BY POSITION

Position	Rating
Quarterbacks	94
Halfbacks	77
Fullbacks	74
Wide Receivers	78
Tight Ends	96
Tackles	81
Guards	88
Centers	86
Defensive Ends	82
Defensive Tackles	71
Outside Linebackers	88
Middle Linebackers	85
Cornerbacks	83
Free Safeties	84
Strong Safeties	76
Kickers	95
Punters	93

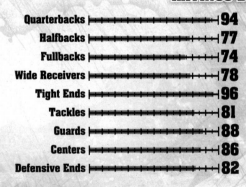

DEPTH CHART

POS	OVR	FIRST NAME	LAST NAME
C	86	Nick	Hardwick
C	73	Scott	Mruczkowski
CB	87	Quentin	Jammer
CB	78	Antoine	Cason
CB	69	Nathan	Vasher
CB	68	Donald	Strickland
CB	64	Dante	Hughes
DT	71	Ian	Scott
DT	71	Ogemdi	Nwagbuo
DT	63	Cam	Thomas
FB	74	Jacob	Hester
FB	74	Mike	Tolbert
FS	84	Eric	Weddle
FS	67	Paul	Oliver
HB	81	Darren	Sproles
HB	77	Ryan	Mathews
HB	66	Marcus	Mason
K	95	Nate	Kaeding
LE	88	Luis	Castillo
LE	66	Alfonso	Boone
LG	93	Kris	Dielman
LG	66	Tyronne	Green
LOLB	91	Shaun	Phillips
LOLB	66	Antwan	Applewhite
LT	89	Marcus	McNeill
LT	69	Brandyn	Dombrowski
MLB	85	Stephen	Cooper
MLB	76	Brandon	Siler
MLB	76	Kevin	Burnett
MLB	72	Donald	Butler
P	93	Mike	Scifres
QB	94	Philip	Rivers
QB	67	Billy	Volek
QB	64	Jonathan	Crompton
RE	75	Jacques	Cesaire
RE	69	Travis	Johnson
RE	67	Ryon	Bingham
RG	83	Louis	Vasquez
ROLB	84	Shawne	Merriman
ROLB	77	Larry	English
ROLB	72	Jyles	Tucker
RT	73	Jeromey	Clary
RT	59	Corey	Clark
SS	76	Kevin	Ellison
SS	68	Steve	Gregory
TE	96	Antonio	Gates
TE	73	Kris	Wilson
TE	54	Dedrick	Epps
WR	90	Vincent	Jackson
WR	76	Malcom	Floyd
WR	69	Legedu	Naanee
WR	68	Buster	Davis
WR	62	Seyi	Ajirotutu

OFFENSIVE STRENGTH CHART

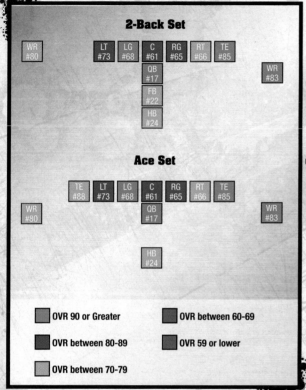

2-Back Set

| WR #80 | | | | | | | | WR #83 |

LT #73 | LG #68 | C #61 | RG #65 | RT #66 | TE #85
QB #17
FB #22
HB #24

Ace Set

TE #88 | LT #73 | LG #68 | C #61 | RG #65 | RT #66 | TE #85

WR #80 | | | | | | WR #83
QB #17
HB #24

- ■ OVR 90 or Greater
- ■ OVR between 80-89
- ■ OVR between 70-79
- ■ OVR between 60-69
- ■ OVR 59 or lower

#17 Philip Rivers
Quarterback (QB)

Overall	94
Throw Power	88
Short Accuracy	96
Medium Accuracy	95
Deep Accuracy	91

#83 Vincent Jackson
Wide Receiver (WR)

Overall	90
Speed	88
Catching	91
Release	98
Jumping	97

#85 Antonio Gates
Tight End (TE)

Overall	96
Speed	84
Catching	92
Catch in Traffic	93
Jumping	92

#93 Luis Castillo
Defensive End (LE)

Overall	88
Speed	65
Strength	97
Finesse Moves	65
Power Moves	90

#95 Shaun Phillips
Linebacker (LOLB)

Overall	91
Speed	84
Awareness	85
Tackle	87
Hit Power	88

#23 Quentin Jammer
Cornerback (CB)

Overall	87
Speed	89
Awareness	82
Man Coverage	92
Zone Coverage	87

DEFENSIVE STRENGTH CHART

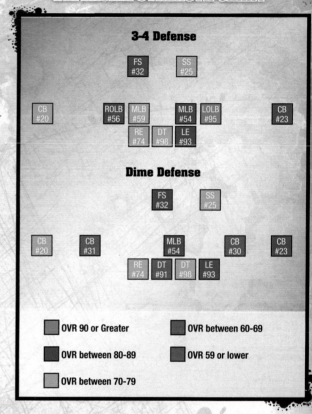

3-4 Defense

FS #32 | SS #25

CB #20 | ROLB #56 | MLB #59 | MLB #54 | LOLB #95 | CB #23
RE #74 | DT #98 | LE #93

Dime Defense

FS #32 | SS #25

CB #20 | CB #31 | MLB #54 | CB #30 | CB #23
RE #74 | DT #91 | DT #98 | LE #93

- ■ OVR 90 or Greater
- ■ OVR between 80-89
- ■ OVR between 70-79
- ■ OVR between 60-69
- ■ OVR 59 or lower

Key Player Substitutions

Position: HB

Substitution: Jacob Hester

When: Deep passing situations

Advantage: Because of the small size of the Chargers running backs, you should bring in Hester to help with any extra rushers that may get through the line. Hester has the size and the strength to slow down anyone coming through.

Key Player Substitutions

Position: DT

Substitution: Cam Thomas

When: Short yardage plays

Advantage: When you are trying to get your defense off the field and your opponent is pounding the ball up the middle play after play, bring in Thomas. His added weight on the offensive line could be enough to stop them.

Playbook Breakdown

The San Diego Chargers are a high-powered offensive team. They have talent all over the field on offense and can literally beat a defense at every offensive position. When using the San Diego Chargers playbook, take into account that the book is designed for an athletic team. That's not to say that other teams don't have athletes, but the Chargers have exceptional talent at their skill positions.

The Chargers playbook is very balanced. Where most playbooks are heavy in one area of passing, the Chargers are evenly spread between standard, shotgun, and play action passes. This makes it hard for a defense to get a feel for what could be coming.

When it comes to the running game, the Chargers are top-heavy in the inside running game. This is also an asset because some of the best running plays in *Madden NFL* start off inside and then break to the outside. Because the Chargers drafted rookie running back Ryan Mathews, they don't lose any talent at the running back position. Even though he isn't L.T., he looks to be a reasonable substitute.

OFFENSIVE FORMATIONS

FORMATION	# OF PLAYS
Gun Doubles	15
Gun Split Slot	12
Gun Split Y-Flex	12
Gun Spread Y-Slot	15
Gun Y-Trips Open	15
I-Form Pro	18
I-Form Tight Pair	12
Singleback Ace	15
Singleback Bunch	15
Singleback Doubles	15
Singleback F Wing	15
Singleback Wing Trio	12
Strong Pro	18
Strong Pro Twins	15
Weak Pro Twins	15
Weak Tight Pair	12

OFFENSIVE PLAYCOUNTS

PLAY TYPE	# OF PLAYS
Quick Pass	13
Standard Pass	48
Shotgun Pass	43
Play Action Pass	50
Inside Handoff	32
Outside Handoff	19
Pitch	5
Counter	7

Singleback F Wing—F Weak Lead

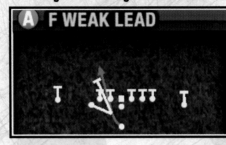

The San Diego Chargers let Tomlinson go over this off-season and looked to the NFL Draft to replace him. Rookie running back Ryan Mathews is a solid young player and has good agility, but he's even better at breaking tackles. We head to the Singleback F Wing—F Weak Lead to showcase our new running back and let our team and fans get behind him.

The fullback sets a key block

The use of automotion with a run play can be a problem at times, but if we mix similar automotion plays together then the defense won't have the chance to get a free pre-snap read on what we're trying to do. On this particular run, we look for the block that the fullback throws, which determines where we run.

House call!

The fullback picks up two blocks on the play and is the sole reason why we're able to take this rushing play to the house. This is also a perfect option for beating a blitzing defense and breaking their spirit early on in the game.

Singleback Wing Trio—Four Verticals

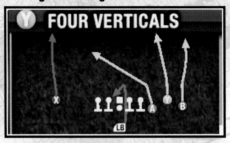

It is necessary to attack the defense down the field when using a team like the Chargers. The size of their receivers alone justifies throwing deep on every play. We like to run Four Verticals because of how easy it makes our pre-snap reads of the defensive coverage. No matter what the defense does, they have to align their safeties, and when they do, we will know which receiver to go to.

The safety has no help underneath

When we set the play in motion, we immediately locate the safety and determine how he is dropping into coverage. He is playing our tight end running the post route pretty well, but without any protection underneath we have a clear passing lane to get the ball to our premier tight end. We will not always be able to go to the tight end, but the safety will always show us the open route.

Gates is a clutch receiver in traffic

The decision to throw the ball to our Pro Bowl tight end was an easy one. The safety broke to play the post, but because of his depth and the lack of coverage underneath him, we were able to go to our tight end. We also had the flanker wide open on the sideline, but we took the easy throw to the post. Always take the smart option.

Strong Pro Twins—Deep Comeback

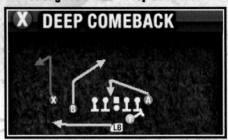

The Strong Pro Twins—Deep Comeback is a solid play to use to help our offense beat an opponent who likes to play with an outside linebacker or safety. The combination of a comeback, post, and flat route can be a little too much for the defense, even when another person is in control of the defense. This play also gives us a route that we have found to be a true quick-pass option.

Here comes the linebacker

When we hike the ball and start the play, we see that the defense is bringing the cornerback and the linebacker on the play. We know that we can hit our split end on his hook route, but we saw the defense drop a defender in a curl/flat zone on the same side. Not to worry—we have our tight end running a spot route just behind the linebackers.

Gates is in the clear

We can use the spot route to the tight end as a quick-pass option as in previous versions of *Madden NFL*. When we see the blitz we immediately pass the ball to the tight end. This can be done faster than you can even picture it. The timing is hike, pass. The tight end is able to slip right by the linebacker and turn downfield right away for more yards.

Weak Tight Pair—HB Power O

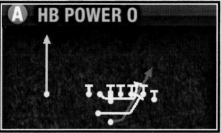

Gun Doubles—Drag Under

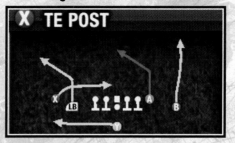

Singleback Doubles—TE Post

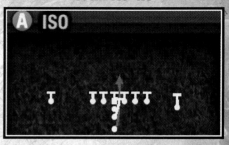

I-Form Pro—Iso

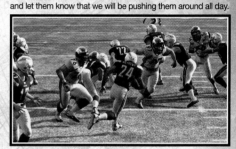

Some of the most memorable moments of a football game come when it looks like everything that could go wrong does, but somehow something amazing comes from the play. Nothing is unexpected in football if you prepare well. The Weak Tight Pair—HB Power O is a play that allows us to put our running backs in position to achieve greatness, but sometimes looking at the way they go about achieving it is a thing of beauty.

Our rookie running back surveys the field

We like this play because of the automotion of the fullback. When the fullback is in position, the blocking we have on this HB Power O play is phenomenal. We have the outside shoulder of the defensive end and the outside linebacker. There is no way for the defense to try to stop our running game if they give us their outside shoulder for us to seal them inside with.

Keep the legs pumping

Rookie running back Ryan Mathews is a stud when running the ball between the tackles. His ability to keep a run alive by pumping his legs is an asset to our offense whenever he runs the ball. If he runs into a defender downfield, there is a strong possibility that he will be able to fight through that tackle and keep churning toward the end zone.

One of the most powerful passing plays in *Madden NFL 11* is in the Gun Doubles formation. The Drag Under has been a dominant force in *Madden NFL* for the past several seasons, and when used with the personnel of the Chargers, this play can be outright scary for a defense. We like to run it with a little motion to help enhance its effectiveness.

No trailing defender signals zone coverage

By putting the flanker in motion before we hike the ball, we get a pre-snap read of the defense and determine that they are in zone coverage. Anything that we can do to help make a quicker decision post-snap will make our offense much more efficient.

Wide open in the flat

The defenders did not come up to play our flanker, and at the start of the play they ran out to cover the deep zones. Our quarterback sees that the defense is not playing anything up front so we decide to throw the ball to our running back in the flat. The closest defender is 20 yards downfield, so this makes the flat throw the best option on the field.

The Gun Doubles and Singleback Doubles are two interchangeable formations. The TE Post lets us take advantage of our great tight end. This play can also be a way to showcase other receivers. We have multiple routes on this play that can damage a defense. The slot receiver is running a corner route and the flanker is running a streak. Consider the size of the Chargers' receivers along with these routes and we have a recipe for success.

Hike the ball when the receiver clears the tight end

We like to make one adjustment on this play and that is to hot route the split end to run a slant and then send him in motion across the formation. Once the split end reaches the tight end, we hike the ball.

Our receiver makes the catch and benefits from a downfield block

By changing the drag route of the split end to a slant, we get an additional step of separation and sling the pass out to him so that he can pick up some quick yards for us. This route works well with the streak by the flanker, who, as soon as we catch the ball, becomes a downfield blocker for us to use.

There is nothing like a good old power running play. Line our best up against their best and let's see who comes out on top. This play allows us to impose our physical will on the defense and let them know that we will be pushing them around all day.

Even though it looks congested we are in control

We enjoy running the Iso because no matter what the defense does, we normally have enough time to make a move and separate from any defenders in pursuit. This can become extremely frustrating for an opponent because every time they get close we are still a step or two just beyond their reach.

The back is already to the third level of the defense

The Chargers playbook features 32 inside handoff running plays. That means the defense will try to collapse the middle of our line in an effort to stop us from gaining yards. With good vision, we're able to overcome the defense and get our running back around the edge of the defense and heading upfield. The I-Form Pro—Iso gives us the opportunity to hit the defense for chunks of yards at a time.

KANSAS CITY CHIEFS

OFFENSIVE SCOUTING REPORT

The Chiefs realized last year that simply adding a talented QB wouldn't magically fix the offense. It would take much longer to get QB Matt Cassel comfortable behind the wheel. Cassel, however, has proved that he can lead the team to victory behind good awareness and precision passing. He's not the most agile QB on his feet, but he's a true pocket passer, making him a great complement to the Chiefs' improved running game. Luckily, Cassel has the services of reliable and sticky-handed WR Dwayne Bowe at his disposal. And 2009's late addition of Chris Chambers proved to be genius as he was a contributor to the offense from the get-go. While the offensive line's pass-blocking leaves something to be desired, the Chiefs have a surprisingly serviceable running game. Emerging running back Jamaal Charles is joined by Thomas Jones to create a serious one-two punch in the backfield. While Jones pounds away to get the tough yardage between the tackles, Charles will provide the high-geared shiftiness to keep defenders guessing.

DEFENSIVE SCOUTING REPORT

Defensively, the Chiefs have not made many changes, save the addition of top-rated safety Eric Berry. That's not to say they're not improving; quite the contrary, the Chiefs have spent the last few seasons piecing together a young defense. This year all those pieces become one defensive unit living up to its potential. Defensive ends Tyson Jackson and Glenn Dorsey return as starters, not as the highest rated, but proficient enough to get the job done, while OLB Tamba Hali's pass-rushing hopefully eases some of the pressure. When acquiring Matt Cassel, the Chiefs also picked up Mike Vrabel, a Pro Bowl–caliber linebacker. Though Vrabel has the skill and knowledge to excel, it is Demorrio Williams who has really begun to shine in the linebacker unit. He is faster and more agile than Vrabel and able to provide more field coverage.

TEAM RATING

71
Overall

KEY ADDITIONS

RB	Thomas Jones
G	Ryan Lilja
DT	Shaun Smith
WR	Jerheme Urban
C	Casey Wiegmann
FS	Eric Berry

KEY DEPARTURES

G	Andy Alleman
S	Mike Brown
TE	Sean Ryan
OL	Wade Smith
WR	Bobby Wade

RATINGS BY POSITION

Position	Rating		Position	Rating
Quarterbacks	78		Defensive Tackles	74
Halfbacks	87		Outside Linebackers	79
Fullbacks	70		Middle Linebackers	82
Wide Receivers	79		Cornerbacks	79
Tight Ends	75		Free Safeties	84
Tackles	77		Strong Safeties	78
Guards	84		Kickers	79
Centers	71		Punters	91
Defensive Ends	77			

DEPTH CHART

POS	OVR	FIRST NAME	LAST NAME
C	85	Casey	Wiegmann
C	71	Rudy	Niswanger
CB	85	Brandon	Flowers
CB	72	Brandon	Carr
CB	71	Javier	Arenas
CB	67	Mike	Richardson
CB	63	Maurice	Leggett
DT	74	Ron	Edwards
DT	72	Shaun	Smith
DT	58	Dion	Gales
FB	70	Mike	Cox
FS	84	Eric	Berry
FS	68	Jon	McGraw
HB	88	Thomas	Jones
HB	87	Jamaal	Charles
HB	68	Kolby	Smith
HB	65	Jackie	Battle
K	79	Ryan	Succop
LE	75	Tyson	Jackson
LE	61	Wallace	Gilberry
LG	85	Brian	Waters
LG	75	Jon	Asamoah
LOLB	77	Mike	Vrabel
LOLB	69	Andy	Studebaker
LOLB	59	Cameron	Sheffield
LT	78	Branden	Albert
LT	68	Barry	Richardson
MLB	82	Demorrio	Williams
MLB	76	Derrick	Johnson
MLB	71	Corey	Mays
MLB	65	Jovan	Belcher
P	91	Dustin	Colquitt
QB	78	Matt	Cassel
QB	65	Brodie	Croyle
QB	58	Matt	Gutierrez
RE	78	Glenn	Dorsey
RE	66	Alex	Magee
RG	82	Ryan	Lilja
RG	56	Colin	Brown
ROLB	80	Tamba	Hali
ROLB	59	Pierre	Walters
RT	76	Ryan	O'Callaghan
RT	68	Ike	Ndukwe
SS	78	Jarrad	Page
SS	67	DaJuan	Morgan
TE	75	Leonard	Pope
TE	69	Tony	Moeaki
TE	66	Brad	Cottam
WR	84	Dwayne	Bowe
WR	82	Chris	Chambers
WR	70	Jerheme	Urban
WR	66	Terrance	Copper
WR	51	Quinten	Lawrence

OFFENSIVE STRENGTH CHART

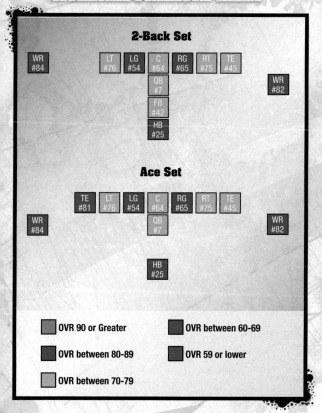

2-Back Set

| WR #84 | | LT #76 | LG #54 | C #64 | RG #65 | RT #75 | TE #45 | | WR #82 |

QB #7
FB #42
HB #25

Ace Set

| TE #81 | LT #76 | LG #54 | C #64 | RG #65 | RT #75 | TE #45 |
WR #84
WR #82

QB #7

HB #25

- OVR 90 or Greater
- OVR between 80-89
- OVR between 70-79
- OVR between 60-69
- OVR 59 or lower

#20 Thomas Jones
Halfback (HB)

Overall	88
Speed	87
Agility	87
Stiff Arm	85
Carrying	95

#25 Jamaal Charles
Halfback (HB)

Overall	87
Speed	97
Agility	96
Stiff Arm	66
Carrying	76

#82 Dwayne Bowe
Wide Receiver (WR)

Overall	84
Speed	86
Catching	81
Release	96
Jumping	96

#24 Brandon Flowers
Cornerback (CB)

Overall	85
Speed	86
Awareness	79
Man Coverage	87
Zone Coverage	88

#29 Eric Berry
Free Safety (FS)

Overall	84
Speed	92
Awareness	55
Tackle	52
Hit Power	90

#53 Demorrio Williams
Linebacker (MLB)

Overall	82
Speed	80
Awareness	86
Tackle	95
Hit Power	74

DEFENSIVE STRENGTH CHART

3-4 Defense

FS #29   SS #44

| CB #39 | | ROLB #91 | MLB #51 | | MLB #53 | LOLB #50 | | CB #24 |

RE #72   DT #95   LE #94

Dime Defense

FS #29   SS #44

| CB #39 | CB #30 | | MLB #53 | | CB #23 | CB #24 |

RE #72   DT #90   DT #95   LE #94

- OVR 90 or Greater
- OVR between 80-89
- OVR between 70-79
- OVR between 60-69
- OVR 59 or lower

Key Player Substitutions

Position: HB

Substitution: Jamaal Charles

When: Global

Advantage: Jamaal Charles is one of the fastest halfbacks in the NFL. Run sweep plays for him and watch him eat up the sidelines with huge runs. Try to avoid huge hits and you should have a great running game.

Key Player Substitutions

Position: MLB

Substitution: Derrick Johnson

When: Global

Advantage: The defense has to have stops for their team to win games, so look to play Johnson more at the middle linebacker spot. His ability to cover receivers in the middle of the field is an added bonus.

Playbook Breakdown

The talent in the NFL is equal in many ways; however, some teams don't perform as well as others. That doesn't mean they are any less talented. The Kansas City Chiefs are in a rebuilding process as far as talent goes, but they have playmakers scattered throughout their roster. As a coach, sitting back to look over this team, you see that you need to feature running back Jamaal Charles. He not only is an asset in the run game but also can help bolster the passing game.

When it comes to the passing game, the Chiefs are led by receiver Dwayne Bowe. At 6'2", Bowe is a good target for the jump ball and has the ratings to prove that he is more than capable of carrying the load for us. The Chiefs also have big tight ends, and they can help add to the passing game by catching or adding protection on the line. The key to using the Chiefs is a solid game plan and fundamental football. We will make sure you have a solid foundation to build upon.

OFFENSIVE FORMATIONS

FORMATION	# OF PLAYS
Full House Normal Wide	9
Gun Doubles	15
Gun Empty Base	9
Gun Split Y-Flex	12
Gun Spread	18
Gun Trips HB Wk	9
Gun Wing Trips Wk	12
I-Form Pro	12
I-Form Tight	12
Singleback Ace	15
Singleback Ace Pair Twins	12
Singleback Bunch	15
Singleback Doubles	15
Singleback Y-Trips	18
Strong Pro	18
Weak Normal	9
Weak Twins Flex	9
Wildcat Chief	3

OFFENSIVE PLAYCOUNTS

PLAY TYPE	# OF PLAYS
Quick Pass	14
Standard Pass	40
Shotgun Pass	47
Play Action Pass	42
Outside Handoff	16
Pitch	10
Counter	7
Draw	9

Strong Pro—Power O

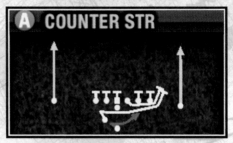

Jamaal Charles is our workhorse and we have no problem feeding him the ball over and over again. With a 97 speed rating, Charles is in the neighborhood of the fastest players in *Madden NFL 11,* and all we need is a tiny crease to get him through and off to the races. We will use the Strong Pro—Power O to give him an opportunity to shine.

The fullback gives us a little daylight

The key to success running the ball is making sure you trust the design of the play. If the play diagram says to run the ball tight to the C gap, then do that. We don't want to get into a habit of taking every run to the sideline and avoiding the blocking scheme of the running play.

The running back doesn't get touched until he's 5 yards downfield

We power forward for a gain of 7 yards on the running play, just by using pure fundamentals. The benefit of using a team that is not rated as high as others is that it forces you to play pure football. When you have to play smart to win, it makes *Madden NFL 11* feel like a real football game and not a video game.

Weak Normal—Counter Str

Make sure you have some virtual fluids for the running back because we're going to run and run and run some more. The Weak Normal—Counter Str pulls the strong-side guard around the edge so he can help with paving an outside running lane for our back. The extra blocking can make it extremely difficult for those scraping linebackers trying to come down the line to make a play.

Both the FB and RG pull on this play

We have the benefit of having both the fullback and right guard pulling on this play. If the defense tries to shoot through the interior of our line, the fullback will be the first to know and he will turn and seal the defender. These counter plays are very effective when used with a fast running back like Jamaal Charles.

The inside is sealed off

Once the right guard comes around the edge and the flanker throws a block on the outside linebacker, we have the green light to the end zone. With a 97 speed rating and a 96 agility rating, even our user control of the running back is enhanced. Use the right thumbstick Locomotion features to juke or dip the back's shoulder to get around a defender.

Singleback Y-Trips—WR Screen

We have two dominant players on our offense. Running back Jamaal Charles is one go-to player for us, and the other is wide receiver Dwayne Bowe. If we plan on moving the ball successfully on offense and sustaining drives then we need to make sure we get the ball in the hands of our stud receiver as well. No offense is good when it is playing one-dimensionally.

Alert, alert, alert, check screen

Whenever the defense comes to the field and leaves our slot uncovered to the flanker side when we are in the Y-Trips, then the screen is a must. If the defense doesn't have a man over top of our slot receiver, then when the slot goes to seal the cornerback we will have an inside line to get down the field with.

Great block by the slot receiver

The Raiders' All-Pro cornerback does not like getting beat, but because of the lack of help to this side of the formation our slot is able to eliminate him from the play. Our receiver takes the catch and turns downfield to pick up more yards. With additional blockers downfield we gain a first down from the catch and run.

I-Form Pro—Bench

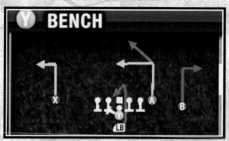

Another play that we like to use when in the Chiefs playbook is the I-Form Pro—Bench. This is a favorite play of many user catchers because the out routes by the flanker and split end are easy to control. We look at this play as an option to get our primary receiver the ball. If we can make the defense see our primary receiver as a threat, it will open up additional opportunities around the field.

The quarterback is reading the coverage

The I-Form Pro—Bench uses a five-step drop by the quarterback. While the quarterback is dropping back, we're scanning the defensive coverage and looking to see if the defense has any defenders sitting in the underneath zone. If the defense leaves the shallow zone clear then we can throw the ball to either the split end or the flanker on their out routes.

You can't defend on your knees

We pass the ball to the flanker just before he breaks on his out route. While the ball is still in the air, we press the Switch Player button to take control of our receiver. With a little bit of practice, you will be able to take control of your receiver, turn him around, and make him aggressively pursue the ball. It is fine to let the computer catch the ball for you, but the higher the level of competition, the less computer assistance you can rely on.

I-Form Tight—Mesh

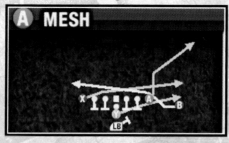

As we beat the defense with our running back and primary receiver they will start to adjust and try to take those players away from us. The Chiefs drafted a good tight end this year in the third round. Tight end Tony Moeaki has an 81 speed rating and can really help our offense out by forcing the defense to account for another target.

The tight end and flanker are running dual crossing routes

The I-Form Tight—Mesh is one of our plays of choice because it allows us to get both of our tight ends on the field and use them in the passing game. We have a tight end running a corner route and our second string tight end running the crossing route. A tight end with an 81 speed rating can control the underneath parts of the defense's coverage.

Perfect spacing

Initially the flanker starts out in automotion, and then when the ball is hiked, he takes off running a crossing route. We see that the defense didn't follow the flanker, so we know they are in zone. Our quarterback rolled out to the right to stretch the zone and then threw the ball to the second string tight end, who was wide open behind the defense's zone.

Gun Split Y-Flex—Scissors Flats

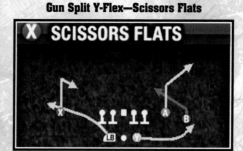

It wouldn't be fair if we left out the quarterback of the team in all of our talk. The Chiefs are led by Matt Cassel, whose success in New England landed him a starting job for the Chiefs last year. We know that Cassel is a solid quarterback when he works from the Gun formations. We look to the Gun Split Y-Flex—Scissors Flats to help our quarterback establish a rhythm and display why he is the leader of the team.

We have options; they will pay for blitzing us

We enjoy running the Scissors Flats because of the protection we have with a split back formation and also because both backs release into the flats and give us quick options vs. the blitz. As soon as the ball is hiked the defense sends a defensive end in on a blitz, but we're not fazed at all because we have a back releasing to the flat.

We deliver a strike to the flanker

Instead of taking the dump-off pass to the back in the flat, we decide to hit the defense for a substantial gain downfield. Many opponents will send pressure, but the pressure is only good if it reaches our quarterback. As long as we have plays like the Gun Split Y-Flex—Scissors Flats then we will always be poised in the pocket.

Gun Trips HB Wk—Curls

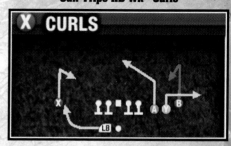

We have presented our running back as a real threat to the defense and have also shown the defense that we can beat them with our tight end and wide receiver. The Gun Trips HB Wk—Curls is the play we use to merge all of these components together and see how much of a nightmare we can be for the defense.

Jamaal Charles is releasing to the flat

We know for a fact that the defense has to respect the speed and pass catching ability of our running back out of the backfield. If they don't, it can cost them seven quick points. We will use this fear as a way to beat the defense and control the adjustments they can make. As soon as they start adjusting to take away the running back, we will have the entire field at our disposal.

The slot receiver is open down the middle

Our opponent recognized the threat of our running back releasing into a pass route and brought a safety down to keep him from gashing the defense. The problem with that is, we have our slot receiver running a post route and as soon as we saw the safety come up on the running back, we let our slot receiver break inside and hit him with a perfect pass down the middle of the field for a touchdown.

INDIANAPOLIS COLTS

OFFENSIVE SCOUTING REPORT

If there is only one word to describe the Colts, it is "consistent." They have reached the playoffs in eight straight years, a league best. The successes, of course, ride on the shoulders of four-time MVP Peyton Manning. It simply does not get much better than Peyton in almost every aspect of the position, especially when it comes to accuracy and running out of the play action pass. The riches of such a great quarterback fall into the laps of his two favorite targets, WR Reggie Wayne and TE Dallas Clark. While many receivers are technically faster than Wayne, it is hard to find one with better hands and ability to catch the ball in stride thanks to the accuracy of Manning. Dallas Clark excels in route running and sniffing out an opening in the red zone to get his sure hands on the ball. Jeff Saturday, the long-time veteran, leads the pass protection on the offensive line and gives Peyton the time he needs in the pocket. If there is a weakness to the offensive machine, it is the run game, but that is more victim of the pass-first philosophy than the talent at the running back position. Joseph Addai and Donald Brown combine for good speed out of the backfield, but also provide another set of hands should Manning need an outlet. Addai is the more elusive and skilled back, but Brown provides the power that Addai lacks.

DEFENSIVE SCOUTING REPORT

Robert Mathis and Dwight Freeney are the most lethal duo of ends in the NFL, making it unsafe for any quarterback lining up for the snap. These two are the foundation of the Colts defense as they are the first line of defense against the run and are relentless at quarterback pressure. The linebacker unit is led by Gary Brackett, a master at play recognition and pursuit, and OLB Clint Session provides the speed against anyone fortunate enough to break through the line. The secondary is filled with strong talent, including a pair of equally fast corners in Kelvin Hayden and Jerraud Powers. Bob Sanders at safety rounds out the depth in the backfield and helps crash the field to help the rush defense, the one area where the Colts have struggled a bit. Teams that find how to beat Freeney and Mathis at the line can find a full day of rushing success against the Colts, so the linebackers with the help of Sanders will need to be on their game.

TEAM RATING

91
Overall

KEY ADDITIONS

G	Andy Alleman
T	Adam Terry
DE	Jerry Hughes

KEY DEPARTURES

DE	Raheem Brock
LB	Freddy Keiaho
LB	Tyjuan Hagler
FS	Marlin Jackson
CB	Tim Jennings
K	Matt Stover

RATINGS BY POSITION

Quarterbacks	99	Defensive Tackles	78
Halfbacks	86	Outside Linebackers	75
Fullbacks	70	Middle Linebackers	87
Wide Receivers	84	Cornerbacks	83
Tight Ends	96	Free Safeties	95
Tackles	84	Strong Safeties	89
Guards	74	Kickers	82
Centers	92	Punters	77
Defensive Ends	96		

DEPTH CHART

POS	OVR	FIRST NAME	LAST NAME
C	92	Jeff	Saturday
C	71	Andy	Alleman
CB	85	Kelvin	Hayden
CB	81	Jerraud	Powers
CB	71	Jacob	Lacey
CB	65	Kevin	Thomas
CB	60	Terrail	Lambert
DT	78	Antonio	Johnson
DT	75	Daniel	Muir
DT	71	Eric	Foster
DT	66	Fili	Moala
FB	70	Gijon	Robinson
FB	68	Jacob	Tamme
FS	95	Antoine	Bethea
HB	86	Joseph	Addai
HB	78	Donald	Brown
HB	65	Mike	Hart
HB	59	Devin	Moore
K	82	Adam	Vinatieri
LE	95	Robert	Mathis
LE	73	Keyunta	Dawson
LE	64	Ervin	Baldwin
LG	76	Mike	Pollak
LG	71	Jamey	Richard
LOLB	70	Philip	Wheeler
LOLB	46	Cody	Glenn
LT	83	Charlie	Johnson
LT	72	Tony	Ugoh
MLB	87	Gary	Brackett
MLB	66	Pat	Angerer
P	77	Pat	McAfee
QB	99	Peyton	Manning
QB	61	Curtis	Painter
RG	72	Kyle	DeVan
RG	62	Jaimie	Thomas
ROLB	80	Clint	Session
ROLB	54	Ramon	Humber
ROLB	50	Brandon	Renkart
RT	85	Ryan	Diem
RT	72	Adam	Terry
SS	89	Bob	Sanders
SS	79	Melvin	Bullitt
SS	65	Jamie	Silva
TE	96	Dallas	Clark
TE	76	Tom	Santi
TE	66	Brody	Eldridge
WR	96	Reggie	Wayne
WR	80	Pierre	Garcon
WR	76	Austin	Collie
WR	75	Anthony	Gonzalez
WR	66	Samuel	Giguere

OFFENSIVE STRENGTH CHART

2-Back Set

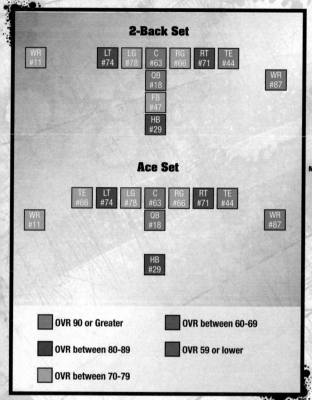

WR #11 | LT #74 | LG #78 | C #63 | RG #66 | RT #71 | TE #44 | WR #87
QB #18
FB #47
HB #29

Ace Set

TE #86 | LT #74 | LG #78 | C #63 | RG #66 | RT #71 | TE #44
WR #11 | WR #87
QB #18
HB #29

- ■ OVR 90 or Greater
- ■ OVR between 80-89
- ■ OVR between 70-79
- ■ OVR between 60-69
- ■ OVR 59 or lower

Key Player Substitutions

Position: HB

Substitution: Devin Moore

When: Screen plays

Advantage: When teams are blitzing you up the middle a lot, try hitting them with a screen play. With Moore's speed all he needs is a few lead blockers, and you could be looking at a TD.

#18 Peyton Manning
Quarterback (QB)

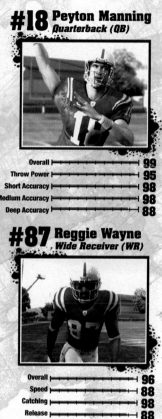

Overall	99
Throw Power	95
Short Accuracy	98
Medium Accuracy	98
Deep Accuracy	88

#87 Reggie Wayne
Wide Receiver (WR)

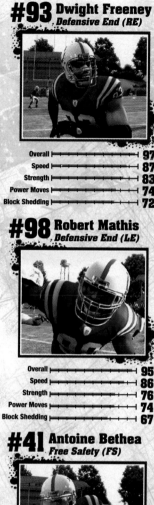

Overall	96
Speed	88
Catching	98
Release	88
Jumping	88

#44 Dallas Clark
Tight End (TE)

Overall	96
Speed	87
Catching	97
Catch in Traffic	88
Jumping	82

#93 Dwight Freeney
Defensive End (RE)

Overall	97
Speed	87
Strength	83
Power Moves	74
Block Shedding	72

#98 Robert Mathis
Defensive End (LE)

Overall	95
Speed	86
Strength	76
Power Moves	74
Block Shedding	67

#41 Antoine Bethea
Free Safety (FS)

Overall	95
Speed	89
Awareness	85
Tackle	82
Play Recognition	84

DEFENSIVE STRENGTH CHART

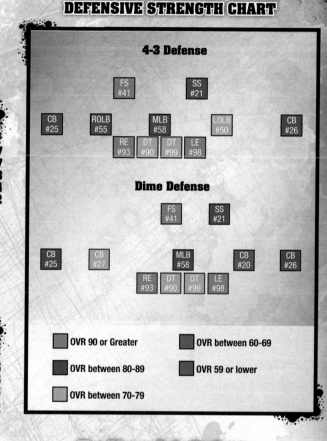

4-3 Defense

FS #41 | SS #21
CB #25 | ROLB #55 | MLB #58 | LOLB #50 | CB #26
RE #93 | DT #90 | DT #99 | LE #98

Dime Defense

FS #41 | SS #21
CB #25 | CB #27 | MLB #58 | CB #20 | CB #26
RE #93 | DT #90 | DT #99 | LE #98

- ■ OVR 90 or Greater
- ■ OVR between 80-89
- ■ OVR between 70-79
- ■ OVR between 60-69
- ■ OVR 59 or lower

Key Player Substitutions

Position: DE

Substitution: Keyunta Dawson

When: Covering the flats

Advantage: If you keep getting beaten in the flats, look to bring Dawson in to better match up in the field, but don't forget to get Mathis back in when you can.

Team Strategy

One of the most the explosive offenses in the league over the last decade deserves to have an explosive playbook represented in *Madden NFL 11*. That's exactly what the Colts playbook is in this year's game—explosive. There are several formations and plays that can make even the most novice of *Madden NFL* players feel like they know how to run a real NFL offense. Formations such as Singleback Deuce, Singleback Dice Slot, Gun Deuce Trips, and Gun Bunch TE all have explosive plays inside them to put points on the board. For those looking to run plays in traditional formations such as the I-Form, Strong, and Weak, this playbook is not for you—the Colts don't utilize the fullback all that much. Most of the formations in the playbook are from the Singleback and Gun. Many of the plays found in those formations are specifically designed for the Colts offense based on the EA SPORTS playbook team spending countless hours watching game-play footage. Give this playbook a try and you will find yourself scoring points in bunches.

OFFENSIVE FORMATIONS

FORMATION	# OF PLAYS
Full House Normal Wide	9
Gun Bunch TE	12
Gun Deuce Trips	12
Gun Dice Slot	24
Gun Dice Slot Wk	21
Gun Empty Trey	9
Gun Split Flex	12
Gun Trips Wk	21
I-Form Tight	12
Singleback Bunch	12
Singleback Deuce	21
Singleback Deuce Slot	18
Singleback Dice Slot	24
Singleback Trips Colt	18

OFFENSIVE PLAYCOUNTS

PLAY TYPE	# OF PLAYS
Quick Pass	9
Standard Pass	36
Shotgun Pass	79
Play Action Pass	38
Outside Handoff	12
Pitch	4
Counter	3
Draw	8

Playbook Breakdown

Singleback Deuce—PA Colt Seam

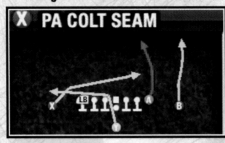

The Colts are one of the best teams at utilizing the play action pass. Trigger man Peyton Manning is a master at the play fake, despite the Colts having an average rushing attack. One of the staple plays that the Colts run is the PA Colt Seam.

Manning masterfully play fakes to Addai

The play's primary receiver is tight end Dallas Clark, who runs a seam route. If Cover 2 zone coverage is called, he is the best option to throw the ball to. If man coverage is called, the split end running the crossing route should be your first read and option. With Clark and Wayne both running streaks down the right hash mark and right sideline, the middle of the field will be open for Anthony Gonzalez to get open as he runs his route underneath them both.

Manning spots Wayne as he comes across the middle

If for some reason he is not open, then look for running back Joseph Addai in the flat. To make this play even more effective, run the HB Dive play from the same formation. It will force your opponent to defend it, which will open more passing lanes to attack.

Singleback Dice Slot—Stretch

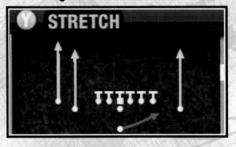

The Singleback Dice Slot—Stretch is a staple running play for the Colts, not only because it works, but also because it sets up the play action bootleg passing game that quarterback Peyton Manning uses so effectively. Stretch runs incorporate zone blocking, which has become increasingly popular on the pro levels over the last several years.

Addai looks to get outside quickly

You see teams abandoning the power run game in order to employ more zone-blocking schemes in their ground attack. The beauty of zone blocking is that it incorporates as many double teams as possible.

A few key blocks are thrown to spring Addai

This makes it a lot easier for Joseph Addai to make it to the outside, because even a good run-stopping defender who has outside containment responsibility will have to beat a double-team block to blow the play up in the backfield. Stretch runs have a longer handoff than other runs to give the play time to develop, and during that time the line throws multiple double-team blocks. Offensive linemen or tight ends move off of the double-team blocks and go up to the second level, allowing the ball carrier to pick up additional yardage.

Gun Split Flex—Colts HB Wheel

A good pass play to get the running back isolated in one-on-one coverage deep down the field is the Gun Split Flex—Colts HB Wheel. This play has running back Joseph Addai running a wheel route out of the backfield down the left sideline. If the defense comes out in Cover 0 or Cover 1, this play is effective, provided you have enough time to wait for Addai to get open.

The FS is locked in man coverage on Addai

Working underneath Addai is split end Reggie Wayne, who runs a spot route. Look for him if Addai doesn't look like he is going to be open based on what the coverage dictates. On the other side, slot receiver Pierre Garcon is running a seam route while Anthony Gonzalez runs a fade.

Manning throws a perfect ball for his receiver

If the defense plays Cover 2 zone, one of those two receivers will be an option to throw to based on where the strong safety plays. Tight end Dallas Clark lines up in the backfield off to the right side of Peyton Manning. He runs a delayed curl route and is the play's check-down receiver.

Gun Dice Slot—PA Colts Seams

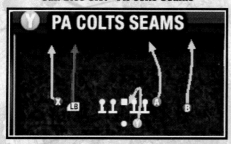

The Gun Dice Slot—PA Colts Seams is an excellent vertical passing concept that can be found in the Indianapolis Colts playbook. This play sends four receivers deep to vertically stretch the coverage. If the defense plays Cover 2 or Cover 3, at least one of the four receivers should be open.

Manning drops back and deciphers the pass coverage

As with any vertical stretch passing concept, the offensive line must give the quarterback time to throw the ball. To help buy Peyton Manning that extra time, play action has been added to slow down the pass rush. If Cover 2 zone coverage is called, watch for one of the outside receivers to be open once they break the press at the line of scrimmage.

Clark goes up and snags the pass between the safeties

Tight end Dallas Clark may also be an option as his seam route has him drifting towards the deep middle of the field. If Cover 3 coverage is called, look for Anthony Gonzalez down the left side running the fade route or else hit Clark down the seam. If you decide to throw to Clark, the passing window is not very big because the ball needs to be thrown underneath the deep coverage.

Gun Dice Slot Wk—Switch

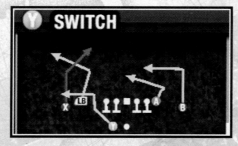

Many offensive coordinators design passing concepts and route combinations to attack both man and zone coverage within the same play. The Colts playbook has several plays that do just that. A good example is the Gun Dice Slot Wk—Switch.

The FS drops over the deep middle, telling Manning Cover 3 is called

On the left side of the field, split end Reggie Wayne and slot receiver Pierre Garcon run a fork concept that attacks deep zone coverage. Wayne runs a post, while Garcon runs a corner. The read is simple to make: If the middle of the field is open, the ball should be thrown to Wayne on the deep post. If the middle of the field is closed, then the ball should be thrown to Garcon.

Manning spots Garcon open on the corner route

If man coverage is called, tight end Dallas Clark should be the first read as he runs the shake route over the middle of the field.

Gun Deuce Trips—Colts Clearout

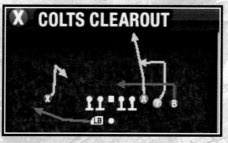

If you are looking for a low-risk passing play to beat zone coverage with, the Gun Deuce Trips—Colts Clearout is a rock solid choice. This play has flanker Reggie Wayne running an in route as the play's primary receiver. The play is designed to have two other routes clear out the underneath pass coverage to allow Wayne to get open for a high percentage pass.

Wayne works underneath the zone coverage to get open

Those two routes are run by the two tight ends that are in the formation. Tight end Dallas Clark lines up on the slot and runs a 10-yard dig route. Tight end Tom Santi runs a seam route. Once the ball is snapped, these two routes drive the zone coverage back, allowing Wayne to work underneath the zone coverage and get open.

Manning throws a strike as Wayne makes his cut underneath the coverage

Peyton Manning's laser accuracy makes this play that much more effective, because his passes are almost always on target. If for some reason Wayne is not open, running back Joseph Addai runs a delayed flat route and is a good choice to at least pick up some yardage.

Gun Bunch TE—Indy Bunch

Another excellent passing play found exclusively in the Colts playbook is the Gun Bunch TE—Indy Bunch. This play abuses pretty much any zone coverage in game by having Anthony Gonzalez get open underneath. His pass route is the first level of the play's design.

Gonzalez uses his route-running ability to get loose underneath

Pierre Garcon is the play's primary receiver. His in route is the second-level route in the play's design. The third-level route is run by Reggie Wayne, who runs a 10-yard in route. Those who like to run the Levels passing concept will feel right at home with this play since it works pretty much the same, except it's run from a Bunch (cluster) formation. Your first read should be Gonzalez.

Manning rifles the football right towards Gonzalez

If you throw to him, expect to pick up 4–6 yards. If you'd rather pick up more yardage, look for Garcon. His route is good for 6–8 yards. Both routes are solid choices when it comes to beating zone coverage. If man coverage is called, Garcon is the best choice to throw to.

DALLAS COWBOYS

OFFENSIVE SCOUTING REPORT

The Cowboys have many weapons surrounding the ever-improving Tony Romo, the clear leader of this blooming offense. Romo has a great arm and is one of the best at throwing on the run, making him hard to contain for opposing defenses. It helps, too, that he stands behind one of the best and largest centers in the game, Andre Gurode. As for weapons around him, none are better and more consistent than go-to guy TE Jason Witten. He has not only the ability to block, but more importantly, the hands to bring in the ball and produce yardage after the catch. While there is no blatant superstar in terms of overall stats at wide receiver, there is plenty of talent in Dallas. Miles Austin and Roy Williams both have areas of greatness, and the anticipated rookie, Dez Bryant, should be considered as a starter. In the backfield, Felix Jones has become the clear-cut starter and had one of the highest per-carry averages in the NFL last season. He has the potential to be a game-breaker with incredible speed and agility. Marion Barber, however, is the end zone magnet for goal line situations.

DEFENSIVE SCOUTING REPORT

When discussing the defense of the Cowboys, you have to start with the defensive captain, DeMarcus Ware. Providing both rush and pass defense, Ware can be a game-changer whenever he is on the field. The physical style of the linebacker corps in Ware, Anthony Spencer, and Bradie James is what made the Cowboys fourth in the league against the run last season. Tackle Jay Ratliff is one of the top defensive linemen in the league and will draw constant attention from the O-line, providing opportunities for the linebackers to make plays on the ball. Spencer benefits from this greatly with opportunities to aggressively rush the quarterback. The secondary is covered well with a pair of equally strong corners in Terence Newman and Mike Jenkins, and the constant pass rush will allow both corners to take chances and capitalize on quarterback mistakes.

TEAM RATING

87
Overall

KEY ADDITIONS

OT	Alex Barron
K	Connor Hughes
WR	Dez Bryant
LB	Sean Lee

KEY DEPARTURES

OT	Flozell Adams
LB	Bobby Carpenter
S	Ken Hamlin
K	Shaun Suisham

RATINGS BY POSITION

Position	Rating
Quarterbacks	90
Halfbacks	83
Fullbacks	76
Wide Receivers	83
Tight Ends	97
Tackles	78
Guards	85
Centers	92
Defensive Ends	77
Defensive Tackles	94
Outside Linebackers	91
Middle Linebackers	85
Cornerbacks	86
Free Safeties	69
Strong Safeties	80
Kickers	68
Punters	92

DEPTH CHART

POS	OVR	FIRST NAME	LAST NAME
C	92	Andre	Gurode
CB	87	Terence	Newman
CB	85	Mike	Jenkins
CB	75	Orlando	Scandrick
CB	64	Jamar	Wall
CB	58	Cletis	Gordon
DT	94	Jay	Ratliff
DT	63	Junior	Siavii
FB	76	Deon	Anderson
FS	69	Alan	Ball
FS	67	Mike	Hamlin
FS	62	Akwasi	Owusu-Ansah
HB	84	Marion	Barber
HB	83	Felix	Jones
HB	77	Tashard	Choice
K	68	David	Buehler
LE	73	Marcus	Spears
LE	59	Jason	Hatcher
LG	80	Kyle	Kosier
LG	66	Travis	Bright
LOLB	84	Anthony	Spencer
LOLB	65	Victor	Butler
LOLB	52	Brandon	Williams
LT	80	Doug	Free
LT	77	Alex	Barron
LT	64	Robert	Brewster
MLB	85	Bradie	James
MLB	84	Keith	Brooking
MLB	70	Sean	Lee
MLB	56	Jason	Williams
P	92	Mat	McBriar
QB	90	Tony	Romo
QB	68	Jon	Kitna
QB	62	Stephen	McGee
RE	80	Igor	Olshansky
RE	58	Stephen	Bowen
RG	89	Leonard	Davis
RG	71	Montrae	Holland
ROLB	97	DeMarcus	Ware
ROLB	62	Steve	Octavien
RT	78	Marc	Colombo
RT	69	Pat	McQuistan
RT	64	Sam	Young
SS	80	Gerald	Sensabaugh
SS	68	Pat	Watkins
TE	97	Jason	Witten
TE	74	Martellus	Bennett
TE	73	John	Phillips
WR	88	Miles	Austin
WR	82	Roy	Williams
WR	80	Dez	Bryant
WR	75	Patrick	Crayton
WR	67	Sam	Hurd
WR	63	Kevin	Ogletree

OFFENSIVE STRENGTH CHART

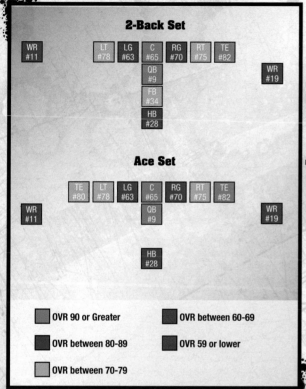

2-Back Set

WR #11		LT #78	LG #63	C #65	RG #70	RT #75	TE #82	
				QB #9				WR #19
				FB #34				
				HB #28				

Ace Set

	TE #80	LT #78	LG #63	C #65	RG #70	RT #75	TE #82	
WR #11				QB #9				WR #19
				HB #28				

▮ OVR 90 or Greater	▮ OVR between 60-69
▮ OVR between 80-89	▮ OVR 59 or lower
▮ OVR between 70-79	

#9 Tony Romo
Quarterback (QB)

Overall	90
Throwing Power	88
Short Accuracy	92
Medium Accuracy	89
Deep Accuracy	83

#82 Jason Witten
Tight End (TE)

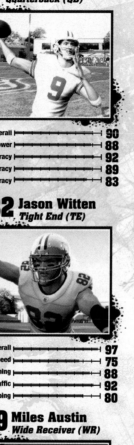

Overall	97
Speed	75
Catching	88
Catch in Traffic	92
Jumping	80

#19 Miles Austin
Wide Receiver (WR)

Overall	88
Speed	94
Catching	89
Release	80
Jumping	88

#94 DeMarcus Ware
Linebacker (ROLB)

Overall	97
Speed	86
Awareness	86
Tackle	88
Hit Power	88

#90 Jay Ratliff
Defensive Tackle (DT)

Overall	94
Speed	70
Strength	87
Power Moves	81
Block Shedding	87

#41 Terence Newman
Cornerback (CB)

Overall	87
Speed	97
Awareness	85
Man Coverage	93
Zone Coverage	85

DEFENSIVE STRENGTH CHART

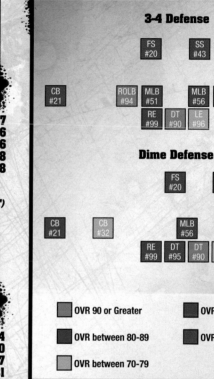

3-4 Defense

			FS #20	SS #43		
CB #21	ROLB #94	MLB #51		MLB #56	LOLB #93	CB #41
		RE #99	DT #90	LE #96		

Dime Defense

		FS #20	SS #43		
CB #21	CB #32		MLB #56	CB #26	CB #41
		RE #99	DT #95	DT #90	LE #96	

▮ OVR 90 or Greater	▮ OVR between 60-69
▮ OVR between 80-89	▮ OVR 59 or lower
▮ OVR between 70-79	

Key Player Substitutions

Position: TE

Substitution: John Phillips

When: Four-wide-receiver sets

Advantage: When you are running four-wide-receiver sets, look to replace Witten with Phillips for better pass blocking. Don't put Phillips in for route running or catching.

Key Player Substitutions

Position: FS

Substitution: Mike Hamlin

When: Blitzing schemes

Advantage: Hamlin is a hard-hitting free safety who can be brought up into the box to stop runs or blitz the QB. Use the double teams that Ware draws to get open lanes to the backfield.

Playbook Breakdown

The Cowboys have been known as America's team for many years and with that popularity many *Madden NFL 11* players gravitate to this playbook. This was also the playbook that the 2010 MLG EA SPORTS Challenge champion used to capture his crown. Because of the many different styles of play that you can utilize with the Cowboys playbook, it is a valuable playbook for anyone who wants a diverse offense.

The Cowboys playbook has 65 shotgun passes for us to throw the ball around to their three very talented receivers. Miles Austin is becoming a threat no matter what team he plays for, and now that Dez Bryant has been drafted, he brings some more talent to the receiving corps.

Even if passing isn't the main focus of your style of play, the Cowboys have a great mix of running plays. Felix Jones and Marion Barber are a solid one-two punch and can exploit the defense with any of the running plays we've found in this book.

OFFENSIVE FORMATIONS

FORMATION	# OF PLAYS
Formation	Number of Plays
Full House Normal Wide	12
Gun Doubles	18
Gun Empty Trips TE	9
Gun Flip Trips	9
Gun Snugs Flip	9
Gun Split Cowboy	12
Gun Spread Y-Slot	12
Gun Trey Open	12
Gun Y-Trips HB Wk	15
I-Form Pro	18
I-Form Tight Pair	12
Razorback Cowboys	3
Singleback Ace	18
Singleback Ace Pair	12
Singleback Bunch	12
Singleback Doubles	15
Singleback Jumbo	9
Strong Close	12
Strong Pro	12

OFFENSIVE PLAYCOUNTS

PLAY TYPE	# OF PLAYS
Quick Pass	15
Standard Pass	35
Shotgun Pass	65
Play Action Pass	41
Inside Handoff	28
Outside Handoff	14
Pitch	9
Counter	5

Singleback Bunch—HB Slash Fk End Ard

Madden NFL has been the best football game for years, because it is just plain fun. The Cowboys playbook has play calls in it that allow us to just have fun playing the game. You always hear players talking about playing loose. Well, the Singleback Bunch—HB Slash Fk End Ard will allow us to loosen up and enjoy beating the defense with a super cool play.

Two running options will confuse the defense

The end around is a beautiful play to behold when it works as designed. We look at the HB Slash Fk End Ard and enjoy it even more because the timing of the animations gives us a perfect mesh between the time the running back gets the ball and when the end runs by for his fake. This is a crucial point in the play and allows us to pre-read where we need to cut once the ball is in our running back's hands.

You're too slow

To enjoy success on this play we need to break a run off with the receiver, and then we can use the HB Slash as a comeback option. This play is strong enough to stand on its own, but we're always thinking about the next play and how we're going to continue to exploit the defense.

Gun Empty Trips TE—Four Verticals

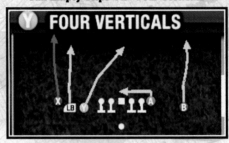

Four Verticals is a play call that we like to run because it is very aggressive and puts a lot of pressure on the defense. With all of our receivers running downfield routes and just the tight end staying shallow, we have a play that can beat man coverage as well as zone. We also like that fact that any slight mistake by the defense could result in a touchdown for us.

Read the angle of the safety's drop

What makes this play so easy to use is the read we get on the deep safety. Even before the snap we can pretty much tell what receiver to look for by looking at where the safety aligns. If he is tight to the hash, then we know we can get to the outside receiver running down the sideline. Then all we need to do is see if he opens to the sideline or the field.

Easy reception by the tight slot receiver

If the safety opens to the sideline, that means he is in a Cover 2 or deep half zone, so we know either inside route will be open. If he opens to the field then we have the skinny post as an option and the deep route just behind the safety. Our tight slot receiver caught the ball in this image but we also have the wide slot as an option sitting in the end zone.

Gun Split Cowboy—Cowboy Curls

The Cowboys playbook was popular last year because of the plays found in the Gun Split Cowboy formation. One of the most used plays was Cowboy Curls. This year, we want to keep the potency of this play at our fingertips. The Gun Split Cowboy—Cowboy Curls gives us the ability to easily start manually catching our passes. This is a technique that needs to be mastered if you want to be among the elite *Madden NFL* players.

The cornerback is playing off of our receiver

All we need to do to make this play work is recognize how the defensive backs are playing our receivers. If the cornerback is laying off then we know the curl is a perfect option because there is no one underneath. If the coverage is tight on the edges then we can look inside to the tight end running the angle route.

We user-control the catch for maximum height

Once we decide on which receiver to go to we let the ball go. While the ball is in the air we can easily click on to control our receiver and turn him around while pressing the Catch button. This will make sure our receiver jumps as high as he can and let us use the height advantage of our tall receivers.

Gun Flip Trips—HB Mid Draw

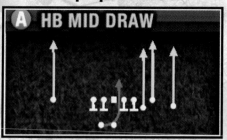

HB MID DRAW

If you watch the Dallas Cowboys then you are very familiar with all of the draw plays that they run. We like this playbook because of how many draw plays we have access to when in the Gun formation. The HB Mid Draw out of the Gun Flip Trips is an exceptional running play because of the tight alignment of two of the receivers to the trips side of the formation.

All the defenders are sealed off

Once we have the ball in the back's hands, we can read the blocks being set by our linemen and receivers. The tight alignment of two of the three receivers to the trips side turns this draw into a run that feels more like a dominant Off Tackle play. We have the size of our linemen and the height and speed of our receivers to help seal the defenders inside and let Felix Jones get around the edge.

Amazing blocks by our receivers

It's rare that we get an aggressive running play out of a Gun formation, and a draw at that. When we can throw a power run game into the mix when running out of the Gun formation, the defense is in for a long day. Use this play to punish an opponent who likes to sit multiple defenders back in coverage.

Gun Flip Trips—Deep Fork

DEEP FORK

There are some plays in the Cowboys playbook that we like simply because they are great football plays. The Gun Flip Trips—Deep Fork is one of these plays. This is a play that we look to when we want to isolate a defender or a human-controlled player and work off of his movements. The Deep Fork has an automotion out route by the flanker, a post by the slot, and a corner route by the tight slot. We also have the luxury of the running back assigned to a circle route.

So many open options

As soon as we hike the ball, we look to see which defender is playing on the hash mark. If the linebacker is on the hash and breaking to the outside like we see in this screenshot, we will have the post as an option. We also see an outside linebacker moving out with our flanker and can take this option because of the speed mismatch.

Send the cart out; the corner just got his ankles broken

We actually have all of our routes open on this play and could beat the defense with any throw we make. We decided on the out route to the flanker because his speed is a mismatch vs. the outside linebacker. We put a move on the cornerback as he tries to make the tackle and pick up additional first down yardage on the play.

Singleback Jumbo—HB Plunge

HB PLUNGE

We have spent a lot of time looking at passing plays in the Cowboys playbook, but everyone knows that the Cowboys can just as well dominate a game by running the ball. We are big fans of pounding the ball and trying to bully our opponent's defense around the field. We can rely on the Singleback Jumbo—HB Plunge to help us set that tone in *Madden NFL 11*.

Use the receiver as an extra blocker

One of the more efficient ways of running the HB Plunge from the Singleback Jumbo formation is to motion the flanker with the intent of using him as an extra blocker. This formation already mirrors the Goal Line formation, and a little motion can really make things hard on the defense to play the run.

Look at the running lane

The motion that we added to the play made a huge difference, as you look at the massive running lane that we have because of it. When we use quick-hitting running plays and enhance them, we can turn an expected 2 yards and a cloud of dust attempt into big play rushing touchdowns. Felix Jones's speed is a serious asset to Cowboys users.

Singleback Doubles—TE Post

TE POST

Jason Witten is the Cowboys' Pro Bowl tight end. It is imperative that we find a way to make sure he is included in our passing attack. When we have a player that is 6'5" and has pretty good speed to work the middle of the field with, it's a given that we need to get him the ball. The Singleback Doubles—TE Post lets us use Witten in the middle of the field and takes advantage of his size and pass-catching abilities to keep the chains moving.

Throw just before he breaks inside

The Singleback Doubles—TE Post has the tight end running a post and the slot receiver running a post. Witten is so good in the middle of the field that we look to him as our first option and only need to make sure there isn't a defender directly underneath him before throwing the ball.

First down!

The pass is thrown perfectly down the middle of the field and Witten makes the catch for first down yardage. Post routes are great options for big tight ends. When you have the talent of a Jason Witten on your team it can make even tight throws over the middle into routine catches.

MIAMI DOLPHINS

OFFENSIVE SCOUTING REPORT

Chad Henne, while he doesn't possess the highest stats, does have one of the biggest arms in terms of throw power. This will need to carry him through the season as the QB position struggled a bit for the Dolphins last year. Henne does have flashes of brilliance and will have a shiny new toy in WR Brandon Marshall. Marshall is a deep threat and a vacuum when it comes to snatching a ball thrown in his direction. This duo will turn some heads this season. Opposite Marshall are WRs Greg Camarillo and Davone Bess, both of whom can bring in the ball on the short slants and through the middle when Marshall is overcovered. Protection will be provided by standout LT Jake Long. Running backs Ronnie Brown and Ricky Williams are always dangerous and have been effective in the past with the Wildcat formation. While defenses around the league are wising up to the Wildcat formation, direct snaps to these two remain a dangerous threat and make for fun plays in the Dolphins' offensive scheme. Brown, the more elusive back, can be subbed out in goal line situations to capitalize on the trucking ability of Williams. Keeping both fresh has led to the success of the Dolphins running game.

DEFENSIVE SCOUTING REPORT

New defensive coordinator Mike Nolan will have his work cut out for him. The Dolphins D is a work in progress, but don't tell that to the new man on campus, Karlos Dansby. He will provide instant upgrades to the linebacker unit. However, he is going to need the help of the line, led by tackle Randy Starks, to control the run effectively. The pass rush will miss Jason Taylor, who left for the Jets. The remaining ends are young and will need to jump in on the quarterback or offenses will be able to challenge the secondary regularly. Corners Will Allen and Vontae Davis, along with strong safety Yeremiah Bell, can make plays, and all possess speed, but without pressure up front they will have a long day come Sunday.

TEAM RATING

79
Overall

KEY ADDITIONS

LB	Karlos Dansby
LB	Tim Dobbins
G	Richie Incognito
WR	Brandon Marshall
DE	Jared Odrick
OLB	Koa Misi

KEY DEPARTURES

LB	Akin Ayodele
WR	Ted Ginn Jr.
S	Nate Jones
LB	Joey Porter
LB	Jason Taylor
S	Gibril Wilson

RATINGS BY POSITION

Position	Rating
Quarterbacks	79
Halfbacks	89
Fullbacks	91
Wide Receivers	80
Tight Ends	79
Tackles	91
Guards	74
Centers	87
Defensive Ends	75
Defensive Tackles	89
Outside Linebackers	71
Middle Linebackers	90
Cornerbacks	81
Free Safeties	66
Strong Safeties	82
Kickers	82
Punters	67

DEPTH CHART

POS	OVR	FIRST NAME	LAST NAME
C	87	Jake	Grove
C	74	Joe	Berger
CB	82	Vontae	Davis
CB	81	Will	Allen
CB	79	Sean	Smith
CB	64	Jason	Allen
DT	89	Randy	Starks
DT	76	Paul	Soliai
DT	56	Ryan	Baker
FB	91	Lousaka	Polite
FS	66	Tyrone	Culver
FS	64	Reshad	Jones
HB	89	Ronnie	Brown
HB	87	Ricky	Williams
HB	66	Lex	Hilliard
HB	65	Kory	Sheets
K	82	Dan	Carpenter
LE	79	Kendall	Langford
LE	75	Phillip	Merling
LG	72	Cory	Procter
LG	65	John	Jerry
LOLB	65	Charlie	Anderson
LOLB	55	Quentin	Moses
LT	96	Jake	Long
LT	66	Andrew	Gardner
MLB	90	Karlos	Dansby
MLB	79	Channing	Crowder
MLB	65	Tim	Dobbins
MLB	62	A.J.	Edds
P	67	Brandon	Fields
QB	79	Chad	Henne
QB	78	Chad	Pennington
QB	66	Pat	White
RE	71	Jared	Odrick
RE	67	Tony	McDaniel
RG	76	Nate	Garner
RG	76	Richie	Incognito
RG	75	Donald	Thomas
ROLB	76	Cameron	Wake
ROLB	67	Koa	Misi
RT	86	Vernon	Carey
RT	65	Lydon	Murtha
SS	82	Yeremiah	Bell
SS	65	Chris	Clemons
TE	79	Anthony	Fasano
TE	68	Joey	Haynos
TE	56	Kory	Sperry
WR	96	Brandon	Marshall
WR	74	Davone	Bess
WR	73	Greg	Camarillo
WR	71	Brian	Hartline
WR	63	Patrick	Turner

OFFENSIVE STRENGTH CHART

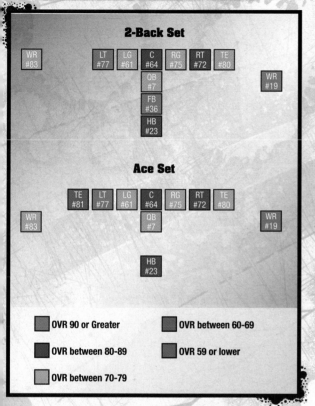

2-Back Set

WR #83							
	LT #77	LG #61	C #64	RG #75	RT #72	TE #80	
			QB #7				WR #19
			FB #36				
			HB #23				

Ace Set

	TE #81	LT #77	LG #61	C #64	RG #75	RT #72	TE #80	
WR #83				QB #7				WR #19
				HB #23				

- ■ OVR 90 or Greater
- ■ OVR between 80-89
- ■ OVR between 70-79
- ■ OVR between 60-69
- ■ OVR 59 or lower

Key Player Substitutions

Position: QB

Substitution: Pat White

When: Rushing with the QB

Advantage: Pat White is one of the fastest QBs in the league. Use his speed in big sets to run to the edges and pick up yards with his feet. When defenses load the box to stop your run, hit them with a pass.

#19 Brandon Marshall
Wide Receiver (WR)

Overall	96
Speed	88
Catching	97
Release	99
Jumping	92

#23 Ronnie Brown
Halfback (HB)

Overall	89
Speed	92
Agility	92
Stiff Arm	78
Carrying	97

#77 Jake Long
Offensive Tackle (LT)

Overall	96
Speed	66
Pass Block	88
Run Block	96
Impact Blocking	93

#58 Karlos Dansby
Linebacker (MLB)

Overall	90
Speed	79
Awareness	88
Tackle	94
Hit Power	88

#21 Vontae Davis
Cornerback (CB)

Overall	82
Speed	92
Awareness	70
Man Coverage	85
Zone Coverage	82

#94 Randy Starks
Defensive Tackle (DT)

Overall	89
Speed	66
Strength	94
Finesse Moves	55
Power Moves	87

DEFENSIVE STRENGTH CHART

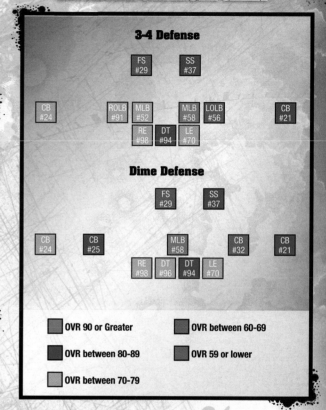

3-4 Defense

	FS #29		SS #37	
CB #24	ROLB #91	MLB #52	MLB #58	LOLB #56	CB #21
	RE #98	DT #94	LE #70	

Dime Defense

	FS #29		SS #37	
CB #24	CB #25	MLB #58	CB #32	CB #21
	RE #98	DT #96	DT #94	LE #70

- ■ OVR 90 or Greater
- ■ OVR between 80-89
- ■ OVR between 70-79
- ■ OVR between 60-69
- ■ OVR 59 or lower

Key Player Substitutions

Position: SS

Substitution: Chris Clemons

When: Nickel and Dime formations

Advantage: With more CBs on the field to man up on wide receivers, use Chris Clemons's speed to help out over the top in Cover 2 defense.

Playbook Breakdown

Last season, the Wildcat offense was introduced to *Madden NFL* football. Other teams had the same version of the Wildcat offense in their playbook, but no team had as many plays as the Dolphins playbook did. For that reason, most players who ran the Dolphins playbook chose it because of the Wildcat formations and plays. Besides the Wildcat, Miami has some strong formations to run from as their offense is built around power running and play action. The I-Form Tight Pair is one of the better running formations in the game, and the Dolphins have several good run and play action plays in that formation alone. The Singleback Ace Pair is another power run formation for those who like to run the ball from one-back sets. If you like to throw the ball, there are some good passing formations from the Gun, such as the Split Slot, Ace Pair Wk, and Empty Trey. Overall this a solid playbook that edges towards the power run game, but with enough passing plays to keep the defense off-balance.

OFFENSIVE FORMATIONS

FORMATION	# OF PLAYS
Gun Ace Pair Wk	9
Gun Doubles	15
Gun Empty Trey	12
Gun Split Slot	15
Gun Y-Trips	15
I-Form Pro	21
I-Form Pro Twins	18
I-Form Tight Pair	12
Singleback Ace	15
Singleback Ace Pair	15
Singleback Bunch	15
Singleback Doubles	18
Singleback Y-Trips	18
Strong Pro	18
Wildcat Normal	6
Wildcat Trips Over	6

OFFENSIVE PLAYCOUNTS

PLAY TYPE	# OF PLAYS
Quick Pass	11
Standard Pass	51
Shotgun Pass	39
Play Action Pass	45
Inside Handoff	32
Outside Handoff	13
Pitch	7
Counter	12

I-Form Tight Pair—Iso

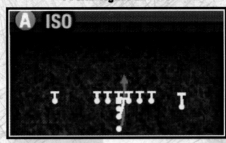

The I-Form Tight Pair—Iso (Isolation) is all about picking up tough yardage inside. The Dolphins offense is built for these types of run plays, so it makes sense to call them. The I-Form Tight Pair—Iso has running back Ronnie Brown following fullback Lousaka Polite through the hole between center Jake Grove and right guard Nate Garner.

Brown looks for the open hole

Both are powerful run blockers who can push the defensive linemen in front of them out of the way. Polite will look to engage the middle linebacker, allowing Brown to pick up yardage. If Brown gets through the hole untouched, he has the speed to pick up yardage in the second and third levels of defense, despite this play not being designed to pick up a ton of yardage.

Brown hits the holes and picks up 5 yards

Consider subbing Ricky Williams in on occasion, as he has the toughness to pick up the tough inside yardage. He may not be as fast as Brown, but he can break a few more tackles and help move the chains.

I-Form Tight Pair—PA Spot

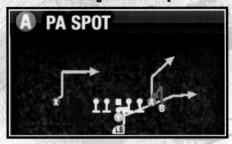

After the I-Form Tight Pair—Iso has been established, a solid play action pass play to run is the PA Spot. The outside tight end runs the spot route, while the inside tight end runs a corner route. His corner route is designed to lift the coverage over the top of the spot route.

Henne surveys the pass coverage while looking for the open receiver

The fullback runs a flat route to the right. His pass route holds the flat defender in check. The lone receiver, who is lined up wide to the left, runs a dig route. We prefer to hot route him on a streak to provide a deep threat down the left side of the field. The play starts off looking like the Iso play. Hopefully this action will get the linebackers to bite.

The TE spots up and Henne throws him a bullet pass

Once the play fake occurs, look to the split end on the left. If he has one-on-one coverage, look to throw deep to him. If not, look to throw to the tight end running the spot route or the fullback in the flat.

Wildcat Normal—Power

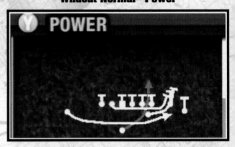

The Dolphins were running over opponents during the first part of the season with Ronnie Brown leading the way in the Wildcat. One of the staple plays from the Wildcat Normal is called Power. This play has Ronnie Brown lined up in the Gun as the quarterback. Fellow running back Ricky Williams lines up out wide on the left.

Williams is sent in motion from left to right

Just before the ball is snapped, Williams is sent in motion towards Brown. Once Brown receives the snap, he has two options; he can either hand the ball off to Williams or keep it himself. Left guard Justin Smiley pulls to the right, where he looks to pancake any blocker who gets in front of him.

Brown looks for a hole to open up inside

If Brown keeps the ball, he looks to run up inside. If he hands it off to Williams, then Williams will look to run outside for positive yardage. Be sure to mix this run play in with other Wildcat Normal plays. Use the PA Jet Sweep to at least make your opponent on defense respect the pass.

Wildcat Normal—Counter

The other Wildcat Normal run play we like to run is the Counter. This play has Ronnie Brown running to the side opposite where the Power run play goes. If the defense starts to overload the side the Power play is run to, use this play to force them to play honestly.

Brown follows his blocks to the left

Ricky Williams does the same automotion as before. This play has right guard Nate Garner and tight end Joey Haynos pulling to the left side as lead blockers for Brown. The option is still there for Brown to hand off to Williams as he comes in motion. If Brown decides to keep the ball, he looks to run to the left behind Garner and Haynos.

Brown picks up 7 yards before finally being tackled

If he can get outside, he has the speed and acceleration to head down the field and pick up a substantial gain. This play is pretty effective once the Power run play has been established. Just as with the Power play, be sure to mix in the PA Jet Sweep to keep your opponent from loading up the box with multiple defenders to stop the run.

Strong Pro—PA Slide

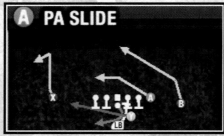

The Dolphins like to use their power run game to set up the play action pass. The Strong Pro—PA Slide is a good example of play action plays that Miami might run on any given Sunday afternoon. The primary receiver for this play is the fullback, who runs a flat route to the left. On top of his pass route, there are two other pass routes that we like to throw to.

Henne boots to the left while looking towards the left side of the field

The tight end runs a shallow cross, and newly acquired receiver Brandon Marshall runs a deep post. If you look closely at the play diagram, you will notice that the three pass routes attack each level of the field.

The ball is thrown on a rope towards Marshall for a big play

One pre-snap adjustment we like to make is to hot route the split end on a streak. We do this to clear out the left side of the field so all of the receivers running their pass routes right to left can work underneath. If Cover 2 is called, we look to throw to Marshall as he heads towards the post.

Gun Doubles—HB Mid Draw

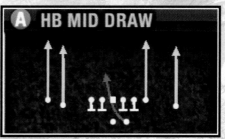

Draw plays are more effective in *Madden NFL 11* because the defensive ends get up the field quicker and farther than in years past. The Gun Doubles—HB Mid Draw is a good run play to call in third and long situations because your opponent won't be expecting it.

The offensive line is in a pass-blocking stance

Ronnie Brown has the speed to rack up this yardage, provided the play is called against the right defense. The offensive line acts like it's pass-blocking in hopes of selling to the defense that a pass play is about to occur.

Brown busts through into the secondary for a big gain

At the last second, the quarterback hands the ball to the running back, who then looks to head up inside, where hopefully a hole has opened up. If the defense calls an inside blitz, chances are the draw is not going to be successful, so watch to see what the defense does before the snap. Are they stacking the middle with defenders or overloading one side of the field? If they stack the middle, consider audibling to a quick inside pass play.

Gun Empty Trey—Strong Flood

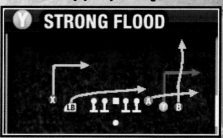

Chad Henne has a strong arm, allowing him to make all the throws that are needed to be a successful quarterback in the NFL. The Gun Empty Trey—Strong Flood showcases his arm strength by showing how quickly he can zip the ball on an out route. This formation (as indicated by its name) empties the backfield.

The slot receiver breaks towards the sideline

On the right side of the field, there is a flood between the tight end, right slot, and flanker. The right slot runs the out route and is the play's primary receiver. The flat route run by the tight end holds the flat defender, while the flanker forces the deep defenders to retreat backwards. Once the right slot breaks towards the sideline, there should be a good-sized passing window for Henne to zip the ball.

Henne shows off his arm strength as he throws a bullet towards the right sideline

If for some reason the out route is covered, look for the left slot receiver on the shallow cross as he should be open underneath. Be prepared to be blitzed when coming out in this formation since there is no back in the backfield to help protect the quarterback.

PHILADELPHIA EAGLES

OFFENSIVE SCOUTING REPORT

The biggest news out of Philly is the loss of Donovan McNabb and the beginning of the Kevin Kolb era. This may mean not as many deep bomb passes to the dynamic DeSean Jackson, but it doesn't mean that the two won't connect often. Expect DeSean Jackson to continue to be the number one target in Philly and continue his rise into the wide receiver elite. Being at the top of the leader board in speed, agility, acceleration, and elusiveness makes Jackson one of the most dangerous men on the field when the ball is in his hands. Kolb will do all he can to get the ball in the hands of this major playmaker. As an outlet, Brent Celek is a receiving tight end with a knack for catching in traffic. Longtime running back Brian Westbrook is also out of Philly, leaving behind a vacancy filled by youngster LeSean McCoy. Fast and agile, McCoy served the Eagles well in his rookie year but is not the large pounding back that Westbrook was; however, McCoy can serve the same role as a receiving running back with quick speed to move the chains.

DEFENSIVE SCOUTING REPORT

Asante Samuel and Trent Cole are the clear superstars of the Philly defense. As a cornerback, Samuel is one of the best and excels in both man and zone coverage. His blistering speed and awareness are always in the minds of opposing quarterbacks, and by himself he can take star receivers out of an opponent's passing game. The other pass threat is sack-monster Cole on the defensive end. With Trent bringing pressure and Samuel stalking the pass, offenses are apt to try and run on the Eagles. This may be the area of concern for Philly, which has no linebackers higher than an overall rating of 83. This didn't stop the defense, however, from finishing last year ninth against the run.

TEAM RATING

80
Overall

KEY ADDITIONS

LB	Alex Hall
RB	Mike Ball
S	Marlin Jackson
LB	Ernie Sims
DE	Darryl Tapp
DE	Brandon Graham

KEY DEPARTURES

QB	Donovan McNabb
RB	Brian Westbrook
WR	Kevin Curtis
WR	Reggie Brown
CB	Sheldon Brown
LB	Chris Gocong

RATINGS BY POSITION

Position	Rating		Position	Rating
Quarterbacks	75		Defensive Tackles	88
Halfbacks	79		Outside Linebackers	77
Fullbacks	90		Middle Linebackers	79
Wide Receivers	83		Cornerbacks	87
Tight Ends	88		Free Safeties	75
Tackles	83		Strong Safeties	83
Guards	85		Kickers	89
Centers	75		Punters	71
Defensive Ends	88			

DEPTH CHART

POS	OVR	FIRST NAME	LAST NAME
C	79	Jamaal	Jackson
C	75	Nick	Cole
CB	94	Asante	Samuel
CB	80	Ellis	Hobbs
CB	74	Joselio	Hanson
CB	72	Macho	Harris
CB	64	Trevard	Lindley
DT	88	Brodrick	Bunkley
DT	83	Mike	Patterson
DT	66	Antonio	Dixon
DT	66	Trevor	Laws
FB	90	Leonard	Weaver
FS	80	Marlin	Jackson
FS	75	Nate	Allen
HB	79	LeSean	McCoy
HB	77	Mike	Bell
HB	68	Eldra	Buckley
K	89	David	Akers
LE	80	Juqua	Parker
LE	78	Brandon	Graham
LE	73	Victor	Abiamiri
LG	89	Todd	Herremans
LG	66	Mike	McGlynn
LOLB	70	Moise	Fokou
LOLB	61	Alex	Hall
LT	88	Jason	Peters
LT	60	King	Dunlap
MLB	79	Stewart	Bradley
MLB	67	Omar	Gaither
MLB	63	Joe	Mays
P	71	Sav	Rocca
QB	75	Kevin	Kolb
QB	73	Michael	Vick
QB	65	Mike	Kafka
RE	95	Trent	Cole
RE	77	Darryl	Tapp
RG	80	Stacy	Andrews
RG	72	Max	Jean-Gilles
ROLB	83	Ernie	Sims
ROLB	79	Akeem	Jordan
RT	77	Winston	Justice
RT	61	Fenuki	Tupou
SS	83	Qunitin	Mikell
SS	67	Qunitin	Demps
TE	88	Brent	Celek
TE	63	Cornelius	Ingram
TE	62	Clay	Harbor
WR	91	DeSean	Jackson
WR	81	Jeremy	Maclin
WR	76	Jason	Avant
WR	65	Hank	Baskett
WR	63	Blue	Cooper

OFFENSIVE STRENGTH CHART

2-Back Set

```
WR
#18
          LT    LG    C    RG    RT    TE
          #71   #79  #59  #76   #74   #87
                      QB                          WR
                      #4                          #10
                      FB
                      #43
                      HB
                      #25
```

Ace Set

```
          TE    LT    LG    C    RG    RT    TE
          #88   #71   #79  #59  #76   #74   #87
  WR                       QB                     WR
  #18                      #4                      #10

                           HB
                           #25
```

- 🟩 OVR 90 or Greater
- 🟥 OVR between 60-69
- 🟦 OVR between 80-89
- 🟥 OVR 59 or lower
- 🟦 OVR between 70-79

#10 DeSean Jackson
Wide Receiver (WR)

Overall	9i
Speed	99
Catching	92
Release	77
Jumping	86

#87 Brent Celek
Tight End (TE)

Overall	88
Speed	78
Catching	89
Catch in Traffic	93
Jumping	75

#43 Leonard Weaver
Fullback (FB)

Overall	90
Speed	79
Agility	75
Stiff Arm	86
Carrying	87

#58 Trent Cole
Defensive End (RE)

Overall	95
Speed	84
Strength	79
Finesse Moves	98
Power Moves	70

#22 Asante Samuel
Cornerback (CB)

Overall	94
Speed	90
Awareness	95
Man Coverage	94
Zone Coverage	98

#97 Brodrick Bunkley
Defensive Tackle (DT)

Overall	88
Speed	62
Strength	96
Power Moves	70
Block Shedding	78

DEFENSIVE STRENGTH CHART

4-3 Defense

```
          FS                    SS
          #29                   #27

 CB      ROLB       MLB        LOLB          CB
 #31     #50        #55        #53           #22
         RE   DT   DT   LE
         #58  #98  #97  #75
```

Dime Defense

```
          FS                    SS
          #29                   #27

 CB      CB        MLB        CB        CB
 #31     #21       #55        #24       #22
         RE   DT   DT   LE
         #58  #98  #97  #75
```

- 🟩 OVR 90 or Greater
- 🟥 OVR between 60-69
- 🟦 OVR between 80-89
- 🟥 OVR 59 or lower
- 🟦 OVR between 70-79

Key Player Substitutions

Position: QB

Substitution: Michael Vick

When: Short yardage

Advantage: Michael Vick is one of the most exciting players in the NFL to watch. Bring Vick in on short yardage situations to keep your opponents wondering if you are going to run or throw it with Vick.

Key Player Substitutions

Position: LOLB

Substitution: Akeem Jordan

When: Global

Advantage: Move Akeem Jordan from ROLB over to LOLB. This will add many strengths overall to your linebackers. With the Eagles' good defensive line, look to move Jordan around to best utilize his speed.

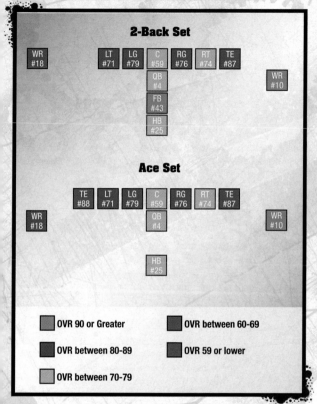
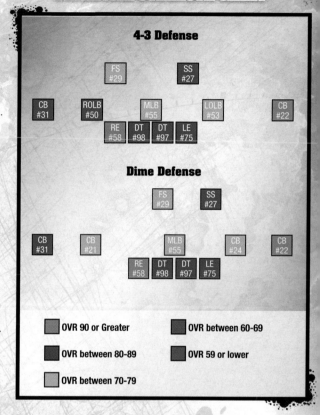

Playbook Breakdown

The Philadelphia Eagles playbook is similar to the play that you would expect to see if you watch them on any given Sunday in the fall. The Eagles have become one of the most pass-happy teams in the NFL and can easily mirror that style in *Madden NFL 11*. With over 70 shotgun plays, this playbook is sure to let you attack the defense through the air with a plethora of passing formations and plays.

When using the Eagles you want to incorporate the screen-passing game, as they are one of the best screen-passing teams in the NFL. This is one of the main draws to this playbook; screen passes are perfect counters to the blitz game and the aggressive defenses that are prominent in the NFC East. The Eagles playbook also gives you the opportunity to make use of the tight end as a dominant factor in your offense.

OFFENSIVE FORMATIONS

FORMATION	# OF PLAYS
Gun Doubles	15
Gun Doubles Wk	12
Gun Empty Trey	9
Gun Snugs Flip	12
Gun Split Offset	18
Gun Spread Flex	12
Gun Trey Open	15
Gun Y-Trips Wk	18
I-Form Pro	21
I-Form Tight Pair	12
Singleback Ace	12
Singleback Ace Pair Twins	15
Singleback Bunch	12
Singleback Double Flex	9
Singleback Eagle Slot	18
Weak Pro	12
Wildcat Philly	3

OFFENSIVE PLAYCOUNTS

PLAY TYPE	# OF PLAYS
Quick Pass	11
Standard Pass	68
Shotgun Pass	86
Play Action Pass	38
Inside Handoff	23
Outside Handoff	22
Pitch	5
Counter	10
Draw	8

Gun Doubles—FL Screen

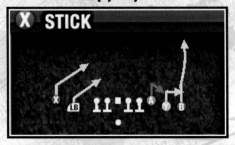

With the kind of speed that you have at the receiver position it is important to get the ball to those receivers to showcase their talent. The Gun Doubles—FL Screen in the Eagles playbook is one of the best screen plays that we have seen in *Madden NFL 11*.

Check, check, check, the slot is uncovered

The benefit of this FL Screen is the bubble screen that the slot receiver runs. Most screen plays outside of the Gun Empty sets don't have two receivers running screen routes. The Gun Doubles—FL Screen not only has a flanker screen, but also makes use of a bubble screen by the slot. This makes it hard for a defense to overplay.

The bubble screen is wide open

If the defense decides to come down or press our flanker we automatically throw the ball to our slot receiver on the bubble screen. Even if they don't overplay the flanker, anytime we see that the slot is uncovered we know we have that quick-pass option. If the defense has the corner sit in a flat zone, with a safety over top, then our split end running a post route becomes our best read.

Gun Empty Trey—Stick

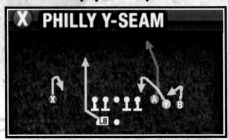

With Kevin Kolb at the helm we want to take advantage of his accuracy and call a play that gets the ball out of his hands quickly so our receivers can get those oh-so-important yards after the catch. The Gun Empty Trey—Stick is a perfect play to start a drive off with because of the dual slants to the back side and the hook, out, and streak combo on the front side.

Front-side route combo: streak, out, hook

We really value this play because of how well it performs after the snap. As we drop back with the quarterback and survey the defense we can see that the defense is in a Cover 2 zone, because of the deep safety and the cornerback in the flat. We can throw the ball to the flanker running the streak or wait for the tight end to turn around on his hook route.

The slot receiver focuses on the ball

Not only do we have solid route options to the front side of the play, but also we have the dual slants to the back side. We have found a lot of success running slants in *Madden NFL* and there is no need to stray away from the easy, yet efficient, slant route.

Gun Trey Open—Philly Y-Seam

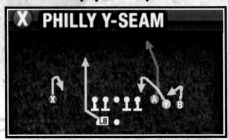

A successful passing game will always have a route designed to hold the safety or prevent a defender in coverage from covering his area completely. The Gun Trey Open—Philly Y-Seam does just that. We like this play to control the movement of both safeties and force them to play tight to the seams or get burned for not doing so.

The defense is blitzing the safety; look for the tight slot receiver

At the snap it looks like the defense is bringing one of the safeties in on a blitz. We like this play because it has our running back assigned to a seam route as well as our tight slot receiver. Any time we face an opponent who likes to blitz from the secondary we can use this play to make quick work of them.

Our receiver gets behind the safety

We make the defense pay for running such a high-risk play against our extremely accurate and efficient quarterback. If we continue to beat the defense with passes downfield they will start to back their coverage off and calm down on the blitzes. But, if they choose to continue in their blitz-happy ways, we will continue to run free downfield.

Singleback Double Flex—Slants

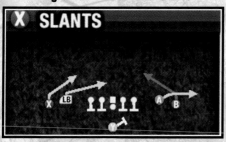

There is no better play in football than a good run play or a good slant route. The Eagles have DeSean Jackson and Jeremy Maclin as their top two receivers, and both are capable of turning a 5-yard slant into a 60-yard touchdown.

Let the first slant go by

The key to success when running the slants is to first be patient. The defense is bringing pressure and dropping into shallow zone over the middle of the field. We read the linebacker and defensive lineman dropping into coverage and let our left slot receiver clear the zone first.

The split end catches the ball in the void of the defense

By letting the slot receiver run through the zone first and not trying to fit a tight pass in to him, we force the defensive lineman and the linebacker to play the slot receiver. Our split end is running a parallel slant route and gets the benefit of a void in the zone because of the slot receiver's work.

Singleback Ace Pair Twins—Eagle Slot Post

There are some plays in the Philadelphia Eagles playbook that we like simply because they are cool. That may seem strange to say when talking about football, but the Eagle Slot Post is a great play because it has two delay pass routes that work as a hidden Levels route option. We can also use these routes to create a middle screen pass option.

Both tight ends turn back to the quarterback

Even though this is not a screen pass play we can get the same effect when running it. The primary tight end will run a normal hook route, followed by the second tight end and then the back. Because the second tight end and back are running delay routes, the defense attacks the quarterback and lets the receivers run their routes. This turns the play into a middle screen to the running back.

What an escort—the tight ends are in position to lead us downfield

Once the running back clears the line of scrimmage we dump the ball off to him. Immediately, our two tight ends turn into blockers and can set downfield blocks for the back, allowing us to maximize our yards from this play.

Singleback Ace Pair Twins—Bubble Screen

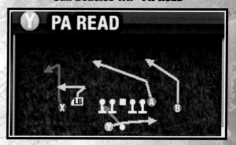

The Bubble Screen from the Singleback Ace Pair Twins is another solid screen play that we find very useful in the Philadelphia Eagles playbook. This slot screen is another quick-hitting pass option that we can attack the defense with. It is also very useful to use when in this formation because we can run the ball successfully when in the Singleback Ace Pair Twins.

Get the receiver the ball quickly

This play is best used when we come to the line of scrimmage and see that the defense has our slot receiver uncovered. We can come out in it and then check into another play or vice versa. Our main thought when running this play is to make sure we punish the defense for allowing us to make a pre-read of their coverage.

Our receiver has already turned the corner

We hike the ball and immediately throw it out to the slot receiver on the bubble screen. When in Twins, the slot receiver is actually the flanker, so this play takes advantage of our top receiver and his ability to punish the defense.

Gun Doubles Wk—PA Read

The Gun Doubles Wk—PA Read is a solid play as it is designed; however, we want to take advantage of the athleticism of our backup quarterback and use this play to give our opponent nightmares. Out of all the Read plays in this formation, we like the PA Read because the computer plays it honest. We know that everyone doesn't play vs. live opponents, so by running this play as a run-first option we can keep the computer honest.

It starts with the ball fake

The success of this play relies on how well the defense reacts to the play action fake to our running back. We are looking at this is a run-first play, but if the defense brings immediate pressure we can easily take advantage of the running back going to the flat or the tight end running a crossing route.

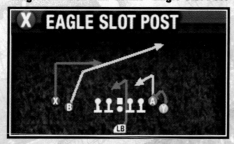

The quarterback breaks off a nice run

Many players cannot handle a solid passing play with the option of a mobile quarterback. The Gun Doubles Wk—PA Read gives us a way to keep the defense off-balance and even helpless at times, when we go back and forth with the run and pass. Don't make this an every down play, but it can definitely serve as a solid tempo-changing option.

ATLANTA FALCONS

OFFENSIVE SCOUTING REPORT

The Falcons offense is built on a power running attack with a bull-dozing little guy, Michael Turner. Turner can run through defenders with his extremely high trucking ability and strong stiff arm. The change-of-pace back is the speedy Jerious Norwood. While not the every-down back like Turner, Norwood is extremely quick to accelerate to a fast top speed and provides a nice outlet in the passing game. Matt Ryan can build the passing game around the ground attack with WR Roddy White and TE Tony Gonzalez acting as the two primary threats. When defenses start to anticipate the run and stack the box, Matt Ryan is a quality quarterback with a dependable arm who can burn the defense with the passing game. Mixing in the pass will be the key to keeping the running attack solid. Center Todd McClure and right guard Harvey Dahl are the two standouts on the line; however, the whole offensive line earned the Falcons 340 yards per game last season.

DEFENSIVE SCOUTING REPORT

The addition of cornerback Dunta Robinson should help the overall defense of the Falcons by providing the secondary threat missing from last year. The secondary, however, cannot truly improve until the front line puts more pressure on the offense. This shouldn't be too much of a problem with tackle Jonathan Babineaux and the return of nose tackle Peria Jerry. If these two can pinch in on offensive lines, John Abraham can get on the quarterback and provide the pass rush they desperately need. Curtis Lofton is a rising star as the Falcons middle linebacker. He is not the fastest linebacker, but his pursuit and play recognition are strong, and hardly anyone tackles as efficiently. The Falcons defense is young and looking for an identity, but the talent is definitely there.

TEAM RATING

83
Overall

KEY ADDITIONS

S	Matt Giordano
CB	Dunta Robinson
LB	Sean Weatherspoon
DT	Corey Peters

KEY DEPARTURES

CB	Tye Hill
CB	Chris Houston
LS	Mike Schneck

RATINGS BY POSITION

Quarterbacks	86
Halfbacks	90
Fullbacks	88
Wide Receivers	79
Tight Ends	98
Tackles	85
Guards	86
Centers	87
Defensive Ends	80
Defensive Tackles	86
Outside Linebackers	79
Middle Linebackers	88
Cornerbacks	80
Free Safeties	77
Strong Safeties	84
Kickers	74
Punters	84

DEPTH CHART

POS	OVR	FIRST NAME	LAST NAME
C	87	Todd	McClure
C	73	Brett	Romberg
CB	85	Dunta	Robinson
CB	77	Brian	Williams
CB	75	Brent	Grimes
CB	72	Chris	Owens
CB	68	Chevis	Jackson
DT	86	Jonathan	Babineaux
DT	78	Peria	Jerry
DT	71	Thomas	Johnson
DT	64	Corey	Peters
FB	88	Ovie	Mughelli
FS	77	Thomas	DeCoud
FS	66	Matt	Giordano
HB	90	Michael	Turner
HB	75	Jerious	Norwood
HB	74	Jason	Snelling
K	74	Matt	Bryant
LE	74	Chauncey	Davis
LE	70	Jamaal	Anderson
LG	85	Justin	Blalock
LG	66	Mike	Johnson
LOLB	82	Mike	Peterson
LOLB	63	Spencer	Adkins
LT	87	Sam	Baker
LT	65	Will	Svitek
MLB	88	Curtis	Lofton
MLB	63	Robert	James
P	84	Michael	Koenen
QB	86	Matt	Ryan
QB	69	Chris	Redman
QB	60	John Parker	Wilson
RE	89	John	Abraham
RE	70	Kroy	Biermann
RE	67	Lawrence	Sidbury
RG	87	Harvey	Dahl
RG	66	Quinn	Ojinnaka
ROLB	75	Sean	Weatherspoon
ROLB	75	Stephen	Nicholas
ROLB	65	Coy	Wire
RT	83	Tyson	Clabo
RT	63	Garrett	Reynolds
SS	84	Erik	Coleman
SS	75	William	Moore
TE	98	Tony	Gonzalez
TE	72	Justin	Peelle
TE	61	Keith	Zinger
WR	93	Roddy	White
WR	78	Michael	Jenkins
WR	67	Brian	Finneran
WR	66	Harry	Douglas
WR	62	Kerry	Meier
WR	58	Eric	Weems

OFFENSIVE STRENGTH CHART

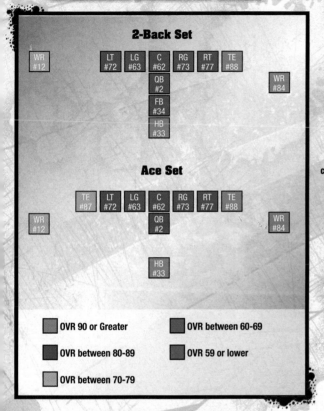

2-Back Set

WR #12	LT #72	LG #63	C #62	RG #73	RT #77	TE #88

WR #84

QB #2

FB #34

HB #33

Ace Set

TE #87	LT #72	LG #63	C #62	RG #73	RT #77	TE #88

WR #12

WR #84

QB #2

HB #33

- ■ OVR 90 or Greater
- ■ OVR between 80-89
- ■ OVR between 70-79
- ■ OVR between 60-69
- ■ OVR 59 or lower

#88 Tony Gonzalez
Tight End (TE)

Overall	98
Speed	82
Catching	95
Catch in Traffic	97
Jumping	90

#84 Roddy White
Wide Receiver (WR)

Overall	93
Speed	94
Catching	89
Release	95
Jumping	94

#33 Michael Turner
Halfback (HB)

Overall	90
Speed	87
Agility	82
Stiff Arm	98
Carrying	95

#50 Curtis Lofton
Linebacker (MLB)

Overall	88
Speed	79
Awareness	85
Tackle	96
Hit Power	90

#23 Dunta Robinson
Cornerback (CB)

Overall	85
Speed	93
Awareness	83
Man Coverage	90
Zone Coverage	80

#55 John Abraham
Defensive End (RE)

Overall	89
Speed	81
Strength	83
Finesse Moves	71
Power Moves	89

DEFENSIVE STRENGTH CHART

4-3 Defense

FS #28   SS #26

CB #20   ROLB #56   MLB #50   LOLB #53   CB #23

RE #55   DT #93   DT #95   LE #98

Dime Defense

FS #28   SS #26

CB #20   CB #21   MLB #50   CB #22   CB #23

RE #55   DT #93   DT #95   LE #98

- ■ OVR 90 or Greater
- ■ OVR between 80-89
- ■ OVR between 70-79
- ■ OVR between 60-69
- ■ OVR 59 or lower

Key Player Substitutions

Position: WR

Substitution: Harry Douglas

When: Global

Advantage: Move Douglas up to the third WR position on your roster. Placing the speedy Douglas on the opposite side of the field from White will stretch the defense and lead to many deep plays.

Key Player Substitutions

Position: LE

Substitution: Lawrence Sidbury

When: Nickel formations

Advantage: Bringing Sidbury in at LE will add much needed speed to the Falcons defensive line. In Nickel formations use Sidbury to put pressure on the quarterback.

Playbook Breakdown

The Atlanta Falcons are a very talented team on offense with third-year quarterback Matt Ryan looking to have a breakout year. Wide receiver Roddy White has proven himself as a top target with back-to-back 1,000-yard seasons. He finished the year with 85 receptions, 1,153 yards, and 11 TDs. Veteran tight end Tony Gonzalez remains a threat; he finished the year with 83 receptions, 867 yards, and 6 TDs. With such targets on offense, you should not have a problem moving the ball through the air. Look at formations where you can get Gonzalez lined up in the slot. The Falcons also love to run the ball with running back Michael Turner, who had a down year last season. Because of injury he rushed for only 871 yards. Pound the ball and feed Michael Turner from the I-Form, Full House, and Strong Slot. In this playbook you will find plenty of run plays that you can use to soften up the defense. Once you do that you can mix in play action passes for your All Pro targets.

OFFENSIVE FORMATIONS

FORMATION	# OF PLAYS
Dirty Bird Normal	3
Full House Normal Wide	12
Gun Doubles On	12
Gun Empty Trio	12
Gun Split Offset	15
Gun Spread Y-Flex	9
Gun Tight Flex	9
Gun Trey Open	12
I-Form Pro	15
I-Form Pro Twins	12
I-Form Tight Pair	15
Singleback Ace	12
Singleback Bunch	15
Singleback Doubles	15
Singleback Jumbo	9
Singleback Y-Trips	15
Strong Pro	15
Strong Slot	9
Weak Tight Twins	9

OFFENSIVE PLAYCOUNTS

PLAY TYPE	# OF PLAYS
Quick Pass	20
Standard Pass	44
Shotgun Pass	47
Play Action Pass	43
Inside Handoff	29
Outside Handoff	6
Pitch	9
Counter	7

I-Form Pro Twins—Atl HB Zone

One of the staple run plays that the Falcons like to use is the Atl HB Zone from the I-Form Pro Twins formation. This is your traditional run play, with Michael Turner following his fullback through the hole. With this play we like to motion the slot receiver to provide additional blocking. Doing this also tells us if the defense is in man or zone.

Look ahead to see who your TE blocks

Matt Ryan hands the ball off to Michael Turner. Turner is being patient and letting his blocks set up in front of him. By being patient, you should see a hole where you can take it up inside between the right tackle and the tight end.

Take it inside or outside

Fullback Ovie Mughelli makes a key block for Michael Turner, and he takes advantage of the opening to pick up 5 yards on the play. When running this play, you always want to count how many men are stacked up in the box. Especially take note of if the defense is stacking up to stop the run on one side of the formation. This is when you want to flip the play.

I-Form Pro Twins—PA Power O

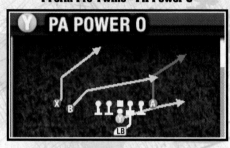

PA Power O is a good play to mix in with Atl HB Zone. In this play, the tight end is your primary target. You have a crossing route, a flat route out the backfield, and a deep post. We focus on the crossing route and the flat route as our main reads for the play.

Avoiding the sack

We begin by motioning the slot receiver just as if we are going to run the ball, but we snap the ball before he gets next to the right tackle. This gives the same look as when running the ball, and it also allows the receiver to get a running start. After the snap, look for the flat and then the crossing route. Matt Ryan sees his target and fires the ball deep.

A catch with room to run

Roddy White makes the catch in stride and picks up 10 yards. With this play, we suggest that you read the fullback first, then the crossing route, and then the tight end last because the corner route takes time to develop downfield.

I-Form Pro—HB Blast

I-Form Pro—HB Blast is a run play that goes to the weak side of the formation behind left tackle Sam Baker and left guard Justin Blalock. This is a good play to mix in with HB Toss and Power O from this formation because it's a run to the weak side of the formation.

Don't worry about the defense coming through the middle

Once the QB snaps the ball, we follow fullback Ovie Mughelli, looking to take the run inside between the left tackle and the left guard. Or if you see that the defense sealed it up pretty well, you can bounce it outside. Patience is the key; you just have to wait for your blockers to set up.

We are taking the ball around the end

Our blocker seals the edge, and Michael Turner has room to run. He takes it outside for a big gain downfield by picking up 10 yards before he is contacted. Because Michael Turner has decent speed, he can take it for a big gain. If needed, he has the power to grind out those important chain-moving first downs as well.

I-Form Pro—PA Falcon

PA FALCON

PA Falcon is designed to get the quarterback outside the pocket. The play has the fullback fake to the left, then go right into the flat on a deep crossing route. The flanker is on a streak route and the tight end is on a delay route. With this play, we are going to use the Dual HB package, which allows us to get more speed on the field.

The quarterback takes a five-step drop

Once you snap the ball, take control of the quarterback and roll out to the right side of the field. Look for the fullback as your primary read, and after that, look for the split end crossing the field. The QB sees his target and fires the ball to him.

The HB is in the flats

Jerious Norwood makes the catch, and because of his speed he gets away from the defender and picks up a big gain. Another suggestion is to keep the tight end in the backfield to block, because his route is designed to go across the field. His route is out of the quarterback's vision.

Full House Normal Wide—HB Slam

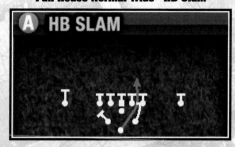

HB SLAM

HB Slam is a great run play from the Full House Normal Wide formation. This formation brings tight end Tony Gonzalez into the backfield with fullback Ovie Mughelli on the right side of the formation. Having two blockers in the backfield and being able to motion them to either side of the formation is great for run blocking.

You can walk through this hole

We begin by motioning the tight end Tony Gonzalez to the right. Snap the ball when he is behind the right guard. After the snap, look to take the run up inside behind right guard Harvey Dahl and left tackle Tyson Clabo.

Let the last blocker engage before you take off

Michael Turner sees a hole and takes the run inside behind his blockers to pick up a good gain. With this play, watch out for the defense stacking up against the run on one side of the formation. If you see this, flip the play and motion your blocker to the other side. Remember that you can motion both guys in the backfield to either side of the formation.

Full House Normal Wide—HB Sweep

HB SWEEP

Use HB Sweep from the Full House Normal Wide formation when the defense is stacking up against the run inside. We like to use the same concept with motioning one of the blockers in the backfield to provide additional blocking.

A good toss from the QB

We begin by motioning tight end Tony Gonzalez to the right. Snap the ball when he is on the outside shoulder of right tackle Tyson Clabo. As you can see, once the quarterback snaps the ball we have our blockers out in front of us. Be careful of outrunning them.

Juke back to the inside

The defenders are picked up and there is plenty of room for Michael Turner to run downfield to pick up some good yards. Remember: Always mix up which side you're going to run the ball to and mix the play in with the inside run. It's all about reading how many defenders you have in the box.

Strong Slot—Slot Streak

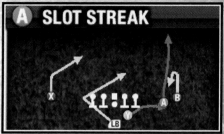

SLOT STREAK

Slot Streak has the running back on a V route out of the backfield, the fullback on a delay flat route, and a streak down the seam by the slot receiver, which opens up the underneath routes. The flanker runs a curl route while the split end is on a post route.

Great block on the edge

After the snap, keep an eye on the running back as your first read; he is the primary target on this play. Matt Ryan sees his target, Michael Turner, and fires the ball to him in the open field.

Catching on the run

He catches the ball in stride and picks up a 5-yard gain. This keeps the chains moving. If you see that the running back is covered, look for the delay route. He should go out on his route about the time the running back is midway through his route. After that, look for the short curl route.

NEW YORK GIANTS

OFFENSIVE SCOUTING REPORT

Eli Manning is getting a reputation as "Mr. Consistent." In football, consistency is often worth more than flashy and occasional brilliance. Eli can scramble when needed, put up the deep pass, or quickly get the ball out of his hands when hurried. While he may not excel in one particular area, he can be counted on to do everything well. The weapons around Eli—young, energetic receivers Steve Smith and Hakeem Nicks—bring the Giants offense to life. Both are good in traffic with sturdy hands. Mario Manningham provides speed and agility to this young corps. TE Kevin Boss is another up-and-comer who is getting increasing looks from Eli and provides a big, capable target. Brandon Jacobs in the backfield is one of the best at running through would-be tacklers and pushing them to the ground as he continually pounds through the line. To keep him fresh and to change speeds, the Giants rely on Ahmad Bradshaw as their speedy and agile back, better at running around defenders rather than through them. The offensive line features Chris Snee, arguably the best guard in the game.

DEFENSIVE SCOUTING REPORT

The Giants' pass-rush, led by defensive end Justin Tuck, is one of the defense's best assets. His constant presence and pressure on the quarterback is the cornerstone of the Giants D. The line also features two strong ends sharing time opposite Tuck in Mathias Kiwanuka and Osi Umenyiora. With relentless pressure on the quarterback, newly acquired Antrel Rolle at safety will have opportunities to make big plays and provide the coverage mid-field that used to be patrolled by MLB Antonio Pierce. With Pierce gone, the linebacker unit's strength is in question, but it's an opportunity for Michael Boley to rise as the Giants' number one tackler. The key for the Giants has been and will continue to be getting pressure on the quarterback and closing holes to running backs. The secondary will most definitely be tested, otherwise.

TEAM RATING

81
Overall

KEY ADDITIONS

P	Jy Bond
S	Deon Grant
S	Antrel Rolle
QB	Jim Sorgi
DE	Jason Pierre-Paul
DT	Linval Joseph

KEY DEPARTURES

S	C.C. Brown
QB	David Carr
LB	Danny Clark
CB	Kevin Dockery
P	Jeff Feagles
LB	Antonio Pierce

RATINGS BY POSITION

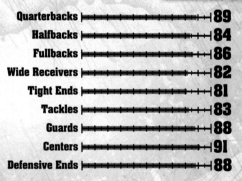

Position	Rating		Position	Rating
Quarterbacks	89		Defensive Tackles	81
Halfbacks	84		Outside Linebackers	78
Fullbacks	86		Middle Linebackers	65
Wide Receivers	82		Cornerbacks	83
Tight Ends	81		Free Safeties	83
Tackles	83		Strong Safeties	78
Guards	88		Kickers	68
Centers	91		Punters	66
Defensive Ends	88			

DEPTH CHART

POS	OVR	FIRST NAME	LAST NAME
C	91	Shaun	O'Hara
C	68	Adam	Koets
CB	89	Corey	Webster
CB	78	Aaron	Ross
CB	77	Terrell	Thomas
CB	75	Bruce	Johnson
DT	81	Barry	Cofield
DT	77	Chris	Canty
DT	76	Jay	Alford
DT	75	Rocky	Bernard
FB	86	Madison	Hedgecock
FS	83	Antrel	Rolle
FS	73	Michael	Johnson
HB	84	Brandon	Jacobs
HB	78	Ahmad	Bradshaw
HB	66	Danny	Ware
K	68	Lawrence	Tynes
LE	92	Justin	Tuck
LE	76	Jason	Pierre-Paul
LE	60	Dave	Tollefson
LG	80	Rich	Seubert
LG	70	Kevin	Boothe
LOLB	84	Michael	Boley
LOLB	64	Chase	Blackburn
LT	84	David	Diehl
LT	76	William	Beatty
MLB	65	Jonathan	Goff
MLB	64	Phillip	Dillard
P	66	Matt	Dodge
QB	89	Eli	Manning
QB	61	Rhett	Bomar
QB	59	Jim	Sorgi
RE	83	Mathias	Kiwanuka
RE	83	Osi	Umenyiora
RG	96	Chris	Snee
RG	64	Mitch	Petrus
ROLB	71	Clint	Smith
ROLB	67	Bryan	Kehl
RT	82	Kareem	McKenzie
RT	73	Guy	Whimper
SS	80	Deon	Grant
SS	78	Kenny	Phillips
SS	66	Chad	Jones
TE	81	Kevin	Boss
TE	63	Bear	Pascoe
TE	63	Travis	Beckum
WR	88	Steve	Smith
WR	81	Hakeem	Nicks
WR	76	Mario	Manningham
WR	72	Domenik	Hixon
WR	65	Derek	Hagan
WR	60	Ramses	Barden

OFFENSIVE STRENGTH CHART

2-Back Set

| WR #88 | | LT #66 | LG #69 | C #60 | RG #76 | RT #67 | TE #89 | | WR #12 |

QB #10
FB #39
HB #27

Ace Set

| | | TE #47 | LT #66 | LG #69 | C #60 | RG #76 | RT #67 | TE #89 | |
| WR #88 | | | | QB #10 | | | | | WR #12 |

HB #27

- ■ OVR 90 or Greater
- ■ OVR between 80-89
- ■ OVR between 70-79
- ■ OVR between 60-69
- ■ OVR 59 or lower

Key Player Substitutions

Position: TE

Substitution: Bear Pascoe

When: Two-tight-end sets

Advantage: Using Pascoe as your second TE in big sets will help in your two-headed running game. You can pound the ball all game long with a blocking TE like Bear.

#10 Eli Manning
Quarterback (QB)

Overall	89
Throw Power	89
Short Accuracy	89
Medium Accuracy	87
Deep Accuracy	85

#76 Chris Snee
Offensive Guard (OG)

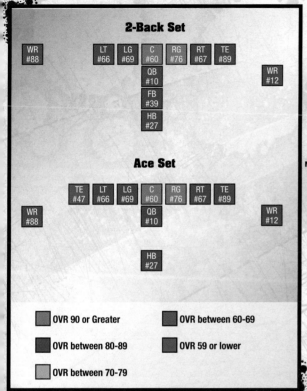

Overall	96
Strength	93
Pass Block	92
Run Block	94
Impact Blocking	92

#12 Steve Smith
Wide Receiver (WR)

Overall	88
Speed	87
Catching	92
Release	79
Jumping	86

#91 Justin Tuck
Defensive End (LE)

Overall	92
Speed	84
Strength	84
Finesse Moves	94
Power Moves	85

#23 Corey Webster
Cornerback (CB)

Overall	89
Speed	87
Awareness	87
Man Coverage	87
Zone Coverage	94

#59 Michael Boley
Linebacker (LOLB)

Overall	84
Speed	83
Awareness	85
Tackle	89
Hit Power	81

DEFENSIVE STRENGTH CHART

4-3 Defense

FS #26			SS #21
CB #24	ROLB #52	MLB #54	LOLB #59	CB #23
	RE #94	DT #93	DT #96	LE #91

Dime Defense

FS #26		SS #21
CB #24	CB #31	MLB #54	CB #25	CB #23
	RE #94	DT #93	DT #96	LE #91

- ■ OVR 90 or Greater
- ■ OVR between 80-89
- ■ OVR between 70-79
- ■ OVR between 60-69
- ■ OVR 59 or lower

Key Player Substitutions

Position: CB

Substitution: Bruce Johnson

When: Nickel formations

Advantage: Use Johnson to cover a team's third wide receiver. His speed should allow man coverage, which allows you to focus on the other two wide receivers.

Playbook Breakdown

Playbooks in *Madden NFL 11* are mirror images of what the team does on Sunday. The Giants playbook is very balanced and it fits the mold of the blue-collar attitude of the New York/New Jersey fan base. When picking out this playbook, you want to think about the style of play that you see from the Giants on Sunday. This book is perfect for the player who expects to run the ball. While most people who play *Madden NFL* stay in some sort of Gun formation, the Giants playbook will let you establish the run to set up the pass. Not only are the Giants a solid running team, but also they have a pretty good passing attack. We're drawn to this book because of the number of plays it has that include the tight end in the passing game. One of the easiest ways to control a defense is by having a good tight end working the inside of the field. Lastly, when using the Giants playbook you will not be stuck feeling one-dimensional; the playbook has a solid mixture of standard pass, gun, and play action passes to keep the defense off-balance.

OFFENSIVE FORMATIONS

FORMATION	# OF PLAYS
Gun Double Flex	15
Gun Doubles Wk	18
Gun Empty Spread	9
Gun Y-Trips Open	12
Gun Y-Trips Wk	15
I-Form Pro	18
I-Form Pro Twins	12
I-Form Tight	15
Singleback Ace	18
Singleback Ace Pair Twins	12
Singleback Bunch	15
Singleback Doubles	18
Singleback Jumbo	12
Singleback Y-Trips	18
Strong Pro	18
Weak Pro	15

OFFENSIVE PLAYCOUNTS

PLAY TYPE	# OF PLAYS
Quick Pass	13
Standard Pass	53
Shotgun Pass	45
Play Action Pass	49
Inside Handoff	34
Outside Handoff	16
Pitch	9
Counter	11

Singleback Jumbo—PA Ctr Waggle

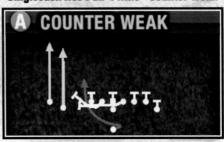

The Singleback Jumbo—PA Ctr Waggle is designed to take advantage of the aggressive nature of the defense. This play is even more potent because of the effectiveness of a solid running back like Brandon Jacobs.

This is the decision point of the play

The crucial part of this play and the reason we like it so much occurs right after the quarterback fakes the handoff and starts to roll out to the right. Even if the defense is in a perfect play call, they will come up to prevent our quarterback from getting out of the pocket. This will play right into the design of our play and give us a wide-open option.

The tight end gets open in the flat

One of the key features in the success of this play is the delay route by the tight end. A solid run fake followed by our quarterback attacking the edge of the defense will force our opponent up to play the quarterback, allowing the tight end to sneak open for the easy catch. This is a solid play to counter edge blitzes.

Singleback Ace Pair Twins—Counter Weak

The running game is a key part of the Giants playbook. One of the better running plays from the book is the Singleback Ace Pair Twins—Counter Weak. This run is a perfect reminder to the defense that even when we come out in a Singleback set, it doesn't mean we can't still pound the ball. It also helps that no matter what side we run to we have two outside blockers at our disposal.

Counters kill speed rushers

When running the Counter Weak we want the defensive end or outside linebacker to come straight upfield at the snap. This puts him in perfect position for our pulling guard to come around and nail him, setting our initial block. As a runner we have to be patient when running the ball and get underneath the block.

Brandon Jacobs is a monster in the open field

The Off Tackle run play was the best running play in *Madden NFL 10*; this year the Counter could return as the dominant run play that it once was throughout the community. Follow the blocks, run according to the design of the play, and the Singleback Ace Pair Twins—Counter Weak could be the staple run play of your offense.

I-Form Pro—Lead Draw

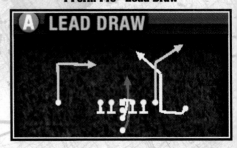

The Giants playbook allows a team with a good running back to dish out some punishment. The I-Form Pro—Lead Draw is a running play that uses automotion from the flanker to bring him just outside the tight end to serve as an extra blocker. We also like this running play because of the pull away motion it has that makes our opponent feel like we're passing the ball.

Here comes the pain

Another reason we love the Lead Draw from the I-Form Pro is that it breaks the routine of the many Off Tackle, Counter, and Sweep running plays that the majority of *Madden NFL 11* players will be used to seeing. The Lead Draw is an A gap running play that is going to let us take our bruising running back and keep establishing a tone for the game.

Brandon Jacobs gives the defense a ride

This running play gives us a good opportunity to maneuver our running back behind the line of scrimmage as he wiggles through the hole. An effective run game is one of the more disheartening things for a defense to deal with. If we continue to dominate our opponent with solid running plays like the Lead Draw, then they could very well surrender to us.

Gun Empty Spread—Stutter Hook

What's not to like about a Gun Empty set? The Gun Empty Spread—Stutter Hook gives us the use of five receivers to send at the defense. We enjoy using this play because of the unique angles of the hook routes by both inside slot receivers. These routes put us in position to handle the blitz as well as base plays that the defense throws at us.

Steve Smith releases to the outside

Because the slot receivers use an inside release and outside release, depending on which side of the line we refer to, we will have perfect spacing to fit the ball in to one of them. There is no way that a defense will call a coverage that has the cornerbacks playing different techniques on the same defense. If the defensive backs or outside linebacker man our receivers up and press, we will always have the left slot available.

Perfect route, great catch

The benefit of the Empty set is that there are times when our offense will force the defense into a mismatch problem. With the defense spread thin and trying to account for all of our weapons, we have forced them into covering our slot receiver with a linebacker. All we have to do to throw this pass to the slot is wait for the linebacker to turn upfield and then hit our receiver as he breaks on his hook.

Gun Empty Spread—Spacing

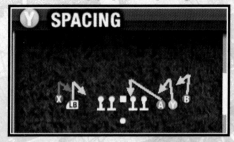

The Gun Empty Spread—Spacing is a mandatory play to run whenever we head to this formation. What is the big deal about all the short curl routes? We like the fact that no matter what defense you throw this against, they will always leave one receiver open. If all we are looking for is an opportunity for success, this play gives us that.

All receivers are coming into focus

Whenever we decide to come out in the Gun Empty, the defense is going to test how well we can handle the blitz. Most players will come out in this formation and immediately use deep routes. We want to establish an efficient passing game first and scare the defense out of trying to blitz us.

Look at the cushion the corner gives us

Spacing is such a good play that it is a must-have, and could really be a one-play offense. We have receivers all over the field open, but instead of throwing to our first look, we took the backside option and hit our split end for an easy pitch and catch. The corner is so worried about deep coverage that he leaves 5 yards between himself and our receiver.

Gun Y-Trips Open—WR Smash

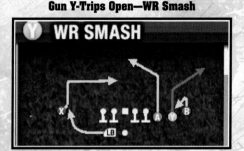

The Gun Y-Trips Open—WR Smash has always been a favorite play of ours because of the route combination to the trips side. This plays uses a hitch, corner, and post combo that can attack any man coverage as well as any zone coverage. When we come to the line of scrimmage to run this play, we aren't worried about anything the defense is doing in the secondary because we have every possibility handled with this play.

The defense is in trouble

As we drop back and survey the field, we can get a quick read on the coverage by watching how the safeties drop. We see that the safety is dropping into a Cover 2 zone, and that tells us immediately that our tight end is open on the post route. We also recognize that the defense is in man coverage, so we have the corner route as an option.

The ball sails over the outstretched arms of the defender

The WR Smash gives us so many different options to beat the defense with that it really makes offense fun. If the defense comes out in a Cover 2 all-around zone, then we will have the post and corner routes open; vs. man, we have the hitch because the defender will lay off. This play is just potent.

Singleback Y-Trips—SE Cross

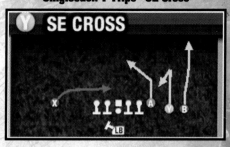

We don't consider any play in our playbook better than another because they all can be schemed to present problems for a defense to handle. The Singleback Y-Trips—SE Cross is a great play to use because we get a quick crossing route by the split end, a post by the tight end, a hook by the slot, and a streak by our flanker.

We recognize the defense in a zone blitz

The actual defensive play call never matters to us because we have to be prepared for anything. After we hike the ball we read some sort of zone blitz that is sending both cornerbacks in to pressure our quarterback. When faced with the blitz the SE Cross shines. Stay calm and look to the slot receiver running the hook route.

The receiver catches the ball in traffic

Each play is different, but we have seen that all of our play calls have given us the opportunity to beat the defense no matter what they are in. Our opponent thought that a little pressure could rattle us, but the Singleback Y-Trips—SE Cross is a play that accounts for the blitz with the hook route. Our receiver caught the ball and gave us first down yardage on the play.

JACKSONVILLE JAGUARS

OFFENSIVE SCOUTING REPORT

Mo-Jo to the rescue! After sharing the field over the past three seasons, Maurice Jones-Drew emerged as the featured back in the Jags offense and flourished. He is the shining star of the offense with his small frame, quick feet, and incredible field vision. Don't bother using Jones-Drew sparingly—he is now the basis of the offense. The passing game of David Garrard is built around the run and features the speed of top receivers Mike Sims-Walker and Mike Thomas. Both Mikes are quick into their routes and have decent hands. The addition of WR Kassim Osgood from San Diego will provide depth. The biggest question on the Jags offense is, can David Garrard step up to truly ignite the passing game? Time will tell, but the potential has always been there, and the weapons around him can be molded to his liking.

DEFENSIVE SCOUTING REPORT

The pass defense of the Jags struggled last season, but an off-season move brought Aaron Kampman from the Packers to help address the problem. In Kampman, the Jags gain a pass-rush threat from someone who has already established himself as capable of reaching the quarterback. The benefactor of the improved pass rush will be CB Rashean Mathis, whose speed and superb zone coverage will allow him to take chances and make a play on the ball from hurried quarterbacks. The secondary as a whole is quick, but it will be up to fellow corner Derek Cox and safety Reggie Nelson to elevate their games to control the pass protection. The linebacker corps of the Jags is solid and provides power and sure tackling, something needed in a rushing defense that sees Titans running back Chris Johnson twice a year. The Jags are still coming into their own but are making strides in the right direction.

TEAM RATING

74
Overall

KEY ADDITIONS

DE	Aaron Kampman
LB	Kirk Morrison
WR	Kassim Osgood
LB	Freddy Keiaho
DT	Tyson Alualu

KEY DEPARTURES

DE	Quentin Groves
DT	John Henderson
WR	Torry Holt
LB	Clint Ingram
LB	Brian Iwuh
OT	Tra Thomas

RATINGS BY POSITION

Position	Rating	Position	Rating
Quarterbacks	79	Defensive Tackles	83
Halfbacks	96	Outside Linebackers	87
Fullbacks	84	Middle Linebackers	82
Wide Receivers	75	Cornerbacks	87
Tight Ends	82	Free Safeties	77
Tackles	82	Strong Safeties	70
Guards	80	Kickers	74
Centers	78	Punters	64
Defensive Ends	79		

DEPTH CHART

POS	OVR	FIRST NAME	LAST NAME
C	78	Brad	Meester
C	78	Uche	Nwaneri
CB	92	Rashean	Mathis
CB	82	Derek	Cox
CB	66	Scott	Starks
CB	63	Don	Carey
CB	60	Tyron	Brackenridge
DT	83	Terrance	Knighton
DT	77	Tyson	Alualu
DT	72	Atiyyah	Ellison
DT	68	D'Anthony	Smith
FB	84	Greg	Jones
FB	68	Montell	Owens
FS	77	Reggie	Nelson
FS	64	Anthony	Smith
HB	96	Maurice	Jones-Drew
HB	69	Deji	Karim
HB	69	Rashad	Jennings
K	74	Josh	Scobee
LE	75	Reggie	Hayward
LE	70	Derrick	Harvey
LG	83	Justin	Smiley
LG	77	Kynan	Forney
LOLB	89	Daryl	Smith
LOLB	65	Russell	Allen
LT	81	Eugene	Monroe
MLB	82	Kirk	Morrison
MLB	65	Teddy	Lehman
P	64	Adam	Podlesh
QB	79	David	Garrard
QB	70	Luke	McCown
RE	87	Aaron	Kampman
RE	67	Julius	Williams
RG	76	Vince	Manuwai
RG	70	Paul	McQuistan
ROLB	85	Justin	Durant
ROLB	65	Freddy	Keiaho
RT	83	Eben	Britton
RT	67	Jordan	Black
SS	74	Gerald	Alexander
SS	70	Sean	Considine
SS	65	Courtney	Greene
TE	82	Marcedes	Lewis
TE	68	Zach	Miller
TE	67	Ernest	Wilford
WR	85	Mike	Sims-Walker
WR	74	Mike	Thomas
WR	68	Troy	Williamson
WR	65	Kassim	Osgood
WR	59	Nate	Hughes
WR	58	Tiquan	Underwood

OFFENSIVE STRENGTH CHART

2-Back Set

WR #80   LT #75 | LG #66 | C #63 | RG #67 | RT #73 | TE #89   WR #11

QB #9

FB #33

HB #32

Ace Set

TE #85 | LT #75 | LG #66 | C #63 | RG #67 | RT #73 | TE #89   WR #11

WR #80

QB #9

HB #32

- ▢ OVR 90 or Greater
- ▢ OVR between 80-89
- ▢ OVR between 70-79
- ▢ OVR between 60-69
- ▢ OVR 59 or lower

Key Player Substitutions

Position: HB

Substitution: Deji Karim

When: Dual-back sets

Advantage: In today's league, running backs are used for more then just running the ball. Karim is a great back who can get the ball in the flats and use his speed to pick up more yards.

#32 Maurice Jones-Drew
Halfback (HB)

Overall	96
Speed	94
Agility	96
Stiff Arm	82
Carrying	79

#11 Mike Sims-Walker
Wide Receiver (WR)

Overall	85
Speed	91
Catching	86
Release	85
Jumping	91

#89 Marcedes Lewis
Tight End (TE)

Overall	82
Speed	72
Catching	78
Catch in Traffic	78
Jumping	78

#74 Aaron Kampman
Defensive End (RE)

Overall	87
Speed	76
Strength	85
Finesse Moves	73
Power Moves	92

#27 Rashean Mathis
Cornerback (CB)

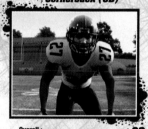

Overall	92
Speed	91
Awareness	85
Man Coverage	88
Zone Coverage	96

#52 Daryl Smith
Linebacker (LOLB)

Overall	89
Speed	78
Awareness	88
Tackle	94
Hit Power	93

DEFENSIVE STRENGTH CHART

3-4 Defense

FS #25 | SS #37

CB #21   ROLB #56 | MLB #57 | MLB #55 | LOLB #52   CB #27

RE #74 | DT #96 | LE #91

Dime Defense

FS #25 | SS #37

CB #21   CB #31   MLB #55   CB #41   CB #27

RE #74 | DT #93 | DT #96 | LE #91

- ▢ OVR 90 or Greater
- ▢ OVR between 80-89
- ▢ OVR between 70-79
- ▢ OVR between 60-69
- ▢ OVR 59 or lower

Key Player Substitutions

Position: LE

Substitution: Larry Hart

When: Long-yardage situations

Advantage: When you don't have to worry about your opponent running the ball, substitute Hart in at LE to use his speed to get around the edge and sack the QB.

Playbook Breakdown

The Jacksonville Jaguars offense revolves around running the ball and high-percentage passing plays. However, this season they want to take some deep shots in hopes of making big plays and to open up running lanes for their talented running back, Maurice Jones-Drew. The Jaguars have a good mix of run, play action, high-percentage passing, and deep passing plays. With that said, there isn't any one formation or play that makes this playbook stand out. This can be a good or bad thing depending on how you look at it. The good thing is your opponent won't be able to tell what playbook you are running since the formations in the book can be found in other playbooks. The bad thing is there isn't a formation that your opponent has to really worry about defending. If you are looking for a balanced playbook that's not flashy, then the Jaguars playbook is a good choice. If you are looking for a playbook with a lot of pizzazz, this one is not for you.

OFFENSIVE FORMATIONS

FORMATION	# OF PLAYS
Gun Doubles	15
Gun Split Slot	12
Gun Spread Y-Flex	15
Gun Trey Open	12
Gun Y-Trips Wk	15
I-Form Pro	21
I-Form Pro Twins	15
I-Form Tight Pair	12
Singleback Ace	18
Singleback Ace Twins	15
Singleback Bunch	15
Singleback Doubles	18
Singleback Y-Trips	15
Strong Pro	18
Strong Tight	9
Weak Pro	15

OFFENSIVE PLAYCOUNTS

PLAY TYPE	# OF PLAYS
Quick Pass	11
Standard Pass	54
Shotgun Pass	42
Play Action Pass	50
Inside Handoff	32
Outside Handoff	17
Pitch	10
Counter	9

I-Form Pro—Comet Pass

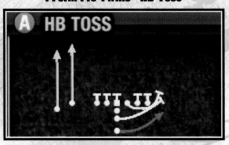

One of the better high-percentage passing plays over the years in *Madden NFL* has been the Comet Pass. This play isn't in many playbooks, so it doesn't get used as much as it once did. We like it because it's simple to run but effective.

Garrard drops back in the pocket looking for his primary receiver

The halfback coming out of the backfield on the circle route is the receiver we look to throw to first regardless of whether man or zone coverage is called. The only pre-snap adjustment we might make is to hot route the tight end on a slant or an in route. If we hot route the tight end on an in route, we must make sure we smart route him so that he runs his route farther down the field.

Jones-Drew reaches out to snag the ball as it closes in

This clears out the zone coverage to ensure that the running back is open as he comes over the short middle of the field. If man coverage is called, wait for the halfback to gain inside position on his man before making the throw.

I-Form Pro Twins—HB Toss

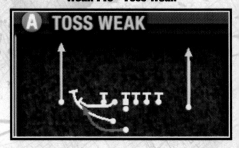

Make no mistake about it; the Jaguars offense revolves around running back Maurice Jones-Drew, and for good reason, as he is one of the fastest and most electric backs in the league. For that reason, finding plays to get him involved in the offense should be your number one priority.

Jones-Drew patiently waits for his blocks to set up

A running play we like to run that showcases his big-time abilities is the I-Form Pro Twins—HB Toss. If your opponent likes to come out in defensive base formations such as the 4–3 Normal and play man coverage, this run play does an excellent job of getting Jones-Drew in open space where can he rack up yardage.

A key block is thrown by the FB to spring Jones-Drew

The key is to not get him out in front of the run blockers. Wait for the pulling right guard and fullback to throw their blocks. Once they do, then get out in front of them and look for open daylight. Jones-Drew is shifty enough once in open space to make a few would-be tacklers miss.

Weak Pro—Toss Weak

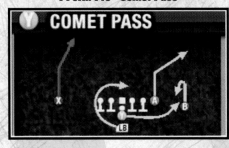

Another outside run play that gets Maurice Jones-Drew in open space is the Weak Pro—Toss Weak. This play is designed to get him into space by running to the weak side. Ideally, to make this play more effective, you want to get the defense over-shifting to the strong side, so that the weak side doesn't have as many defenders in that area of the field.

The ROLB is blocked by the FB

For instance, if you run the Power O and Stretch plays first, your opponent might shift the linebackers to the tight end side. Once you notice this, it's time to run the Toss Weak. Once the ball is snapped, the play's success depends on if the fullback can seal off the outside defender or not.

The RB uses a juke to get by the defender

If he does, then there should be running room to the outside for Jones-Drew. If not, then you will have to bounce him back inside and try to pick up what you can with this play. If zone coverage is called, consider motioning the flanker to the other side so he becomes an additional blocker.

Singleback Ace—PA Ctr Waggle

The Singleback Ace—PA Ctr Waggle is a perfect way to get quarterback David Garrard out of the pocket while giving him downfield targets to beat the pass coverage. The play's primary receiver is Mike Sims-Walker, who is lined up at the flanker position. He runs a deep hitch route.

Garrard throws the ball downfield while on the run

If you have strong stick control, his route can be difficult to defend if man coverage is called. The other option is the backside tight end running the crossing route. Watch for him if man coverage is called. Tight end Marcedes Lewis runs a delayed flat route and is a good choice to dump the ball to if the first two reads are not open. Running the deep post on the backside is split end Mike Thomas.

The backside TE makes the catch as his man lags behind

If no safety drops over the deep middle, Thomas is an option to throw to. Just keep in mind that although he's accurate on shorter passes, Garrard's deep accuracy is not the best, so the ball may not travel fast enough or be accurate enough to prevent a defender from stepping in front and picking the pass off.

Gun Doubles—HB Angle

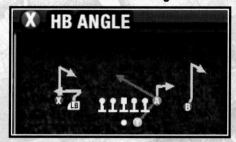

A good play to take advantage of Maurice Jones-Drew's abilities to catch the ball out of the backfield is the Gun Doubles—HB Angle. As the play suggests, the running back runs an angle route out of the backfield. If man coverage is called, Jones-Drew can gain separation due to his speed and acceleration ratings.

Jones-Drew cuts over the middle of the field to get open

Wait for him to make his break over the middle before throwing. If zone coverage is called, we like to hot route the tight end on a slant in. The idea is to force to the hook zone defenders to drop back to cover the tight end's slant route, allowing Jones-Drew to get open underneath the coverage. This is a solid red zone play, especially when just outside of the end zone.

The ball is about to be caught on the run for a solid gain

Another route worth noting is the whip route run by the slot receiver. If man coverage is called, look for him once he breaks towards the sideline. Consider hot routing the split end on a streak to clear room for the slot.

Gun Spread Y-Flex—HB Off Tackle

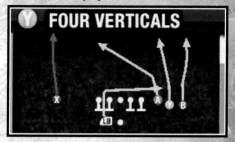

Spreading out the defense is a good choice when trying to create running lanes for Maurice Jones-Drew to attack. The Gun Spread Y-Flex—HB Off Tackle is an excellent play to attack Dollar and Quarter defenses.

Plenty of holes open up for the RB to run through

We like this play because we can run up inside or run outside with Jones-Drew depending on what the defense dictates. As long as the blocks hold up, there will be running room to maneuver Jones-Drew through to pick up yardage.

Jones-Drew runs off tackle into daylight for a big pickup

Something to consider when zone coverage is called is sending the right slot or flanker in motion to the other side of the field to add an extra running blocker as long as zone coverage is called. If man coverage is called, snap the ball before the receiver gets all the way across.

Gun Trey Open—Four Verticals

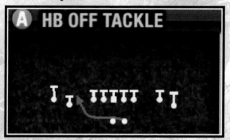

The Jaguars are looking to open up the offense by throwing deep more often. The idea is to help open up running lanes for Maurice Jones-Drew by preventing the defense from stacking the box. A good play to call out of the Gun Trey Open is the Four Verticals.

The slot receiver gets open as the FS cheats towards the right side

This play sends four receivers deep that vertically stretch the passing coverage. The play's primary receiver is split end Mike Thomas, who runs a go route down the left sideline. The receiver that we tend to look for is Troy Williamson, who runs a slice route over the deep middle. Even if a safety plays the deep middle, he will be open because the safety will cheat towards Kassim Osgood, who runs a seam route.

The catch is made between two defenders over the deep middle

If Cover 2 man coverage is called, Williamson will be open as long as he can get separation from the defender covering him. The only pass coverage that might prevent him from being open is Cover 4.

NEW YORK JETS

OFFENSIVE SCOUTING REPORT

QB Mark Sanchez will have a lot of weapons this year. The Jets' improved passing game this season will include wide receivers Jerricho Cotchery, Braylon Edwards, and newly acquired Santonio Holmes. With Sanchez's ever-improving ratings, opposing defenses will have their hands full against air attacks because any of those receivers can be dangerous. The offensive line is built tough and anchored by the best center in the league, Nick Mangold, further providing time and protection for Sanchez and his talented receiver corps. The loss of RB Thomas Jones was immediately followed by the addition of RB LaDainian Tomlinson. This will add excitement to the running game and force defenses to anticipate the run, again opening the field for Sanchez. The Jets are aligning themselves offensively to be a contender in the AFC.

DEFENSIVE SCOUTING REPORT

The Jets have the top-ranked defense. With the return of Kris Jenkins at tackle and Shaun Ellis looking to continue his solid defensive end performance of last year, the Jets line is one of the best. At corner, Antonio Cromartie comes to the Jets this year to join the top-rated Darrelle Revis to make a formidable pair in the secondary. Opposing receivers will have a hard time beating these shutdown corners. The linebacker corps is also nothing to sneeze at. Expect plenty of pressure on the QB and plenty of sacks with this group of men, consisting of Calvin Pace, David Harris, and the newly acquired LOLB Jason Taylor. Taylor is an effective pass rusher and should strengthen the Jets' already formidable defense.

TEAM RATING

89
Overall

KEY ADDITIONS

CB	Antonio Cromartie
WR	Santonio Holmes
S	Brodney Pool
LB	Jason Taylor
RB	LaDainian Tomlinson
CB	Kyle Wilson

KEY DEPARTURES

G	Alan Faneca
K	Jay Feely
RB	Thomas Jones
S	Kerry Rhodes
CB	Lito Sheppard
RB	Leon Washington

RATINGS BY POSITION

Position	Rating
Quarterbacks	82
Halfbacks	80
Fullbacks	94
Wide Receivers	86
Tight Ends	82
Tackles	90
Guards	82
Centers	97
Defensive Ends	75
Defensive Tackles	94
Outside Linebackers	81
Middle Linebackers	91
Cornerbacks	91
Free Safeties	77
Strong Safeties	85
Kickers	73
Punters	64

DEPTH CHART

POS	OVR	FIRST NAME	LAST NAME
C	97	Nick	Mangold
CB	99	Darrelle	Revis
CB	83	Antonio	Cromartie
CB	76	Kyle	Wilson
CB	74	Dwight	Lowery
CB	61	Drew	Coleman
DT	94	Kris	Jenkins
DT	72	Sione	Pouha
FB	94	Tony	Richardson
FB	67	John	Conner
FS	77	Eric	Smith
FS	72	Brodney	Pool
HB	83	LaDainian	Tomlinson
HB	80	Shonn	Greene
HB	69	Joe	McKnight
HB	62	Chauncey	Washington
K	73	Nick	Folk
LE	86	Shaun	Ellis
LE	75	Vernon	Gholston
LE	60	Ropati	Pitoitua
LG	75	Vladimir	Ducasse
LG	65	Matt	Slauson
LOLB	82	Jason	Taylor
LOLB	77	Bryan	Thomas
LT	91	D'Brickashaw	Ferguson
LT	67	Wayne	Hunter
MLB	91	David	Harris
MLB	89	Bart	Scott
MLB	50	Lance	Laury
P	64	Steve	Weatherford
QB	82	Mark	Sanchez
QB	70	Kellen	Clemens
QB	54	Erik	Ainge
RE	64	Mike	Devito
RE	47	Rodrique	Wright
RG	88	Brandon	Moore
RG	63	Robert	Turner
ROLB	85	Calvin	Pace
ROLB	58	Jamaal	Westerman
RT	89	Damien	Woody
SS	85	Jim	Leonhard
SS	59	James	Ihedigbo
TE	82	Dustin	Keller
TE	64	Ben	Hartsock
WR	87	Santonio	Holmes
WR	85	Braylon	Edwards
WR	85	Jerricho	Cotchery
WR	69	Brad	Smith
WR	68	David	Clowney
WR	49	Danny	Woodhead

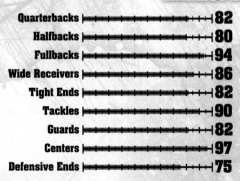

OFFENSIVE STRENGTH CHART

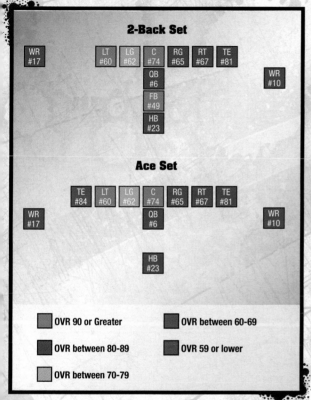

2-Back Set

| WR #17 | | | | | | | | | |
| LT #60 | LG #62 | C #74 | RG #65 | RT #67 | TE #81 | | WR #10 |

QB #6
FB #49
HB #23

Ace Set

| TE #84 | LT #60 | LG #62 | C #74 | RG #65 | RT #67 | TE #81 |
| WR #17 | | | | | | WR #10 |

QB #6

HB #23

- OVR 90 or Greater
- OVR between 80-89
- OVR between 70-79
- OVR between 60-69
- OVR 59 or lower

Key Player Substitutions

Position: WR

Substitution: David Clowney

When: Four-wide-receiver sets

Advantage: Speed is everything when it comes to four-wide-receiver sets. Clowney's speed on the outside will make it much tougher for defenses to double on one WR and leave a linebacker to cover another.

#74 Nick Mangold
Center (C)

Overall	97
Strength	94
Pass Block	93
Run Block	92
Impact Blocking	91

#10 Santonio Holmes
Wide Receiver (WR)

Overall	87
Speed	94
Catching	90
Release	77
Jumping	88

#49 Tony Richardson
Fullback (FB)

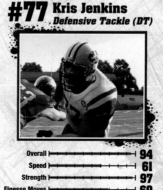

Overall	94
Speed	75
Agility	75
Stiff Arm	85
Carrying	84

#24 Darrelle Revis
Cornerback (CB)

Overall	99
Speed	93
Awareness	90
Man Coverage	98
Zone Coverage	95

#52 David Harris
Linebacker (MLB)

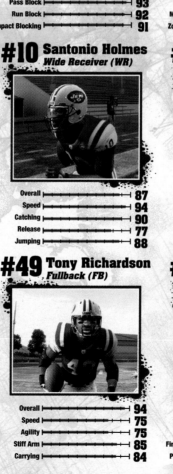

Overall	91
Speed	79
Awareness	88
Tackle	97
Hit Power	91

#77 Kris Jenkins
Defensive Tackle (DT)

Overall	94
Speed	61
Strength	97
Finesse Moves	69
Power Moves	94

DEFENSIVE STRENGTH CHART

3-4 Defense

FS #33   SS #36

| CB #31 | | ROLB #97 | MLB #57 | | MLB #52 | LOLB #99 | | CB #24 |
| | | | RE #70 | DT #77 | LE #92 | | | |

Dime Defense

FS #33   SS #36

| CB #31 | | CB #26 | | MLB #52 | | CB #20 | | CB #24 |
| | | | RE #70 | DT #91 | DT #77 | LE #92 | | |

- OVR 90 or Greater
- OVR between 80-89
- OVR between 70-79
- OVR between 60-69
- OVR 59 or lower

Key Player Substitutions

Position: FS

Substitution: Brodney Pool

When: Situational

Advantage: When you need to bring a lot of heat from your safeties, try letting Pool use his speed to get into the backfield. Only use him in blitz situations.

Playbook Breakdown

One thing we know for sure is that teams that do well in the real NFL season before the new *Madden NFL* game comes out generally get an upgrade in their offensive playbook. The Jets are no exception, and we have a funny feeling that their offensive and defensive playbooks will get plenty of attention once the game is dropped. The offensive playbook is one of the most balanced in the game, just like the real Jets offense. If you like to pound the rock, the I-Form Tackle Over, I Form Twin TE, and Strong Close are all excellent choices. If you'd rather pass the ball, check out the Gun Split Jet, Gun Jets Wing Trips, and Gun Spread Y-Slot; these formations have man coverage beaters that will make your opponent's head spin. As an added bonus for those of you who are Wildcat users, the Jets have their own version of it, which is called Wildcat Jet. The three run plays in that formation are Counter, Jet Sweep, and Power.

OFFENSIVE FORMATIONS

FORMATION	# OF PLAYS
Gun Bunch Wk	12
Gun Doubles Wk	15
Gun Jets Wing Trips	12
Gun Split Jet	12
Gun Spread Y-Slot	15
I-Form Pro	12
I-Form Tackle Over	9
I-Form Twin TE	9
Singleback Ace	12
Singleback Ace Pair	12
Singleback Bunch Base	9
Singleback Doubles	15
Singleback Y-Trips	12
Strong Close	12
Strong Pro	15
Strong Y-Flex	12
Weak Pro	12
Weak Pro Twins	12
Wildcat Jet	3

OFFENSIVE PLAYCOUNTS

PLAY TYPE	# OF PLAYS
Quick Pass	15
Standard Pass	39
Shotgun Pass	43
Play Action Pass	47
Inside Handoff	36
Outside Handoff	10
Pitch	12
Counter	8

I-Form Tackle Over—HB Slam

The I-Form Tackle Over formation has the left tackle lined up next to the right tackle. The tight end moves over to where the left tackle would normally line up. The other tight end lines up in a wing position next to the left tackle. As one might expect, this formation is about the power run game.

Greene follows his blocks, looking to pick up yardage

Shonn Greene and LaDainian Tomlinson are both effective when running between the tackles. A good inside run play to call from the I-Form Tackle Over for either of them is the HB Slam. This play has the fullback lead-blocking for the halfback. The fullback looks to attack one of the linebackers, allowing the halfback to run through the open hole that is created between the right guard and right tackle.

Greene bounces outside to open daylight

What we like about this play is that the ball carrier can easily be bounced outside, where positive yardage can often be found. If you really want to get creative with this play, sub in another tackle at the wing tight end position to add even more power in the run game.

Strong Close—Quick Toss

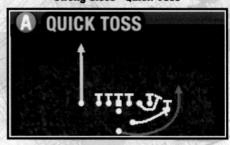

In *Madden NFL 10*, the Strong Close formation was one of the most used in the game due to the Off Tackle and Quick Toss plays. The Jets playbook has the Strong Close but does not have the Off Tackle. However, it does have the Quick Toss.

Sanchez tosses the ball to Greene

Neither Shonn Greene nor LaDainian Tomlinson has great speed, but because the run blocking is so good in this play, they are both effective enough to pick up yardage. The Strong Close has the flanker and split end lined up tighter. The right guard and fullback both are the lead blockers for the ball carrier. The key to running this play successfully is to not outrun the blockers in front.

One more key block and Greene is on his way in for 6

Let the blocks set up first. Once they do, get outside into the open field to pick up yardage. If for some reason the outside is shut down, cut back inside and pick up what you can. Whatever you do, don't try to make something happen or you'll end up losing yardage.

Strong Close—Y Trail

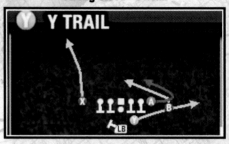

One passing play that we like to run out of the Strong Close against zone coverage is the Y Trail. Those familiar with the Texas passing concept will feel right at home because this play works pretty much the same way. Braylon Edwards runs a quick slant over the middle.

Sanchez looks for his primary receiver over the short middle of the field

Tight end Dustin Keller trails underneath Edwards. The idea is to have Holmes's route force the hook zone defenders to drop back to cover him, allowing Keller to work underneath and get open for a quick pass.

Keller is open for a bullet pass as he makes his cut over the middle

This play is not designed to pick up a lot of yardage, but it will limit the chances of the ball being picked off and will consistently pick up 4–7 yards against most zone coverages in the game. In our book, we will take that type of pass yardage all day long. If man coverage is called, look for Edwards because he often gains separation once he cuts towards the middle of the field.

Gun Split Jet—HB Power O

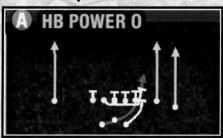

In last year's game, many top players started to run the ball from various Gun formations because of how effective they were. In *Madden NFL 11*, Gun run plays are just as effective, or even more so than in last year's game. A run play we like out of the Jets playbook in the Gun Split Jet is the HB Power O.

The left guard pulls as one of the lead blockers for Greene

This Gun formation has the running back lined up to the left of the quarterback and the tight end lined up to right. The left guard and tight end are the running back's lead blockers. How the defense decides to play will determine if the ball is run to the inside or to the outside.

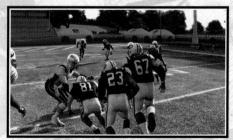

Greene lowers his shoulders, looking to bang out some tough yardage

Once the ball is snapped, watch to see where the holes open up. Generally at least one will open up inside where you can slip through with the running back for positive yardage. If not, look to bust it outside to pick up some yardage.

Gun Doubles Wk—Jets Y-Cross

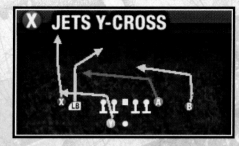

The Gun Doubles Wk—Jets Y-Cross is an excellent play to call if your opponent likes to call man coverage as the primary way of defending the pass. The play's primary receiver is tight end Dustin Keller, who runs a shallow crossing route. His speed and acceleration make him a matchup nightmare to cover for most linebackers and safeties in the game.

Keller is open over the short middle of the field for a quick bullet pass

Look for him first as he comes across over the middle. Another pass route we like is the deep crossing route run by Santonio Holmes, who is lined up out wide in the flanker position. Once he makes his cut towards the deep middle of the field, he should be open for a hard bullet pass.

Sanchez throws a dart to Holmes as he comes across the deep middle

What helps get these two receivers open is two routes run by the slot and the split end on the left side of the field. Both of their pass routes drive the deep pass coverage farther back, allowing Keller and Holmes to work underneath in one-on-one coverage. If for some reason neither of those two receivers is open, look for Greene in the flat.

Gun Jets Wing Trips—Stutter Curl Seam

The Jets have some new plays that were added this year. One of them is the Gun Jets Wing Trips—Stutter Curl Seam. This passing play is very efficient at beating man coverage. The play's primary receiver is Braylon Edwards, who lines up in the slot on the right.

Edwards takes a few stutter steps before he curls back towards the QB

If you look closely at the play diagram, you will notice he runs a curl route. Unlike with most curl routes in the game, he stutter-steps before turning around on his curl route. By stutter-stepping, he can free himself from his defender in man coverage. The pass can be thrown to him at two different points during his pass route: while he is stutter-stepping or right as he curls back. If the ball is thrown during the stutter-step, there is a chance of the ball being picked off.

Sanchez lets the ball fly once he spots his primary target open

If the ball is thrown just as he curls back, it is almost impossible for the defender to pick it off because Edwards can get enough cushion to make the catch.

Gun Spread Y-Slot—Jet Seams

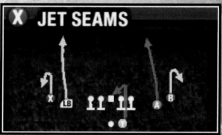

An effective pass play to call that attacks Cover 2 man and zone coverages is the Gun Spread Y-Slot—Jet Seams. This play has the two outside receivers running hook routes to the outside while the two inside receivers run seam routes.

Holmes jumps up and snags the ball

The running back runs a delayed curl route and is the play's check-down receiver. If Cover 2 man is called, the outside hook routes are pretty much money as long as the throw is timed properly. Wait for the receivers to get about 7 yards down the field. At this point throw a high bullet pass towards the sideline. If it's thrown correctly, you should see the intended receiver separate himself enough from the cornerback to make an easy catch for a 7- to 10-yard pickup. If the pass is thrown late, the cornerback in coverage might pick it off.

Keller gets inside position on the SS just before making the catch

If Cover 2 zone coverage is called, look for the tight end lined up on the right slot. When making the throw, put the ball inside where he can go grab it.

DETROIT LIONS

OFFENSIVE SCOUTING REPORT

The Lions offense has one of the best all-around receivers in the game in Calvin Johnson Jr. He is a large target with explosive speed and agility, not to mention his ability to jump for a spectacular catch and come down with a big play. Matthew Stafford, in his sophomore year, has the big throwing power to get it to Calvin Johnson, as long as the offensive line provides enough time for the play to develop. The Lions added Nate Burleson to the wide receiver unit to give Stafford another quality target and to help free Johnson Jr. from a constant double team. The acquisition of TE Tony Scheffler allows the Lions to work in two-tight-end sets to further open up the passing game for Stafford. To help get the passing game going, the Lions have to mix in the running of Kevin Smith and rookie Jahvid Best. Smith is the larger of the two backs, with more trucking power, but look to the rookie for speed and agility and more potential to break a long run.

DEFENSIVE SCOUTING REPORT

After finishing the year with the worst passing defense in the league and a run defense that was not much better, the Lions made a lot of off-season moves to the overall improvement of both. Former Titan Kyle Vanden Bosch provides decent strength at RE and can put pressure on opposing QBs, while rookie Ndamukong Suh provides grade A stats in strength, hit power, and block shedding at the tackle position. Julian Peterson at linebacker should benefit from the new strength on the front line. Despite all the improvements on the defensive line for the Lions, the secondary only has one player with an overall rating over 80, and that is free safety Louis Delmas. Speedy corner Chris Houston was brought to the Lions to also provide deep coverage. Delmas and Houston will have to provide the coverage needed to make up for the secondary's shortcomings.

TEAM RATING

68
Overall

KEY ADDITIONS

WR	Nate Burleson
TE	Tony Scheffler
HB	Jahvid Best
CB	Chris Houston
DE	Kyle Vanden Bosch
DT	Ndamukong Suh

KEY DEPARTURES

CB	Phillip Buchanan
LB	Larry Foote
CB	Anthony Henry
LB	Ernie Sims
DT	Grady Jackson
OL	Daniel Loper

RATINGS BY POSITION

Position	Rating
Quarterbacks	80
Halfbacks	80
Fullbacks	78
Wide Receivers	80
Tight Ends	82
Tackles	77
Guards	80
Centers	83
Defensive Ends	75
Defensive Tackles	85
Outside Linebackers	78
Middle Linebackers	75
Cornerbacks	70
Free Safeties	85
Strong Safeties	72
Kickers	89
Punters	73

DEPTH CHART

POS	OVR	FIRST NAME	LAST NAME
C	83	Dominic	Raiola
C	68	Dylan	Gandy
CB	71	Chris	Houston
CB	68	Eric	King
CB	65	Dante	Wesley
CB	65	Jonathan	Wade
CB	60	Jack	Williams
DT	85	Ndamukong	Suh
DT	78	Corey	Williams
DT	75	Sammie Lee	Hill
DT	64	Landon	Cohen
FB	78	Jerome	Felton
FS	85	Louis	Delmas
FS	73	Ko	Simpson
HB	80	Kevin	Smith
HB	75	Jahvid	Best
HB	74	Maurice	Morris
HB	67	Aaron	Brown
K	89	Jason	Hanson
LE	71	Jared	DeVries
LE	70	Jason	Hunter
LE	68	Turk	McBride
LG	82	Rob	Sims
LG	65	Manny	Ramirez
LOLB	86	Julian	Peterson
LOLB	66	Zack	Follett
LT	80	Jeff	Backus
LT	66	Jason	Fox
MLB	75	Deandre	Levy
MLB	59	Jordon	Dizon
P	73	Nick	Harris
QB	80	Matthew	Stafford
QB	70	Shaun	Hill
QB	61	Drew	Stanton
RE	80	Kyle	Vanden Bosch
RE	76	Cliff	Avril
RG	78	Stephen	Peterman
ROLB	69	Landon	Johnson
ROLB	58	Ashlee	Palmer
RT	74	Gosder	Cherilus
RT	74	Jon	Jansen
SS	72	Marquand	Manuel
SS	66	Marvin	White
TE	82	Brandon	Pettigrew
TE	74	Tony	Scheffler
TE	70	Will	Heller
WR	91	Calvin	Johnson Jr.
WR	78	Nate	Burleson
WR	70	Bryant	Johnson
WR	66	Dennis	Northcutt
WR	62	Derrick	Williams
WR	60	Brian	Clark

OFFENSIVE STRENGTH CHART

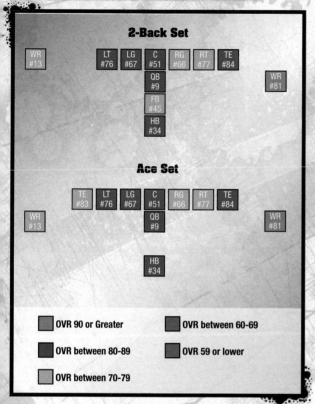

2-Back Set

	WR #13								
LT #76	LG #67	C #51	RG #66	RT #77	TE #84		
		QB #9				WR #81
		FB #45			
		HB #34			

Ace Set

TE #83	LT #76	LG #67	C #51	RG #66	RT #77	TE #84
WR #13		QB #9				WR #81
		HB #34			

■ OVR 90 or Greater	■ OVR between 60-69
■ OVR between 80-89	■ OVR 59 or lower
■ OVR between 70-79	

#81 Calvin Johnson Jr.
Wide Receiver (WR)

Overall	91
Speed	95
Catching	90
Release	95
Jumping	99

#34 Kevin Smith
Halfback (HB)

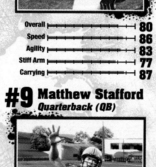

Overall	80
Speed	86
Agility	83
Stiff Arm	77
Carrying	87

#9 Matthew Stafford
Quarterback (QB)

Overall	80
Throw Power	97
Short Accuracy	81
Medium Accuracy	76
Deep Accuracy	80

#59 Julian Peterson
Linebacker (LOLB)

Overall	86
Speed	84
Awareness	87
Tackle	84
Hit Power	84

#90 Ndamukong Suh
Defensive Tackle (DT)

Overall	85
Speed	71
Strength	95
Power Moves	85
Block Shedding	92

#93 Kyle Vanden Bosch
Defensive Tackle (DT)

Overall	80
Speed	69
Strength	83
Power Moves	85
Block Shedding	85

DEFENSIVE STRENGTH CHART

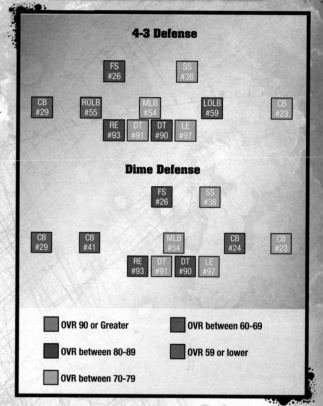

4-3 Defense

	FS #26			SS #36		
CB #29	ROLB #55		MLB #54		LOLB #59	CB #23
		RE #93	DT #91	DT #90	LE #97	

Dime Defense

	FS #26			SS #36		
CB #29	CB #41		MLB #54		CB #24	CB #23
		RE #93	DT #91	DT #90	LE #97	

■ OVR 90 or Greater	■ OVR between 60-69
■ OVR between 80-89	■ OVR 59 or lower
■ OVR between 70-79	

Key Player Substitutions

Position: TE

Substitution: Tony Scheffler

When: Global

Advantage: Tony Scheffler is a great tight end to get into the flats or hit across the middle. Because he's one of the faster tight ends in the league, linebackers have problems keeping up with him in the field.

Key Player Substitutions

Position: DE

Substitution: Cliff Avril

When: Blitzing situations

Advantage: Avril is a change of pace over Vanden Bosch. Blitz Avril around the outside and watch his finesse moves get him to the quarterback.

Playbook Breakdown

The Lions playbook is based on a power running game and vertical passing. This is the type of playbook that if you want to run a spread-based concept you can. It allows you to use teams that have three solid wideouts with tight ends that are weapons in your passing attack. You can use the halfback well in this playbook also. We will show you key passing plays that allow you to get downfield and put the defense in trouble. We will also show you how to use your rushing attack within your passing scheme. This playbook allows you to force opponents to use more passing-based defenses so that you can establish your power rushing attack. The upgrade to the HB Draw gives you a dual threat from the Gun and keeps you in a nice flow throughout the game.

OFFENSIVE FORMATIONS

FORMATION	# OF PLAYS
Gun Doubles	15
Gun Snugs Flip	9
Gun Split Lion	12
Gun Spread Flex Wk	15
Gun Trips Open	15
Gun Y-Trips Wk	15
I-Form Pro	15
I-Form Pro Twins	15
I-Form Twin TE	12
Singleback Ace	18
Singleback Bunch	12
Singleback Doubles	15
Singleback Tight Slots	9
Singleback Y-Trips Lion	15
Strong Twins	12
Weak Pro	15

OFFENSIVE PLAYCOUNTS

PLAY TYPE	# OF PLAYS
Quick Pass	17
Standard Pass	46
Shotgun Pass	57
Play Action Pass	38
Outside Handoff	10
Pitch	7
Counter	5
Draw	9

Gun Snugs Flip—Mesh Switch

This play gives you three hot reads. You have the dig, the drag, and the flat route. Then this play provides you with two deep reads, the streak in the seam and the corner route. Your progression will be flat, drag, dig, corner, and streak. When you read heat, look at the three hot reads right off the break. If you have time or see a key pre-snap read you can switch to your deep reads. This progression is easy, so once you lab the play you will have them down in no time.

Nice picks and rubs

Compressed sets allow you to get picks and rubs. If the defense uses press coverage you will see the men in the middle get picked. Look for the player who gets picked and then hit him. The dig is coming open via the pick inside.

Great catch and possible YAC

This play attacks man, zone, and heat very well. Whenever you add a play to your play calling you must make sure you can make quick progressions and that they can work against the different defenses you will see coming your way.

Gun Snugs Flip—PA X Clown

This play is a nice one that you only have to make one adjustment to. You have to hot route your halfback to run a drag. This play works better without play action than if you allow it to be a play action play. Your progression should be the out, dig, flat, post, and then the delay route. When you read pressure, look for the flat, the dig, and the quick out. The delay route is a nice check-down because the receiver pass-blocks and then releases. The post is your deep read if you have time or you see something pre-snap that leads you to believe it will be open.

The safety is sitting over top of the post—time to check down

Once you hike the ball look for heat. If you see no pressure take a look downfield. If you see any defenders sitting over top of the post route, check down to your shorter routes.

The quick out is a hard route to sit on

The quick out is a great route against man coverage. It will also get open in zone when you have a deeper route on that side with a player working the flat.

Gun Snugs Flip—HB Mid Draw

The HB Mid Draw is a nice play to add here to establish your power rushing attack. You don't have to be in double-tight-end sets or power-rushing sets to get a good rushing attack going. The key is that if you come out in a power set, the defense will make adjustments to that set. When you use the Snugs Flip, it allows you to get a better matchup so you can run the ball down their throats. Why run against a 4–6 when you can pound against a Quarter or Nickel package?

Holes open up while the wideouts are locking up on the DBs

When you run the HB Mid Draw, you will get a better seal than with the other draws from the Gun. The main reason is the 2 × 2 setup. The wideouts protect the edge so you can concentrate on the middle of the field.

Our favorite dessert: pound cake

Once you hit the hole, get those yards. The defense has to choose their poison for how they will defend you.

Gun Snugs Flip—Mesh

The Mesh is a great play and will work off the same look as the Mesh Switch. This is a play you go to when you're facing an opponent who is generating pressure. You want to get in the Gun and work the short game. What you're hoping is that you can get a one-on-one and take the ball to the house. This play also allows you to get a feel for what your opponent is doing to you. You have three hot reads, the drags and the flat route. Then you have two deep reads—the streak in the seam and the corner route. Brees made a living eating up heat by attacking the seams.

Routes are opening the field up

You can see here how this play works well against man, zone, or pressure with combo coverage.

Attacking the seam with size

When you attack the seams look off the safety. If no one is in the lane and the safety drifts, fire the ball. When you have a player with size this can be a nice play for you.

Gun Trips Open—Four Verticals

This is a nice formation to use to cause mismatch problems. You can run an isolation to the right side, and then you have the trips to the left of the formation. This really spreads the defense out and makes them account for everyone. One of the best ways to beat zone is to use Four Verticals because it applies pressure on the coverage and exposes the soft spots of the zone. You read the dig and then look off the streak to see if you have an opening in the seams. In interviews, Drew Brees has talked about how he loves to expose the seams and that they are his first read. If you attack the seams it forces the defense to account for them and open the outside up. He won a Super Bowl, so why not listen to the man?

The dig is coming open in the middle of the field

The streak route opens up the dig route for you. It pushes the defensive coverage back. This way you can work underneath. You have the streak open as well.

Great catch and some room for YAC

Four Verticals will put a great deal of pressure on your opponent's coverage schemes and stick skills. It's a great play to add to your play calling.

Gun Trips Open—Deep Attack

Now it's time to work that isolation. When you have a great wideout, you want to isolate him so that he can work on a weaker defensive player or work one-on-one with a great defender. Trips sets cause problems; we have seen that already. In addition, we are attacking from a spread formation, which will really stretch the defense from side to side. Our key here is to work the post route first. If the post is covered, then check down to the dig and in combo. The dig-in combo works like this: The dig will draw coverage and allow the in route to get open against most zones. You should first read the post and then the dig-in; finally, you have a check-down with the delay route.

Here is an overhead shot of all your reads

This is a Cover 3 shell. The key to attacking this shell is working the side the FS will drift away from. The streak will draw him over more to allow the post to come open. If you don't like the read, you dump to the delay route.

Nice catch

The post came open because of the streak. If pressure had been coming in your face, you could have hit the dig route to escape the heat.

Gun Trips Open—Lions Iso Fade

This play allows the isolated receiver to run a fade route over a smaller defender. If your fade read is covered you then have a nice combo to the left. It's very hard to defend a post and a corner route at the same time. Next you have a delay route and a quick in route for heat. This play works well against man, zone, and combo pressure. You look off the fade, and if it's covered you make your deep read with the post-corner combo. If you don't like the read, you have the in and the delay route.

Our downfield reads are covered—time for a check-down

When you don't see a wideout open downfield, check down to your shorter reads. There is no need for a loss of yards or to force a turnover. There is no way that the defense can cover everything. Just make your progressions and trust your reads.

The delay was wide open and primed for a nice gain

Since everyone is downfield, your halfback can do what he does best. Be sure to come back with draw plays to support your passing attack and keep the defense from dropping everybody back into coverage.

GREEN BAY PACKERS

OFFENSIVE SCOUTING REPORT

Aaron Rodgers leads the offensive charge for the Green Bay Packers again this year after a stellar performance last year, catapulting him to one of the elite QBs in the league. Now ranked among the top five QBs, Rodgers can be trusted to throw the ball with precision and, in a pinch, scramble with the best of them. Greg Jennings remains one of the top WRs in the league and the primary target for Rodgers, but don't overlook Donald Driver's ability to cross the middle on a slant for big yardage. Ryan Grant returns as the primary back; he has the ability to break a run at any time, especially when following the blocking schemes of Green Bay's fullbacks. The return of Chad Clifton and Mark Tauscher to the offensive line should help protect Rodgers, but beware; the Packers gave up 50 sacks last year, which is the biggest obstacle to becoming one of the league's top offenses.

DEFENSIVE SCOUTING REPORT

The Packers' 3–4 defense features the 2009 Defensive Player of the Year, Charles Woodson, at CB. Woodson is a stalking vacuum waiting for a QB to try to force a ball into coverage. Al Harris lines up opposite Woodson to make one of the strongest CB tandems in the league; however, Green Bay has shown weaknesses in pass defense when opposing teams can effectively spread the defenders. When it comes to run defense, on the other hand, Green Bay led the league and has the ability to do so again with a solid linebacker unit led by Nick Barnett. B.J. Raji and Clay Matthews will continue to provide defensive pressure, closing holes and forcing opposing quarterbacks out of the pocket and into a waiting linebacker.

RATINGS BY POSITION

Position	Rating
Quarterbacks	94
Halfbacks	88
Fullbacks	73
Wide Receivers	84
Tight Ends	86
Tackles	84
Guards	79
Centers	76
Defensive Ends	82
Defensive Tackles	79
Outside Linebackers	80
Middle Linebackers	87
Cornerbacks	91
Free Safeties	93
Strong Safeties	79
Kickers	71
Punters	49

TEAM RATING

87
Overall

KEY ADDITIONS

P	Chris Bryan
OT	Bryan Bulaga
DE	Mike Neal

KEY DEPARTURES

OLB	Aaron Kampman
DE	Mike Montgomery
P	Jeremy Kapinos
FS	Matt Giordano

DEPTH CHART

POS	OVR	FIRST NAME	LAST NAME
C	76	Scott	Wells
C	65	Evan	Dietrich-Smith
CB	97	Charles	Woodson
CB	85	Al	Harris
CB	75	Tramon	Williams
CB	63	Jarrett	Bush
CB	67	Brandon	Underwood
DT	79	B.J.	Raji
DT	63	Anthony	Toribio
FB	73	John	Kuhn
FB	72	Korey	Hall
FS	93	Nick	Collins
FS	65	Derrick	Martin
HB	88	Ryan	Grant
HB	70	Brandon	Jackson
HB	65	James	Starks
K	71	Mason	Crosby
LE	77	Ryan	Pickett
LE	75	Johnny	Jolly
LE	60	Jarius	Wynn
LG	80	Jason	Spitz
LG	75	T.J.	Lang
LG	70	Daryn	Colledge
LOLB	73	Brad	Jones
LT	84	Chad	Clifton
LT	78	Bryan	Bulaga
MLB	87	Nick	Barnett
MLB	79	A.J.	Hawk
MLB	70	Desmond	Bishop
MLB	72	Brandon	Chillar
P	49	Tim	Masthay
QB	94	Aaron	Rodgers
QB	57	Matt	Flynn
RE	87	Cullen	Jenkins
RE	62	Justin	Harrell
RE	67	Mike	Neal
RG	78	Josh	Sitton
RG	64	Marshall	Newhouse
ROLB	86	Clay	Matthews
ROLB	68	Brady	Poppinga
RT	83	Mark	Tauscher
RT	60	Allen	Barbre
SS	79	Atari	Bigby
SS	70	Morgan	Burnett
TE	86	Jermichael	Finley
TE	77	Donald	Lee
TE	62	Spencer	Havner
WR	90	Greg	Jennings
WR	89	Donald	Driver
WR	73	James	Jones
WR	70	Jordy	Nelson
WR	66	Brett	Swain

OFFENSIVE STRENGTH CHART

2-Back Set

WR #80   LT #76   LG #72   C #63   RG #71   RT #65   TE #88   WR #85
QB #12
FB #30
HB #25

Ace Set

TE #86   LT #76   LG #72   C #63   RG #71   RT #65   TE #88
WR #80   QB #12   WR #85
HB #25

- ■ OVR 90 or Greater
- ■ OVR between 80-89
- ■ OVR between 70-79
- ■ OVR between 60-69
- ■ OVR 59 or lower

#12 Aaron Rodgers
Quarterback (QB)

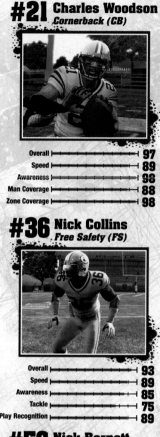

Overall	94
Throw Power	94
Short Accuracy	93
Medium Accuracy	89
Deep Accuracy	86

#21 Charles Woodson
Cornerback (CB)

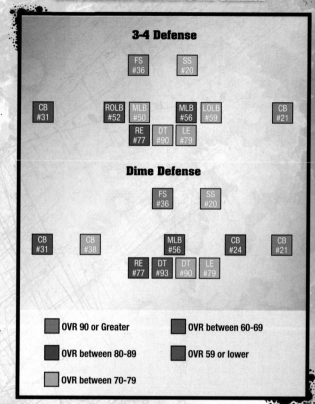

Overall	97
Speed	89
Awareness	98
Man Coverage	88
Zone Coverage	98

#25 Ryan Grant
Halfback (HB)

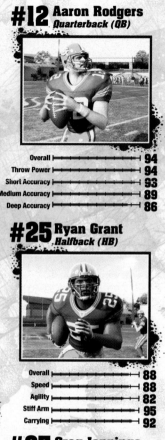

Overall	88
Speed	88
Agility	82
Stiff Arm	95
Carrying	92

#36 Nick Collins
Free Safety (FS)

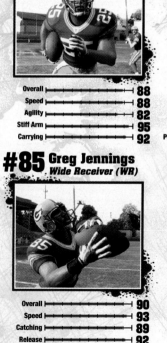

Overall	93
Speed	89
Awareness	85
Tackle	75
Play Recognition	89

#85 Greg Jennings
Wide Receiver (WR)

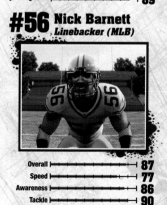

Overall	90
Speed	93
Catching	89
Release	92
Jumping	91

#56 Nick Barnett
Linebacker (MLB)

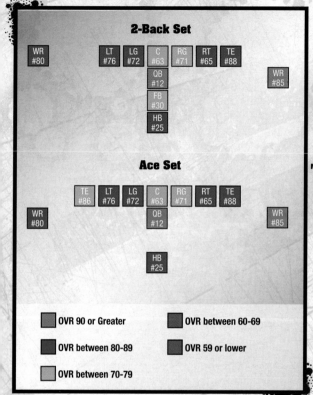

Overall	87
Speed	77
Awareness	86
Tackle	90
Hit Power	78

DEFENSIVE STRENGTH CHART

3-4 Defense

CB #31   FS #36   SS #20   CB #21
ROLB #52   MLB #50   MLB #56   LOLB #59
RE #77   DT #90   LE #79

Dime Defense

FS #36   SS #20
CB #31   CB #38   MLB #56   CB #24   CB #21
RE #77   DT #93   DT #90   LE #79

- ■ OVR 90 or Greater
- ■ OVR between 80-89
- ■ OVR between 70-79
- ■ OVR between 60-69
- ■ OVR 59 or lower

Key Player Substitutions

Position: FB

Substitution: Quinn Johnson

When: Global

Advantage: : Bringing Johnson up the depth chart will help in both run and pass blocking. This will help Grant have a clean hole to hit and keep Rodgers on his feet.

Key Player Substitutions

Position: SS

Substitution: Morgan Burnett

When: Situational

Advantage: If you keep getting beaten with the deep ball, insert Burnett at the strong safety position. His added speed will help slow down the deep passes and keep the wide receivers in front of you.

Over the years, Green Bay has always been a West Coast Offense team. Nothing has changed much in this playbook in regards to quick passing and a balanced rushing attack to move the ball. This playbook is more of a timing-based book that allows you to have a steady flow in your attack. You can use any team with an accurate quarterback to be effective with this playbook. This playbook is also halfback-friendly. In any West Coast–based playbook the use of the backs in the passing game allows you to get favorable matchups for your talented backfield. In this breakdown we will walk through a few sets that allow you to both pass and run well. These plays will keep your opponents off-balance a bit as you keep a nice steady flow with your passing and rushing attack. We will also show some Gun sets that will provide added pass protection.

OFFENSIVE FORMATIONS

FORMATION	# OF PLAYS
Full House Wide	9
Gun Bunch Wk	9
Gun Double Flex	12
Gun Doubles Flex Wing	9
Gun Doubles On	18
Gun Flex Trey	12
Gun Pack Trips	18
Gun Y-Trips Wk	15
I-Form Pro	18
I-Form Slot Flex	12
I-Form Tight	12
I-Form Tight Pair	12
Singleback Ace	15
Singleback Ace Twins	12
Singleback Flex	15
Singleback Tight Flex	9
Strong Close	12

OFFENSIVE PLAYCOUNTS

PLAY TYPE	# OF PLAYS
Quick Pass	10
Standard Pass	35
Shotgun Pass	62
Play Action Pass	47
Inside Handoff	28
Outside Handoff	15
Pitch	4
Counter	3

Playbook Breakdown

Singleback Tight Flex—Off Tackle

This formation has been one of the best-kept secrets in the game for some time now. The Off Tackle play in this formation is great. You can flip the play and keep your opponents on their toes the whole game. You can run inside or outside based on your reads. Your key read is the defensive end. If he slants inside you will bounce the ball outside. If the defensive end comes upfield or slants out, pound the ball inside. The improved run blocking makes this a great play to use when under center.

The defensive end slants inside and gets sealed

Make the right reads and you can get a nice gain. If you see inside pressure, turn the ball inside and square your running back's shoulders up. You don't want to take a big loss. This isn't a quick handoff.

There are solid blocks down the field

When your blocking wideouts are up to the task, you can get nice gains on the ground. Just make your reads and mix this play in with your other plays.

Singleback Tight Flex—Slot Corner

This is another oldie but goodie. Remember that it's hard to defend a post and a corner route. This play has both routes and two nice hot reads. You have the drag, flat, and quick in route. First make your hot reads, then look deep. Because you are under center, you need to make the short-then-long-read progression. Most people you play will send pressure at you under center until you show them you can handle it. A nice weapon to pull out is a play that has great hot reads, beats man, and beats zone. You are just begging then for your opponent to send pressure at you. Then you can flip the play as well to keep them off-balance.

These are your hot reads

This play opens the field up quickly. When you don't read heat, look downfield quickly to your post and then your corner route.

Post routes give big receivers plenty of leverage

When you have bigger wideouts, you have an advantage when you run post routes. When they get inside position it's a wrap.

Singleback Tight Flex—HB Slam

When you run the ball you need two types of running plays in your tool box: You need one that attacks the perimeter and one that attacks the inside. We showed you the Off Tackle; now let's look at the HB Slam. This play is a B gap running play that is designed to get those tough yards inside. Once you beat down your opponent with the passing game and Off Tackle play, you should be able to add this in and exploit the soft middle of the defense.

Making a strong inside cut

Your main read is the defensive tackle. If the defensive tackle slants inside, bang the ball out to the B and C gaps. If the defensive end slants away, hit the A gap hard. In this screenshot, you can see that the defensive tackle took an outside angle because you have killed them with the Off Tackle. So you must square up and cut the ball inside. You can do this by simply flicking your left thumbstick to make the quick cut.

Nice gain off the cut

Our runner gets a great gain after the cut and now the defense has to close that line off a bit to slow down our inside rushing attack.

Singleback Tight Flex—Mesh

The Mesh gives you three hot reads and two deep reads. Your passing progression will be your dual drags first, and then the flats. Then progress to your streak and the corner route. The crossing routes inside will provide a pick or rub for you. Again, you're under center so you don't have time in the pocket like you would in the shotgun. So you need plays that open quickly in case pressure comes. If you have time, take your shot downfield. If you have been successful with your Off Tackle and HB Slam plays, you should have some room to go deep.

We have great protection and time to look deep

Your underneath routes are open, but you have enough time to take a shot downfield. If no defenders get over the top of the corner route, hit it. If you see no one in the seam you can attack the open area of the field with the streak.

Great grab by our receiver

Again, big bodies make a difference when you have to climb that ladder and get the ball. This is a great complement to the other plays you have run in this scheme so far and will give opponents fits.

Gun Double Flex—Slot Outs

This is a nice play to run as a base play to set up your attack. You can audible up to the Singleback Tight Flex when you need extra protection. The Singleback Tight Flex is a compressed set. The Gun Double Flex is a spread set. Moving back and forth allows you to see where the pressure is coming from, and you don't lose a thing with personnel. You just hit your audibles and go up to this formation. You have two quick outs, two streaks, and a monster route for the HB that is your main read.

The HB is working the middle of the field

You must work the HB into the passing attack. This is one of those plays; it opens the field up and allows you to attack any coverage and beat heat well.

An easy catch for the back

The HB made the easy grab and now you have shown that you will eat up any pressure that comes your way. Your opponent will have to sit on the HB, which opens other areas up.

Gun Double Flex—HB Mid Draw

The draw works well in spread sets because the spread sets open the field up for better rushing lanes for you. Once you pass from this set a few times, the defense will have to account for those wideouts out there. So when they respect your passing attack you can go to this play and get your pound game going to move the chains. Not many players can deal with a four-wide spread with 4-3 personnel on the field.

Look at those holes!

This is why the play is a very nice add when you run spread. There are two reasons why players use spread sets: One is to run the ball. The other is to isolate good players in space. Most people you play won't be able to make good open-field tackles. If they miss, you can get a good gain. So in this case we use spread sets to open up a rushing attack.

The draw play breaks free for a nice gain

When you get the ball, get what you can and just move the chains. You now have a nice balanced system working to torment opposing defenses.

Gun Doubles Flex Wing—Slot Cross

This is another set that isn't in any other playbook. You can add it to your audibles as well. You keep the same personnel, but you're giving them another look. The TE being off the line provides a nice option in your pass protection and allows him to get off clean on press coverage. This play is a great one that works with the dig-in route combo. The dig will clear for the in route. You now have your TE running a delay route to help open up the flats if the dig-in combo is covered.

The dig route is open

The dig is a hard route to contain with either man or zone coverage. If you don't see anyone sitting in the middle you must throw this route early and often.

Great snag downfield

If the coverage had stayed with the dig, the in or delay route would have come open. Don't take a loss or force the ball downfield for a turnover. Make sure you package a good route runner into the formation with routes like this, because poor route runners can be knocked off their routes easily and mess with your timing.

CAROLINA PANTHERS

OFFENSIVE SCOUTING REPORT

One of the best backfield tandems in the league resides in Carolina. DeAngelo Williams and Jonathan Stewart compose a one-two punch from the line of scrimmage. Both eclipsed the thousand-yard mark last season. There should be no reason not to regularly switch these two in and out of the game to keep the running game fresh, wearing down the opposing defense. The running game has always been the focus in Carolina, and with new starting QB Matt Moore, this trend should continue. While Moore does have the arm to get the ball into the phenomenal hands of Steve Smith, he should not be counted on to run the offense with a pass-first mentality. And likely, with no other Carolina receiver anywhere near as fast or talented, watch for Smith to get bogged down by the opposing team's best cornerbacks. On the positive side, the Carolina offensive line is one of the best at creating opportunities for what the Panthers do best—run!

DEFENSIVE SCOUTING REPORT

The defense for the Panthers saw many changes over the off-season, including the loss of Julius Peppers and Na'il Diggs. In fact, no one on the defensive line has an overall rating higher than 75. Don't let this discourage you, however; middle linebacker Jon Beason is an animal and can provide coverage if and when the line fails. Thomas Davis is also a solid linebacker who can help keep the offensive gains to a minimum. The secondary is led by CBs Chris Gamble and Richard Marshall, who both have great speed for corners and will continue to keep the pass defense Carolina's strong suit. Use the linebackers effectively to minimize the run and the secondary should balance the defensive efforts to hold teams to minimal scoring. However, should the line fail and linebackers get tied up in the middle of the field, Carolina could find themselves chasing running backs down the field all game long.

TEAM RATING

75
Overall

KEY ADDITIONS

S	Aaron Francisco
CB	Marcus Hudson
DT	Ed Johnson
LB	Jamar Williams
WR	Wallace Wright
QB	Jimmy Clausen

KEY DEPARTURES

QB	Jake Delhomme
LB	Na'il Diggs
SS	Chris Harris
DE	Julius Peppers
DT	Damione Lewis
DT	Maake Kemoeatu

RATINGS BY POSITION

Position	Rating	Position	Rating
Quarterbacks	76	Defensive Tackles	69
Halfbacks	92	Outside Linebackers	78
Fullbacks	66	Middle Linebackers	96
Wide Receivers	75	Cornerbacks	87
Tight Ends	73	Free Safeties	75
Tackles	91	Strong Safeties	75
Guards	80	Kickers	87
Centers	90	Punters	76
Defensive Ends	75		

DEPTH CHART

POS	OVR	FIRST NAME	LAST NAME
C	90	Ryan	Kalil
C	70	Steve	Justice
CB	91	Chris	Gamble
CB	82	Richard	Marshall
CB	72	Captain	Munnerlyn
CB	62	C.J.	Wilson
CB	58	Marcus	Hudson
DT	70	Tank	Tyler
DT	69	Louis	Leonard
DT	69	Nick	Hayden
DT	62	Corvey	Irvin
FB	66	Tony	Fiammetta
FS	75	Sherrod	Martin
FS	68	Jordan	Pugh
HB	92	DeAngelo	Williams
HB	88	Jonathan	Stewart
HB	65	Mike	Goodson
HB	65	Tyrell	Sutton
K	87	John	Kasay
LE	74	Tyler	Brayton
LE	70	Charles	Johnson
LG	83	Travelle	Wharton
LOLB	87	Thomas	Davis
LOLB	66	Jamar	Williams
LOLB	57	Jordan	Senn
LT	95	Jordan	Gross
LT	63	Garry	Williams
MLB	96	Jon	Beason
MLB	56	Brett	Warren
P	76	Jason	Baker
QB	76	Matt	Moore
QB	74	Jimmy	Clausen
QB	65	Tony	Pike
RE	75	Everette	Brown
RE	61	Hilee	Taylor
RG	76	Mackenzy	Bernadeau
RG	68	Duke	Robinson
ROLB	69	James	Anderson
ROLB	67	Eric	Norwood
ROLB	65	Dan	Connor
RT	86	Jeff	Otah
RT	69	Geoff	Schwartz
SS	75	Charles	Godfrey
SS	63	Aaron	Francisco
TE	73	Jeff	King
TE	71	Gary	Barnidge
TE	70	Dante	Rosario
WR	92	Steve	Smith
WR	71	Brandon	LaFell
WR	64	Armanti	Edwards
WR	63	Dwayne	Jarrett
WR	63	Kenny	Moore
WR	63	Wallace	Wright

OFFENSIVE STRENGTH CHART

2-Back Set

WR #80					
	LT #69	LG #70	C #67	RG #73	RT #79	TE #47
			QB #3			WR #89
			FB #42			
			HB #34			

Ace Set

TE #88	LT #69	LG #70	C #67	RG #73	RT #79	TE #47
WR #80			QB #3			WR #89
			HB #34			

- ■ OVR 90 or Greater
- ■ OVR between 80-89
- ■ OVR between 70-79
- ■ OVR between 60-69
- ■ OVR 59 or lower

Key Player Substitutions

Position: QB

Substitution: Jimmy Clausen

When: Global

Advantage: Even though Clausen dropped in the draft, he landed on a team where he could end up being a starter. With the unknown play of Moore, don't be afraid to play Clausen.

#34 DeAngelo Williams
Halfback (HB)

Overall	92
Speed	94
Agility	97
Stiff Arm	67
Carrying	96

#89 Steve Smith
Wide Receiver (WR)

Overall	92
Speed	97
Catching	90
Release	88
Jumping	91

#28 Jonathan Stewart
Halfback (HB)

Overall	88
Speed	90
Agility	86
Stiff Arm	92
Carrying	90

#52 Jon Beason
Linebacker (MLB)

Overall	96
Speed	85
Awareness	93
Tackle	97
Hit Power	94

#20 Chris Gamble
Cornerback (CB)

Overall	91
Speed	92
Awareness	80
Man Coverage	95
Zone Coverage	89

#58 Thomas Davis
Linebacker (LOLB)

Overall	87
Speed	88
Awareness	75
Tackle	90
Hit Power	96

DEFENSIVE STRENGTH CHART

4-3 Defense

		FS #23		SS #30	
CB #31	ROLB #50	MLB #52	LOLB #58	CB #20
		RE #91	DT #94	DT #98	LE #96	

Dime Defense

		FS #23		SS #30	
CB #31	CB #41	MLB #52	CB #27	CB #20
		RE #91	DT #94	DT #98	LE #96	

- ■ OVR 90 or Greater
- ■ OVR between 80-89
- ■ OVR between 70-79
- ■ OVR between 60-69
- ■ OVR 59 or lower

Key Player Substitutions

Position: ROLB

Substitution: Eric Norwood

When: Situational

Advantage: When you are getting beaten on the right side, try bringing Norwood in. With his speed and strength, you will be able to control that side of the field again. Make sure that he is not dropping back into coverage.

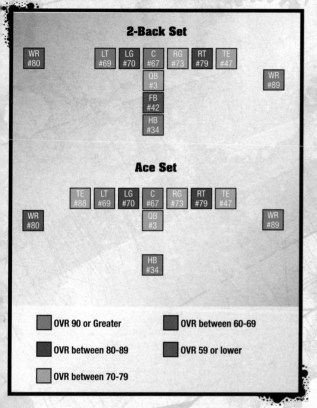

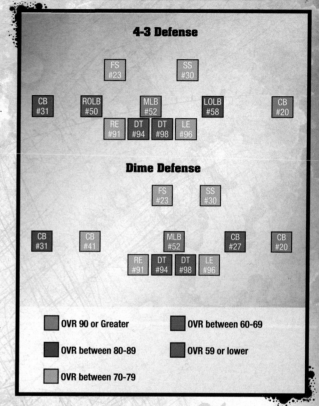

The Carolina Panthers finished last year third in rushing with a total of 2,498 yards as a team. The Panthers have two of the best running backs in the league: DeAngelo Williams and Jonathan Stewart. Both of them rushed for over 1,000 yards last year. Williams finished with 1,117 yards, 7 TDs, and a 5.2 carry average, and Stewart finished with 1,133 yards, 11 TDs, and a 5.1 carry average. The team is all about using the run to set up the pass and playing solid defense. Quarterback Matt Moore takes over for Jake Delhomme, so the ground game is important in protecting this young quarterback. With plenty of running formations to choose from in this playbook, such as three I-Form sets and Full House Philly, there are enough formations to get that run-first attack going on. The Carolina Panthers also like to mix in the play action pass game once they get their ground game going. Look to set up Steve Smith for the deep ball.

OFFENSIVE FORMATIONS

FORMATION	# OF PLAYS
Full House Philly	12
Gun Empty Base	9
Gun Split Slot	15
Gun Spread Y-Slot	12
Gun Y-Trips Open	18
I-Form Pro	18
I-Form Pro Twins	12
I-Form Tight Pair	12
Singleback Ace	18
Singleback Bunch	12
Singleback Panther Doubles	15
Singleback Spread Flex	12
Singleback Tight Slots	12
Singleback Twin TE	12
Singleback Twin TE Flex	12
Weak Twins	9
Wildcat Panther	3

OFFENSIVE PLAYCOUNTS

PLAY TYPE	# OF PLAYS
Quick Pass	16
Standard Pass	47
Shotgun Pass	38
Play Action Pass	37
Inside Handoff	33
Outside Handoff	7
Pitch	8
Counter	6

Playbook Breakdown

I-Form Pro—Inside Zone

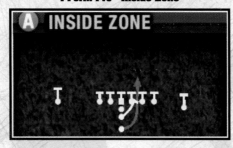

The I-Form Pro—Inside Zone is a run play designed to go behind right tackle Jeff Otah and right guard Mackenzy Bernadeau with fullback Tony Fiammetta leading the way. In this formation, we want use the flanker to get extra blocking by motioning him to the left and snapping the ball when he is still behind the line of scrimmage.

Determine early if you are going to bounce it outside

Quarterback Matt Moore hands the ball off to the back. Williams follows his fullback's lead. He is being patient and letting his blockers set up out in front of him.

A sealed edge helps here

Because of his patience, he has plenty of room to run because of his blockers. The running back takes the ball outside and uses his speed for a big gain downfield; we pick up about 15 yards. This play works very well to pick up tough yards, or you can take it outside if the edge is clear. Remember to use motion and also to flip the play if you see that the defense is stacked on one side of the formation.

I-Form Pro—Iso Weak

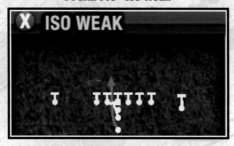

The I-Form Pro—Iso Weak is a run play designed to go to the weak side of the formation. For this play we are going to use backup HB Jonathan Stewart as he has a bit more power than Williams.

Wait for the blocks to set

We motion the flanker to provide extra blocking and snap the ball when he gets past the center. The quarterback hands the ball off to the running back, who follows his blockers up inside.

Running over a linebacker

Because of his size and power, Stewart's escape route pushes the pile for 4 yards. Once you soften up the defense with a running game, mix in play action passes such as PA Power O, PA Boot, and PA Scissors. Getting your play calling right is the key; this all comes from reading the defense correctly.

I-Form Pro Twins—HB Power O

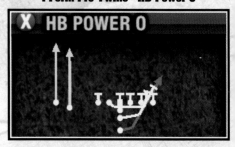

HB Power O from the I-Form Pro Twins formation is a run play where the left guard pulls to the right side of the formation. You also have a fullback that pulls and blocks alongside the right tackle. This type of run gives you the option of taking it inside or outside.

Follow your pulling lineman

The quarterback hands the ball off to the running back. As you can see, we have the left guard and the fullback out in front. This gives the runner two running lanes to choose from. You can choose to run behind your blockers inside or, if you see the edge sealed, you can bounce it outside. It's all about being patient in reading the defense.

Turn on the jets

DeAngelo Williams chooses to take it outside because he sees plenty of room to run. With his speed, he picks up 20 yards before being tackled. Using motion and choosing which side to run the ball to is the key. When using this play, look carefully at the blocking assignments so you know where to go with the ball.

I-Form Pro Twins—PA Boot

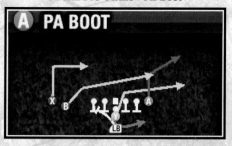

Play action is always good to use after you have weakened the defense with the run game because you'll have everyone committed to stuff the line. PA Boot has the tight end as the primary target. On this play he is running a corner route; you also have a fullback who comes out of the backfield and a crossing route.

Look at both receivers

We like to motion the slot receiver and snap the ball once he gets next to the left tackle. The quarterback rolls outside the pocket. Look for the fullback in the flats first, then the crossing route. If there is too much pressure on you, throw the ball away. We have two targets in sight in this example.

Always look to get the ball in Smith's hands

Wide receiver Steve Smith makes the catch for a 5-yard gain—it's all about moving the ball downfield and getting positive yards. Once you get outside the pocket, your first two reads are right in front of you. Then, if you have time, wait for the corner route to develop so you can go deep.

I-Form Tight Pair—HB Sweep

HB Sweep from the I-Form Tight Pair formation is a run play that we like to use to get outside once we have the defense committed to the inside run. With run plays such as HB Power O, Counter Wk, and Iso, you should be able to set the table for your outside runs.

Stay behind your FB

The quarterback tosses the ball to the running back. The right guard and the fullback are pulling outside to seal the edge. Be patient in letting the blocks develop. Sometimes, if you see the defense is overpursuing, you can cut back inside.

A blocker to the end zone

With fullback Tony Fiammetta leading the way, running back DeAngelo Williams has plenty of room to run. With his speed, he takes the ball the distance for a TD. Another suggestion is to motion the tight end to the other side and flip the play if you see that the defense is favoring one side of the formation.

Full House Philly—HB Slam

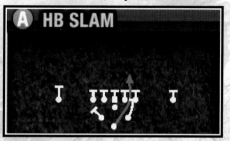

Full House Philly is a run formation that brings the tight end into the backfield as a blocker. One thing that the formation provides is the option of motion. Both the blockers are behind the line of scrimmage to either side of the formation. The HB Slam is designed to run between the right tackle and left guard.

The hole is wide open

We motion the tight end and snap the ball once he is behind the left guard. After the quarterback hands the ball off, we can see the running lane developing. With power runner Jonathan Stewart, we should pick up those tough yards inside.

The FB is the key to this play

Jonathan Stewart follows fullback Tony Fiammetta up inside the hole for a tough 5-yard gain. The key to using this play is reading the defensive front. Sometimes you want to snap the ball in different spots depending on where you see defenders stacked. Also remember that because you can motion blockers to each side of the formation, you can flip it as well.

Full House Philly—Slants

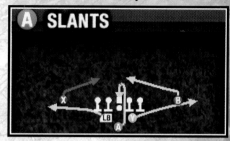

Full House Philly—Slants has two flat routes out of the backfield with a curl route. The split end is the primary target on display. The flat route coming out of the backfield and the slant route give you a nice combination to read the field one-half at a time.

Getting the ball out quick

The quarterback sees his target and fires the ball to wide receiver Steve Smith. Notice how we have the fullback open in the flats as well. This combination of routes forces the defense to overcompensate in coverage.

Eyeing the ball in

Steve Smith makes the catch for a quick 5 yards. Sometimes, if the defense blitzes with man coverage behind, you will have a big gain after the catch. With someone like Steve Smith, you can take it the distance for a TD. Another way that we like to disguise this play pre-snap is to use motion just as if we are going to run the ball. Getting the defense to shift here can open up the field for us.

NEW ENGLAND PATRIOTS

OFFENSIVE SCOUTING REPORT

The Patriots offense revolves around one star, Tom Brady. Brady's packing one of the best arms in the game, fueled with power, accuracy, and the ability to deliver the deep pass with precision. His main targets this year should remain receivers Wes Welker and Randy Moss. Brady's deep threat, Moss, continually finds the end zone and breaks out a spectacular catch like no one else can. Moss's weakness, if you can find one, is his ability to catch in mid-field traffic, but with his wheels, does he really need to? Moss will continue to juice his way down the field to be on the receiving end of a Brady bomb. Veteran Torry Holt joins Brady's arsenal of receivers this year but will play behind Welker and Edelman to start the season. But his addition does allow Brady to continue doing what he does best: spreading the ball. Hoping to keep the opposing defenses honest, RB Laurence Maroney is a strong and sturdy runner, capable of getting the short yardage with his power or breaking to the outside with decent speed. The Patriots, however, are built for the pass and have one of the best protecting lines in the game.

DEFENSIVE SCOUTING REPORT

Nose tackle Vince Wilfork leads the Patriots defense. He is a big body with a lot of power. Ends Ty Warren and Mike Wright will try to fill the shoes of the departed Richard Seymour and Jarvis Green. While not as impenetrable as in years past, they should be able to get the job done. Brandon Meriweather provides great speed and coverage in the backfield at safety. Meriweather's Pro Bowl season should propel him into this season with some big plays and hits. Leigh Bodden is the Patriots' best cornerback, but the secondary could be tested this year as there is a lot of youth playing opposite Bodden.

TEAM RATING

86
Overall

KEY ADDITIONS

TE	Alge Crumpler
WR	Torry Holt
DT	Damione Lewis
LB	Marques Murrell
DL	Gerard Warren
CB	Devin McCourty

KEY DEPARTURES

TE	Chris Baker
DE	Jarvis Green
P	Chris Hanson
LB	Junior Seau
LB	Adalius Thomas
TE	Benjamin Watson

RATINGS BY POSITION

Position	Rating
Quarterbacks	95
Halfbacks	78
Fullbacks	80
Wide Receivers	87
Tight Ends	74
Tackles	84
Guards	89
Centers	88
Defensive Ends	78
Defensive Tackles	95
Outside Linebackers	75
Middle Linebackers	86
Cornerbacks	79
Free Safeties	77
Strong Safeties	88
Kickers	91
Punters	69

DEPTH CHART

POS	OVR	FIRST NAME	LAST NAME
C	88	Dan	Koppen
C	61	Ryan	Wendell
CB	82	Leigh	Bodden
CB	76	Darius	Butler
CB	74	Devin	McCourty
CB	68	Jonathan	Wilhite
CB	62	Terrence	Wheatley
DT	95	Vince	Wilfork
DT	68	Myron	Pryor
DT	66	Ron	Brace
FB	80	Sammy	Morris
FS	80	James	Sanders
FS	77	Brandon	McGowan
HB	78	Laurence	Maroney
HB	77	Fred	Taylor
HB	75	Kevin	Faulk
HB	69	BenJarvus	Green-Ellis
K	91	Stephen	Gostkowski
LE	84	Ty	Warren
LE	62	Brandon	Deaderick
LE	62	Darryl	Richard
LG	95	Logan	Mankins
LG	65	Rich	Ohrnberger
LOLB	71	Rob	Ninkovich
LOLB	67	Pierre	Woods
LT	89	Matt	Light
LT	79	Sebastian	Vollmer
MLB	86	Jerod	Mayo
MLB	75	Gary	Guyton
MLB	72	Brandon	Spikes
MLB	64	Tyrone	McKenzie
P	69	Zoltan	Mesko
QB	95	Tom	Brady
QB	63	Brian	Hoyer
QB	59	Zac	Robinson
RE	72	Damione	Lewis
RE	71	Mike	Wright
RG	83	Stephen	Neal
RG	70	Dan	Connolly
ROLB	79	Tully	Banta-Cain
ROLB	64	Jermaine	Cunningham
RT	78	Nick	Kaczur
RT	65	Mark	LeVoir
SS	88	Brandon	Meriweather
SS	76	Pat	Chung
TE	77	Rob	Gronkowski
TE	74	Alge	Crumpler
TE	68	Aaron	Hernandez
WR	95	Randy	Moss
WR	91	Wes	Welker
WR	79	Torry	Holt
WR	76	Julian	Edelman
WR	68	Brandon	Tate
WR	65	Taylor	Price

OFFENSIVE STRENGTH CHART

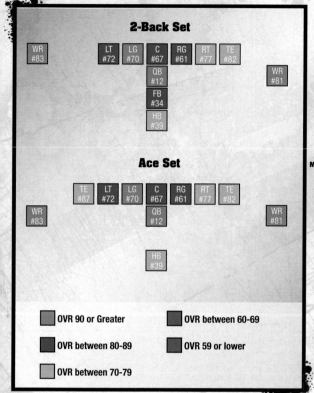

2-Back Set

WR #83		LT #72	LG #70	C #67	RG #61	RT #77	TE #82		
				QB #12				WR #81
				FB #34				
				HB #39				

Ace Set

		TE #87	LT #72	LG #70	C #67	RG #61	RT #77	TE #82	
WR #83				QB #12				WR #81
				HB #39				

- ■ OVR 90 or Greater
- ■ OVR between 80-89
- ■ OVR between 70-79
- ■ OVR between 60-69
- ■ OVR 59 or lower

#12 Tom Brady
Quarterback (QB)

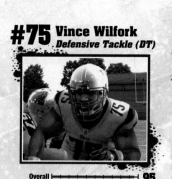

Overall	95
Throw Power	94
Short Accuracy	93
Medium Accuracy	91
Deep Accuracy	89

#81 Randy Moss
Wide Receiver (WR)

Overall	95
Speed	96
Catching	95
Release	88
Jumping	99

#70 Logan Mankins
Offensive Guard (OG)

Overall	95
Strength	92
Pass Block	85
Run Block	95
Impact Blocking	89

#75 Vince Wilfork
Defensive Tackle (DT)

Overall	95
Speed	55
Strength	97
Power Moves	92
Block Shedding	97

#51 Jerod Mayo
Linebacker (MLB)

Overall	86
Speed	85
Awareness	76
Tackle	89
Hit Power	87

#31 Brandon Meriweather
Strong Safety (SS)

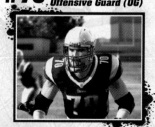

Overall	88
Speed	91
Awareness	79
Tackle	66
Hit Power	81

DEFENSIVE STRENGTH CHART

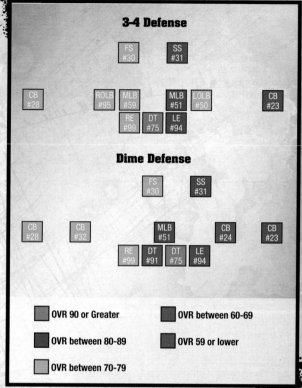

3-4 Defense

	FS #30		SS #31	
CB #28	ROLB #95	MLB #59	MLB #51	LOLB #50	CB #23
	RE #99	DT #75	LE #94	

Dime Defense

	FS #30	SS #31	
CB #28	CB #32	MLB #51	CB #24	CB #23
	RE #99	DT #91	DT #75	LE #94	

- ■ OVR 90 or Greater
- ■ OVR between 80-89
- ■ OVR between 70-79
- ■ OVR between 60-69
- ■ OVR 59 or lower

Key Player Substitutions

Position: TE

Substitution: Aaron Hernandez

When: Global

Advantage: The Patriots can see Aaron Hernandez as their starting tight end for many years to come. When Hernandez gets his hands on the ball you'd better watch out.

Key Player Substitutions

Position: DT

Substitution: Ron Brace

When: Situational

Advantage: Getting Brace on the field strengthens an already huge line. With Brace and Wilfork on the line at the same time, teams will find it almost impossible to run the ball up the middle.

In *Madden NFL 10*, the Patriots playbook was one of the most popular offensively because of the number of Gun formations. In *Madden NFL 11*, there are not as many Gun formations as last season, but the playbook still ranks among the top Gun formation books. Players who are pass happy and like to throw from the Gun won't find too many other playbooks in the game that are as fun to run as this one. Some new plays have been added to the playbook this year, such as Gun Pats Wing TE—Pats Slot Trail, Gun Pats Wing TE—Pats Slot Whip, and Gun Pats Wing TE—Pats Slot Bubble. For those who want to call plays under center, there are enough plays to run for that style of play, but then again if you are running the Patriots playbook, you are likely doing so because of the Gun formations.

OFFENSIVE FORMATIONS

FORMATION	# OF PLAYS
Gun 5WR Patriot	12
Gun Empty Y-Flex	9
Gun Normal Flex Wk	12
Gun Pats Wing TE	21
Gun Pats Wing Trips	24
Gun Snugs Flip	9
Gun Split Patriot	12
Gun Spread Flex	12
Gun Trips Open	9
Gun Trips TE	12
I-Form TE Flip	12
I-Form Tight	12
I-Form Twin TE Strg	9
Singleback Ace Pair Twins	12
Singleback Bunch	9
Singleback Deuce Wing	15
Singleback Doubles Pats	15

OFFENSIVE PLAYCOUNTS

PLAY TYPE	# OF PLAYS
Quick Pass	12
Standard Pass	17
Shotgun Pass	95
Play Action Pass	36
Inside Handoff	22
Outside Handoff	10
Pitch	5
Counter	2

Playbook Breakdown

Gun Pats Wing TE—Whip Unders

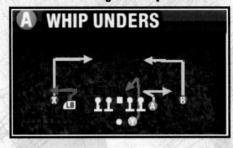

Of all the offensive formations in the Patriots playbook, the Gun Pats Wing TE has some of the best plays. One of those plays we really like is the Whip Unders. This play has the slot receiver and tight end both running whip routes, while the two outside receivers run in routes over the top.

Welker breaks hard towards the left sideline to get open

The running back runs a delayed curl route out of the backfield and is the play's check-down receiver. What makes this play so effective against man coverage is Wes Welker lined up in the slot. There are very few cornerbacks in the game that can cover him. He starts off by going up the field about 3 yards and pivoting before breaking towards the sideline.

Brady delivers a well-thrown ball towards Welker

At this point he gains separation from his man and gets open. Once he's open, we throw him a hard bullet pass. If the catch is made on the run, chances are we are going to pick up some yards after the catch.

Gun Normal Flex Wk—Patriots Spot

The Gun Normal Flex Wk—Patriots Spot is a play we like to run to beat both man and zone coverage. We like it because we know where to go with the ball before the quarterback ever touches it. To set the play up, we hot route the slot receiver on a curl route and then extend it by smart routing.

Welker is about to show Brady his numbers as he spots up

Keep in mind that we only want to smart route his curl if it's more than 7 yards for the first down. To prevent our opponent from being tipped off, we take control of the split end and make it look like we are manually sending him in motion.

The linebacker drops back to cover Edelman, leaving Welker open

As the split end is sent in automotion, we want to see if the right cornerback follows him or not. If he doesn't, then it's zone coverage. We look to throw to the split end once he spots up. If the right cornerback follows him, then it's man coverage. We then look to throw to the tight end or running back.

Gun Pats Wing Trips—Double Ins

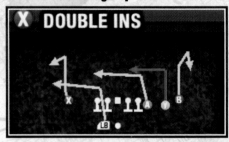

A play we like to showcase some of our user stick control with is the Gun Pats Wing Trips—Double Ins. This play has Wes Welker lined up in the slot running an in route; he is the primary receiver. Tight end Alge Crumpler also runs an in route, but his route runs underneath Welker's.

Brady throws a high bullet pass to Moss just before he curls back

On the outside of the trips, Randy Moss runs a deep hook route. His route is very effective against man coverage and is the route we can use stick control with to help ensure he makes the catch. If man coverage is called, we look for Moss. The key to making the throw is to release the pass when Moss makes his break towards the sideline, but before he hooks back.

Moss goes up in the air and snags the pass in front of the cornerback

We throw a high bullet pass. While the ball is up in the air, we take control of Moss and bring him back towards the quarterback. As the ball comes down, we hold the Catch button. If you time it properly, Moss will go up and make the catch.

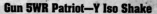

Gun Trips TE—Pats Slot Screen

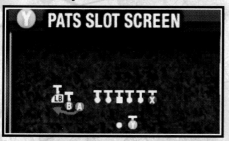

Those of you who ran the Patriots playbook last season know there was a formation called Gun Trips TE. Within that formation there was a play named Slot Screen. That play is still in the game, but another slot screen has been added to the formation; it's called Pats Slot Screen.

Brady sets up and is ready to fire the ball to Welker

The main difference between the two is that no offensive linemen pull when you call Pats Slot Screen. Instead, two receivers line up next to the slot receiver running the screen. By default they will serve as blockers; however, we like to hot route the middle receiver on a slant out instead.

Moss is out in front ready to throw a block for Welker

We do this to draw the coverage away from the slot receiver. We still have the outside receiver blocking. This play might not pick up as many yards as the Slot Screen does, but for the most part it picks up positive yardage. The other advantage is we have more time to make the throw since none of the offensive linemen pull. This play works best if the defense sends a blitz on the same side as the screen is being run towards.

Gun Spread Flex—HB Draw

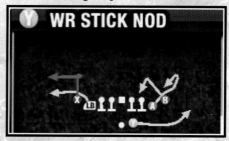

The Patriots don't run the ball too much, just enough to force the defense to respect it. A solid run play out of the Gun Spread Flex is the HB Draw. This draw play, also known as a delayed handoff, has the offensive linemen momentarily showing pass block.

Brady hands off to the RB as the defensive ends head up the field

It is designed to show pass to the defense so that the defensive ends will charge up the field after the quarterback, thus creating inside running lanes for the running back to run through. The four receivers run clear-out routes downfield to take the defensive backs clear out of the play, allowing for even more running room.

Maroney finds a big open hole to burst through to pick up yardage

If zone coverage is called, we like to send one of the receivers in motion and snap the ball when he gets inside. This action adds an extra run blocker for us to move our running back behind. If man coverage is called, we won't snap the ball until the receiver sets. We do this so we don't bring an unwanted defender where we are running the ball.

Gun Snugs Flip—WR Stick Nod

The Patriots playbook is chock-full of passing plays that beat man coverage. The Gun Snugs Flip—WR Stick Nod is another good example.

Moss plants his feet and then breaks towards the sideline

Not only is this play effective against man coverage, but it's equally as effective against zone coverage. If man coverage is called, we hot route the left inside receiver on a streak. We do this to clear room for the left outside receiver, so that he can run his whip route and get open once he breaks towards the sideline.

Moss accelerates and gains a few steps on his man

If zone coverage is called, we don't need to make any pre-snap adjustments. Just look for the left outside receiver once he fakes the stick route and then breaks towards the sideline. The Gun Snugs Flip—WR Stick Nod is one of those plays you are going to want to add to your playbook, because it works against both man and zone coverage and it's very easy to execute with a high percentage of success.

Gun 5WR Patriot—Y Iso Shake

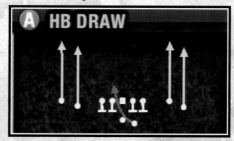

Another play that beats man coverage consistently out of the Patriots playbook is the Gun 5WR Patriot—Y Iso Shake. This play has Wes Welker lined up in the inside slot position on the right, where he runs a shake route. There are no third or fourth string defensive backs in the game that can match Welker's speed or acceleration rating.

Welker makes a few sudden jukes to shake loose from his man

To run this play, we hot route both receivers on the left on streaks to clear route room so that Welker can work over the middle in one-on-one coverage. Once he is open, the ball should be thrown hard in his direction.

Brady delivers a strike to Welker as he comes across the middle of the field

After Welker makes the catch, there will be additional yardage to pick up because of the cleared out coverage. Since this is an Empty formation, expect your opponent to call a blitz to try to force you to throw the ball quicker than you want.

OAKLAND RAIDERS

OFFENSIVE SCOUTING REPORT

The JaMarcus Russell experiment is over in Oakland. In place of the first overall pick of the 2007 NFL Draft is Jason Campbell, formerly of the Redskins, where he showed flashes of poise and precision. Look for Campbell to make Darrius Heyward-Bey a favorite target down the field. D.H.B.'s speed is the perfect weapon against skilled cornerbacks. To that point, every single wide receiver in the Raiders' stable posts a speed rating of 90 or higher, allowing any combination to stretch the field in a hurry and wear down opposing defenses. TE Zach Miller was a standout receiver for Russell and can be a good outlet for Campbell as well, especially in the quick post routes in the middle of the field. With Darren "Run DMC" McFadden and Michael Bush, the Raiders backfield has enough juice to grind out victories on the ground, though both have yet to truly prove themselves on the field. Unfortunately, the offensive line is still shuffling to find consistency, offering little chance for improvement.

DEFENSIVE SCOUTING REPORT

Few players can be so good that they're a bright spot of shining light in the black hole. CB Nnamdi Asomugha is one such player. Perhaps the best cornerback in the NFL, Asomugha is a true shutdown corner capable of making a team's best wide receiver a non-issue. Offenses should simply not throw the ball in his direction. SS Tyvon Branch ended the season with the second most tackles on the team, proving he is capable of making hits and rounding out the pass defense. With last year's addition of DE Richard Seymour, a tried and true Super Bowl talent, the Raiders vastly improved their run defense. This year's addition of Kamerion Wimbley at ROLB, however, should help support a once-spotty defensive line, turning the Raiders into a solid defensive unit.

TEAM RATING

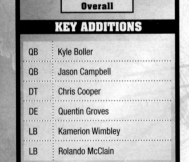

71
Overall

KEY ADDITIONS

QB	Kyle Boller
QB	Jason Campbell
DT	Chris Cooper
DE	Quentin Groves
LB	Kamerion Wimbley
LB	Rolando McClain

KEY DEPARTURES

DE	Greg Ellis
RB	Justin Fargas
OT	Cornell Green
LB	Kirk Morrison
QB	JaMarcus Russell
WR	Javon Walker

RATINGS BY POSITION

Position	Rating
Quarterbacks	83
Halfbacks	77
Fullbacks	60
Wide Receivers	72
Tight Ends	86
Tackles	78
Guards	80
Centers	79
Defensive Ends	82
Defensive Tackles	78
Outside Linebackers	80
Middle Linebackers	79
Cornerbacks	87
Free Safeties	72
Strong Safeties	86
Kickers	90
Punters	98

DEPTH CHART

POS	OVR	FIRST NAME	LAST NAME
C	79	Samson	Satele
C	71	Chris	Morris
CB	98	Nnamdi	Asomugha
CB	76	Chris	Johnson
CB	67	Stanford	Routt
CB	64	Walter	McFadden
CB	56	Joey	Thomas
DT	78	Tommy	Kelly
DT	70	Lamarr	Houston
DT	66	Desmond	Bryant
DT	66	William	Joseph
FB	60	Luke	Lawton
FS	78	Michael	Huff
FS	72	Hiram	Eugene
HB	77	Darren	McFadden
HB	77	Michael	Bush
HB	69	Rock	Cartwright
K	90	Sebastian	Janikowski
LE	92	Richard	Seymour
LE	71	Jay	Richardson
LG	82	Robert	Gallery
LG	77	Langston	Walker
LOLB	78	Thomas	Howard
LOLB	77	Trevor	Scott
LT	79	Mario	Henderson
LT	72	Bruce	Campbell
MLB	79	Rolando	McClain
MLB	70	Ricky	Brown
MLB	50	Isaiah	Ekejiuba
P	98	Shane	Lechler
QB	83	Jason	Campbell
QB	67	Bruce	Gradkowski
QB	63	Charlie	Frye
RE	72	Matt	Shaughnessy
RE	68	Quentin	Groves
RG	78	Cooper	Carlisle
RG	67	Brandon	Rodd
ROLB	82	Kamerion	Wimbley
ROLB	63	Sam	Williams
ROLB	56	Slade	Norris
RT	76	Khalif	Barnes
RT	70	Erik	Pears
RT	68	Jared	Veldheer
SS	86	Tyvon	Branch
SS	68	Mike	Mitchell
TE	86	Zach	Miller
TE	69	Tony	Stewart
TE	66	Brandon	Myers
WR	75	Louis	Murphy
WR	73	Chaz	Schilens
WR	70	Johnnie Lee	Higgins
WR	68	Darrius	Heyward-Bey
WR	60	Jacoby	Ford
WR	52	Todd	Watkins

OFFENSIVE STRENGTH CHART

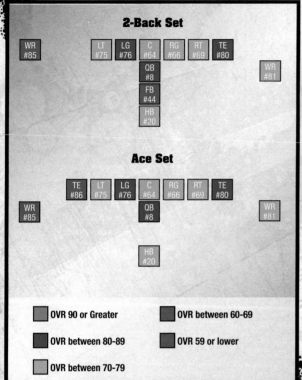

2-Back Set

WR #85

LT #75 | LG #76 | C #64 | RG #66 | RT #69 | TE #80

QB #8

FB #44

HB #20

WR #81

Ace Set

TE #86 | LT #75 | LG #76 | C #64 | RG #66 | RT #69 | TE #80

WR #85

QB #8

WR #81

HB #20

- ■ OVR 90 or Greater
- ■ OVR between 80-89
- ■ OVR between 70-79
- ■ OVR between 60-69
- ■ OVR 59 or lower

#80 Zach Miller
Tight End (TE)

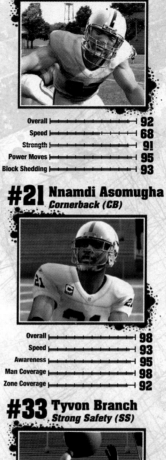

Overall	86
Speed	78
Catching	87
Catch in Traffic	88
Jumping	85

#8 Jason Campbell
Quarterback (QB)

Overall	83
Throw Power	92
Short Accuracy	85
Medium Accuracy	78
Deep Accuracy	79

#76 Robert Gallery
Offensive Guard (OG)

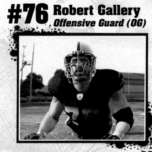

Overall	82
Strength	89
Pass Block	75
Run Block	91
Impact Blocking	89

#92 Richard Seymour
Defensive End (DE)

Overall	92
Speed	68
Strength	91
Power Moves	95
Block Shedding	93

#21 Nnamdi Asomugha
Cornerback (CB)

Overall	98
Speed	93
Awareness	95
Man Coverage	98
Zone Coverage	92

#33 Tyvon Branch
Strong Safety (SS)

Overall	86
Speed	93
Awareness	75
Tackle	79
Hit Power	78

DEFENSIVE STRENGTH CHART

3-4 Defense

FS #31 | SS #33

CB #37

ROLB #96 | MLB #57 | MLB #55 | LOLB #91

CB #21

RE #77 | DT #93 | LE #92

Dime Defense

FS #31 | SS #33

CB #37 | CB #26

MLB #55 | CB #22 | CB #21

RE #77 | DT #90 | DT #93 | LE #92

- ■ OVR 90 or Greater
- ■ OVR between 80-89
- ■ OVR between 70-79
- ■ OVR between 60-69
- ■ OVR 59 or lower

Key Player Substitutions

Position: HB

Substitution: Darren McFadden

When: Global

Advantage: Darren McFadden can help the Raiders put points on the board. Focus on trying to get the ball to McFadden where he can bounce it to the outside.

Key Player Substitutions

Position: DE

Substitution: Quentin Groves

When: Situational

Advantage: When lined up with Seymour on the defensive line, Groves has the speed to beat any tackle around the edge, and he has the finesse moves to get him all the way to the quarterback.

Playbook Breakdown

The Raiders are a team built for speed, and when using them we must consider calling plays that showcase their ability to run away from defenders. The Raiders were one of the most used teams in *Madden NFL* last season, and it was simply because of how fast their personnel is on both sides of the ball.

Our only concern is the offense, and we have weapons with track athlete–type speed in almost every skill position. Every receiver on the team has a 90 or better speed rating. When we have an offense with these types of threats to go to, there aren't many defenses that can keep up with us.

In previous years, the Raiders have been down on their luck at the quarterback position, but with Jason Campbell now running the show, people who like to play with the Raiders will have a quarterback who can deliver the ball. As we look over the Raiders' style of play, we see that they are a team that incorporates a lot of play action passing. We have to be sure to feed the running back so that the play action can work. Overall, the Raiders have a pretty balanced playbook.

OFFENSIVE FORMATIONS

FORMATION	# OF PLAYS
Gun Doubles On	15
Gun Snugs	9
Gun Split Y-Flex	12
Gun Spread Flex	9
Gun Trey Open	12
Gun Y-Trips Wk	15
I-Form Pro	15
I-Form Pro Twins	15
I-Form TE Flip	12
I-Form Tight	12
I-Form Tight Pair	9
Singleback Ace	15
Singleback Ace Twins	15
Singleback Bunch Base	12
Singleback Doubles	15
Singleback Wing Trio	15
Strong Tight Pair	12
Wildcat Trio	3

OFFENSIVE PLAYCOUNTS

PLAY TYPE	# OF PLAYS
Quick Pass	15
Standard Pass	39
Shotgun Pass	45
Play Action Pass	52
Inside Handoff	29
Outside Handoff	15
Pitch	7
Counter	4

Gun Spread Flex—Quick Slants

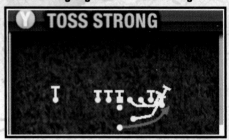

The Raiders have always been a team that believes in the value of speed. This team is extremely fast, and one great way to attack the defense right away is with the Gun Spread Flex—Quick Slants. This has always been a quick-hitting pass play that gives the receivers a chance to catch the ball and run away from the defenders. With all the speed on the Raiders roster, that is very likely to happen.

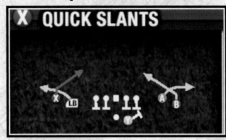

The flanker is open on the slant

All we need is a small void in the defense's coverage, and with the speed of our receivers we can get the ball to them and let them make a play. The defense is showing lax coverage here, and with no defenders underneath they don't have a chance against the slants.

The flanker catches the ball

The pass to the flanker on the slant route is the perfect decision and results in a 14-yard gain on the play. As an offense, any time we can get big chunks of yards on minimal-risk passing plays, we will continue to go to those plays.

Gun Trey Open—Double Post

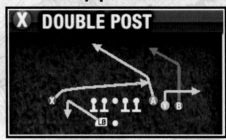

The luxury of having so much speed on the field whenever we come out in a Gun formation is addictive. We can turn routine passing plays into big-play passing opportunities. We have found that the Gun Trey Open—Double Post is a play that can do just that. This play is a nightmare for any man or zone coverage to face. And if the defense blitzes, just put 7 on the board for our offense.

The deep safety will always tell us who to throw to

As we scan the field and identify what the defense is doing coverage-wise, we see that they have decided to drop the safety back in a Cover 1 zone. He has already turned to the opposite sideline, so we know that the post route by our tight slot is wide open. We also always have the luxury of the drag route by our split end.

Easy touchdown

To say it was a footrace would be a misrepresentation of what really happened. We actually saw the tight slot receiver open on the post, threw him the ball, and then watched him effortlessly jog into the end zone.

Strong Tight Pair—Toss Strong

The Strong Tight Pair—Toss Strong is a play that gets our running back to the edge of the defense quickly. With all the speed we have in the backfield, this running play is a must-have in our offensive attack. Darren McFadden has a 97 speed rating, so all we need is a sliver of space and then it's off to the races.

We have a wall of blockers

The blocking that we enjoy when running this play gives it that much more of a reason to continue to go to it. One common mistake that people make when running the toss is to string the play out to the sideline. The best way to run the toss is to run it inside out, cut upfield as soon as you can, and then hit the sideline.

McFadden sprints down the sideline

The benefit of cutting the run up first is that it prevents the defense from scraping down the line and meeting us before we turn upfield. Once we cut upfield, the defense has to change their pursuit angle, which allows us to get more yards from our run. We burn them for a 15-yard gain on this play.

I-Form Tight Pair—Raider Blast

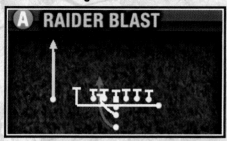

The run has always been an important part of the Raiders offense. The Silver and Black have always delighted fans with amazing runs from backs like Marcus Allen and Bo Jackson. The Raider mystique can continue here with solid running plays like the I-Form Tight Pair—Raider Blast. This automotion run will give us a chance to put up serious yards with Darren McFadden or whatever back we decide on.

The automotion tight end makes the key block

This running play is special because the automotion by the pair tight end is done in normal speed. Many times when you run an automotion play, the motion is different than if we were to set the player in motion. The fact that the automotion is in regular speed prevents the defense from knowing what play we have called.

McFadden bursts through the line

The block that our tight end makes after going in automotion is the reason we can get our running back through this hole and up the field. All we ask for from our line is a half a second, so we can burst through the hole. McFadden takes this opportunity and gets through the hole and down the field for a 13-yard gain.

Singleback Bunch Base—End Around Lead

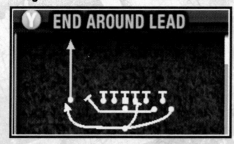

Madden NFL 11 is still a very fun game to play, and there are plays that are just flat out a blast to run. Even though a play may be fun, it doesn't mean it's not solid. The Singleback Bunch Base—End Around Lead is a play that fits perfectly in the design of our personnel and offensive scheme. Get the ball to the fastest players on the field and see what they can do.

Our lead blocker is the key to success on this play

There are multiple end around plays in *Madden NFL 11*, but the Raiders have one of the best. The Singleback Bunch Base—End Around Lead is unique because it actually has a lead blocker. Most end around plays in *Madden NFL 11* simply rely on the speed of the receiver to outrun the defenders. This end around gives us an opportunity on offense to make a play because of the additional blocker.

We pick up a critical downfield block

The advantage of that lead blocker is seen here as we pick up a critical block that helps our receiver change direction to get around the approaching safety. Schilens has a 92 speed rating, and if he has blocking in front of him, he can easily gouge the defense for big yards.

Gun Snugs—Bench

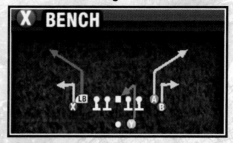

Many times when playing *Madden NFL 11*, we feel like we have to set each play up and have it work within a scheme. But to be honest, the only scheme we need is to score; everything we do should be designed around scoring on the play. The Gun Snugs—Bench will get our fastest receivers on the field and put them in position to beat the defense for a score.

Our quarterback is looking for Heyward-Bey

When running the Gun Snugs we can get an early read on the defense based on their alignment. There aren't too many defenses that can afford to play zone and have their men aligned far outside of our men. When we set the play in motion, we already know the defense is in zone coverage and wait to see what route will be open.

Our receiver beats the cornerback for a touchdown

The cornerback didn't adjust quickly enough and found himself out of position against one of the fastest receivers in the NFL. With the kind of speed we have on the field, we can stay aggressive and throw bombs downfield for our receivers to run under when we see defensive backs out of position.

Gun Doubles On—PA FL Fly

The Gun Doubles On—PA FL Fly lets us stay aggressive with our attack on the defense and still add a little element of balance with the fake to the running back. If the defense decides to disregard the fake to our running back, we can come back to that and run the ball later. We will no longer give the defense a chance to think they can hang with us; we want them in retreat mode from the start of the game.

Read the defense while the play action fake is happening

One of the weaknesses of running play action is that a good blitz can make us pay for running it. We can handle that threat by hot routing our back to block. We see that the defense is bringing pressure and also notice that they are sending pressure at us without any coverage behind it. Big mistake.

Our tight end scores easily

The blatant disrespectfulness of the defense to send a zero blitz at us cost them dearly. We know that we have an option to protect us against the blitz, and even with the threat of a blitz we were not worried about the defense reaching us because of the quick-throw options to the post or the split end on a slant hook. Nonetheless, we spot our tight end down the center of the field and hit him for an uncontested touchdown pass.

ST. LOUIS RAMS

OFFENSIVE SCOUTING REPORT

The Rams picked quarterback Sam Bradford with the first overall pick in this year's draft. Bradford will come in as an instant starter, hitting the ground running. In Bradford, the Rams get a strong, accurate arm and someone capable of throwing on the run. The team indeed needs all the help it can get after averaging only 10.9 points per game in 2009. Last year's pick, LT Jason Smith, should add some much-needed protection for the young quarterback, who hopes to find speed-burner WR Donnie Avery or sure-handed rookie Mardy Gilyard. Both of these receivers are quick off the line, with Avery posing the most problems for defenses to contain. Thankfully for Bradford, the young line, and receiving corps there's the Rams' biggest asset, Steven Jackson. He's a huge running back who seems to look for contact and breaks defenses down over the course of a game. Nothing will open up opportunities like a 6' 2", 236-pound freight train. Jackson should run early and often in this offense and is as elite a running back as the NFL has to offer. He's also a rarity in the NFL now as an every-down back, as evidenced by his stamina rating.

DEFENSIVE SCOUTING REPORT

The defense for the Rams is promising. There are some really nice pieces here for the team to build upon for the foreseeable future. Starting up at the front line is the constant motor of RE Chris Long. There's no quit in the Long family and that eventually wears on offensive linemen. The Rams also have one of the best tacklers in linebacker James Laurinaitis. Broken tackles are rare for this guy, and the addition of Na'il Diggs will solidify this team as a threat mid-field. James Butler provides the protection in the secondary as the strong safety. The Rams are not a lockdown defense, but they are an up-and-coming defense led by gritty head coach Steve Spagnuolo that could surprise some teams.

RATINGS BY POSITION

Position	Rating
Quarterbacks	80
Halfbacks	95
Fullbacks	85
Wide Receivers	71
Tight Ends	66
Tackles	77
Guards	81
Centers	89
Defensive Ends	72
Defensive Tackles	77
Outside Linebackers	72
Middle Linebackers	85
Cornerbacks	72
Free Safeties	67
Strong Safeties	80
Kickers	87
Punters	94

TEAM RATING

66
Overall

KEY ADDITIONS

LB	Bobby Carpenter
LB	Na'il Diggs
WR	Mardy Gilyard
C/G	Hank Fraley
S	Kevin Payne
QB	Sam Bradford

KEY DEPARTURES

QB	Kyle Boller
QB	Marc Bulger
TE	Randy McMichael
OT	Alex Barron
LB	Paris Lenon
CB	Jonathan Wade

DEPTH CHART

POS	OVR	FIRST NAME	LAST NAME
C	89	Jason	Brown
C	78	Hank	Fraley
CB	81	Ronald	Bartell
CB	70	Jerome	Murphy
CB	68	Bradley	Fletcher
CB	66	Quincy	Butler
CB	63	Justin	King
DT	80	Fred	Robbins
DT	77	Cliff	Ryan
DT	68	Gary	Gibson
DT	64	Darell	Scott
FB	85	Mike	Karney
FS	71	Kevin	Payne
FS	67	Craig	Dahl
HB	95	Steven	Jackson
HB	66	Kenneth	Darby
HB	64	Chris	Ogbonnaya
K	87	Josh	Brown
LE	69	Victor	Adeyanju
LE	66	George	Selvie
LE	64	Hall	Davis
LG	85	Jacob	Bell
LG	73	Mark	Setterstrom
LOLB	70	Bobby	Carpenter
LOLB	63	Chris	Chamberlain
LOLB	60	Larry	Grant
LT	83	Jason	Smith
MLB	85	James	Laurinaitis
MLB	56	Dominic	Douglas
P	94	Donnie	Jones
QB	80	Sam	Bradford
QB	66	A.J.	Feeley
QB	60	Keith	Null
RE	76	James	Hall
RE	75	Chris	Long
RE	65	C.J.	Ah You
RG	76	Adam	Goldberg
RG	75	John	Greco
ROLB	74	Na'il	Diggs
ROLB	68	David	Vobora
RT	71	Rodger	Saffold
RT	60	Phil	Trautwein
SS	80	James	Butler
SS	63	David	Roach
TE	69	Darcy	Johnson
TE	68	Billy	Bajema
TE	66	Daniel	Fells
WR	75	Donnie	Avery
WR	71	Brandon	Gibson
WR	70	Laurent	Robinson
WR	70	Mardy	Gilyard
WR	67	Danny	Amendola
WR	67	Keenan	Burton

OFFENSIVE STRENGTH CHART

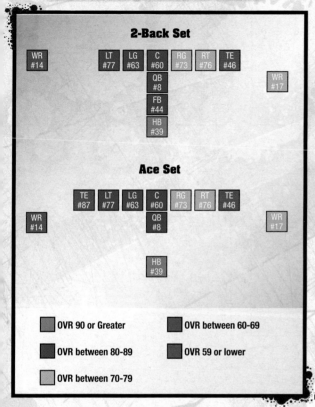

2-Back Set

WR #14		LT #77	LG #63	C #60	RG #73	RT #76	TE #46
			QB #8			WR #17
			FB #44			
			HB #39			

Ace Set

	TE #87	LT #77	LG #63	C #60	RG #73	RT #76	TE #46
WR #14			QB #8			WR #17
			HB #39			

- ■ OVR 90 or Greater
- ■ OVR between 80-89
- ■ OVR between 70-79
- ■ OVR between 60-69
- ■ OVR 59 or lower

#39 Steven Jackson
Halfback (HB)

Overall	95
Speed	87
Agility	87
Stiff Arm	97
Carrying	90

#60 Jason Brown
Center (C)

Overall	89
Strength	93
Pass Block	84
Run Block	93
Impact Blocking	93

#8 Sam Bradford
Quarterback (QB)

Overall	80
Throw Power	87
Short Accuracy	95
Medium Accuracy	87
Deep Accuracy	72

#55 James Laurinaitis
Linebacker (MLB)

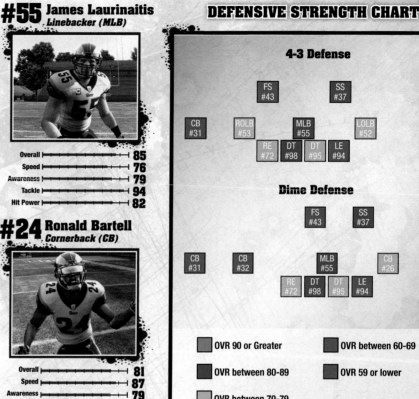

Overall	85
Speed	76
Awareness	79
Tackle	94
Hit Power	82

#24 Ronald Bartell
Cornerback (CB)

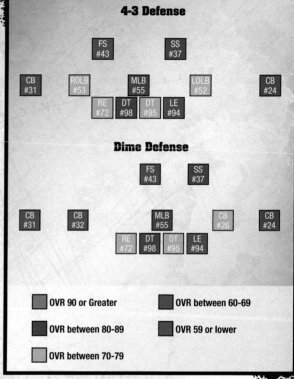

Overall	81
Speed	87
Awareness	79
Man Coverage	83
Zone Coverage	86

#37 James Butler
Strong Safety (SS)

Overall	80
Speed	80
Awareness	75
Tackle	73
Hit Power	69

DEFENSIVE STRENGTH CHART

4-3 Defense

	FS #43		SS #37	
CB #31	ROLB #53	MLB #55	LOLB #52	CB #24
	RE #72	DT #98	DT #95	LE #94	

Dime Defense

	FS #43		SS #37	
CB #31	CB #32	MLB #55	CB #26	CB #24
	RE #72	DT #98	DT #95	LE #94	

- ■ OVR 90 or Greater
- ■ OVR between 80-89
- ■ OVR between 70-79
- ■ OVR between 60-69
- ■ OVR 59 or lower

Key Player Substitutions

Position: WR

Substitution: Laurent Robinson

When: Three-wide-receiver sets

Advantage: Moving Robinson up to the number three slot on the depth chart will add much-needed speed to the receiver group. Robinson's high acceleration will help him get space from the cornerback.

Key Player Substitutions

Position: CB

Substitution: Justin King

When: Nickel and Dime formations

Advantage: With a 95 speed rating, King is capable of running the field with a wide receiver. Keeping King in man coverage will help him stay with whomever he's guarding.

Playbook Breakdown

The Rams' second-year coach, Steve Spagnuolo, drafted rookie quarterback Sam Bradford in the first round to go with already-proven stud running back Steven Jackson. Sam Bradford was the number one pick from Oklahoma even after suffering a shoulder injury in his last season of college football. With a rookie quarterback, the offense will be centered on running back Steven Jackson. Jackson is one of the best running backs in the league, with five straight thousand-yard seasons. To get the ground game going you can use formations such as Strong Twins Flex, I-Form Pro, and I-Form Twin TE. Between these three formations you have more than 15 run plays, including Sweeps, Counters, Dives, and Draws. You also have a decent number of play action passes out of all these formations, which are good to use after you soften up the defense with the run game. This playbook has eight Gun formations with a good variation of compressed and spread sets. You have Gun Split Offset, Gun Snugs Flip, and Gun Trey Open, to name a few.

OFFENSIVE FORMATIONS

FORMATION	# OF PLAYS
Gun Doubles On	15
Gun Empty Trey	9
Gun Snugs Flip	12
Gun Split Offset	18
Gun Spread Y-Slot	12
Gun Trey Open	15
Gun Y-Trips Wk	15
I-Form Pro	18
I-Form Slot Flex	12
I-Form Twin TE	12
Singleback Ace Pair Twins	12
Singleback Big	12
Singleback Doubles	18
Singleback Jumbo	9
Singleback Y-Trips	15
Strong Twins Flex	12

OFFENSIVE PLAYCOUNTS

PLAY TYPE	# OF PLAYS
Quick Pass	13
Standard Pass	32
Shotgun Pass	66
Play Action Pass	41
Inside Handoff	25
Outside Handoff	12
Pitch	5
Counter	5

Strong Twins Flex—HB Off Tackle

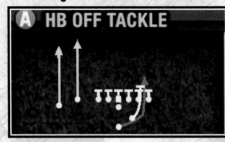

The Rams have one of the top running backs in the NFL with Steven Jackson. The Strong Twins Flex—HB Off Tackle is the perfect run to get this power back going. This type of run was widely used in *Madden NFL 10* and we expect that to be no different this year in *Madden NFL 11*.

Handing it to the beast

One thing we like to do with this play is motion the slot receiver to the right side of the field and snap the ball when he is behind the line of scrimmage to provide extra blocking. After we hand the ball off to Steven Jackson our blocks are set up perfectly out in front of us.

Setting up the block

Steven Jackson finds a hole inside behind right guard Adam Goldberg and right tackle Rodger Saffold. This type of run is very hard to stop because you have the choice to take it up inside or bounce it outside if you see the defense overpursuing the run. You will be sure to give the defense fits with this run mixed into your offensive game plan.

Strong Twins Flex—Curl Flat

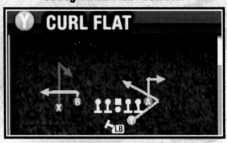

Strong Twin Flex—Curl Flat allows you to get your short passing game on with quick reads to the slot receiver and the fullback out the backfield. The play design has the split end as the primary target, but what we like to do is use the out route run by the slot receiver as our first read.

Good blocking up front

With a formation such as Strong Twins Flex we can tell before we hike the ball whether the defense is in man or zone. The defense is in zone here and decides to blitz off the left side of the field. This makes it an easy decision for Sam Bradford.

An outside block will lead to 6 points

He finds his target, Keenan Burton, for the catch. Wide receiver Donnie Avery makes a key block downfield. Burton picks up 9 yards before being tackled. If you see that the defense is playing man, this is when it's a good time to look at the fullback on the V route out the backfield as your second read.

I-Form Twin TE—HB Power O

I-Form Twin TE has been a widely used formation in *Madden NFL* for years. HB Power O is a perfect run to use that complements Steven Jackson's power running style. With the tight end lined up on the right side of the field, you can motion him behind the line of scrimmage to provide extra blocking.

Look at all of your gap options

Once you motion the tight end to the right, wait until he is behind the left tackle before you snap the ball. Sam Bradford hands the ball off to Jackson, and his blocks are set up perfectly in front of him. With left guard Jacob Bell pulling and fullback Mike Karney out in front, Jackson sees the hole.

Ripping though would-be tacklers

The blocker seals the edge and Jackson bounces it outside with his speed and picks up 10 yards before he is tackled. If you see the defense overload one side of the formation, flip the play and run it to the other side.

I-Form Twin TE—PA Waggle

The I-Form Twin TE—PA Waggle works alongside the HB Power O. This play allows the tight end to get involved in the passing game. He goes deep on a corner route. You also have the other tight end, who acts like a blocker then sneaks out into the flat.

Freeze the linebackers

The QB fakes the handoff to Jackson as if he is running the ball to the left. This allows him to roll out to the right side of the field. The play is all about misdirection—getting the defense to anticipate the run one way while you pass to the other side of the field. Make sure you take control of the QB after the handoff, then roll to the right. If you don't have the tight end open, look short or take off with him.

Hitting your receiver on the sidelines

Sam Bradford spots tight end Daniel Fells downfield and throws a bullet pass to him down the right sideline. The game plan with this scheme is to soften the defense up with the run and then mix in this play action play.

I-Form Slot Flex—HB Blast

The I-Form Slot Flex formation spreads the defense out. The HB Blast from this formation is designed to run to the weak side behind left tackle Jason Smith. This is a solid run that moves the chains and works well with the other runs from this formation.

Follow your FB

The QB hands the ball off to Steven Jackson as he follows fullback Mike Karney. Left tackle Jason Smith and left guard Jacob Bell are holding their blocks as well. You can choose to cut it up inside between them or, if the edge is sealed, take it outside. It's all about being patient and reading the defense.

A good WR block

The edge is sealed and Steven Jackson bounces it outside for a 5-yard gain before being tackled. Another suggestion with this run is to use motion and flip the play, depending on which side the defense overloads. Again, this is a very good run that picks up positive yards.

Gun Split Offset—FL Spot

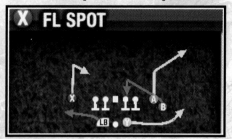

FL Spot is a favorite play of ours from the Gun Split Offset formation. The play design has the receivers compressed, and this makes the play unique because it is hidden within this formation. Because this is a compressed set, you can easily tell if the defense is playing man or zone.

Bradford makes a quick-release throw

We motion the flanker to the left side of the field. If the defense plays zone, the flanker will be open on the left sideline. Sam Bradford sees that his target, wide receiver Donnie Avery, is open so he fires the ball to him down the sideline.

Keeping two feet in bounds

Avery makes the catch for a 10-yard gain, which keeps the chains moving. If the defense is playing man, this is when you want to look for one of the running backs out of the backfield. You have the delay route and the flat route as potential targets. After that, you can look toward the slot receiver and the split end.

Gun Split Offset—Curls

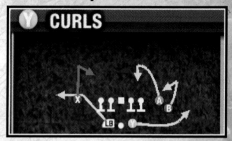

Curls is another play that is part of the hidden plays in this formation. It has all three receivers on short curl routes with two routes out of the backfield. This play kills man or zone and is a good play to use to keep the chains moving. It's what we call a money play.

Viewing the field

With this play, we motion the flanker inside and snap the ball. Once he gets behind the right tackle, this creates a flood. Look for the flat route and the two curl routes with three receivers in one area. It's hard for the defense to cover this no matter if they are in man or zone coverage.

Hitting the quick slant

The QB finds his target, Donnie Avery. Avery makes the grab and has plenty of room to get some good yards after the catch before he is tackled. Another suggestion is to put the slot receiver on a streak. This will pull the coverage and open up the underneath routes even more. Also, don't forget about the running back and the split end on the left side of the field.

BALTIMORE RAVENS

OFFENSIVE SCOUTING REPORT

QB Joe Flacco showed great promise in his rookie season and he's been building from that base ever since. Now in his third year, Flacco is no longer a rookie or second-year question mark, but rather the tried and true leader of the Ravens offense. Young and athletic, Flacco has a great arm and legs to go with it. He's not a scrambling quarterback like Vince Young or even Aaron Rodgers, but he's shifty when he needs to be. With the recent acquisition of one of the most talented wide receivers in the league, Anquan Boldin, the Ravens' WR corps gets an immediate star-level upgrade. Use Boldin to confound cornerbacks and make critical catches; he's the very definition of clutch. While 2009 began with questions as to who would start at running back, it ended with a definite, resounding answer: RB Ray Rice. He's tough, agile, and has speedy acceleration, and best of all, he's got surprising vision for someone so young. Much of Rice's success can be attributed to the offensive line of LT Michael Oher, LG Ben Grubbs, and C Matt Birk.

DEFENSIVE SCOUTING REPORT

If there is one thing you can always count on in the NFL, it's legendary MLB Ray Lewis rallying his men and being the core of a stout Ravens defense. This year is no different. Ray Lewis is the heart of the defense—the entire team, for that matter—and should be your go-to guy. Terrell Suggs is a ridiculous talent at OLB and can provide instant pressure from anywhere on the field. Be it hawking or sacking, Suggs always makes his presence felt on opposing QBs. If the Ravens D has a weakness, it's their secondary. With the exception of super safety Ed Reed, the defensive backfield can be exploited by big-play WRs. Support this chink in the armor by keeping a constant pressure on opposing QBs with the likes of all-star RE Haloti Ngata and plugging holes when they open up. After all, if the Ravens can't get the stop up front, then the secondary is the least of their worries.

TEAM RATING

90
Overall

KEY ADDITIONS

WR	Anquan Boldin
DE	Cory Redding
WR	Donté Stallworth
OLB	Sergio Kindle

KEY DEPARTURES

DT	Justin Bannan
DE	Dwan Edwards
TE	L.J. Smith
T	Adam Terry
WR	Kelley Washington
TE	Quinn Sypniewski

RATINGS BY POSITION

Position	Rating
Quarterbacks	87
Halfbacks	90
Fullbacks	90
Wide Receivers	84
Tight Ends	83
Tackles	88
Guards	87
Centers	91
Defensive Ends	88
Defensive Tackles	84
Outside Linebackers	86
Middle Linebackers	94
Cornerbacks	77
Free Safeties	97
Strong Safeties	82
Kickers	70
Punters	86

DEPTH CHART

POS	OVR	FIRST NAME	LAST NAME
C	91	Matt	Birk
C	70	David	Hale
CB	82	Domonique	Foxworth
CB	74	Lardarius	Webb
CB	72	Fabian	Washington
CB	65	Chris	Carr
CB	58	Cary	Williams
DT	84	Kelly	Gregg
DT	72	Terrence	Cody
DT	65	Brandon	McKinney
FB	90	Le'Ron	McClain
FS	97	Ed	Reed
FS	76	Tom	Zbikowski
HB	90	Ray	Rice
HB	83	Willis	McGahee
HB	66	Jalen	Parmele
K	70	Billy	Cundiff
LE	82	Trevor	Pryce
LE	76	Cory	Redding
LG	94	Ben	Grubbs
LOLB	82	Jarret	Johnson
LOLB	78	Sergio	Kindle
LOLB	72	Antwan	Barnes
LT	89	Michael	Oher
LT	61	Tony	Moll
MLB	94	Ray	Lewis
MLB	71	Dannell	Ellerbe
MLB	70	Tavares	Gooden
MLB	63	Jameel	McClain
P	86	Sam	Koch
QB	97	Joe	Flacco
QB	67	Troy	Smith
QB	58	John	Beck
RE	94	Haloti	Ngata
RE	55	Lamar	Divens
RG	80	Marshal	Yanda
RG	76	Chris	Chester
ROLB	90	Terrell	Suggs
ROLB	72	Paul	Kruger
RT	86	Jared	Gaither
RT	68	Oniel	Cousins
SS	82	Dawan	Landry
SS	66	Haruki	Nakamura
TE	83	Todd	Heap
TE	65	Ed	Dickson
TE	62	Dennis	Pitta
WR	91	Anquan	Boldin
WR	85	Derrick	Mason
WR	76	Mark	Clayton
WR	68	Donté	Stallworth
WR	67	Demetrius	Williams
WR	58	David	Reed

OFFENSIVE STRENGTH CHART

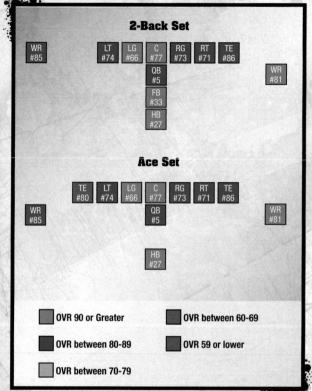

2-Back Set

| WR #85 | | LT #74 | LG #66 | C #77 | RG #73 | RT #71 | TE #86 | |
| QB #5 |
| FB #33 |
| HB #27 |
| | | | | | | | | WR #81 |

Ace Set

		TE #80	LT #74	LG #66	C #77	RG #73	RT #71	TE #86
WR #85			QB #5					WR #81
			HB #27

■ OVR 90 or Greater	■ OVR between 60-69
■ OVR between 80-89	■ OVR 59 or lower
■ OVR between 70-79	

Key Player Substitutions

Position: WR

Substitution: Donté Stallworth

When: Situational

Advantage: Donté Stallworth is the fastest wide receiver on the Ravens' depth charts. Use screen plays and short crossing routes to get the ball in Stallworth's hands, and watch him turn the ball up the field.

#27 Ray Rice
Halfback (HB)

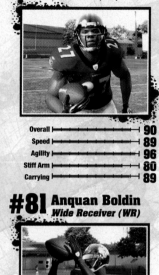

Overall	90
Speed	89
Agility	96
Stiff Arm	80
Carrying	89

#81 Anquan Boldin
Wide Receiver (WR)

Overall	91
Speed	87
Catching	93
Release	91
Jumping	87

#5 Joe Flacco
Quarterback (QB)

Overall	87
Throw Power	96
Short Accuracy	87
Medium Accuracy	85
Deep Accuracy	80

#52 Ray Lewis
Linebacker (MLB)

Overall	94
Speed	82
Awareness	99
Tackle	95
Hit Power	96

#20 Ed Reed
Free Safety (FS)

Overall	97
Speed	93
Awareness	94
Tackle	59
Hit Power	75

#55 Terrell Suggs
Linebacker (ROLB)

Overall	90
Speed	84
Awareness	86
Tackle	81
Hit Power	79

DEFENSIVE STRENGTH CHART

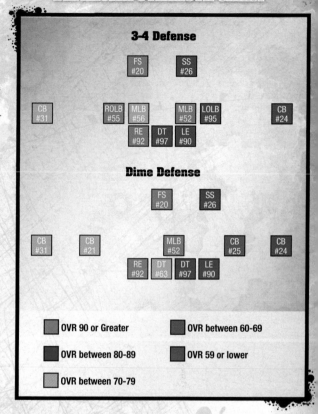

3-4 Defense

		FS #20		SS #26		
CB #31	ROLB #55	MLB #56		MLB #52	LOLB #95	CB #24
		RE #92	DT #97	LE #90		

Dime Defense

		FS #20		SS #26		
CB #31	CB #21		MLB #52		CB #25	CB #24
		RE #92	DT #63	DT #97	LE #90	

■ OVR 90 or Greater	■ OVR between 60-69
■ OVR between 80-89	■ OVR 59 or lower
■ OVR between 70-79	

Key Player Substitutions

Position: CB

Substitution: Fabian Washington

When: Global

Advantage: Moving Washington up on your depth chart will help keep fast wide receivers from getting open. Keeping in front of wide receivers for an extra second will let one of the best linebackers get to the quarterback.

Playbook Breakdown

The Ravens have made some upgrades to the team via draft and free agency. The Ravens were one of the hottest teams last season, more so when Ray Rice became the main offensive threat. Now with the free agent additions at wideout, the Ravens are a balanced team capable of running a balanced attack. No team will be able to drop 8–9 players down in the box to stop the run with the new tools that were added. Joe Flacco is coming into his own as a solid QB. Be creative with your packages and sets to force matchup problems throughout the passing game. Then, when you have numbers, pound the rock with Rice. Rice is a great option at wideout as well. Move him around to look for mismatches for him. In this breakdown, we show sets that are new or cause major problems for people to defend when used correctly. Let's look at what the Ravens playbook can bring to the table.

OFFENSIVE FORMATIONS

FORMATION	# OF PLAYS
Gun Raven Empty	12
Gun Raven Trips	9
Gun Split Raven	12
Gun Spread Y-Flex	12
Gun Wing Trips	15
I-Form Pro	18
I-Form Tight Pair	12
I-Form Twins Flex	12
Singleback Big	12
Singleback Bunch	12
Singleback Doubles Flex	18
Singleback F Pair Twins	15
Singleback Jumbo	12
Singleback Trey Open	9
Singleback Y-Trips	12
Strong H Twin TE	9

OFFENSIVE PLAYCOUNTS

PLAY TYPE	# OF PLAYS
Quick Pass	16
Standard Pass	36
Shotgun Pass	39
Play Action Pass	47
Outside Handoff	20
Pitch	9
Counter	6
Draw	7

Strong H Twin TE—Ravens Curls

The curl-flat read is easy. You look for the flat route, and if anyone sits on the flat you drive the curl route. This is a running set, so throwing the ball will catch your opponent off guard. Once you have run the ball a few times, you need quick-hitting plays to move the chains and keep your down and distance short. The curl-flat read works against all zones and man coverage. You have two hot reads to your backs with three short curls.

The linebacker gets picked by our TE

This play really opens up the field quickly. Your overload is to the right side of the field. You read the flat, the inside curl, and then the outside curl. As you can see, the linebacker got picked by the twin TEs going into their routes. When you see this happen, you must hit the flats.

The FB gets good yards for our team

When you hit the uncovered wideout, it forces the defense to make adjustments to cover everyone. You must punish the defense every time they leave a player open. Make them accountable for every player on the field, every single play.

Strong H Twin TE—Power O

The Power O is a good play by itself, but when you run it to a twin tight end side you have something special. You have two tight ends to seal the edge, and you have a guard pulling from the back side of the play to kick out and drive to the second level between the tackle and the guard. You should read the inside first and stay with the guard. If the hole is filled you must go to the edge and bounce it outside.

The TE gets a nice seal block

The best thing to do is stay with your guard and lead fullback. The guard will stop pulling if someone leaks through. Then you have to read your fullback. If you're lucky, the guard will pull and reach to the second level, with the fullback cleaning up the mess.

Breaking outside to daylight

If your inside gaps are filled, bounce the ball outside. The key is that you have to stay with your blocks and, if your inside holes are filled, cut it outside. The defenders flow well, so if you step outside you may get hit for a loss.

Strong H Twin TE—PA Power O

When you have gotten your Power O going well, you need to take advantage of an aggressive defensive adjustment to stop your run. The use of play action passing bodes well when you have set up your rushing attack. This is what you call "letting the run set up your pass." This play will have the same backfield movement, to sell the Power O, and then the defense will flow to the ball. Once they do, you should have some nice opportunities to take shots downfield.

The defense is flowing to the Power O fake

The defense is biting hard on the play fake. Now it's time to look downfield and take a shot. Your pass progression should be the dig from the wideout, then the corner route by the tight end, then the flat route by the fullback. The fullback is open most of the time, but you want to take a shot downfield if you have an opening.

Todd Heap is wide open for an easy catch

You have to like the matchup of a tight end vs. any defender. This is a great one-two punch with the run and PA fake.

Gun Raven Trips—Verticals

One set you won't see in any other playbook is this offset formation with trips to the right side. The purpose of the offset line is to force the defense to slide over and adjust to the overload to the right side of the line. Then you have the tight end to the weak side. Three-way and four-way floods are hard to defend. You want to flood a side with routes that expose a weakness in the defensive coverage. Your progressions should be the dig, the streaks, and then the tight end doing his quick out. When you're facing zone coverage, you will find holes. If you're facing man coverage, the dig and out will come open quickly.

Here is a look at the dig and the out routes

The dig and the out are coming open quickly. The streaks are pushing the secondary back to open up the shorter routes.

TEs in the slot create great mismatches

Any time we can get our TE lined up in the slot there is potential for a mismatch. We make a great catch here to keep the chains moving.

Gun Raven Trips—HB Mid Draw

We may sound like a broken record, but you have to be able to run and pass out of any sets that you use. In the long run this will keep your opponents off-balance so they have to play you honestly. The offset line is a really big factor in your rushing attack. If they don't adjust to your offset line, you run towards the overloaded side. If they make the adjustment, you can run to the weak side where you have a tight end and a guard. The best plan is just to hit the first hole you see when you hike the ball. The fake pass-blocking will force the defense to assume you're passing. When the coverage drops back, you take advantage and hit the hole for yards.

The Ravens are parting the Red Sea

You see the inside hole and have to take it. If there isn't a hole inside, look to cut the ball outside quickly.

Rice gets downfield

Now your wideouts are blocking downfield. This is a nice change-of-pace play to call when you're in this formation.

Gun Wing Trips—Empty BAL Smash

This is a formation within a formation. You will find, at times, that you have a hidden formation within a set. These hidden formations have a slightly different alignment. An example of this is the Empty BAL Smash. Since Rice is a great option as a wideout, the formation moves him from the backfield to the outside, which gives you a five-wide look. You want to catch the defense off-balance if they don't account for him outside. If he's uncovered you must hit him. When you get Rice in open space like this, magic happens. If the defense accounts for him, you now have a better wideout inside against a weaker defender. This is a nice changeup.

The HB and slot receiver are uncovered pre-snap

When you hike the ball, you want to hit the uncovered player from your pre-snap read. If you don't, then you're wasting your time even running this play or using this formation. This alignment is supposed to put the defense in conflict. So when it does you must expose them.

Rice is out!

Just pitch, catch, and get what you can get down the field.

Gun Wing Trips—Empty BAL Screens

You have to love this play. This play allows you to run a screen to either side of the field. If your opponent is using a lot of zone coverage, then this play is a nice changeup when you have exposed the defense deep out of this formation. You have your halfback and your flanker set up for the screen. Look for the uncovered wideout and hit that person. If they both are covered, then hit the open screen side.

Both options are open

Just pick a side to attack and hit it. Make sure that the blockers have set their blocks. If the screens aren't open, take off with the QB or throw the ball away. No need to take a loss or force a turnover.

Mason is out!

Get the ball to your playmaker in open space and let him do what he does best. This is a nice play to have in your audibles when you're using this playbook.

WASHINGTON REDSKINS

OFFENSIVE SCOUTING REPORT

Welcome, Donovan McNabb and head coach Mike Shanahan. The Redskins will be sporting a new offense this season now that a new quarterback and head coach have come to town. Donovan McNabb still has plenty in his tank and should make the receivers around him better. This is good news for the speedy receiving corps of Santana Moss, Devin Thomas, and Joey Galloway, since they have a quarterback with the arm and accuracy to provide the deep bombing pass they all thrive on. Clinton Portis is a dependable back who will also thrive with the sudden threat of the deep pass, allowing him to run against a defense that hasn't stacked the front line to stop him. Willie Parker provides the speed that Clinton Portis lacks for the change of pace and long third downs. At the goal line, Redskins have the heavy steamroller in Larry Johnson. The one continuing performer is TE Chris Cooley, whose productivity will remain intact no matter who takes the snaps. A trio of capable and sturdy running backs, a trusty tight end, and a proven quarterback at the helm will help bring the offense back to life, provided the suspect offensive line can create time for plays to develop.

DEFENSIVE SCOUTING REPORT

The Redskins defense is solid against both the rush and the pass. It doesn't hurt that they have one of the largest men in the league taking up one whole side of the defensive line. Albert Haynesworth is listed at 350 pounds and has the strength to match his size. He excels at power moves, and no one sheds a block better. With this kind of pressure on the QB and the run, star linebacker London Fletcher is free to roam and fill in and shoot the gaps. The secondary is quite solid with speedy corner DeAngelo Hall and the hard hitting of corner Carlos Rogers. Safety LaRon Landry polishes the secondary with his size and speed. Offenses will focus on tying up Haynesworth and reaching midfield from the opposite side, where the line is weaker, leaving linebacker Brian Orakpo to provide the stop. Otherwise, the Redskins could have a weakness exposed.

TEAM RATING

76
Overall

KEY ADDITIONS

RB	Larry Johnson
RB	Willie Parker
QB	Donovan McNabb
CB	Phillip Buchanon
LB	Chris Draft
LT	Trent Williams

KEY DEPARTURES

QB	Jason Campbell
RB	Rock Cartwright
WR	Antwaan Randle El
LT	Chris Samuels
DT	Cornelius Griffin
P	Hunter Smith

RATINGS BY POSITION

Position	Rating	Position	Rating
Quarterbacks	89	Defensive Tackles	76
Halfbacks	85	Outside Linebackers	81
Fullbacks	84	Middle Linebackers	91
Wide Receivers	76	Cornerbacks	82
Tight Ends	89	Free Safeties	69
Tackles	73	Strong Safeties	87
Guards	80	Kickers	61
Centers	74	Punters	80
Defensive Ends	80		

DEPTH CHART

POS	OVR	FIRST NAME	LAST NAME
C	74	Casey	Rabach
C	65	Will	Montgomery
CB	85	DeAngelo	Hall
CB	79	Carlos	Rogers
CB	74	Phillip	Buchanon
CB	72	Justin	Tryon
CB	63	Kevin	Barnes
DT	76	Ma'ake	Kemoeatu
DT	73	Kedric	Golston
DT	66	Howard	Green
FB	84	Mike	Sellers
FS	69	Reed	Doughty
FS	68	Kareem	Moore
HB	85	Clinton	Portis
HB	81	Larry	Johnson
HB	77	Willie	Parker
K	61	Graham	Gano
LE	74	Adam	Carriker
LE	73	Phillip	Daniels
LG	80	Derrick	Dockery
LG	58	Edwin	Williams
LOLB	85	Brian	Orakpo
LOLB	58	Chris	Wilson
LT	80	Trent	Williams
LT	60	Clint	Oldenburg
MLB	91	London	Fletcher
MLB	79	Rocky	McIntosh
MLB	61	H.B.	Blades
MLB	59	Robert	Henson
P	80	Josh	Bidwell
QB	89	Donovan	McNabb
QB	65	Rex	Grossman
QB	59	Colt	Brennan
RE	86	Albert	Haynesworth
RE	69	Jeremy	Jarmon
RG	80	Mike	Williams
RG	72	Chad	Rinehart
ROLB	76	Andre	Carter
ROLB	61	Lorenzo	Alexander
RT	66	Artis	Hicks
RT	66	Stephon	Heyer
SS	87	LaRon	Landry
SS	72	Chris	Horton
TE	89	Chris	Cooley
TE	76	Fred	Davis
TE	72	Sean	Ryan
WR	83	Santana	Moss
WR	74	Devin	Thomas
WR	73	Joey	Galloway
WR	70	Bobby	Wade
WR	70	Malcolm	Kelly

OFFENSIVE STRENGTH CHART

2-Back Set

WR #11

LT #72 | LG #66 | C #61 | RG #71 | RT #74 | TE #47

QB #5

FB #45

HB #26

WR #89

Ace Set

WR #11

TE #86 | LT #72 | LG #66 | C #61 | RG #71 | RT #74 | TE #47

QB #5

WR #89

HB #26

- OVR 90 or Greater
- OVR between 80-89
- OVR between 70-79
- OVR between 60-69
- OVR 59 or lower

Key Player Substitutions

Position: TE

Substitution: Sean Ryan

When: Two-tight-end sets

Advantage: With Chris Cooley leaving the line on most passing plays, you will want to have another tight end to stay home and block for McNabb. Ryan is the blocking backup tight end on the depth chart.

#5 Donovan McNabb
Quarterback (QB)

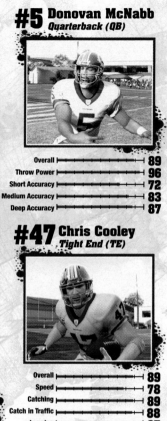

Overall	89
Throw Power	96
Short Accuracy	72
Medium Accuracy	83
Deep Accuracy	87

#47 Chris Cooley
Tight End (TE)

Overall	89
Speed	78
Catching	89
Catch in Traffic	88
Jumping	85

#26 Clinton Portis
Halfback (HB)

Overall	85
Speed	87
Agility	88
Stiff Arm	73
Carrying	86

#59 London Fletcher
Linebacker (MLB)

Overall	91
Speed	79
Awareness	98
Tackle	99
Hit Power	81

#30 LaRon Landry
Strong Safety (SS)

Overall	87
Speed	92
Awareness	71
Tackle	80
Hit Power	97

#23 DeAngelo Hall
Cornerback (CB)

Overall	85
Speed	97
Awareness	79
Man Coverage	90
Zone Coverage	84

DEFENSIVE STRENGTH CHART

3-4 Defense

FS #37 | SS #30

CB #22 | ROLB #99 | MLB #52 | MLB #59 | LOLB #98 | CB #23

RE #92 | DT #96 | LE #93

Dime Defense

FS #37 | SS #30

CB #22 | CB #38 | MLB #59 | CB #20 | CB #23

RE #92 | DT #64 | DT #96 | LE #93

- OVR 90 or Greater
- OVR between 80-89
- OVR between 70-79
- OVR between 60-69
- OVR 59 or lower

Key Player Substitutions

Position: MLB

Substitution: Perry Riley

When: Situational

Advantage: The Redskins' weaker defensive line can be helped out by adding Riley to the middle linebacker position. His speed and strength will go along way towards plugging line gaps.

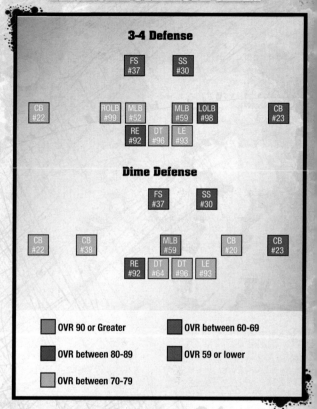
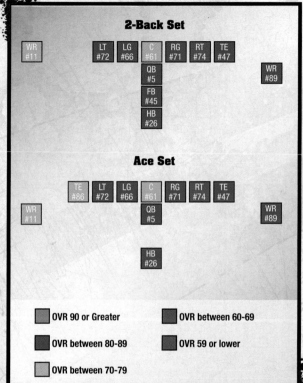

Playbook Breakdown

The Redskins playbook has been revamped this year, and if it looks attractive to you, that's because it is similar to the popular Texans playbook of last year. Mike Shanahan is back in the coaching ranks, and one of the first people he called on was his son, who left the Texans and will be the offensive coordinator of the Redskins. This means there will be plenty of opportunities for us to get the ball into the hands of our skilled players.

We know for a fact that a Mike Shanahan team will have some of the better Bunch and Trips receiver plays in the game. We look to use this playbook to take advantage of those tight groupings and how they make our speedy receivers even better. If the pass doesn't make you ready to jump on this game, then the zone-blocking run plays will be a perfect option for you. The Redskins have numerous zone run plays that resemble the infamous tackle running plays from *Madden NFL 10*.

OFFENSIVE FORMATIONS

FORMATION	# OF PLAYS
Gun Doubles	15
Gun Empty Y-Flex	9
Gun Snugs Flip	9
Gun Split Texan	12
Gun Spread Flex Wk	12
I-Form Close	12
I-Form Pro	15
I-Form Twins Flex	9
Singleback Ace	18
Singleback Ace Pair	12
Singleback Ace Twins	12
Singleback Bunch	15
Singleback Tight Doubles	12
Singleback Y-Trips	18
Strong Close	15
Weak Pro	18

OFFENSIVE PLAYCOUNTS

PLAY TYPE	# OF PLAYS
Quick Pass	18
Standard Pass	99
Shotgun Pass	50
Play Action Pass	39
Inside Handoff	32
Outside Handoff	24
Pitch	16
Counter	9
Draw	7

Singleback Bunch—PA Waggle

The first thing we want to do when looking at the Redskins playbook is focus in on a play that uses the skills of their new Pro Bowl quarterback, Donovan McNabb. The PA Waggle is going to be a serious play threat for defenses to defend when facing the Redskins because of all the solid run plays this playbook has.

Start thinking about the defensive coverage at this point

Immediately after the play fake to the running back we need to focus in on the defense to determine their coverage. If we recognize shallow zones then we know our crossing route by the split end will come open as it crosses between the zones. If we see man, then we look for our tight end running the whip route.

The split end prepares for the ball

The defense sat in a Cover 2 zone with the linebackers in hook zones. We continued to roll the quarterback out, which forced the linebackers to roll their zones. When our receiver crossed the zones with the most space between them, we threw the ball to him for the catch and first down pickup on the play.

Singleback Bunch—Double Drags

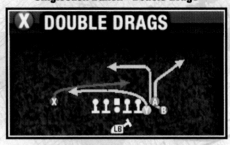

We expect greatness from the Bunch formations in the Redskins playbook, and we are pleased with what we see already. The Singleback Bunch—Double Drags is sure to shred man coverage because of the crossing routes, and also zone coverage for the same exact reason. This play works against the fundamentals of zone defense because if they don't jump any of the routes we will pick them apart all day.

The split end receiver clears the zones

Even though we are focused in on the split end as he runs his crossing route, we are really looking downfield at the defensive coverage. We notice that the defense has a void in the coverage and is leaving the seam-crossing route that our flanker is running open. There is no chance for the defense to stop us when we see coverage like this being played.

Santana Moss prepares for the easy catch

As soon as we recognize the bad coverage by the defense we throw the ball to our flanker for the downfield catch. This play has so many weapons in its design, and when you add the speed and catching ability of the Redskins receiving corps we could have the chance to light up a scoreboard.

Singleback Tight Doubles—HB Stretch

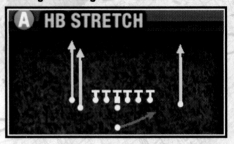

Running the ball is a key element to the success of any offensive game plan. The Redskins run the ball a good deal, and now that they have an offense that fits Clinton Portis's running style perfectly, we're sure to enjoy some good running play calls. The Singleback Tight Doubles—Stretch can establish our running game.

The tight end is motioned to the fullback position

We find this play valuable because it lets us beat the defense from either side of the formation. We use motion to get the tight end to line up in the fullback position and then we playmaker the run to the left side. We can even fake the playmaker and use it to throw off the defense.

Portis is reading his downfield blocks

The NFC East has some of the best right defensive ends in all of football. We use the extra blocking by our tight end to help make sure the defensive end or outside linebacker can't make an easy play on our ball carrier. The result is a perfect initial block and tons of daylight for the back to run to.

I-Form Close—Spacing

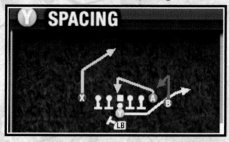

There are no left out players when it comes to the Redskins playbook. We focus in on the I-Form Close—Spacing so we can get a chance to work our fullback into the mix. The fullback runs an automotion quick out to the flat that normally gets open because of a mesh with the routes of the flanker and tight end.

The flanker has cleared a passing lane to the fullback

Our initial draw to this play was the oddity of the flanker route continuing to pop open and the defense not recognizing it. There could be times when we you see the flanker wide open in a voided zone. The defense is currently in man coverage, and because of that we have our fullback wide open.

The fullback fights for more yards after the catch

The decision to throw the ball to the fullback is an easy one. We get him the ball and fight for as many yards as possible on this quick flat route. When the defense finally gets our fullback to the ground we have gained 9 yards on the play.

Singleback Ace Twins—PA Skins Wheel

The Singleback Ace Twins—PA Skins Wheel is a favorite of ours because of the wheel route. We have been fans of the wheel route for years because it normally gives us great spacing to fit the ball into our receiver. You can also set pass combos around this route and really work the defense over. We like this particular play so much because the wheel route in this play starts off flat and then turns up.

The linebacker is attacking the flat

Because the flanker starts off on the wheel route as if it were a flat route or a quick out, it forces the defender to come up and try to cut off the passing lane at the line of scrimmage. This is a big mistake and will give us perfect spacing later on in the route.

Moss makes the catch between the zones

As soon as the defender aggressively attacked the flats we knew that the wheel route was going to torch the defense's coverage. Even if the defense adjusted and covered the wheel route, they would then leave open the split end, who is running a hook route. These two routes paired together in this play make the Singleback Ace Twins—PA Skins Wheel a solid play choice.

Singleback Ace—Skins Drive

The Singleback Ace—Skins Drive can start off a drive or a multiplay scheme during the game. The automotion by the flanker gives the play a unique feel, and we can use this same automotion in other play calls throughout the formation to keep the defense from guessing what we're doing.

We get the defense confused

The automotion of the flanker creates a mesh point a few yards downfield. Once the flanker crosses over the tight end, the running back also releases to the area the flanker just came from. The defenders will start to scurry to cover the open area and create additional openings as they do. We just sit back and wait to see which receiver will pop open for us to throw the ball to.

Portis looks at the slower linebacker in pursuit

We have multiple options open on this play but we decide to go with the running back in the flat. The closest defender capable of catching him was a safety 20 yards downfield. We juked around the linebacker and rattled off an additional 12 yards before meeting the safety 15 yards downfield.

Gun Spread Flex Wk—Slot Post

The best thing we can say about any play in our playbook is that it is reliable. The Gun Spread Flex Wk—Slot Post is a reliable play call. We have a play that protects us from the blitz by giving us a quick out with the running back and a quick slant hook with the right slot. We can also attack man and multiple coverage zones with the post, hook, and streak by our three remaining receivers.

Here comes the blitz

The defense sends an outside linebacker and a defensive back in on a blitz from the strong side of our formation. We immediately see this threat and know that we have the slot receiver, to the right, running a quick slant hook route. This route is an outlet route, specifically for this scenario.

Our receiver secures the ball to beat the blitz

Pressure can be a major obstacle to deal with, but because we put in so much practice time, there is no way a little pressure will make us uncomfortable. The only thing we need to make sure we do is catch the ball. The Gun Spread Flex Wk—Slot Post gives us an opportunity to stand tall in the midst of pressure from the defense because we know we have open routes.

NEW ORLEANS SAINTS

OFFENSIVE SCOUTING REPORT

The Super Bowl Champions, the New Orleans Saints, have an explosive offense that can score points seemingly at their leisure. Drew Brees leads that high-energy offense with the highest QB overall rating and unmatched accuracy in short, medium, and deep passing situations. Wideouts Marques Colston, Devery Henderson, and Robert Meachem, along with TE Jeremy Shockey and RB Reggie Bush, provide plenty of targets for Brees to hit on any down at any time. While none of them post elite overall ratings, all account for solid production since Brees can place the ball anywhere on the field. Pierre Thomas provides the brunt of the run game behind the All Pro offensive line led by two of the best guards in the business, Jahri Evans and Carl Nicks. Take advantage of the talented backfield of the Saints by subbing the HBs to suit their strengths.

DEFENSIVE SCOUTING REPORT

The defense for the Saints is led by a solid defensive line backed by middle linebacker Jonathan Vilma. And Will Smith can penetrate through the offensive line to put pressure on opposing quarterbacks as well as shred blocks to place a hit on the rush. In the secondary, free safety Darren Sharper provides the best zone coverage of anyone in his position. Allow him to roam to continually come up with big plays and break open the defense. Tracy Porter and Jabari Greer make a formidable duo at corners, but with Sharper behind them, the secondary remains strong enough to make the offense think twice before sending out a deep pass. The defense overall is good with a few exceptional standouts, but it is not the shutdown defense afforded by some other teams. Rather, be prepared to keep the offense scoring big and allow the defense to contain the opposing team to a minimal score.

TEAM RATING

92
Overall

KEY ADDITIONS

DE	Alex Brown
DE	Jimmy Wilkerson
CB	Patrick Robinson
OT	Charles Brown

KEY DEPARTURES

RB	Mike Bell
LB	Scott Fujita
DE	Charles Grant
OG	Jamar Nesbit

RATINGS BY POSITION

Position	Rating	Position	Rating
Quarterbacks	99	Defensive Tackles	88
Halfbacks	84	Outside Linebackers	72
Fullbacks	82	Middle Linebackers	90
Wide Receivers	84	Cornerbacks	86
Tight Ends	86	Free Safeties	94
Tackles	91	Strong Safeties	82
Guards	95	Kickers	76
Centers	81	Punters	75
Defensive Ends	85		

DEPTH CHART

POS	OVR	FIRST NAME	LAST NAME
C	81	Jonathan	Goodwin
C	65	Nick	Leckey
CB	87	Jabari	Greer
CB	85	Tracy	Porter
CB	76	Malcolm	Jenkins
CB	75	Patrick	Robinson
CB	75	Randall	Gay
DT	88	Sedrick	Ellis
DT	76	Remi	Ayodele
DT	74	Anthony	Hargrove
DT	65	DeMario	Pressley
FB	82	Heath	Evans
FS	94	Darren	Sharper
FS	68	Usama	Young
HB	84	Pierre	Thomas
HB	83	Reggie	Bush
HB	69	Lynell	Hamilton
K	76	Garrett	Hartley
LE	80	Alex	Brown
LE	76	Jimmy	Wilkerson
LG	91	Carl	Nicks
LOLB	73	Clint	Ingram
LOLB	66	Jo-Lonn	Dunbar
LOLB	57	Troy	Evans
LT	91	Jammal	Brown
LT	75	Jermon	Bushrod
LT	74	Charles	Brown
MLB	90	Jonathan	Vilma
MLB	58	Marvin	Mitchell
P	75	Thomas	Morstead
QB	99	Drew	Brees
QB	64	Sean	Canfield
QB	62	Chase	Daniel
RE	90	Will	Smith
RE	76	Bobby	McCray
RE	62	Jeff	Charleston
RG	98	Jahri	Evans
RG	60	Tim	Duckworth
ROLB	77	Scott	Shanle
ROLB	56	Anthony	Waters
RT	90	Jon	Stinchcomb
RT	66	Zach	Strief
SS	82	Roman	Harper
SS	63	Chip	Vaughn
SS	63	Chris	Reis
TE	86	Jeremy	Shockey
TE	78	David	Thomas
TE	64	Jimmy	Graham
WR	89	Marques	Colston
WR	82	Devery	Henderson
WR	82	Robert	Meachem
WR	75	Lance	Moore
WR	63	Courtney	Roby
WR	50	Adrian	Arrington

OFFENSIVE STRENGTH CHART

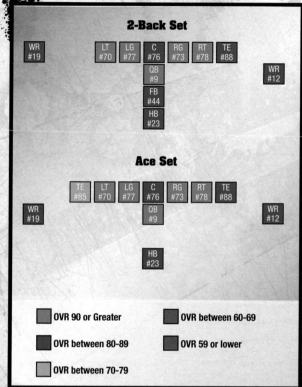

2-Back Set

| WR #19 | | LT #70 | LG #77 | C #76 | RG #73 | RT #78 | TE #88 | | WR #12 |

QB #9
FB #44
HB #23

Ace Set

| TE #85 | LT #70 | LG #77 | C #76 | RG #73 | RT #78 | TE #88 |

WR #19
QB #9
WR #12
HB #23

- ■ OVR 90 or Greater
- ■ OVR between 80-89
- ■ OVR between 70-79
- ■ OVR between 60-69
- ■ OVR 59 or lower

#9 Drew Brees
Quarterback (QB)

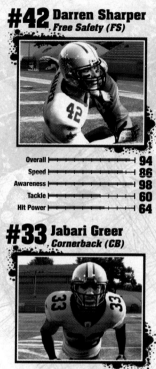

Overall	99
Throw Power	88
Short Accuracy	99
Medium Accuracy	98
Deep Accuracy	92

#73 Jahri Evans
Offensive Guard (OG)

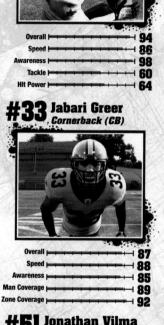

Overall	98
Strength	96
Pass Block	94
Run Block	95
Impact Blocking	88

#42 Darren Sharper
Free Safety (FS)

Overall	94
Speed	86
Awareness	98
Tackle	60
Hit Power	64

#33 Jabari Greer
Cornerback (CB)

Overall	87
Speed	88
Awareness	85
Man Coverage	89
Zone Coverage	92

DEFENSIVE STRENGTH CHART

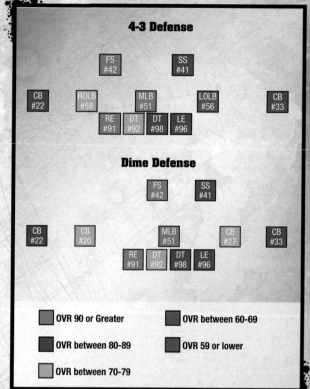

4-3 Defense

FS #42		SS #41
CB #22	ROLB #58	MLB #51	LOLB #56	CB #33
RE #91	DT #92	DT #98	LE #96

Dime Defense

FS #42		SS #41
CB #22	CB #20	MLB #51	CB #27	CB #33
RE #91	DT #92	DT #98	LE #96

- ■ OVR 90 or Greater
- ■ OVR between 80-89
- ■ OVR between 70-79
- ■ OVR between 60-69
- ■ OVR 59 or lower

Key Player Substitutions

Position: HB

Substitution: Reggie Bush

When: Third down situations

Advantage: Reggie Bush is one of the most explosive backs in the game. Bring Bush in on third downs to have more of a threat in the flats. Bush has some of the best hands in the league for running backs.

#12 Marques Colston
Wide Receiver (WR)

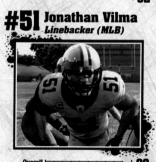

Overall	89
Speed	84
Catching	94
Release	92
Jumping	90

#51 Jonathan Vilma
Linebacker (MLB)

Overall	90
Speed	84
Awareness	92
Tackle	93
Hit Power	84

Key Player Substitutions

Position: CB

Substitution: Tracy Porter

When: Situational

Advantage: Try placing Porter on the league's best receivers. With his speed and strength, Porter makes it very hard for wide receivers to get off the line free, and if they do he has the speed to stay with them.

The New Orleans Saints had the number one offense in the NFL last year, racking up 403 yards a game. Most of those yards came through the air via the arm of quarterback Drew Brees; he was the number-one-rated quarterback in the league. Drew Brees passed for 4,388 yards, 34 TDs, and only 11 interceptions. With targets such as Marques Colston, Devery Henderson, Robert Meachem, Jeremy Shockey, and Reggie Bush, the Saints have plenty of weapons. Their playbook has only one new formation added to it this year: I-Form Tight replaces I-Form Tight Pair. The rest of the playbook has all the same formations from last year, but there are plenty of new plays (over 15) throughout the playbook. The Saints playbook still has a lot of Gun formations (9 total); however, there are plenty of run sets in the playbook to get the ground game going. With Strong Close, I-Form Tight, I-Form Twins Flex, and I-Form Pro, there are plenty of formations to run a good under-center game with.

OFFENSIVE FORMATIONS

FORMATION	# OF PLAYS
Gun 4WR Saints Trey	12
Gun Doubles Wk	15
Gun Empty Trey	12
Gun Empty Y-Saints	9
Gun Split Offset	12
Gun Spread Y-Slot	12
Gun Tight	9
Gun Wing Trio Wk	12
I-Form Pro	15
I-Form Tight	12
I-Form Twins Flex	18
Singleback Ace	18
Singleback Snugs Flip	18
Singleback Twin TE Flex	12
Singleback Y-Trips	12
Strong Close	12
Weak H Twins	12

OFFENSIVE PLAYCOUNTS

PLAY TYPE	# OF PLAYS
Quick Pass	9
Standard Pass	42
Shotgun Pass	65
Play Action Pass	36
Inside Handoff	24
Outside Handoff	10
Pitch	9
Counter	3

Playbook Breakdown

Gun Empty Trey—Stick

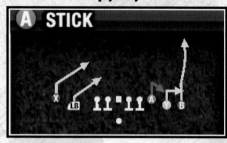

Gun Empty Trey is all about spreading the defense out with four wide receivers and one tight end. Stick has tight end Jeremy Shockey as the primary read. You have an out route and streak route on the right side of the formation to take the coverage deep. On the left side, you have two slant routes that go over the middle of the field.

Sit in the pocket and look for open receivers

Once you snap the ball, look over the middle of the field for the slot receiver on a slant route and the short curl route that Shockey runs as your first two reads for this play. Quarterback Drew Brees has two targets to choose from. On this play, he fires the ball over the middle of the field to Shockey.

Hit Shockey with a bullet pass

We complete the pass to tight end Jeremy Shockey for a quick 5-yard gain. When you use a spread set such as Gun Empty Trey, most defenses will blitz, so you have to make quick reads.

Gun Doubles Wk—Angle Smash

Gun Doubles Wk—Angle Smash has the running back on an angle route out of the backfield; he is the primary target. You also have tight end Jeremy Shockey on the out route. These two routes are the main reads for this play because they flood one area of the field. Before we begin, we are going to sub running back Reggie Bush into the backfield.

Zoning in on a receiver

As you can see, once the ball is snapped you have two targets right in front of you. Both are crossing the same area of the field. Brees has his eyes on his target and fires over the middle.

Using the TE as a pick

Running back Reggie Bush makes the grab and picks up 5 yards. Another suggestion for this play is to put slot receiver Robert Meachem on a slant over the middle; also put flanker Marques Colston on a slant. Motion him to the left and snap the ball once he gets next to the tight end. This adjustment floods the middle of the field and gives you four targets in one area.

Gun Tight—Saints HB Wheel

Gun Tight—Saints HB Wheel has a wheel route that comes out of the backfield with two crossing routes run by this flanker and the split end. We like to hot route the flanker on a slant to the outside and the slot receiver next to him on a streak down the middle of the field.

Look at the HB; he is wide open

Once the ball is snapped, the flanker on the slot on the sideline is in front of the running back. We have Reggie Bush open and quarterback Drew Brees throws him the ball.

Now you have a blocker in front

Bush makes the catch and the flanker makes a key block. Bush picks up 10 yards before being contacted. Sometimes you will be able to take the play the distance by getting a key block. The slot receiver should be your next read if you see that the coverage goes towards the flat. Finally, you have your split end on a drag route coming across the middle as your last read.

Gun Spread Y-Slot—Saints Y-Under

Y SAINTS Y-UNDER

Gun Spread Y-Slot—Saints Y-Under has tight end Jeremy Shockey on the crossing route as the main target with halfback Reggie Bush on an out route out of the backfield. These two targets are your main reads for the play. The flanker and the split end are on deep streak and fade routes. Their routes are designed to pull the coverage deep.

Our TE is open across the middle

Once the ball is snapped, quarterback Drew Brees has two targets in front of him with Reggie Bush and Jeremy Shockey crossing each other. It becomes an easy one-two read. Brees fires the ball to Shockey across the middle.

Time to get some yards after the catch

Jeremy Shockey makes the catch for a 5-yard gain. One other option for this play is to put the slot receiver on the left on a slant route over the middle. This will give you two crossing routes over the middle plus the out route out of the backfield. It does not matter if the defense is playing man or zone; one of the routes should be open.

Gun 4WR Saints Trey—Saints Stick

X SAINTS STICK

Gun 4WR Saints Trey—Saints Stick has wide receiver Marques Colston on a short stick route. He is the primary read on this play. However, the split end and the running back are also good targets on this play. Running back Reggie Bush runs an out route and split end Robert Meachem runs inside then cuts deep on a streak.

Good protection for Brees

The quarterback sees his target wide receiver Marques Colston as the quick read. Notice that in this screenshot running back Reggie Bush breaks towards the outside and is open. Next to your primary target you have a short out route that can be another read as well.

Another first down for the Saints

The pass is completed for a quick 5 yards. The route that split end Robert Meachem is on can be used as a quick slant. Once he cuts inside, throw a bullet pass and press up on the analog stick. Reading the left side of the field should be the second step in your progression.

Gun Empty Y-Saints—Saints Fork

Y SAINTS FORK

Gun Empty Y-Saints has three wide receivers, as well as one running back split out wide to the left with one tight end. With this formation you can tell right away if the defense is playing man or zone coverage. Saints Fork from this formation has the split end as the primary target; however, we are going to switch up the progression a bit.

A good passing lane for Brees

The QB sees his target to the left with his running back Reggie Bush on the quick slant. While you're looking at him, it's good to keep an eye out for slot receiver Devery Henderson; this is your progression on the left side of the field.

Get the ball to the HB quickly

Bush makes the catch in stride and has plenty of room to run before being tackled. On the right side of the field, look for the flat route and corner route as your next two reads.

Gun Split Offset—Close Shake

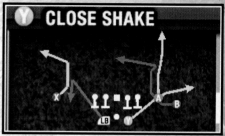

Y CLOSE SHAKE

The Gun Split Offset formation in the Saints playbook has what we call a hidden formation. Close Shake is one of the plays from this formation. The play has the flanker and the slot receiver compressed next to each other on the right side of the field.

This is a two-back Gun set

The flanker in this play is the primary read; however, we want to key in on the running back's delay route out of the backfield. His route tends to release quickly, as you can see in the screenshot. Also notice the flanker and the other back that comes out of the backfield. These are your other targets.

Attack the field with the HB

We find our target, Reggie Bush, and he makes the catch. With his speed in the open field, he picks up a good gain before being tackled. Sometimes with this play the running back tends to stay in the backfield if the defense is blitzing. If you see this, look towards the other side of the field.

187

SEATTLE SEAHAWKS

OFFENSIVE SCOUTING REPORT

The Seahawks are led by quarterback Matt Hasselbeck, who's battled injuries the past couple of seasons. However, he's a dangerous quarterback with a strong arm and one of the best from the play action. Hasselbeck has a healthy amount of talent around him with the likes of wide receivers T.J. Houshmandzadeh, Deion Branch, and draft pick Golden Tate. Tate, the rookie, has the speed that the Seahawks may have been missing to help stretch the defenders. The team added one of the top prospects from the draft, Russell Okung, to the line to play alongside another young talent, Max Unger, providing protection and decent run blocking. The running game is led by Julius Jones and solidified by third down back Leon Washington. Jones should finally get his chance to shine as the everyday back if he can remain healthy, while Washington can provide a spark catching out of the backfield. As always seems to be the case with the Seahawks, the potential for the offense is there.

DEFENSIVE SCOUTING REPORT

There are those names you hear that immediately garner your respect, like Lawyer Milloy. In his 15th season Milloy is still a formidable defensive back who's sure to play a role in the Seahawks defense. Playing inside of him are linebackers Aaron Curry and Lofa Tatupu. These are the playmakers and the ones who'll either cause or recover turnovers. A healthy Marcus Trufant and steady Josh Wilson at cornerback will offer solid defense in the secondary. The question mark for this defense is the line that only managed 28 sacks last season and lost ends Patrick Kerney (retirement) and Darryl Tapp (trade). Brandon Mebane remains at tackle and provides the most strength to the line. The Seahawks as a whole are a solid team with potential, despite no player on either side of the ball possessing an overall ranking over 88.

TEAM RATING

75
Overall

KEY ADDITIONS

DE	Chris Clemons
RB	Leon Washington
TE	Chris Baker
DE	Robert Henderson
G/C	Ben Hamilton
LT	Russell Okung
WR	Golden Tate

KEY DEPARTURES

WR	Nate Burleson
LT	Walter Jones
DE	Patrick Kerney
CB	Ken Lucas
QB	Seneca Wallace
S	Deon Grant

RATINGS BY POSITION

Position	Rating		Position	Rating
Quarterbacks	79		Defensive Tackles	86
Halfbacks	77		Outside Linebackers	82
Fullbacks	77		Middle Linebackers	88
Wide Receivers	76		Cornerbacks	85
Tight Ends	84		Free Safeties	81
Tackles	80		Strong Safeties	77
Guards	80		Kickers	82
Centers	79		Punters	80
Defensive Ends	76			

DEPTH CHART

POS	OVR	FIRST NAME	LAST NAME
C	79	Chris	Spencer
C	73	Steve	Vallos
CB	87	Marcus	Trufant
CB	82	Josh	Wilson
CB	72	Kelly	Jennings
CB	62	Roy	Lewis
CB	60	Walter	Thurmond III
DT	86	Brandon	Mebane
DT	76	Colin	Cole
DT	66	Red	Bryant
DT	65	Kevin	Vickerson
DT	60	Craig	Terrill
FB	77	Owen	Schmitt
FS	81	Earl	Thomas
FS	81	Jordan	Babineaux
HB	80	Leon	Washington
HB	77	Julius	Jones
HB	76	Justin	Forsett
HB	58	Louis	Rankin
K	82	Olindo	Mare
LE	79	Lawrence	Jackson
LE	57	E.J.	Wilson
LG	81	Ben	Hamilton
LG	66	Mike	Gibson
LOLB	83	Aaron	Curry
LOLB	60	Matt	McCoy
LT	82	Russell	Okung
LT	69	Ray	Willis
MLB	88	Lofa	Tatupu
MLB	80	David	Hawthorne
P	80	Jon	Ryan
QB	79	Matt	Hasselbeck
QB	71	Charlie	Whitehurst
QB	66	J.P.	Losman
RE	72	Chris	Clemons
RE	65	Nick	Reed
RG	79	Max	Unger
RG	69	Mansfield	Wrotto
ROLB	81	Leroy	Hill
ROLB	59	Wil	Herring
RT	78	Sean	Locklear
SS	77	Lawyer	Milloy
SS	67	Kam	Chancellor
SS	58	Jamar	Adams
TE	84	John	Carlson
TE	77	Chris	Baker
TE	64	Anthony	McCoy
WR	87	T.J.	Houshmandzadeh
WR	75	Golden	Tate
WR	69	Deion	Branch
WR	67	Deon	Butler
WR	66	Sean	Morey
WR	58	Benjamin	Obomanu

OFFENSIVE STRENGTH CHART

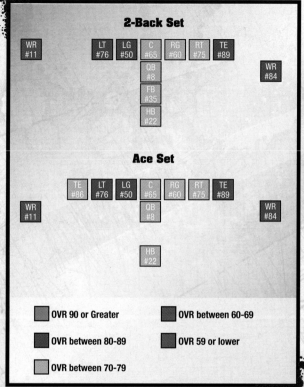

2-Back Set

WR #11 | LT #76 | LG #50 | C #65 | RG #60 | RT #75 | TE #89
QB #8
FB #35
HB #22
WR #84

Ace Set

TE #86 | LT #76 | LG #50 | C #65 | RG #60 | RT #75 | TE #89
QB #8
WR #11
WR #84
HB #22

- OVR 90 or Greater
- OVR between 80-89
- OVR between 70-79
- OVR between 60-69
- OVR 59 or lower

Key Player Substitutions

Position: HB

Substitution: Justin Forsett

When: Two-back sets

Advantage: If you are going to run a two-back set with the Seahawks, try inserting Forsett in the starting lineup. Having Forsett and Washington both coming out of the backfield creates matchup problems for the defense.

#84 T.J. Houshmandzadeh
Wide Receiver (WR)

Overall	87
Speed	84
Catching	92
Release	84
Jumping	78

#33 Leon Washington
Halfback (HB)

Overall	80
Speed	93
Agility	94
Stiff Arm	66
Carrying	76

#89 John Carlson
Tight End (TE)

Overall	84
Speed	74
Catching	86
Catch in Traffic	87
Jumping	80

#51 Lofa Tatupu
Linebacker (MLB)

Overall	88
Speed	79
Awareness	93
Tackle	95
Hit Power	85

#23 Marcus Trufant
Cornerback (CB)

Overall	87
Speed	88
Awareness	84
Man Coverage	93
Zone Coverage	86

#92 Brandon Mebane
Defensive Tackle (DT)

Overall	86
Speed	64
Strength	91
Power Moves	87
Block Shedding	83

DEFENSIVE STRENGTH CHART

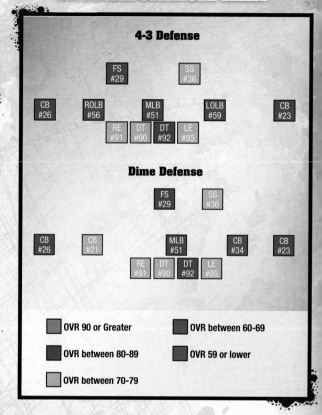

4-3 Defense

FS #29 | SS #36
CB #26 | ROLB #56 | MLB #51 | LOLB #59 | CB #23
RE #91 | DT #90 | DT #92 | LE #95

Dime Defense

FS #29 | SS #36
CB #26 | CB #21 | MLB #51 | CB #34 | CB #23
RE #91 | DT #90 | DT #92 | LE #95

- OVR 90 or Greater
- OVR between 80-89
- OVR between 70-79
- OVR between 60-69
- OVR 59 or lower

Key Player Substitutions

Position: ROLB

Substitution: David Hawthorne

When: Global

Advantage: If your opponents are having their way passing the ball on you, try moving Hawthorne from MLB to ROLB. He is faster and better at covering his zones on the field.

Pete Carroll takes over the Seattle Seahawks after many years of success at USC. The Seahawks use a power run game mixed in with play action passing once the defense is softened up by the game on the ground. The Seahawks use a dual-running-back system like a lot of teams do in the NFL today. Their runners are Julius Jones and speed back Leon Washington, who came from the Jets. With both of these two talented runners splitting carries out of the backfield in two-back sets, their primary focus will be ball control. With the Seahawks playbook you can do just that with I-Form formations such as Normal, Tight, and Slot Flex. This playbook also has the Strong I Normal and Strong I Twin TE. This gives you plenty of run plays and play action passes to choose from. If you're a person who likes to have a lot of Gun formations to pass out of, then this is not the playbook for you; it's all about ground and pound with a smidgen of the short passing game with this book.

OFFENSIVE FORMATIONS

FORMATION	# OF PLAYS
Gun 4WR Hawk Trips	15
Gun Normal Flex Wk	12
Gun Spread	15
I-Form Normal	21
I-Form Slot Flex	12
I-Form Tight	15
Singleback Ace	18
Singleback Ace Pair Twins	12
Singleback Bunch	15
Singleback Double Flex	12
Singleback Slot	18
Singleback Snugs	9
Strong I Normal	15
Strong I Twin TE	12
Weak I Twins	15
Wildcat Seahawk	3

OFFENSIVE PLAYCOUNTS

PLAY TYPE	# OF PLAYS
Quick Pass	16
Standard Pass	49
Shotgun Pass	31
Play Action Pass	45
Inside Handoff	34
Outside Handoff	9
Pitch	9
Counter	8

Playbook Breakdown

I-Form Tight—HB Off Tackle

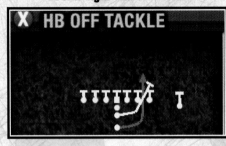

One of the staple run plays the Seahawks like to run out of I-Form Tight is the HB Off Tackle. This play involves fullback Owen Schmitt pulling and trying to seal the edge behind right tackle Sean Locklear. With this play, we are going to bring the flanker, T.J. Houshmandzadeh, in motion to provide additional blocking.

Clean handoff to Julius Jones

Once the flanker is behind the line of scrimmage, snap the ball. Once the ball is snapped, the quarterback Matt Hasselbeck hands the ball off to running back Julius Jones. This is when you want to follow your blockers to the inside, or if you see that the line sealed the edge you can bounce it outside.

Cutting to the outside

Julius Jones sees a hole and takes the run inside behind his blockers to pick up a 5-yard gain. With this play, you can keep the defense guessing as to which side you're going to run the ball by flipping the plays and sending the flanker in motion.

I-Form Tight—PA Boot Slide

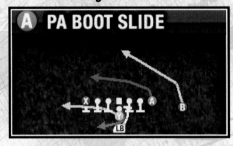

The PA Boot Slide is a good play action play that works with any of the runs from I-Form Tight. This play is a fake handoff to running back Julius Jones, which allows the quarterback to roll out to the left. You have a crossing route over the middle of the field and the fullback on a flat route out of the backfield.

Wait for the TE to get open

Quarterback Matt Hasselbeck fakes the handoff to the running back and scans the field. Once you roll out to the left, you should look over the middle of the field for your tight end running a deep crossing route. Next you want to look for the fullback out of the backfield as your secondary read. Your last read for this play is to keep an eye out for the deep crossing route that the flanker is running.

Push to get to the end zone

We complete a pass to our tight end down the field for a 15-yard gain. Another thing to consider for maximum protection is to motion the flanker behind the line of scrimmage; this gives you maximum protection and gives the same look as if you were running the ball.

Strong I Twin TE—Power O

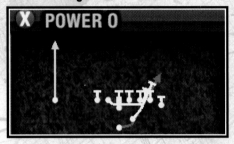

Strong I Twin TE is a formation that is not widely used in *Madden NFL*. Power O is a perfect run to use out of this formation with Julius Jones's running style. With the tight end lined up on the right side of the field, you can motion him behind the line of scrimmage to provide extra blocking.

Running the ball with Jones

Once you motion the tight end to the right, wait until he is behind the left tackle before you snap the ball. The QB hands the ball off to the running back, and he follows his blockers in front of him. With left guard Ben Hamilton pulling and fullback Owen Schmitt out in front, Julius Jones sees the hole.

Looking to pound the ball

The blocker seals the edge, and Jones bounces it outside with his speed and picks up 10 yards before he is tackled. If you see the defense overload one side of the formation, flip the play and run it to the other side. Be sure to motion the fullback to the left.

Strong I Twin TE—PA FB Fake

The Strong I Twin TE—PA FB Fake works alongside the Power O. This play allows the tight end to get involved in the passing game. He goes deep on a corner route. You also have the running back sneaking out into the flat area as well as a deep crossing route.

Leaving the TE in to block

The QB fakes the handoff to the fullback as if he is running the ball to the right. This allows the running back to get out to the right side of the field. After the handoff, you want to look deep for the tight end, but the running back is your first read. He is open vs. most defenses that you will see.

Trying to break away

The QB spots his target—it's the running back in the flat, and he is ready to deliver the ball to him. The key to this play is to soften the defense up with the run, and then you can mix in this play action play. Because this is a fake handoff to the fullback, this play action is very quick.

I-Form Slot Flex—HB Blast

The I-Form Slot Flex formation spreads the defense out a bit. The HB Blast from this formation is designed to run to the weak side behind the left tackle. This is a solid run that moves the chains and works well with the other runs from this formation.

Man-on-man blocking

The QB hands the ball off to the running back, who follows his fullback. Left tackle Russell Okung and left guard Ben Hamilton are holding their blocks as well. You can choose to cut it up inside between them or, if the edge is sealed, take it outside. It's all about being patient and reading the defense.

Outrunning the linebackers

The edge is sealed and Leon Washington bounces it outside for a 5-yard gain before being tackled. Another suggestion with this run is to use motion and flip the play depending on which side the defense overloads. Again, this is a very good run that picks up positive yards.

I-Form Slot Flex—Smash

Smash is a good play to use out of the Slot Flex formation. It consists of the running back running a circle route out of the backfield, a deep corner route, a short curl that the flanker runs, and an in route. The flanker is the primary read but the circle route is the key to this play.

Quick pass

The QB has his target in sight once you snap the ball. The first read is the circle route. This route kills both man and zone coverage and is a very quick read. Notice how the defender is out of position. This is when you want to throw the ball to the running back.

Picking up first down yardage

Leon Washington makes the catch for a 5-yard gain before being contacted by the defense. Another suggestion is to motion the flanker as if you're going to run the ball, and snap it once he is next to the right tackle. This gives you two reads right in front of you.

I-Form Normal—Hawks HB Angle

Angle routes have been effective out of the backfield for many years in *Madden NFL*. You will see this play in a lot of West Coast playbooks, such as the Seahawks, 49ers, and Chiefs. You can use this play and mix it in with the run plays from this formation.

A good pocket to sit in

With this play, your first two reads should be the halfback and the fullback coming out of the backfield. You should see the running back come open against just about any defense. If the defense has him covered, look for the fullback going to the left side of the field. You also have to keep an eye out for the flanker on the short curl route.

Cover the ball to avoid a strip by the defense

The QB passes the ball to the running back. He makes the catch, turns downfield, and picks up 5 yards. Once you get the defense to worry about the HB, this is when you want to get either your fullback or flanker involved into the play.

PITTSBURGH STEELERS

OFFENSIVE SCOUTING REPORT

Despite having a less-than-stellar offensive line—they allowed 50 sacks in 2009—the Steelers have one of the toughest QBs in the league. QB Ben Roethlisberger has as much talent in his throwing arm as he has letters in his last name. Use Roethlisberger as a mobile quarterback. He's got scrambling skills galore—he'll need them with his offensive line—and can easily chuck the ball when needed, sporting one of the highest throw on the run stats in the game. RB Rashard Mendenhall returns as the Steelers' starter. With the departure of "Fast" Willie Parker, Mendenhall finally takes the lead spot in the backfield, granting the Steelers a solid running game. He's not a prototypical outside runner, but that's never been the Steelers' style. Run Mendenhall between the tackles and wear away at opposing defensive lines. Despite losing Super Bowl MVP Santonio Holmes, the Steelers still have Hall of Fame shoe-in Hines Ward. He's a hard-hitting wide receiver with amazing route-running ability. For speed, sophomore receiver Mike Wallace has the wheels to streak downfield and stretch the opposing secondary for a constant deep ball threat. The recipe is simple: Ward gets the yardage, and Wallace wears down the secondary, all while Mendenhall puts the hurt on the defensive line.

DEFENSIVE SCOUTING REPORT

The Steelers are a bit of a puzzle on defense. When safety superman Troy Polamalu is on the field, opposing teams can forget about throwing the ball. He's a ball-hungry hawk capable of shutting down entire WR corps with just his presence on the field. His level of play reduces dynamic pass-happy teams to one-dimensional junior varsity squads. When he's not on the field, however, the Steelers become an above-average defense with an average secondary. Aside from Polamalu, the strength of the defense is its linebackers. James Harrison can drop back into coverage just as easily as he can pressure the line. James Farrior and LaMarr Woodley provide excellent depth while Casey Hampton holds the line at the center. Offenses will be pressed to run the ball against this defense, but with Polamalu on the prowl, they'll have little choice.

TEAM RATING

84
Overall

KEY ADDITIONS

S	Will Allen
C	Maurkice Pouncey
LB	Larry Foote
QB	Byron Leftwich
CB	Bryant McFadden
WR	Antwaan Randle El

KEY DEPARTURES

S	Tyrone Carter
WR	Santonio Holmes
DE	Travis Kirschke
RB	Willie Parker
G	Darnell Stapleton
CB	Deshea Townsend

RATINGS BY POSITION

Position	Rating
Quarterbacks	88
Halfbacks	87
Fullbacks	58
Wide Receivers	80
Tight Ends	90
Tackles	84
Guards	78
Centers	81
Defensive Ends	85
Defensive Tackles	91
Outside Linebackers	94
Middle Linebackers	88
Cornerbacks	81
Free Safeties	79
Strong Safeties	97
Kickers	75
Punters	79

DEPTH CHART

POS	OVR	FIRST NAME	LAST NAME
C	81	Justin	Hartwig
C	76	Maurkice	Pouncey
CB	83	Ike	Taylor
CB	79	Bryant	McFadden
CB	69	William	Gay
CB	66	Joe	Burnett
CB	61	Keenan	Lewis
DT	91	Casey	Hampton
DT	74	Chris	Hoke
DT	63	Scott	Paxson
FB	58	Frank	Summers
FS	79	Ryan	Clark
FS	70	Will	Allen
HB	87	Rashard	Mendenhall
HB	74	Mewelde	Moore
HB	67	Jonathan	Dwyer
K	75	Jeff	Reed
LE	87	Aaron	Smith
LE	72	Ziggy	Hood
LG	79	Chris	Kemoeatu
LG	64	Ramon	Foster
LOLB	91	LaMarr	Woodley
LOLB	70	Thaddeus	Gibson
LT	85	Max	Starks
LT	70	Tony	Hills
MLB	88	James	Farrior
MLB	82	Lawrence	Timmons
MLB	79	Larry	Foote
MLB	73	Keyaron	Fox
P	79	Daniel	Sepulveda
QB	88	Ben	Roethlisberger
QB	69	Byron	Leftwich
QB	64	Dennis	Dixon
RE	82	Brett	Keisel
RE	58	Nick	Eason
RG	77	Trai	Essex
RG	67	Kraig	Urbik
ROLB	97	James	Harrison
ROLB	65	Jason	Worilds
RT	82	Willie	Colon
RT	69	Jonathan	Scott
SS	97	Troy	Polamalu
SS	58	James	Harrison
TE	90	Heath	Miller
TE	68	Sean	McHugh
TE	66	Matt	Spaeth
WR	89	Hines	Ward
WR	78	Mike	Wallace
WR	73	Antwaan	Randle El
WR	72	Arnaz	Battle
WR	66	Emmanuel	Sanders

OFFENSIVE STRENGTH CHART

2-Back Set

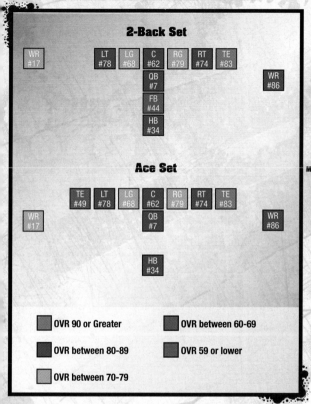

| WR #17 | | LT #78 | LG #68 | C #62 | RG #79 | RT #74 | TE #83 | |
| QB #7 | | | | | | | | WR #86 |
| FB #44 |
| HB #34 |

Ace Set

		TE #49	LT #78	LG #68	C #62	RG #79	RT #74	TE #83
WR #17				QB #7				WR #86
				HB #34

■ OVR 90 or Greater	■ OVR between 60-69
■ OVR between 80-89	■ OVR 59 or lower
■ OVR between 70-79	

#7 Ben Roethlisberger
Quarterback (QB)

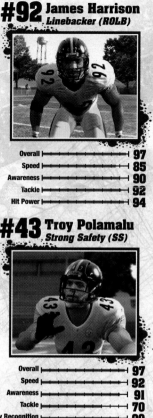

Overall	88
Throw Power	93
Short Accuracy	85
Medium Accuracy	82
Deep Accuracy	76

#86 Hines Ward
Wide Receiver (WR)

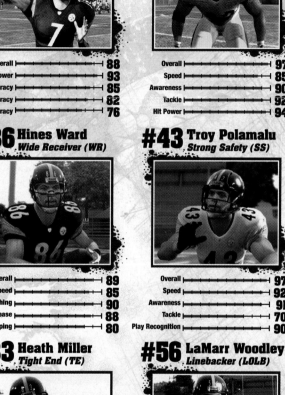

Overall	89
Speed	85
Catching	90
Release	88
Jumping	80

#83 Heath Miller
Tight End (TE)

Overall	90
Speed	72
Catching	88
Catch in Traffic	90
Jumping	75

#92 James Harrison
Linebacker (ROLB)

Overall	97
Speed	85
Awareness	90
Tackle	92
Hit Power	94

#43 Troy Polamalu
Strong Safety (SS)

Overall	97
Speed	92
Awareness	91
Tackle	70
Play Recognition	90

#56 LaMarr Woodley
Linebacker (LOLB)

Overall	91
Speed	85
Awareness	85
Tackle	92
Hit Power	94

DEFENSIVE STRENGTH CHART

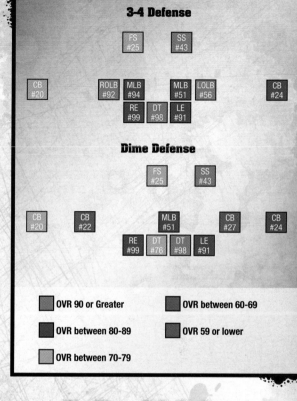

3-4 Defense

		FS #25		SS #43		
CB #20		ROLB #92	MLB #94	MLB #51	LOLB #56		CB #24
			RE #99	DT #98	LE #91	

Dime Defense

		FS #25		SS #43		
CB #20	CB #22		MLB #51		CB #27	CB #24
		RE #99	DT #76	DT #98	LE #91	

■ OVR 90 or Greater	■ OVR between 60-69
■ OVR between 80-89	■ OVR 59 or lower
■ OVR between 70-79	

Key Player Substitutions

Position: TE

Substitution: David Johnson

When: Situational

Advantage: The Steelers are known for always having great wide receivers. If you are looking to use them more, put Johnson in to stay on the line and block for Roethlisberger.

Key Player Substitutions

Position: CB

Substitution: Crezdon Butler

When: Dime formations

Advantage: Butler is a player you want to have on the field when the offense comes out in four-wide-receiver sets. Butler can match up on lesser receivers all day long.

Playbook Breakdown

The days of pounding the ball in Pittsburgh are over. Now the Steelers are using more of a one-back, passing-attack-based offensive scheme. You will find some great passing sets to use with the good weapons that the Steelers have on offense now. You can still pound a bit out of this playbook. This playbook will serve you well as a come-from-behind book because it provides you with so many sets to force defensive conflicts. You just have to use your packages well and move people around to generate mismatches, forcing players to adjust to your alignments. If they refuse to make changes, attack them till they do. You can still use HB Draws from these sets to generate a solid rushing attack. We will look at some sets you can pound out of because you need that to close games out or if your passing attack is slipping a bit. Then we will look at some nice alignments to help you create mismatches in the passing game.

OFFENSIVE FORMATIONS

FORMATION	# OF PLAYS
Gun Bunch Wk	9
Gun Doubles On	9
Gun Empty Steeler	12
Gun Snugs	9
Gun Spread Y-Slot	15
Gun Trio	15
Gun Y-Trips Wk	15
I-Form Tight	15
I-Form Tight Pair	12
Singleback Ace	15
Singleback Ace Pair Twins	15
Singleback Bunch	12
Singleback Jumbo	12
Singleback Pitt Doubles	18
Singleback Pitt Y-Trips	12
Strong Close	12
Weak Flex Twins	15

OFFENSIVE PLAYCOUNTS

PLAY TYPE	# OF PLAYS
Quick Pass	15
Standard Pass	37
Shotgun Pass	59
Play Action Pass	39
Inside Handoff	29
Outside Handoff	8
Pitch	9
Counter	10

Strong Close—Quick Toss

This playbook has some nice compressed sets. Compressed sets allow you to get offensive overloads and force the defense to adjust. You're able to read the coverage easily, as well. With compressed sets your personnel is lined up tight to the line of scrimmage. This allows you to get decent double teams when you run the ball. If you want to attack the perimeter quickly this play fits the bill.

The Steelers are getting outside to the perimeter

This is a quick pitch outside where you just have to read your blocks. If you see a flow hard to the outside, cut the ball inside. If you see that you have numbers outside, stay with your blocks until you get outside.

We have plenty of room to run

When you allow your blocks to set up, you can get a nice gain from this play. Again, you have to use your judgment and make solid reads.

Strong Close—PA Scissors

You need a quick play action play when you have established your rushing attack. When you see that people are flowing hard to your toss play, you know it's time to go with the play action passing attack. This is a nice call if you just broke a long run and your opponents are still heated about the big chunk of yards they gave up to you from the toss play. This is a good hurry-up call for this set as well. When you call plays, it's about down and distance, adjustments to your play calling, and setting up the next play. Your reads are the corner, the post, and then the flat route.

The defense flows hard to the play action fake

Now you have two seconds to get a look downfield or dump the ball off. If no one is open downfield, run with the QB and then slide. You can also throw the ball away to prevent taking a loss in yards.

Our tight end made a nice catch downfield

A strong tight end is a very hard matchup for any defender. It's hard to defend both a corner and a post route, so one should get open.

Strong Close—Inside Post

This is a nice five-step passing play. You're attacking the defense the same way as you did in the play action play. You have a corner and a post route in this play, and you also have dual flat routes. These will be your hot reads. You just need to read the coverage shell over top and it will tell you where to go with the ball.

The inside post route opens the field up

These types of plays open the field up quite a bit. These route combos make it easy for you to make reads downfield. You're peeking to see if you have room inside for the post, or if you have room outside for the corner route. If you read heat, you can tear up the flats.

Squeeze the pass in between two defenders

Once you make your read, trust it and throw the ball. The defenders react to the ball quickly this season, so when you have a window, hit it quickly. Make sure you have a QB who throws well downfield as well. The ball will hang longer with weaker-armed QBs.

Gun Trio—WR Screen

Trips sets are just plain hard to defend. You want the defense to adjust to your Trips. If they don't, plays like the WR Screen allow you to throw a quick pass and take advantage of the numbers outside. Once they cover your Trips set, you can attack other areas.

The slot receiver is wide open for the screen

Wait until your wideouts set their blocks. Just a side note: This play kills zone coverage. If the defense is in man you can get it off, but not as well because the defender will read the screen and try to jump it. Make sure your man is open and pass the ball. If he's covered you throw the ball away or run with the QB.

We are out of here!

The blocks are set up nicely and you've now extended your rushing attack with the use of screens. Screen plays are good to mix in once you have attacked the defense deep with other plays in this formation.

Gun Trio—Scat

The Scat is a new play this season. It gives you a bubble screen feel. Your reads are easy: You read the streak, slant, and then the bubble flat route. You also have the HB flowing to the other side for a hot read, along with your tight end. You need to key in on the alley defender. If he drops back you use the bubble route. If he flares out, you hit the slant. If you see no one sitting outside deep you can attack the streak.

The alley defender flares and the corner drops deep with streak

When you see that the alley defender drops back or sits, you throw to the bubble route. This is a quick and easy read. If he flares out, you just hit the slant and attack the area he left open.

Eat some grass, please

The key here is to get the ball to your playmaker in open space. When you can do that you have a chance to generate a big gain. It is always to your advantage to isolate a playmaker in open space to make a play.

Gun Trio—HB Delay

Now what's our rule in regards to choosing formations? You guessed it—when you pass from a set you must be able to run from it as well. You want to use specific sets to get the defense in matchup problems. Once they adjust, attack the new areas of weakness. The key to the Trips/Trio is to get someone from the middle to slide over and defend those three wideouts. Once that's done, you should have a lighter box to run on.

Read from inside to outside

You should get a good seal to the tight end side. You have to read the middle first. If you have no inside gaps, bounce the ball outside. With three wideouts sitting outside, you should have plenty of help to get the ball downfield.

We have a nice gain in the works

This play really works well against Nickel and Dime packages. You don't want your wideouts trying to block linebackers out there. The linebackers will get the wideouts out of the way quicker to make a play than if you are attacking a DB.

Gun Bunch Wk—Steelers Cross

This is another set where our offensive overloads put the defense in a quandary. The Gun Bunch Wk gives you three wideouts on one side with an isolation to the back side. This is a play that's not in any other playbook. You use this play in conjunction with other schemes from this set to make up a nice series. The crossing routes work well against man or zone. The delay route to the TE is sick. Most of the time the tight end will be open. You read the crossing routes, and if no one is open, pop the delay route. The HB's route is great as well. His route works like a C route and is solid option against heat.

The HB gets open out of the backfield

The defense came with pressure, so we check down to the HB. The crossing routes will often get picks and rubs for you. When you see a pick, get ready to pop it to the open receiver.

An easy catch for our receiver

Get the ball out to your playmaker in open space to strike fear in the defense.

HOUSTON TEXANS

OFFENSIVE SCOUTING REPORT

The Texans quietly led the league in passing yards last season as the relationship between QB Matt Schaub and WR Andre Johnson flourished. Fast, extremely sure-handed in every situation, and one of the best at creating space between him and the cornerback, Andre Johnson is the biggest star in Texas. And with the emergence of Kevin Walter as the number two receiver, Andre Johnson is no longer the full focus of defenses, not that it would matter. Owen Daniels has also become a strong receiver at tight end, and at 6'3", he makes a large target in the end zone and down the middle of the field. It is obvious that the Texans are a pass-first team, but that doesn't mean the elusive speed-burner Steve Slaton can't get his fair share of touches. He should be mixed into the offensive game plan to stop defenses from depending on the Nickel cover packages. The only offensive concern is whether the line can protect Schaub long enough for him to throw, but they seem to get it done without the overly impressive stats.

DEFENSIVE SCOUTING REPORT

The defense of the Texans is centered around the strong pass rush and presence on the line of Mario Williams. He is fast and strong with the ability to consistently get to the quarterback in a hurry. DeMeco Ryans at middle linebacker provides the strength against the run, while Brian Cushing provides the speed of the linebacker corps. Together they account for the best rushing defense in the AFC South. The secondary, again fueled by the pressure from Mario Williams, consists of young cornerbacks who will get tested often and could become a liability. Safety Bernard Pollard can pick up the slack with good awareness and positioning. In all, the Texans have a well-rounded defense but should be mindful of getting pressure on the quarterback early and often to avoid getting burned by their inexperienced corners.

TEAM RATING

78
Overall

KEY ADDITIONS

LB	Darnell Bing
QB	John David Booty
K	Neil Rackers
G	Wade Smith
CB	Kareem Jackson
RB	Ben Tate

KEY DEPARTURES

QB	Rex Grossman
G	Chester Pitts
CB	Dunta Robinson

RATINGS BY POSITION

Position	Rating
Quarterbacks	89
Halfbacks	78
Fullbacks	77
Wide Receivers	80
Tight Ends	87
Tackles	82
Guards	75
Centers	74
Defensive Ends	89
Defensive Tackles	74
Outside Linebackers	79
Middle Linebackers	90
Cornerbacks	72
Free Safeties	79
Strong Safeties	84
Kickers	71
Punters	72

DEPTH CHART

POS	OVR	FIRST NAME	LAST NAME
C	74	Chris	Myers
C	63	Chris	White
CB	76	Glover	Quin Jr.
CB	73	Kareem	Jackson
CB	68	Brice	McCain
CB	68	Jacques	Reeves
CB	66	Fred	Bennett
DT	74	Amobi	Okoye
DT	73	Shaun	Cody
DT	63	Frank	Okam
DT	62	DelJuan	Robinson
FB	77	Vonta	Leach
FS	79	Eugene	Wilson
HB	78	Steve	Slaton
HB	72	Ben	Tate
HB	68	Ryan	Moats
HB	67	Arian	Foster
K	77	Neil	Rackers
K	71	Kris	Brown
LE	82	Antonio	Smith
LE	64	Tim	Bulman
LG	78	Kasey	Studdard
LG	72	Wade	Smith
LOLB	87	Brian	Cushing
LOLB	87	Zac	Diles
LOLB	75	Danny	Clark
LT	79	Duane	Brown
LT	69	Rashad	Butler
MLB	90	DeMeco	Ryans
MLB	61	Kevin	Bentley
P	72	Matt	Turk
QB	89	Matt	Schaub
QB	63	Dan	Orlovsky
QB	53	John David	Booty
RE	95	Mario	Williams
RE	71	Connor	Barwin
RG	73	Antoine	Caldwell
RG	71	Mike	Brisiel
ROLB	71	Xavier	Adibi
ROLB	60	Darryl	Sharpton
RT	85	Eric	Winston
SS	84	Bernard	Pollard
SS	68	Dominique	Barber
TE	87	Owen	Daniels
TE	72	James	Casey
TE	70	Joel	Dreessen
WR	98	Andre	Johnson
WR	77	Kevin	Walter
WR	70	Jacoby	Jones
WR	64	David	Anderson
WR	63	Andre	Davis
WR	52	Trindon	Holliday

OFFENSIVE STRENGTH CHART

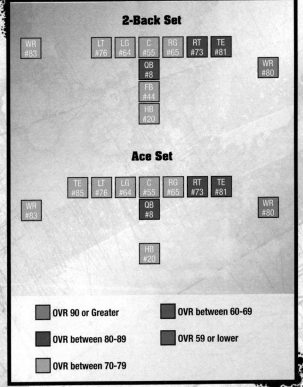

2-Back Set

WR #83 | LT #76 | LG #64 | C #55 | RG #65 | RT #73 | TE #81 | WR #80
QB #8
FB #44
HB #20

Ace Set

TE #85 | LT #76 | LG #64 | C #55 | RG #65 | RT #73 | TE #81
WR #83 | QB #8 | WR #80
HB #20

■ OVR 90 or Greater
■ OVR between 80-89
■ OVR between 70-79
■ OVR between 60-69
■ OVR 59 or lower

Key Player Substitutions

Position: WR

Substitution: : Trindon Holliday

When: Situational

Advantage: With Olympic-caliber speed, Holliday can be used in many different parts of your passing game. Run him on screen plays or end-arounds. You are going to want to hit the edges as fast as he can run there, and try to avoid big hits.

#80 Andre Johnson
Wide Receiver (WR)

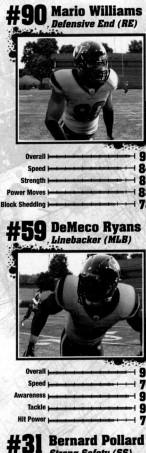

Overall	98
Speed	94
Catching	95
Release	96
Jumping	95

#8 Matt Schaub
Quarterback (QB)

Overall	89
Throw Power	88
Short Accuracy	94
Medium Accuracy	92
Deep Accuracy	81

#81 Owen Daniels
Tight End (TE)

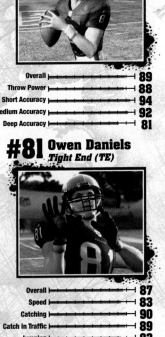

Overall	87
Speed	83
Catching	90
Catch in Traffic	89
Jumping	83

#90 Mario Williams
Defensive End (RE)

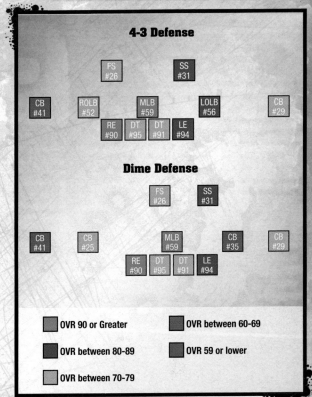

Overall	95
Speed	84
Strength	85
Power Moves	88
Block Shedding	78

#59 DeMeco Ryans
Linebacker (MLB)

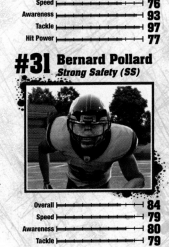

Overall	90
Speed	76
Awareness	93
Tackle	97
Hit Power	77

#31 Bernard Pollard
Strong Safety (SS)

Overall	84
Speed	79
Awareness	80
Tackle	79
Play Recognition	80

DEFENSIVE STRENGTH CHART

4-3 Defense

FS #26 | SS #31
CB #41 | ROLB #52 | MLB #59 | LOLB #56 | CB #29
RE #90 | DT #95 | DT #91 | LE #94

Dime Defense

FS #26 | SS #31
CB #41 | CB #25 | MLB #59 | CB #35 | CB #29
RE #90 | DT #95 | DT #91 | LE #94

■ OVR 90 or Greater
■ OVR between 80-89
■ OVR between 70-79
■ OVR between 60-69
■ OVR 59 or lower

Key Player Substitutions

Position: DE

Substitution: Connor Barwin

When: Situational

Advantage: With one of the league's best right ends in Mario Williams, you can move Barwin to the left end and increase the speed coming from that side. This will help you get to the quarterback.

Playbook Breakdown

The Houston Texans like to attack the defense by using a zone running game mixed in with the bootleg passing game. Those types of plays are well-represented throughout the playbook. They also have the ability to stretch the defense vertically thanks largely to having one the best receivers in the game in Andre Johnson. Those of you who ran the Texans playbook in *Madden NFL 10* should feel right at home; most of the formations and plays made it to *Madden NFL 11*. Formations such as I-Form Close, Strong Close, Singleback Tight Doubles, and Gun Snugs Flip are all back for another season. Two new formations have been added to the Texans playbook this year. One is called Singleback Jumbo Z. This formation gets three tight ends on the field, making it very effective to run from. The other formation is Singleback Ace Close. This formation has the two receivers lined up closer to the tight ends on both sides of the field. Overall this is one of the better balanced playbooks in the game and will certainly garner its share of usage from players this season.

OFFENSIVE FORMATIONS

FORMATION	# OF PLAYS
Gun Bunch	15
Gun Doubles	15
Gun Empty Y-Flex	9
Gun Snugs Flip	9
Gun Split Texan	12
Gun Y-Trips HB Wk	15
I-Form Close	12
I-Form Pro	15
I-Form Tight Pair	12
I-Form Twins Flex	9
Singleback Ace	12
Singleback Ace Close	9
Singleback Ace Twins	18
Singleback Jumbo Z	9
Singleback Tight Doubles	12
Singleback Wing Trio	12
Strong Close	15
Weak Pro	18

OFFENSIVE PLAYCOUNTS

PLAY TYPE	# OF PLAYS
Quick Pass	16
Standard Pass	43
Shotgun Pass	57
Play Action Pass	47
Outside Handoff	17
Pitch	8
Counter	3
Draw	7

I-Form Pro—PA Boot

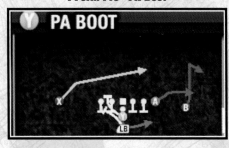

The Texans use a lot of bootleg action to get quarterback Matt Schaub out of the pocket where he can find open receivers. The I-Form Pro—PA Boot is the type of boot action play that you might see the Texans run on any given Sunday. The primary receiver is Andre Johnson, who is lined up in the flanker position. His pass route is a hitch to the outside.

Schaub bootlegs out of the pocket while looking for the open receiver

If man coverage is called, you will need to take control of the receiver and bring him forward towards the ball to make sure he makes the catch. Another option is the split end running the crossing route. Tight end Owen Daniels leaks out into the flat on a delayed flat.

Johnson gets some separation from his man as he goes for the catch

He should be your third option if none of the other receivers are open after you make your reads. The running play that coincides with the PA Boot is the Iso Weak. This play has the fullback lead-blocking for running back Steve Slaton between the center and left guard. Be sure to work these in combination.

I-Form Close—PA Texans Clear

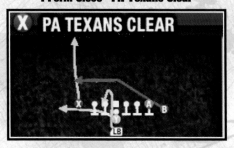

Another play action that gets the Texans' top receiver Andre Johnson involved in the offense is the I-Form Close—PA Texans Clear. This play has Johnson running a crossing route from right to left.

Johnson breaks across the middle on his crossing route

Split end Kevin Walter runs a go route and clears out the pass coverage down the left side of the field. His route will help create space for Johnson to work underneath in one-on-one coverage. Fullback Vonta Leach leaks out in the left flat and is one of two check-down options. The other check-down option is running back Steve Slaton, who hooks back towards the quarterback just a few yards past the line of scrimmage. The run play this pass works alongside is the I-Form Close—Texans HB Zone.

The pass is thrown on target from Schaub

That run play is a staple play of the Texans offense that aims to get Slaton positive yardage on the ground. The play is designed to have him run behind his fullback and between the left guard and left tackle.

Strong Close—Dbl Stutter Go

Andre Johnson is one of the best receivers in the NFL, and finding ways to get him open deep down the field is a must to open up the running game and the short passing game. The Strong Close—Dbl Stutter Go has Johnson and Kevin Walter running go routes but with an added twist: They both stutter about 12 yards down the field.

The QB unloads the ball deep as the defenders close in

Their stutter is an attempt to shake loose from their defenders. Whether or not it works is another story, but it does make your opponent have to leave at least one safety over the top in case it does work. If you have good user stick control, you can come up with some nice catch animations such as the one we show here.

Johnson skies up in the air to make the grab

If neither of them is open, tight end Owen Daniels spots up underneath and fullback Vonta Leach runs a flat route. Both are good options if there is nowhere else to go with the ball.

Singleback Jumbo Z—PA Zone Wk

A brand-new formation has been added to the Texans playbook this year: Singleback Jumbo Z. This formation has three tight ends in it. Two of the tight ends line up on the right, while the third tight end lines up on the left.

Schaub sprints out to the right while scanning the field for an open receiver

The PA Zone Wk is a play action play that is specifically designed to suit the Texans' offensive style. Tight end James Casey is lined up at the wing position on the right. He is sent in automotion to the left before the ball is snapped. Initially, the play looks like it's going to be a run play to the right as quarterback Matt Schaub fakes the handoff to Steve Slaton.

The ball is thrown towards Johnson as he breaks towards the corner

After the play fake, Schaub rolls to the right, looking for one of three receivers. Flanker Andre Johnson runs a corner route and is the play's primary receiver. His next option is tight end Joel Dreessen, who runs a crossing route. His third option is Casey, who runs a flat route. The run play that works best with the PA Zone Wk is H Zone Wk. Combo these plays together for maximum effect.

Singleback Tight Doubles—Texan Cross

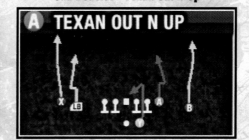

The Singleback Tight Doubles—Texan Cross does an excellent job of attacking man coverage by getting Andre Johnson open as he comes across over the middle of the field. Two other routes that help get him open belong to split end Kevin Walter and the slot receiver.

Schaub drops back in the pocket while his offensive line protects him

Walter runs a go route while the slot receiver runs a post route. Tight end Owen Daniels runs a wheel route and running back Steve Slaton runs an out route. The only downside of this play is there are only two other plays in the formation where Johnson lines up tighter inside—the Texan Under and Texan Curl—so your opponent knows a pass play is called.

The ball is thrown over the middle as Johnson gets open

This play is one that you will only be able to run once or twice if you are playing against a human. If you are playing against the CPU, then it won't matter as much. If Cover 2 zone coverage is called, look for the slot receiver. If Cover 3 coverage is called, look for the split end or tight end Owen Daniels.

Gun Doubles—Texan Out N Up

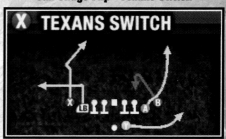

The Gun Doubles—Texan Out N Up is a vertical stretch play we can use to attack deep zone coverage. This play has Kevin Walter and Andre Johnson running go routes on the outside. The inside slot receiver and tight end Owen Daniels run out-n-up routes.

Walters breaks towards the sideline as if he is running an out route

Against Cover 2 and Cover 3, one of the two inside receivers is open. The primary receiver is Daniels, and he is the receiver we generally look to first. If neither of them are open, look to one of the outside receivers. Running back Steve Slaton runs a delayed curl route out of the backfield and is the play's check-down receiver.

Walters breaks down the field, where the ball is delivered on time

For this play to have a chance to succeed, Matt Schaub needs time in the pocket. If a blitz is called, you won't be able to wait until they get deep. Watch for the slot or tight end to get open shortly after the ball is snapped—one of them should be accessible to throw to.

Gun Snugs Flip—Texans Switch

One of our favorite high-percentage passing plays that gets Kevin Walters involved in the offense is the Gun Snugs Flip—Texans Switch. This play has Walters hooking back towards the quarterback. The inside receiver runs a wheel route and clears out the pass coverage so that Walters can get open underneath.

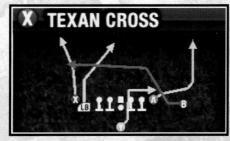

Walters spots up in front of the hook zone defenders

If man coverage is called, look for Walters before he hooks back, or find the inside receiver just before he goes downfield. The post corner route run by the outside receiver is also an option if Cover 2 zone coverage is called.

The pass is thrown on time for a 6-yard pickup

Finally, one more option is Steve Slaton out of the backfield running the swing route to the right side. Look for him if the defense calls a blitz and you don't have time to wait for Walters to spot up.

TENNESSEE TITANS

OFFENSIVE SCOUTING REPORT

With 2,000 yards rushing last season, Chris Johnson became the league's best running back and should be showcased during each game played in your *Madden NFL* campaign. No running back can match his explosive speed and ability to find an open lane. However, with such a golden egg, defenses will attempt to stack the line and focus all of their efforts to block his path. This is where Vince Young and receivers Kenny Britt and Nate Washington excelled last season. When the defenses crowd the box, the speed of the Titans receivers would make them pay by quickly finding the openings in the midfield, moving the chains. Once defenses were made to stay honest, the Chris Johnson clinic would begin again. Left tackle Michael Roos should be thanked by Johnson for providing excellent run blocking throughout the season, and he and the rest of the line return this year to do it again.

DEFENSIVE SCOUTING REPORT

The Titans defensive line lost Kyle Vanden Bosch in the off-season, putting a lot of pressure on defensive end William Hayes to fill his shoes. And without the presence of a high-quality pass rusher, the Titans could struggle against the pass, spelling trouble considering the division they're in has two of the highest-rated passing offenses. Fortunately, there is a lot of speed in the secondary with CBs Cortland Finnegan and Tye Hill and safety Michael Griffin. Both Griffin and Finnegan excel in zone coverage, which will compensate well for the Texans' lack of pass rush. The middle of the field will be covered nicely by Will Witherspoon, fresh from Philly, which will more than help contain the run, something that the Texans can do well, in part by tackle Tony Brown.

TEAM RATING

77
Overall

KEY ADDITIONS

DE	Jason Babin
CB	Tye Hill
QB	Chris Simms
LB	Will Witherspoon
DE	Derrick Morgan

KEY DEPARTURES

TE	Alge Crumpler
P	Craig Hentrich
C	Kevin Mawae
DE	Kyle Vanden Bosch
RB	LenDale White

RATINGS BY POSITION

Position	Rating
Quarterbacks	79
Halfbacks	99
Fullbacks	84
Wide Receivers	78
Tight Ends	81
Tackles	92
Guards	82
Centers	80
Defensive Ends	75
Defensive Tackles	83
Outside Linebackers	81
Middle Linebackers	77
Cornerbacks	80
Free Safeties	86
Strong Safeties	84
Kickers	93
Punters	68

DEPTH CHART

POS	OVR	FIRST NAME	LAST NAME
C	80	Eugene	Amano
CB	92	Cortland	Finnegan
CB	70	Roderick	Hood
CB	70	Tye	Hill
CB	68	Jason	McCourty
CB	63	Ryan	Mouton
DT	83	Tony	Brown
DT	78	Jovan	Haye
DT	77	Jason	Jones
DT	68	Sen'Derrick	Marks
FB	84	Ahmard	Hall
FS	86	Michael	Griffin
FS	72	Vincent	Fuller
FS	64	Robert	Johnson
HB	99	Chris	Johnson
HB	67	Javon	Ringer
HB	66	Alvin	Pearman
HB	65	LeGarrette	Blount
K	93	Rob	Bironas
LE	71	William	Hayes
LE	69	Jason	Babin
LG	78	Leroy	Harris
LOLB	79	David	Thornton
LOLB	65	Jamie	Winborn
LOLB	64	Rennie	Curran
LT	95	Michael	Roos
LT	68	Michael	Otto
MLB	77	Stephen	Tulloch
MLB	57	Colin	Allred
P	68	Brett	Kern
QB	79	Vince	Young
QB	72	Kerry	Collins
QB	68	Chris	Simms
RE	79	Derrick	Morgan
RE	79	Jacob	Ford
RE	66	Dave	Ball
RG	85	Jake	Scott
RG	57	Fernando	Velasco
ROLB	82	Will	Witherspoon
ROLB	73	Gerald	McRath
ROLB	61	Stanford	Keglar
RT	89	David	Stewart
RT	69	Troy	Kropog
SS	84	Chris	Hope
SS	55	Donnie	Nickey
TE	81	Bo	Scaife
TE	70	Craig	Stevens
TE	68	Jared	Cook Jr.
WR	82	Kenny	Britt
WR	77	Justin	Gage
WR	76	Nate	Washington
WR	71	Damian	Williams
WR	62	Lavelle	Hawkins
WR	52	Dominique	Edison

OFFENSIVE STRENGTH CHART

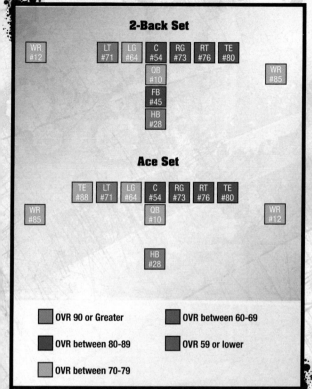

2-Back Set

WR #12		LT #71	LG #64	C #54	RG #73	RT #76	TE #80	
				QB #10				WR #85
				FB #45				
				HB #28				

Ace Set

	TE #88	LT #71	LG #64	C #54	RG #73	RT #76	TE #80	
WR #85				QB #10				WR #12
				HB #28				

- ■ OVR 90 or Greater
- ■ OVR between 80-89
- ■ OVR between 70-79
- ■ OVR between 60-69
- ■ OVR 59 or lower

Key Player Substitutions

Position: WR

Substitution: Damian Williams

When: Run blocking situations

Advantage: With the top running back in the NFL in the backfield, you have to use every player on the field to block for Chris Johnson. Sub Williams in for Washington for better blocking on the edges.

#28 Chris Johnson
Halfback (HB)

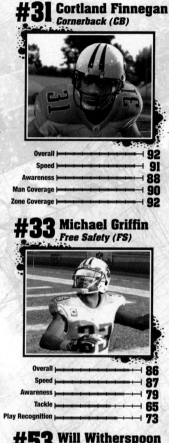

Overall	99
Speed	99
Agility	88
Stiff Arm	74
Carrying	96

#71 Michael Roos
Offensive Tackle (OT)

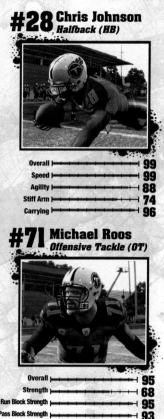

Overall	95
Strength	68
Run Block Strength	95
Pass Block Strength	93
Impact Blocking	90

#18 Kenny Britt
Wide Receiver (WR)

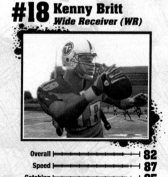

Overall	82
Speed	87
Catching	85
Release	94
Jumping	88

#31 Cortland Finnegan
Cornerback (CB)

Overall	92
Speed	91
Awareness	88
Man Coverage	90
Zone Coverage	92

#33 Michael Griffin
Free Safety (FS)

Overall	86
Speed	87
Awareness	79
Tackle	65
Play Recognition	73

#53 Will Witherspoon
Linebacker (ROLB)

Overall	82
Speed	84
Awareness	84
Tackle	86
Hit Power	72

DEFENSIVE STRENGTH CHART

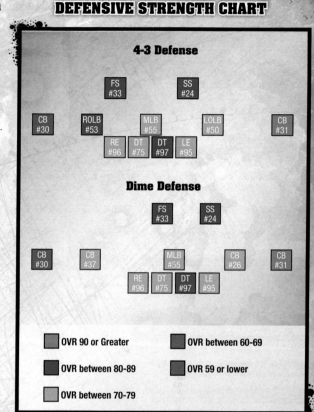

4-3 Defense

	FS #33			SS #24	
CB #30	ROLB #53	MLB #55	LOLB #50	CB #31
	RE #96	DT #75	DT #97	LE #95	

Dime Defense

	FS #33		SS #24	
CB #30	CB #37	MLB #55	CB #26	CB #31
	RE #96	DT #75	DT #97	LE #95	

- ■ OVR 90 or Greater
- ■ OVR between 80-89
- ■ OVR between 70-79
- ■ OVR between 60-69
- ■ OVR 59 or lower

Key Player Substitutions

Position: LOLB

Substitution: Gerald McRath

When: Situational

Advantage: Moving McRath to the left-side linebacker position strengthens the Titans' ability to put pressure on the quarterback. His speed helps him get into the backfield and create losses.

Playbook Breakdown

The Tennessee Titans playbook features a lot of run heavy plays and play action with rollouts, which is what they do in real life. A few of the run heavy formations that we like are the I-Form H Pro, I-Form H Twins, I-Form H Tight, Strong H Pro, and Singleback Ace. Each one has some strong inside and outside run plays, plus play action plays that get the quarterback out of the pocket to find the open receiver. For those who like to call plays from the Gun, there are six formations to choose from. The Doubles Wk, Bunch, and Snugs are all good choices. Inside a few of those Gun formations, you will find a play called Tenn Read Option. This play is effective because it allows Vince Young or Chris Johnson to pick up yardage on the ground based on what the defense does, particularly the backside defensive end. Overall, we like this playbook, but there are better run and play action books in the game. Still, the Titans playbook is worth checking out, especially if you plan on using the Tennessee Titans team.

OFFENSIVE FORMATIONS

FORMATION	# OF PLAYS
Gun Bunch	12
Gun Doubles Wk	18
Gun Snugs	12
Gun Split Slot	15
Gun Spread Wk	15
Gun Trips Y-Flex	12
I-Form H Pro	18
I-Form H Tight	15
I-Form H Twins	15
Singleback Ace	18
Singleback Ace Pair Twins	12
Singleback Doubles	18
Singleback Spread	12
Singleback Y-Trips	18
Strong H Pro	15
Weak H Pro	15

OFFENSIVE PLAYCOUNTS

PLAY TYPE	# OF PLAYS
Quick Pass	12
Standard Pass	44
Shotgun Pass	48
Play Action Pass	48
Inside Handoff	26
Outside Handoff	16
Pitch	5
Counter	15

I-Form H Pro—HB Lead Draw

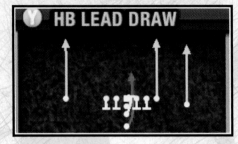

With the improvement of offensive line run blocking, draw plays are now more effective than in past editions of the game. A really good draw play to call under center is the HB Lead Draw out of I-Form H Pro. Throw in Titans running back Chris Johnson and the offensive line, and this play just screams with big-play potential.

Young drops back as if he is about to pass

This play has the offensive line setting up like a pass while Vince Young drops looking like he is going to throw the ball. The defensive ends tend to get up the field quickly going after the passer. This movement provides plenty of inside running lanes for Johnson to run through. What really we like about this play is that while the quarterback is dropping back we have time to look over which running lanes are opening up. Once we spot the open hole, we burst through it looking to pick up yardage.

Johnson finds plenty of running room

With Johnson's high speed and acceleration ratings, there is a chance he could break off a long run if you maneuver him correctly.

Strong H Pro—Toss Sweep

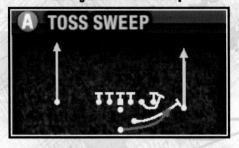

There is no doubt about it—Chris Johnson is the main focus of the Titans' offensive game plan. Getting him the ball multiple times is a must for success with the Titans. The Strong H Pro—Toss Sweep allows him to use his speed, shiftiness, and acceleration to break off long runs at any given moment.

Two blockers are out in front of Johnson

Pulling right guard Jake Scott and fullback Ahmard Hall lead the way for Johnson to the outside. Both are powerful run blockers and have a knack for opening lanes to the outside for Johnson. Make sure while controlling Johnson not to get out in front of your blockers.

The FB throws a key block that springs Johnson to the outside

Allow them time to set up their blocks. Once they do, look to bust it outside, where there should be plenty of running room. If man coverage is called, send the flanker in motion and wait for him to set on the other side. By doing this, there will be one less defender you have to worry about once you get Johnson outside.

Singleback Spread—Inside Zone

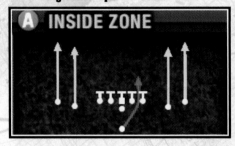

Not only does Chris Johnson have the speed and finesse to run outside, he also has enough power to run inside between the tackles to pick up yardage. The Singleback Spread—Inside Zone is an excellent inside run play to spread the defense out, allowing Johnson to use power and quickness to gain yardage.

The Titans O-line gets a big push and opens running lanes

This play can be run inside or outside depending on how the blocking sets up. Don't get cute with jukes and spins. Make one cut and then head down the field looking to pick up yardage. Some players use motion to add an extra run blocker into the mix.

Johnson uses his vision to find room to run

Only use motion if zone coverage is called, because you don't want to add any extra defenders into the mix. If the defense stacks the inside with extra defenders, consider audibling to a pass play to take advantage of the defensive alignment.

I-Form H Tight—PA FB Slide

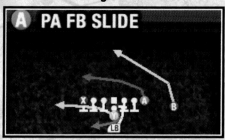

There is no doubt that quarterback Vince Young has the talent to succeed in the NFL, as he showed last season. With that said, he is a mobile quarterback who needs to get out of the pocket to show off his passing skills.

Young play fakes to Johnson to the right side

The I-Form H Tight—PA FB Slide gets him outside of the pocket, where he can use his legs and arm to make positive things happen on the field. Tight end Bo Scaife is Young's primary target for this play. Scaife runs a shallow crossing route from right to left. Fullback Ahmard Hall leaks out of the backfield and is a good option if Scaife is not open.

Young throws a dart towards Scaife for a big play down the field

The play's deep threat is Justin Gage, who runs towards the post. The HB Stretch works well with this play so that the defense can't just sit on the play action pass play. Use these two plays to give the defense fits and keep them on their heels.

Gun Doubles Wk—Tenn Read Option

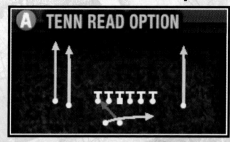

The Titans' two best offensive players are running back Chris Johnson and quarterback Vince Young. The Gun Spread Doubles Wk—Tenn Read Option ensures that one of them is going to have the ball when running this play. The formation spreads the defense out with four receivers.

The RE crashes down and chases Johnson

Spreading the defense out to defend more of the field isolates the defenders in space. The Tenn Read Option with the right personnel is a very lethal play even in the NFL. This run play is effective, yet easy to run. If you see that the unblocked backside defensive end is crashing down towards the ball carrier, you keep it and take off with your quarterback.

Young keeps the ball and takes off in the other direction

If you see that the unblocked backside defensive end sits back and stays home, then you hand off to your running back. As long as you make the right read, this run play is very difficult to defend even if the defense knows it's coming towards them.

Gun Bunch—Verticals

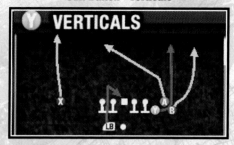

Very few quarterbacks in the game possess the speed that Vince Young has. Rather than showing off his arm, we are going to show a way we like to use his legs to pick up yardage on the ground. The play is Gun Bunch—Verticals. We chose this play because there are four receivers running vertical routes.

Young sits back in the pocket, waiting for receivers to get down the field

This means we don't have hot route on streaks to clear out room for us to take off and run with Young. The only eligible receiver we need to hot route is the running back. We motion him to the left and then hot route him on a streak. By having all five receivers run deep routes, there won't be much in the way of our picking up yardage with Young once we take off and run with him.

He tucks the ball down and takes off running

We can either take off, run him outside, or look to the inside. In this case, we run inside between the tackles. Once through the line of scrimmage, we look to pick up yardage.

Gun Spread Wk—HB Slip Screen

The Gun Spread Wk—HB Slip Screen is one of our favorite plays because it has three other routes that you can throw to if the screen is covered. As always, screens are good to mix into any offensive scheme. We hot route the left slot receiver on a slant route to provide us with yet another option if the screen is covered.

The blocking is set up as Young throws the ball

We wait for our blocks to set up before making the throw. We also want to let defensive linemen get up the field as much as they can so they can't go back to make the tackle. Once Johnson makes the catch, we watch to see how the blocks set up before taking off full speed. As you can see, the HB Slip Screen remains one of the most effective screen plays in the game no matter what formation you're using.

Johnson follows his blocks and picks a good chunk of yardage

If Johnson is covered, look for the left slot receiver on the slant out as he may be open depending on the pass coverage. Don't forget that if you read zone pre-snap, you should hot route the right slot and flanker on drags to add extra blockers to the play once the catch is made.

MINNESOTA VIKINGS

OFFENSIVE SCOUTING REPORT

With Adrian Peterson and Brett Favre, Minnesota has arguably the best of air and ground in terms of offensive weapons. Peterson is undeniably a premier back in the NFL and has the ability to create a run out of the smallest of opportunities. Stellar awareness, agility, and vision, teamed with the highest rated juke and stiff arm moves, make Peterson the cornerstone of the offense and a go-to guy when needing to move the chains. Favre complements the run game with the threat of the deep pass to his favorite target, Percy Harvin. Utilizing the pass prevents defenses from stacking the box to stop the run. Wide receiver Sydney Rice and tight end Visanthe Shiancoe can be counted on for shorter routes and dump passes when Brett becomes pressured. With well-rounded play calling, the Minnesota Vikings led by Brett Favre and Adrian Peterson are practically unstoppable.

DEFENSIVE SCOUTING REPORT

The Vikings excel in rushing defense, in part because of the tackle duo of Pat Williams and Kevin Williams. These two put a lot of pressure on offensive lines, often drawing double teams, which allows the linebackers to make plays. Should Kevin Williams be left to single coverage by the line, look for him to continually make big plays as both a run stopper and a threat to the QB on a pass-rush. The pass rush is also where RE and sack-monster Jared Allen shines. His ability to never stop charging landed him 14.5 sacks last season. Use him as a constant threat to any quarterback who decides to drop back for a pass. While the front line is strong, the secondary is a little thin when it comes to pass defense. And while corners Cedric Griffin and Antoine Winfield do have strong overall ratings (80–89), they'll have their work cut out for them to make up for the Vikings' lack of depth at the safety positions.

TEAM RATING

88
Overall

KEY ADDITIONS

K	Rhys Lloyd
CB	Lito Sheppard
DE	Mike Montgomery
CB	Chris Cook
RB	Toby Gerhart

KEY DEPARTURES

OL	Artis Hicks
RB	Chester Taylor
CB	Karl Paymah

RATINGS BY POSITION

Position	Rating		Position	Rating
Quarterbacks	92		Defensive Tackles	97
Halfbacks	98		Outside Linebackers	84
Fullbacks	76		Middle Linebackers	85
Wide Receivers	83		Cornerbacks	85
Tight Ends	86		Free Safeties	74
Tackles	85		Strong Safeties	75
Guards	84		Kickers	92
Centers	77		Punters	75
Defensive Ends	92			

DEPTH CHART

POS	OVR	FIRST NAME	LAST NAME
C	77	John	Sullivan
C	63	Jon	Cooper
CB	88	Antoine	Winfield
CB	82	Cedric	Griffin
CB	77	Lito	Sheppard
CB	70	Chris	Cook
CB	69	Benny	Sapp
DT	97	Kevin	Williams
DT	88	Pat	Williams
DT	73	Jimmy	Kennedy
DT	60	Fred	Evans
DT	58	Letroy	Guion
FB	76	Naufahu	Tahi
FS	74	Madieu	Williams
FS	63	Husain	Abdullah
HB	98	Adrian	Peterson
HB	71	Toby	Gerhart
HB	66	Albert	Young
HB	64	Ian	Johnson
K	92	Ryan	Longwell
LE	85	Ray	Edwards
LE	68	Mike	Montgomery
LG	97	Steve	Hutchinson
LOLB	80	Ben	Leber
LOLB	62	Erin	Henderson
LT	90	Bryant	McKinnie
LT	62	Drew	Radovich
MLB	85	E.J.	Henderson
MLB	69	Jasper	Brinkley
P	75	Chris	Kluwe
QB	92	Brett	Favre
QB	71	Tarvaris	Jackson
QB	69	Sage	Rosenfels
RE	99	Jared	Allen
RE	69	Brian	Robison
RG	70	Anthony	Herrera
RG	63	Chris	DeGeare
ROLB	88	Chad	Greenway
ROLB	68	Heath	Farwell
RT	79	Phil	Loadholt
RT	67	Ryan	Cook
SS	75	Tyrell	Johnson
SS	71	Jamarca	Sanford
TE	86	Visanthe	Shiancoe
TE	74	Jim	Kleinsasser
TE	63	Jeff	Dugan
WR	90	Sidney	Rice
WR	84	Percy	Harvin
WR	75	Bernard	Berrian
WR	66	Greg	Lewis
WR	55	Jaymar	Johnson

OFFENSIVE STRENGTH CHART

2-Back Set

WR #87		LT #74	LG #76	C #65	RG #64	RT #71	TE #81
				QB #4			WR #18
				FB #38			
				HB #28			

Ace Set

	TE #40	LT #74	LG #76	C #65	RG #64	RT #71	TE #81
WR #87				QB #4			WR #18
				HB #28			

- ■ OVR 90 or Greater
- ■ OVR between 80-89
- ■ OVR between 70-79
- ■ OVR between 60-69
- ■ OVR 59 or lower

#28 Adrian Peterson
Halfback (HB)

Overall	98
Speed	97
Agility	98
Stiff Arm	99
Carrying	62

#4 Brett Favre
Quarterback (QB)

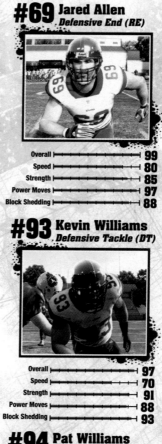

Overall	92
Throw Power	95
Short Accuracy	88
Medium Accuracy	87
Deep Accuracy	84

#18 Sidney Rice
Wide Receiver (WR)

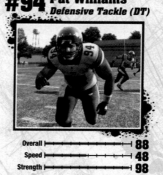

Overall	90
Speed	89
Catching	90
Release	95
Jumping	97

#69 Jared Allen
Defensive End (RE)

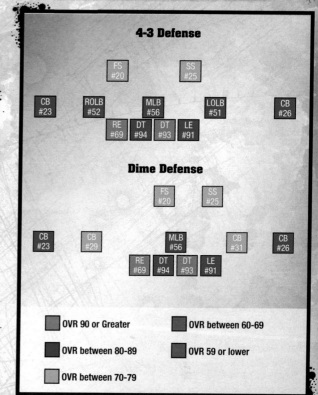

Overall	99
Speed	80
Strength	85
Power Moves	97
Block Shedding	88

#93 Kevin Williams
Defensive Tackle (DT)

Overall	97
Speed	70
Strength	91
Power Moves	88
Block Shedding	93

#94 Pat Williams
Defensive Tackle (DT)

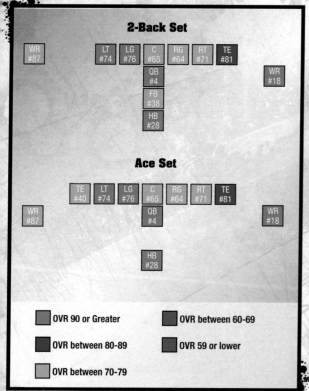

Overall	88
Speed	48
Strength	98
Power Moves	87
Block Shedding	96

DEFENSIVE STRENGTH CHART

4-3 Defense

		FS #20			SS #25		
CB #23	ROLB #52		MLB #56		LOLB #51		CB #26
		RE #69	DT #94	DT #93	LE #91		

Dime Defense

		FS #20		SS #25		
CB #23	CB #29		MLB #56		CB #31	CB #26
		RE #69	DT #94	DT #93	LE #91	

- ■ OVR 90 or Greater
- ■ OVR between 80-89
- ■ OVR between 70-79
- ■ OVR between 60-69
- ■ OVR 59 or lower

Key Player Substitutions

Position: HB

Substitution: Toby Gerhart

When: Situational

Advantage: You may want to hand the ball off to Gerhart at the end of a game when you are trying to run the clock out.

Key Player Substitutions

Position: CB

Substitution: Asher Allen

When: Dime and Dollar formations

Advantage: Allen can be brought on in Dime and Dollar formations to help when you are facing four- or five-wide-receiver sets. Try to keep him in zone coverage when he is in the game.

When you first think of the Vikings playbook, you would imagine that it would really focus on runs. This isn't the case at all. This is a very balanced playbook that can fit anyone's needs. You have the quick-passing attack that the West Coast Offense provides, as well as a healthy rushing attack. Then you also have some nice five-wide formations that with the right athletes can do some major damage as a changeup. There are spread concepts as well. The main personnel requirement for using this playbook is to have an accurate QB, because the West Coast Offense hinges on that point alone. You also need decent route runners and backs that can be showcased in the passing attack. This playbook is tight-end friendly as well. So teams like the Vikings, Skins, Colts, Cowboys, Chargers, and a few others would fit nicely with this playbook.

OFFENSIVE FORMATIONS

FORMATION	# OF PLAYS
Gun Double Flex	15
Gun Doubles On	18
Gun Empty Trey	12
Gun Split Viking	12
Gun Trey Open	15
Gun Y-Trips Wk	15
I-Form Pro	18
I-Form Slot Flex	15
I-Form Tight Pair	12
Singleback Ace	15
Singleback Ace Pair Twins	12
Singleback Ace Twins	15
Singleback Doubles	18
Singleback Jumbo Z	9
Singleback Y-Trips	15
Strong Flex Twins	12
Weak Normal	9

OFFENSIVE PLAYCOUNTS

PLAY TYPE	# OF PLAYS
Quick Pass	17
Standard Pass	42
Shotgun Pass	59
Play Action Pass	41
Inside Handoff	32
Outside Handoff	13
Pitch	8
Counter	7

Playbook Breakdown

Strong Flex Twins—Outside Zone

The Outside Zone is a great play. When you put it in a twin-receiver set, you have a nice combo. The Twins set forces the defense to make critical decisions right off the bat. If they're in man coverage you will see that your running side will be wide open on the perimeter. If it's zone, all you have to do is motion your slot wideout over and allow him to set to kick out on the DB. In addition, you have the option of simply flipping the play to the side away from the DB if it's zone. You're playing a numbers game with the defense.

Plenty of open field for our back

When you run the Outside Zone your key read is the edge defender. If he slants inside, you cut the ball outside. If the end slants outside or comes upfield, you cut the ball inside. There is zone blocking up front. So allow your men to set blocks and then make your read.

We are out!

When you make the right reads you can do some serious damage.

Strong Flex Twins—HB Dive

When you run the ball you have to attack two areas. You have to attack the perimeter, but you also need to attack the teeth of the defense inside. The Outside Zone provides you with the perimeter attack. It's time to set up shop inside. Your key read is the defensive tackle. If the defensive tackle slants inside, you bang the ball through the B gap. If the defensive tackle slants away or upfield, you shoot through the A gap. You have to trust your reads and hit the hole aggressively.

The defensive tackle slants inside

When you read this move, you must cut to the next hole away from the tackle. Stay with your blocks and trust your read. If you make a mistake, this play can be a loss of yards or, worse, a turnover. You just want to move the chains and keep the defense off-balance with your attack.

We get downfield with a lead blocker

This is a nice play call to go in short yardage situations or when your opponent overplays the outside zone. The best way to have a solid rushing attack is to make sure you attack those two areas. You can also add a counter play for misdirection.

Strong Flex Twins—PA Boot Slide

One of the best parts of a healthy rushing attack is that it opens up opportunities to use play action passing. When your rushing attack is really on fire, there is nothing like a nice play action play. One of the best times to call a play action play is after a really nice gain. The person you're playing is heated at this point, and if you have this play in your audibles it would be a nice time to run no-huddle and dial this one up. This isn't an every down play. You pick and choose the right time to do this.

The defense bites hard on the action

You can see that the defense is flowing heavily to the strong side of your formation. This will open up your passing lanes quickly. Make your reads quickly and take your shot if you have time.

The FS bites, leaving the streak open

If the FS drifts, hit the streak. If he sits on the streak, you have the post. You also have the dig route if both deep routes are covered. The flat route will usually be open.

Strong Flex Twins—WR Streak

This is the West Coast Offense at its best here. This is a great play for using backs in the passing attack, and more so if you're playing an opponent who likes to send heat your way when you're under the center. Your progression should be your backs, the post, the out, and then the streak. These out-of-the-backfield routes are very hard to contain and work well with Dual HB packages.

The defense is sitting on the C route

If you have time, hit the post route. If you feel any pressure and the middle is covered then fire the ball out to the flat.

A great read by our QB results in a completion

Let your playmaker do what he does best. When you're in open space with a stud back, you can make magic happen. Most people you will play don't think you will be content with just taking short gains to the flats. If this is what they're giving you, take it. Make them defend every inch of the field. When you do this they will overcompensate and open another area for you to attack.

Gun Empty Trey—Jet Sweep

The Jet Sweep is a nice play to call when you want to change up the pace a bit. When you have players like Harvin, this can be a nice gain because it will catch most people off guard. You look to get outside, but if you see the defense flow outside, you can cut the ball back inside. Let's take a look at this play in action.

The defensive end slants outside

The blocking up front is outside zone–based. So you make the same reads you would if you were running the Outside Zone play. In this case the defensive end isn't giving up the edge, so you just cut the ball back inside.

And we're out!

Once you get out of the backfield, it's a wrap, pretty much. When you come out in an Empty set your opponent will either bring pressure or come out in a pass-based set (Dime or Nickel package).

Gun Empty Trey—PA Jet Sweep

You know that we won't leave you hanging without a complementary play to the Jet Sweep. You need a complementary play to take advantage of the defense overplaying the jet motion. When they do you can kill them over the top with the play action pass in this play. Unlike with the Wildcat, there isn't a threat to throw most of the time. In this case you have a good QB who can punish anyone who wants to use an all-out blitz to slow you down.

The defense chases the jet motion

You see that the defender is flowing with the jet motion. If you read pressure just drop the ball off to the jet motion wideout. If you have time, look down the field. In most cases, your opponent will run down with a defender to crack the wideout. When you read this, look deep.

Hit the deep out when you have time in the pocket

The secondary shifts with the flow of the jet motion, and that left the SE one-on-one with his defender. When a defense overcompensates to cover a specific area, attack the area that they just vacated.

Gun Empty Trey—WR Screen

When you're in an Empty set, you need quick hitters. This is one of the best plays to use, mainly because it gets your stud playmaker in open space to make plays. The Empty Trey has one of the best screen setups in the game. Since you have attacked with the Jet Sweep, you can work in the screen game. The screen is no more than a basic running play for this formation.

Look at those wideouts setting up the blocking

When you see that your wideouts have set their blocks you must fire the ball. Don't hike and throw, as you may throw a pick. You see here that the defender is in position to make a play. You have to wait until your slot wideouts drift over to block him.

Time to get busy, son!

This is a short pass, but many of them have been turned into highlight reel plays in games over the years. Just make sure you see that the slot wideouts drift out and made contact before you throw. If you misread this play, you will be the highlight reel, but from throwing a pick 6 instead of a touchdown.

BALANCED PLAYBOOK BREAKDOWN

A balanced offensive attack can be used to set up the run, or the run can set up a balanced offensive attack. With the Balanced playbook you can come out in a Gun formation to air it out; there are five Gun sets to choose from: Gun Split Slot, Gun Y-Trips HB Wk, Gun Snugs Flip, Gun Spread, and Gun Empty Trey. Plays are WR Post Corner, Bench Swap, X Follow, and 619 Sail, to name a few. This playbook has two I-Form sets to choose from to get that ground game going. All the basic run plays are available, such as the Power O, HB Toss, Iso, and Dive. There are also plays that give you that West Coast quick passing. There are four Singleback formations; our favorite set is Singleback Trips Open. We like that it gives you the ability to spread the defense out so you can make quick easy reads if you choose to pass, and by spreading the defense out you can also run the ball.

OFFENSIVE FORMATIONS

FORMATION	# OF PLAYS
Full House Normal Wide	9
Gun Empty Trey	12
Gun Snugs Flip	12
Gun Split Slot	15
Gun Spread	15
Gun Y-Trips HB Wk	21
I-Form Pro	15
I-Form Tight	12
Singleback Ace	15
Singleback Doubles	21
Singleback Jumbo	12
Singleback Trips Open	12
Strong Pro	15
Weak Pro Twins	12

OFFENSIVE PLAY COUNTS

PLAY TYPE	# OF PLAYS
Quick Pass	10
Standard Pass	47
Shotgun Pass	57
Play Action Pass	32
Inside Handoff	24
Outside Handoff	7
Pitch	5
Counter	6

Gun Split Slot—WR Post Corner

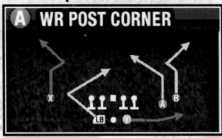

WR Post Corner has been a popular play for many years in *Madden NFL*. It is always a good play to run because it doesn't require many adjustments. The split end is the primary target on this play; however, we like to use the running backs as the primary targets. The post route can be used as the second read in this play. We are going to smart route the slot receiver's route to shorten it, then motion him and snap the ball once he gets to the right tackle.

The quarterback has his target

The slot receiver stutter-steps then runs a slant over the middle. The running back and slot receiver are your first two reads for this play. Also keep an eye out for the fullback on the delay route out of the backfield.

The pass is completed to the slot receiver

The slot receiver makes the catch for a 5-yard gain; this gets us a first down and keeps the chains moving. Because the slot receiver takes a stutter step, his route goes underneath the zone coverage and kills man defense as well.

Gun Snugs Flip—Bench Swap

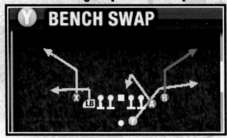

Bench Swap was a very effective play last year because it gave you the option of attacking the defense short and deep. This year, the play is still very effective because of the slant curl route and the running back's flat route from the backfield, which can be used as two quick reads. Then the corner routes, if given time to develop, can still pick up big chunks of yardage.

The QB sees the weakness in the defense

The defense is playing zone and the quarterback has two quick options: the slot receiver and the running back are both open as you can see in the screenshot. The defender sitting underneath is out of position, so the quarterback throws his receiver the ball.

The receiver makes the catch over the middle of the field

One final suggestion with this play is to hot route the slot receiver on a slant to the inside. This gives us two options right in front of us, which makes for easy reads.

Gun Spread—X Follow

Gun Spread—X Follow is a play with the flanker running a streak route as the primary target on this play. We like the running back's out route and the slot receiver's drag route, which come across the middle of the field.

The quarterback notices the linebacker out of position

As you scan the field with the quarterback, notice that against man or zone the running back and the crossing route will get open. The QB has his target crossing over the middle of the field, and notice how you have the running back coming open; these are two good reads right in front of you.

The pass is completed to our receiver over the middle of the field for a quick 5-yard gain

Another suggestion is to put the other slot receiver on the right side of the field on a slant route over the middle of the field.

I-Form Pro—Angle

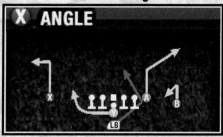

Angle routes have been effective out of the backfield for many years in *Madden NFL*. You will see this play in a lot of West Coast teams' playbooks. This play is very effective when mixed in with run plays from this formation.

The quarterback notices the blitzer coming off the edge

With this play, your first two reads should be to look at the halfback and the fullback coming out of the backfield. You should see the running back come open against just about any defense. If the defense has him covered, look for the fullback going to the left side of the field. You also have to keep an eye out for the flanker on the short curl route.

The pass is dumped off to a running back

The QB passes the ball to the running back; he makes the catch and turns downfield for a 5-yard pickup. Once you get the defense worrying about the HB, this is when you want to get either your fullback or flanker involved in the play.

I-Form Pro—Power O

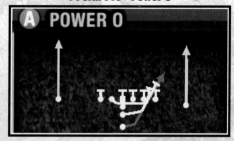

Power O is a perfect run to use out of the I-Form Pro formation. This play is designed for the left guard to pull to the right while the right guard and right tackle block down with the fullback as the lead blocker for the running back. For this play, we bring the flanker in motion to provide extra blocking.

The ball is handed off to the running back

The halfback then proceeds to follow the fullback's lead behind the right tackle and the right guard. Letting your blockers clear the path is the key to running this play effectively. You should see a hole to the inside of the tight end.

The running back follows the pulling left guard through the hole

He uses his speed to burst up inside and pick up 10 yards. If you see the defense overload one side of the formation, this is when you want to flip the play and run it to the opposite side. Counting how many defenders are in the box is the key to running this play effectively.

Strong Pro—Comet Pass

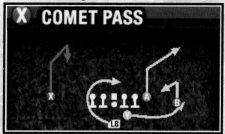

The Comet Pass is an effective play to run from the Strong Pro formation. What we like about this play is that you have three quick options. The running back runs a circle route, the fullback runs a flat route, and the flanker is on a short curl. While the tight end is running a deep corner route, the split end is the primary target; we like to hot route him on a slant.

The quarterback sees the linebacker blitzing

If the defense decides to drop back into zone coverage or even man, the circle route is usually open. We like to motion the flanker inside and snap the ball once he gets next to the tight end. Because his route is short, it gives us another option directly in our sight.

The running back makes the catch

He quickly gets away from the linebacker and picks up 10 yards before being tackled from behind. The progress of this play is the running back first, split end second, and then you can turn your attention to the right side of the formation.

Strong Pro—HB Blast

The Strong Pro—HB Blast is designed to run to the strong side behind the right tackle. This is a solid run that moves the chains and works well with the other runs from this formation. The right tackle and right guard block down on this play, while the fullback is designed to lead-block between them.

The quarterback hands the ball off

With this play, we like to motion the flanker from the left to the right side of the field to provide extra blocking. This gives the same look as if we were running Comet Pass, and it also tells us if the defense is playing man or zone.

The fullback makes a key block on a linebacker

The halfback then uses his speed to quickly burst through the hole and pick up 8 yards. Remember to always use motion, because it gives the defense the same look on every play, whether you are using play action or any other play from this formation.

PASS BALANCED PLAYBOOK BREAKDOWN

The Pass Balanced playbook was very popular last year in *Madden NFL 10*. If you were a fan of the playbook last year and would like to run the same offense you can do so because most of the playbook has not changed at all. You can have a run-first offense with formations such as I-Form Pro, I-Form Tight Pair, or the very popular Strong Close (and its go-to play, the HB Off Tackle). This set was very popular among top *Madden NFL* players. With how effective the running game is this year, we predict that most players will use the same approach. This playbook also has four Singleback sets, including the in-demand Singleback Tight Flex. With plenty of Gun formations (six in total: Doubles, Empty Trey, Snugs Flip, Split Cowboy, Spread Y-Slot, Y-Trips HB Wk) you have plenty to choose from. We like the versatility that this playbook gives you, whether you like to ground and pound or spread the defense out in four- or five-wide-receiver sets. It can all be done in the Pass Balanced playbook.

OFFENSIVE FORMATIONS

FORMATION	# OF PLAYS
Gun Doubles	24
Gun Empty Trey	12
Gun Snugs Flip	9
Gun Split Cowboy	18
Gun Spread Y-Slot	18
Gun Y-Trips HB Wk	18
I-Form Pro	21
I-Form Tight Pair	12
Singleback Ace	21
Singleback Ace Twins	15
Singleback Spread Flex	15
Singleback Tight Flex	9
Split Slot	12
Strong Close	12
Weak Pro	12

OFFENSIVE PLAY COUNTS

PLAY TYPE	# OF PLAYS
Quick Pass	6
Standard Pass	53
Shotgun Pass	72
Play Action Pass	38
Inside Handoff	22
Outside Handoff	15
Pitch	3
Counter	5

Gun Split Cowboy—TE Out

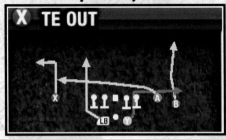

The Split Cowboy formation is very similar to Gun Split Offset; the only difference is that there is a tight end in the backfield instead of a fullback. You still have the option of using the dual halfback or fullback package. In this play, the tight end is running an out route and the halfback is on a fade out of the backfield. The tight end is the primary target; however, both routes can be used as primary reads.

The quarterback has three options in front of him

We really like this play because it's easy to read the three receivers that are in one area, as you can see in the screenshot. The two backs in the backfield can be two quick and easy reads, while you have the slot receiver running a drag route in the middle of the field.

The pass is completed to the tight end

Tight end Travis Beckum makes the catch for a 5-yard gain. The route combinations in this play are very hard to defend. They kill man, zone, and the blitz. This is a very good play to use to keep the chains moving.

Gun Split Cowboy—Slot Post

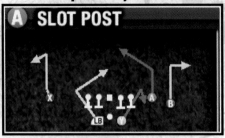

Slot Post is another play we like from the Gun Split Cowboy formation. The primary target on this play is the slot receiver, but you also have the running back coming with an angle route out of the backfield. The fullback is on a delay route. The way we set up this play is to smart route the slot receiver's route.

The quarterback sees his running back open and throws the ball

After the snap, notice how quickly the running back comes out of the backfield. He is the primary target on this play. Also notice that the slot receiver is getting separation from the defender covering him. By this time, the fullback should come out of the backfield on the delay route.

The pass is completed to Brandon Jacobs

With plenty of room to run, Brandon Jacobs picks up 10 yards and a first down. Another suggestion is to use motion with this play. This tells you if the defense is in man or zone. Against most coverages, the angle route is very effective.

Gun Empty Trey—Quick Slants

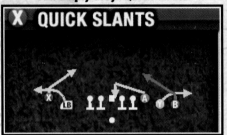

The Gun Empty formation is all about spreading the defense out with five receivers on the line of scrimmage. Quick Slants is a play that we like to use from this formation because it gives us a slant and flat combo. This route combination is very hard for a defense to cover.

The quarterback has his eye on his target

Eli Manning notices that the defense is playing man coverage, and he sees that the split end has separation on the defender. With the defender a step behind him, he throws a bullet pass.

Hakeem Nicks stretches out for the catch

Any time the defense is playing man there is a chance for a big gain. Against the zone, the slot receiver is left open for a quick pass to the flat. Sometimes you might see a Cover 2 coverage; if you notice this type of coverage, you can hot route your outside receivers on streaks and throw the ball in the window between the corner and the safety.

Gun Doubles—Texas

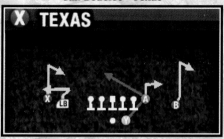

The Texas play has the running back on an angle route out of the backfield; he is the primary target. You also have the tight end on an out route. These two routes are the main reads for this play because they flood one area of the field.

The quarterback has two targets in front of him

Once the ball is snapped, focus on this area of the field. Both are crossing the same region of the field. Quarterback Eli Manning throws a bullet pass to Brandon Jacobs. Against most coverages this route combination works.

Brandon Jacobs makes the catch

Jacobs picks up a tough 5 yards. We suggest putting the slot receiver on a slant over the middle. This will give you another target in the same area of the field, and that is very hard for any defense to cover. Putting the flanker on a streak to push the coverage back for the shorter out route is another suggestion.

Gun Snugs Flip—WR In

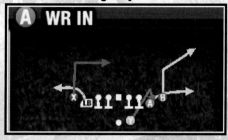

Gun Snugs Flip is a very popular formation. WR In has the split end as the primary target, with two flat routes, a delay route out of the backfield, and a corner route that the split end runs. We hot route both outside receivers on slant routes over the middle.

Eli Manning throws the ball to Steve Smith

With the defender a step behind the slot receiver, quarterback Eli Manning throws the ball. We also have the running back sneaking out of the backfield while the flanker is running the slant over the middle. This is a very hard route combination for the defense to cover.

Steve Smith makes the catch

Smith uses his speed to turn the corner and run away from the defender, picking up 15 yards. It is very easy to tell what type of coverage the defense is playing from this formation. If it's man, once you break the huddle the corners will be lined up directly over the receivers. If it's zone, the corners will start from the outside and come in.

Strong Close—HB Off Tackle

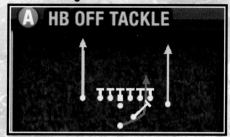

HB Off Tackle is still a very effective run from the Strong Close formation and is one of the sets we like to get our ground game going with. This play can be deadly with a power runner such as Brandon Jacobs, because you can just take it up inside and pick up tough yards.

The quarterback hands the ball off

The fullback is leading the way. Follow him and read off of his blocking to see if you can cut it up inside or take it outside. This run play is so versatile that either option will work. You just have to watch to see if the defense is overpursuing or not.

Brandon Jacobs uses his power to break a tackle

With the fullback getting a key block on the linebacker and the right tackle blocking the defensive linemen, Jacobs picks up a tough 5 yards. After breaking the first tackle, he picks up another 5 yards before getting tackled.

Strong Close—PA Deep Cross

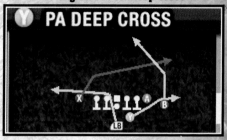

PA Deep Cross is a very effective play action play that we like to use from the Strong Close. It has the tight end blocking with both the fullback and the halfback going out on pass routes. The split end is the primary target on this play, with a crossing route. The flanker runs a deep post route that pulls the coverage back to open up the shorter routes.

The quarterback fakes the handoff

After the handoff, look for the short routes first out of the backfield, then the deeper routes after that. For maximum protection, keep the flanker in to block. This is a good thing to do because it gives the play the same look as if you're running the ball.

The quarterback fires the ball downfield

Wide receiver Steve Smith uses his superior route running to gain separation from the defender. He picks up a 15-yard gain downfield. Having this play to go along with the HB Off Tackle makes it a very good one-two punch to give just about any defense fits.

RUN BALANCED PLAYBOOK BREAKDOWN

A balanced offensive attack is all about being able to run the ball and pass the ball. Many teams in the NFL take this type of approach, and this is no different from a lot of *Madden NFL* players. The Run Balanced playbook is for the person who chooses to run a balanced attack that includes having the run set up the pass. For a run-first type of approach, you can use formations such as I-Form Pro, I-Form Tight Pair, Strong Pro, and Weak Tight Twins. You also have the Full House Normal, which you can use to showcase a different type of running approach. Once you establish your ground game, you can pass out of the five Singleback sets in this playbook. If you choose to pass from the Gun, there are three formations to choose from: Gun Split Offset (which also has a hidden compressed set), Gun Doubles On, and Gun Spread. We really like the versatility of this playbook.

OFFENSIVE FORMATIONS

FORMATION	# OF PLAYS
Full House Normal	12
Gun Doubles On	12
Gun Split Offset	21
Gun Spread	18
I-Form Pro	24
I-Form Tight Pair	15
Singleback Ace	24
Singleback Ace Twins	15
Singleback Flex	21
Singleback Wing Trio	12
Singleback Y-Trips	21
Strong Pro	18
Weak Tight Twins	9
Wildcat Normal	3

OFFENSIVE PLAY COUNTS

PLAY TYPE	# OF PLAYS
Quick Pass	13
Standard Pass	61
Shotgun Pass	34
Play Action Pass	47
Outside Handoff	13
Pitch	6
Counter	8
Draw	7

I-Form Pro—Inside Zone

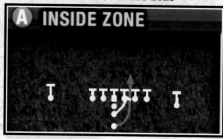

One of the staple run plays from the I-Form Pro formation is the Inside Zone. This year it is still a very effective run play. With this play we are going to motion the flanker receiver over to provide additional blocking. Also, doing this tells us if the defense is in man or zone coverage.

The quarterback hands the ball off

The center and the right guard double-team the defensive tackle while the fullback leads the way up inside the hole. The ball carrier then looks to run up inside between the right tackle and the right gaurd. This zone blocking scheme is designed to create double-team blocks.

The running back sees a hole and uses his speed to burst through it

Once the running back gets through the hole, he runs over a defender and picks up some tough yards. We have solid blocking up front, which creates a nice running lane for the running back. This really helps to make this play successful.

I-Form Pro—Stretch

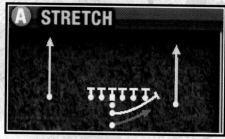

Stretch from the I-Form Pro formation works well in combination with the Inside Zone. This is a zone-blocking scheme designed to give the running back the option of cutting inside or bouncing it outside. Every offense can benefit from this type of run scheme; it is widely used in the NFL today by many teams.

The quarterback stretches out and hands the ball off to his runner

This zone-blocking scheme is designed for double teams by the right guard and center. The tight end and right tackle look to do the same. The runner has to see the hole and wastes no time running through it.

The runner sees a hole and bursts through it

With the ball in his hand, he picks up a little tough yardage inside before being tackled. Consider using motion on this play just as with the Inside Zone, giving the defense the same look. Counting the defensive front is also a plus when using this play. If you see an overload, flip the play and run to the other side.

I-Form Pro—Corner Strike

The run plays we have been throwing at the defense really make the Corner Strike work well. We give the defense the same look with this pass play by motioning the flanker. Note that this play is a formation audible, so you don't have to pick it at the Play Call screen. Before we snap the ball, we are going to hot route the flanker on a slant route.

The QB notices the defense is playing zone

The circle route out of the backfield is the primary option. The other key route to look out for is the flat route that the tight end runs. After that, turn your attention to the flanker running the slant route. The quarterback sees his target and throws the ball.

The pass is completed to the running back

The runner gets into the open field for a 5-yard gain before being tackled. You might also consider putting the split end on a slant route; this gives you another option. You can mix this play in with the play action plays from this formation to develop a nice little series.

Weak Tight Twins—Spacing

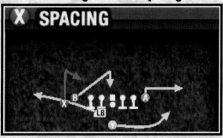

Using a compression formation such as Weak Tight Twins allows you to tell whether the defense is playing man or zone pre-snap. Spacing is one of our favorite plays from this formation because we can make quick reads. On this play, both backs run flat routes while the flanker and the split end run short curls. The tight end is on an out route.

The quarterback reads the coverage as he is standing inside the pocket

Having the flat route and two short routes on one side of the field creates a flood that is very hard for any type of defense to cover. This should be the first area we look for as we go through our progression. The quarterback has his eye on the fullback and throws the ball.

The pass is completed to the fullback

The fullback catches the ball and picks up 5 yards. This scheme is used by many teams in the NFL today.

Gun Spread—Inside Cross

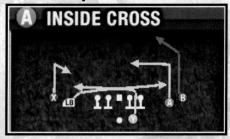

Gun Spread—Inside Cross has the flanker on a streak route as the primary target. We really like the running back's out route and the slot receiver's drag route, which come across the middle of the field.

The QB scans the field and is reading the defense

As you scan the field with the quarterback, notice that against both man and zone coverage the running back and the crossing route will get open. The quarterback sees his target crossing over the middle of the field and gets ready to deliver the ball. Also, notice in the screenshot how you have the running back coming open. There are two good reads right in front of you.

The pass is completed to the running back out of the backfield

Our running back makes the catch for a quick 5 yards. Another suggestion is to hot route the other slot receiver on the right side of the field to a slant route over the middle of the field. Once you do that, you can motion him to give him a running start. This creates a flood over the middle of the field, with three targets in one area.

Gun Split Offset—Deep Comeback

Gun Split Offset—Deep Comeback has the flanker on a deep streak route as the primary target. However, we like to make our backs out of the backfield our primary targets for this scheme. The slot receiver runs a deep post up the seam. We are going to smart route him to make his route shorter, which gives us another option over the middle.

The quarterback is scanning the field for targets

If zone coverage is called look for both routes from the backfield. The fullback usually releases quickly into his route. While you're looking at your backs, keep an eye out for the post route that the slot receiver runs.

The pass is completed to the halfback

The halfback breaks a tackle and picks up an additional 10 yards. These routes by the backs can be very difficult for a defense to cover, even against the man coverage.

Gun Split Offset—Slants Middle

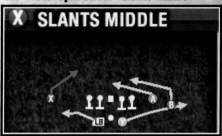

Gun Split Slot—Slants Middle has three receivers running slant routes with two backs on flat routes out of the backfield. With three receivers flooding the middle of the field, this play kills man defense and is very effective against zone defense as well.

The quarterback spots his receiver with inside position

The QB fires the ball over the middle of the field. Take note of the defender blitzing off of the edge; when you see this quickly release the pass to the halfback.

The pass is completed to the slot receiver over the middle of the field

Our slot receiver breaks a tackle and picks up 5 additional yards. Another suggestion is to use motion with this play. This tells you if the defense is in man or zone. If your opponent is playing man coverage, then it's a good idea to throw the ball to one of the backs out of the backfield. Having two backs with speed in the backfield also helps. You can audible to this play from a four-wide-receiver set to get speed in the backfield.

RUN HEAVY PLAYBOOK BREAKDOWN

The Run Heavy playbook is all about playing smashmouth football. Any *Madden NFL* player who likes to pound the ball and manage the clock can do so from all the available run formations in the playbook: I-Form Tight, I-Form Twin TE, Strong I Twin TE, Strong I Normal, and Singleback Twin TE, to name a few formations that you can get your ground game going with. You also have three Singleback Big formations to choose from. All of these sets have plenty of play action plays that you can mix in with all the running plays at your disposal. We particularly like the I-Form Twin TE as the main running formation; there are nine run plays and three play action plays. Another very good run formation is Strong I Twin TE, with plays such as Power O, Toss Strong, and Counter Weak. With the ability to run the ball from all the formations available in this book, you should have no problem playing a ball control offensive approach.

OFFENSIVE FORMATIONS

FORMATION	# OF PLAYS
Full House Wide	9
I-Form Normal	18
I-Form Tight	15
I-Form Twin TE	15
Shotgun Normal Slot	12
Shotgun Wing Trips	15
Singleback 4WR	12
Singleback Big	18
Singleback Big 3TE	15
Singleback Big Twin WR	18
Singleback Trips Bunch	15
Singleback Twin TE	12
Strong I Normal	18
Strong I Twin TE	12
Weak I Twin WR	12

OFFENSIVE PLAY COUNTS

PLAY TYPE	# OF PLAYS
Quick Pass	18
Standard Pass	64
Shotgun Pass	22
Play Action Pass	36
Inside Handoff	54
Outside Handoff	39
Pitch	16
Counter	19

I-Form Twin TE—HB Blast

I-Form Twin TE has been a very popular formation for many years in *Madden NFL*, and with how effective the ground game is this year, it is no different. HB Blast is designed for the halfback to run between the center and left guard. We are going to motion the inside tight end to the right for extra blocking.

The halfback takes the handoff from the quarterback

Ray Rice is waiting for his blocks to set up. He is a patient runner with great vision. He sees a lane developing right in front of him. Rice is following fullback Le'Ron McClain inside the running lane.

McClain makes a key block on a linebacker

Ray Rice takes advantage of this great block and picks up the tough yards. The solid blocking up front is what creates this nice running lane for Rice to run through. The defense will have to respect the threat of giving up these yards. This is smashmouth football at its best.

I-Form Twin TE—HB Sweep

Now that you have the defense worried about the inside running game, it is time to mix in HB Sweep. This play is designed for the left guard to pull outside while the fullback is supposed to block the inside linebacker. We suggest using the Strategy Pad to have the offensive line block to the left.

The quarterback tosses the ball to the halfback

With the ball in your hands, you want to follow the lead of the left guard and your fullback. Look to cut the ball inside or take it outside, depending on how the defense is pursuing.

Left guard Ben Grubbs makes a key block on the linebacker

Ray Rice then uses his speed to turn the corner for a big gain. A versatile back like Rice is very hard for any defense to deal with. You have to be patient when using this play; do not rush outside and outrun your blockers. Another suggestion is to use motion as if you're going to run the ball inside, then snap the ball.

I-Form Tight—HB Power O

The I-Form Tight formation gives us the ability to motion the flanker from one side of the field to the other while flipping our run plays. This concept is very effective when facing a loaded defensive front. HB Power O is the main run play that we like to use from this formation. It really allows us to play smashmouth football. We begin by bringing the flanker in motion and snapping the ball once he is behind the line of scrimmage.

Joe Flacco hands the ball off to Ray Rice

After the snap, we follow the lead of fullback Le'Ron McClain and left guard Ben Grubbs. The halfback has the choice of taking the ball through the interior of the defense or bouncing it outside. Ray Rice has an opening and wastes no time taking advantage of it. The fullback handles the linebacker.

With a nice running lane, Rice uses his speed and turns the corner

He then uses his speed to get away from the linebacker and picks up a big gain downfield.

I-Form Tight—PA Power O

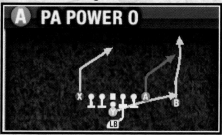

With the defense worrying about the run this is a perfect opportunity to use play action. PA Power O has the tight end running a corner out as the primary target. While the other tight end runs a deep post the flanker has a streak route that pulls the coverage deep. The fullback has a flat route that provides a safety valve for the play.

The quarterback fakes the handoff

We are going to take control of the quarterback and roll outside the pocket so that we can buy time while the tight end runs his route downfield. With this extra time, if the defense bites on the fake there is an opening for the QB to take off. You can choose to do so if there are no open options.

Todd Heap makes the catch downfield

Heap picks up an 18-yard gain, which gets us a first down and keeps the chains moving. It was a mistake leaving the linebacker in coverage with Heap; the defense now has to worry about the run and the pass from this formation.

Strong I Twin TE—FB Dive

FB Dive is still a very effective run from the Strong I Twin TE formation, and is one of the sets we like to get our ground game going with. This play can be deadly in combination with the dual halfback package with Willis McGahee subbed in at fullback. With his power, he can just take it up inside and pick up tough yards.

Joe Flacco hands the ball off to the fullback

To have success running the fullback dive, you have to make a pre-snap read. If you see that the defense is overloading the side that you're running on, flip the play. You must waste no time in bursting through it.

The halfback wastes no time getting into the hole

Willis McGahee is no stranger to contact. He's a very physical runner who can pick up those tough yards inside. Making good pre-snap reads of the defense results in a very effective run play. Now the defense has to worry about the fullback running the ball, which makes it easier to run the other run plays from this set.

Strong I Twin TE—PA FB Flat

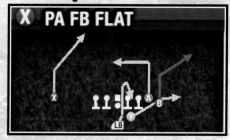

PA FB Flat is our favorite play action play from this formation because it's a fake handoff to the fullback. You get to take control of the quarterback quickly. The play design has the tight end as the primary target. One adjustment we like is to put the inside tight end on a streak; this opens up the underneath for the corner route. We also substitute our best tight end on the outside; in this case, it is Todd Heap.

The quarterback fakes the handoff to the fullback

After the snap, keep an eye out for the fullback in the flat. He's what we call a bailout option. It is good to throw to him if the quarterback feels pressure. Joe Flacco sees his tight end getting separation from the linebacker, and he throws a bullet pass to the corner.

The linebacker is trailing and is out of position

Todd Heap makes the catch for a 15-yard gain.

Gun Wing Trips—Strong Flood

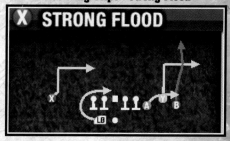

The Run Heavy playbook has only two Shotgun formations. Our favorite of the two is Wing Trips; this has two receivers and one tight end on the right side. Strong Flood is one of the main plays we like to use from this formation because it floods the right side of the field. A deep streak and a 10-yard in route that opens up the flat route underneath flood this area of the field.

The quarterback scans the field and finds his target

Another valuable option on this play while scanning the field is to look for the circle route that the halfback is running from the backfield. His route is very hard for the defense to cover. These two routes are the first two reads for this play; it doesn't matter whether it's man or zone.

The pass is completed to the tight end

Heap then turns the corner and picks up an 8-yard gain before being tackled by the defense.

WEST COAST PLAYBOOK BREAKDOWN

The West Coast Offense was popularized by the late Bill Walsh. He used this offense to win Super Bowls in the 1980s. Quarterbacks such as Brett Favre and Donovan McNabb have had great success with this offense in the NFL today. Using it in *Madden NFL* can be very effective; just like in the NFL, it requires you to make quick decisions because most of the plays are short and quick (usually no longer than 15 yards). The quarterback has to be very accurate. The West Coast playbook has plenty of short, quick passing routes that you can use. With formations such as Near Pro, Far Pro, Far Tight Twins, and Singleback Tight Doubles at your disposal, you have everything that you need to run a successful scheme. You can even apply this concept in I-Form Pro and Weak Flex Twins. This book also has four Gun sets to choose from. Overall, this is a very balanced playbook and you should have no problem coming up with a good offensive scheme.

OFFENSIVE FORMATIONS

FORMATION	# OF PLAYS
Far Pro	12
Far Tight Twins	12
Gun Bunch Wk	15
Gun Empty Trey	9
Gun Snugs Flip	12
Gun Split Offset	21
I-Form Pro	18
I-Form Tight Pair	12
Near Pro	12
Singleback Ace	18
Singleback Bunch Swap	12
Singleback Flex	18
Singleback Spread	15
Singleback Tight Doubles	9
Singleback Y-Trips	18
Weak Flex Twins	15

OFFENSIVE PLAY COUNTS

PLAY TYPE	# OF PLAYS
Quick Pass	20
Standard Pass	110
Shotgun Pass	47
Play Action Pass	33
Inside Handoff	33
Outside Handoff	25
Pitch	10
Counter	9

Near Pro—Texas

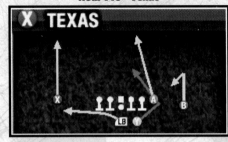

The Near Pro formation has been very popular in the West Coast Offense for many years in the NFL. Texas is one of the staple plays from this formation. The halfback is the primary target on this play. The tight end's route is designed to pull the coverage for the halfback; we suggest putting the split end on a slant route so that we can have a slant or flat combo on the left side of the field. By doing this, we now have three options for the play.

The quarterback scans the field and notices that the defense is playing zone

After the snap look for the heavy halfback first. His circle route will be open against most coverages and is very difficult to cover. After that look left for the fullback and the slant route. As you can see, the defense has dropped back into a Cover 4 coverage. The quarterback sees this and quickly finds his target.

Clinton Portis makes the catch and quickly picks up the 5-yard gain

Near Pro—HB Inside

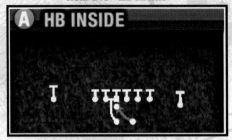

Near Pro—HB Inside is designed for the halfback to run the ball up inside between the left guard and center. With solid blocking up front, the offensive line should create a running lane for the halfback to exploit. We suggest bringing the flanker in motion to provide an extra blocker up front.

The quarterback hands the ball off to the runner

As you take control of the halfback, you should have two running lanes to choose from depending on the defensive front. With that extra blocker (the flanker) in, you should have no problem picking up yards. You must not hesitate in choosing which lane to run through; this is the key for this play to be effective.

Clinton sees the hole and uses his speed to burst through it

He breaks a tackle and picks up a tough 5 yards before being tackled. Another way we like to run this play is to motion the fullback to the right side of the formation and snap the ball once he is behind the right guard and in front of the halfback.

Near Pro—PA Strong Flow

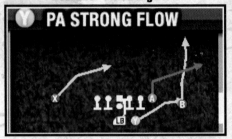

PA Strong Flow works well. The play has the tight end as the primary target while the halfback sneaks out into the flat. The flanker runs a streak route so that the tight end can come open underneath. You also have the split end on a deep crossing route.

The quarterback fakes the handoff to the fullback

After the snap, look for the halfback in the flat area as your first read, because the tight end's corner route takes time to develop. Another option is to take control of the quarterback after the snap and roll outside the pocket. As the quarterback rolls outside of the pocket, he sees his tight end coming open.

Chris Cooley is too fast for the linebacker covering him

Cooley picks up 15 yards downfield. Reading the defensive front is key to knowing when to use the play action play. If you see nine in the box, that's a perfect time to call the play.

Far Tight Twins—Flats

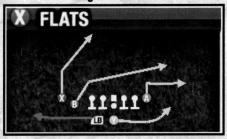

Far Tight Twins is a compression formation used in the West Coast system; it has two receivers lined up on the left side of the formation and the halfback on the left side as well. The Flats play has both running backs going into the flat with a deep post route and a crossing route over the middle of the field, while the tight end runs an in route. The halfback is the primary target on this play. This play is very effective because it requires no adjustments at all.

The quarterback sees the corner blitzing from the edge

After three steps, look over the middle for the crossing route and post if you notice that the defense is dropping back into coverage, then look for the back in the flat. The halfback is open and McNabb throws the ball.

Clinton Portis makes the catch

Portis catches the pass and then uses his speed to turn the corner and pick up 10 yards before he is tackled. If you notice that the defense is playing Cover 2 coverage, look for the deep post route.

Far Tight Twins—Quick Toss

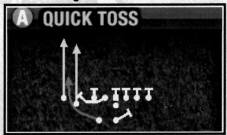

Quick Toss is a run play that is designed to have the left guard pulling outside while both receivers look to seal the edge. This play works very well with the FB Dive from this formation. To have success, this play requires more of a pre-snap read of the defense. If you notice that the defense is playing man, motion the split end to the right. This is very easy to tell because the corners will line up directly in front of the receivers.

The quarterback tosses the ball

With left guard Derrick Dockery out in front, Clinton Portis looks for an opening. If you notice that the defense is overpursuing, look to cut back inside. Portis has great vision and the speed to do so.

Left guard Derrick Dockery throws a key block on a linebacker

Portis uses his speed to pick up 8 yards.

Singleback Tight Doubles—Curl Drag

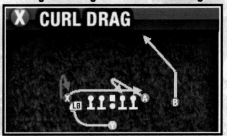

Singleback Tight Doubles has two receivers compressed to the left side of the formation, while the flanker is spread out wide to the right. Curl Drag is a base play that we like to use from this set. The play as designed has two curls with the slot receiver doing a drag across the middle. The split end is the primary target on this play.

The quarterback takes a three-step drop

You have to trust the play's design. Look for the halfback and the flat as your first read, then the middle of the field. This play is very effective against man or zone. McNabb notices that the defense is playing man and fires the ball to his halfback.

The linebacker is a few steps behind

Clinton Portis uses his speed to turn the corner and pick up 10 yards before being tackled.

Singleback Tight Doubles—Stick

Stick gives you a curl and flat combo on one side of the field with a slant and flat combo on the other. For this play, we bring the flanker in motion and snap the ball once he gets next to the tight end. The right side of the formation will be the first step in our progression.

The defense drops back into coverage

McNabb sees his tight end get open quickly in the flat area after the ball is snapped. Chris Cooley ran out to the open area, and McNabb quickly delivers the ball to him.

Cooley makes the catch in the open field

He has space to run after the catch, and he then picks up 8 yards. Now remember, the right side of the field is the first step in your progression for this play. Then, on the other side, the curl and flat combo is also very hard for the defense to stop in man or zone. Reading the defensive alignment pre-snap is a requirement. It is very easy to tell the difference between man and zone.

RUN N GUN PLAYBOOK BREAKDOWN

The Run N Gun playbook has been very popular among *Madden NFL* players for years. This is because the playbook gives you a wide variety of formations to choose from. Whether you are the type of player who likes to pass from the gun or under center, it's all available to you in this playbook. There are five Gun formations; three are spread sets. This playbook also has Gun Tight Flex, which was used by many top *Madden NFL* players last year. Under center, Strong Pro and Strong Tight help you to get your ground game going. You also have Weak Tight Twins and Weak Tight Pair. The Full House Normal Wide has always been a popular formation because of the ability to run and pass from it. In the end, this is a very balanced book that can fit any offensive style because of its versatility. This continues to be one of our favorite playbooks in *Madden NFL*.

OFFENSIVE FORMATIONS

FORMATION	# OF PLAYS
Full House Normal Wide 12	12
Gun Doubles On	12
Gun Empty Trio	12
Gun Spread	18
Gun Tight Flex	12
Gun Trey Open	18
I-Form Pro	18
I-Form Pro Twins	15
Singleback Ace	21
Singleback Ace Twins	15
Singleback Y-Trips	24
Singleback Trips Open	12
Strong Pro	18
Strong Tight	9
Weak Tight Pair	12
Weak Tight Twins	9

OFFENSIVE PLAY COUNTS

PLAY TYPE	# OF PLAYS
Quick Pass	17
Standard Pass	104
Shotgun Pass	55
Play Action Pass	41
Inside Handoff	31
Outside Handoff	23
Pitch	11
Counter	6

Gun Empty Trio—Spacing

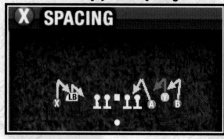

The Gun Empty Trio has five wide receivers spread out wide. This tells us what type of defense we are going to face. Spacing is a play that has five short curl routes. This play design is very effective against a blitzing defense, whether it's man or zone. This play is a quick audible for this formation.

The quarterback scans the field

Quarterback Tony Romo has three options open underneath on the right side of the formation, as you can see in the screenshot. He fires the ball to veteran wide receiver Patrick Crayton. Getting the ball to the right receiver vs. man or zone is the key; it's all about making a quick decision.

Patrick Crayton makes the catch and picks up a quick 5 yards

We suggest mixing up your hot route adjustments by putting one or both of your outside receivers on slant routes or streaks; this adds versatility to the play.

Gun Empty Trio—Stick

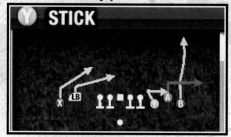

Stick is a play that we like to mix in with Spacing. Slot receiver Patrick Crayton is the primary target on this play, while flanker Roy Williams runs a deep streak that pulls the coverage deep. You also have Sam Hurd running a short out route. The two out routes are designed to flood the right side of the field. On the left side of the field, you have two slant routes, one short and one deep.

The defense is showing man coverage

Quarterback Tony Romo sees the defender out of position and has his eye on his target. It's rookie wide receiver Dez Bryant; he throws him a bullet pass.

The catch is made for 10 yards downfield

You have to know your options when facing an aggressive defense, and you must anticipate where your wide receivers will be located. Any one of the underneath receivers can be your primary target for the play; it's all about making the correct pre-snap read and understanding what coverage the defense is playing.

Gun Trey Open—Strong Flood

Gun Trey Open is a spread formation that is designed with three wide receivers on the right, flooding one side of the field. There is a deep, midrange, and short route combination. The flanker is the primary target; however, we like to use either the flat route or the circle route as our primary option.

The defense is showing man

The quarterback scans the field. The defense drops back into coverage and quarterback Tony Romo has his eye on slot receiver Patrick Crayton. The pass is thrown to the slot receiver in the flat.

The pass is completed

Patrick Crayton makes the catch. He uses his speed to get away from the defender and picks up 5 yards and a first down. Anticipating the slot receiver being open is the key. With the correct timing, you can pick up a big gain.

Gun Tight Flex—WR Cross

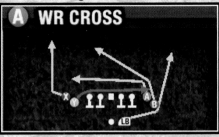

Gun Tight Flex is a formation that has four wide receivers compressed. WR Cross has two crossing routes, a post, and a wheel route out of the backfield that we like to use as our primary options on this play, depending on the coverage we see. This play can be run without any hot route adjustments at all. You can just come to the line and snap the ball—it's what we call a money play.

The defense is showing zone coverage

With a defender blitzing off the edge, the halfback is another option. This is an added advantage to this play. Wide receiver Roy Williams appears to have found a weak spot in the coverage. Quarterback Tony Romo sees him and throws him the ball.

The pass is completed, which results in a 10-yard gain

These reads are simple and quick to make. It doesn't matter if the defense is in man or zone or if they are blitzing.

Strong Tight—Power O

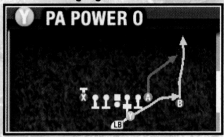

The Strong Pro formation allows you to get that ground game going. This is where we can use our smash football approach. The left guard, Kyle Kosier, pulls to the right side of the formation, while lead blocker Deon Anderson leads the way for halfback Felix Jones. We like the versatility that this play gives you. You can choose to run it up inside behind the right tackle and right guard.

The quarterback hands the ball off

Halfback Felix Jones takes the handoff and is being patient and letting his blocks develop. He sees a hole and uses his speed to burst through it.

Fullback Deon Anderson makes a key block on the linebacker

Jones is no stranger to picking up tough yards inside. A halfback like him is so valuable to his team. Consider bringing the flanker in motion to provide extra blocking. You also should read the defensive alignment pre-snap. If you see nine men in the box, flip the play and run to the other side.

Strong Tight—PA Power O

PA Power O works once you have the defense worried. The play has three receivers out on pass routes. For this play, the tight end is the primary target. The flanker's streak brawl route is designed to pull the coverage deep, and the fullback sneaks out into the flat.

The quarterback fakes the handoff to the halfback

After the snap, look for the fullback in the flats first, and then look for the tight end downfield. Another suggestion is to take control of the quarterback and roll out to the right. This gives you the option to take off running or to throw the ball away if there's nobody open. Tony Romo spots his tight end downfield and throws a bullet pass.

Jason Witten makes the catch for 15 yards

A skilled tight end like Jason Witten is very hard for linebackers to cover. This is why he is an All-Pro player. This play can pick up big chunks of yards if the defense is overplaying the run.

Full House Normal Wide—Slants

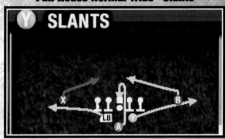

Full House Normal Wide—Slants has two flat routes out of the backfield with a curl route. The split end is the primary target on display. Because you have a flat route coming out of the backfield and a slant route, you have a nice combination that allows you to read the field one half at a time.

The quarterback sees his target

The quarterback fires the ball to wide receiver Miles Austin. Notice how we have the fullback open in the flats as well. This combination forces the defense to overcompensate in coverage.

Miles Austin makes the catch for a quick 5 yards

Sometimes, if the defense blitzes and it's man coverage, you will have a big gain after the catch. With someone like Miles Austin, you can take it the distance for a TD. One way that we like to disguise this play pre-snap is to use motion to keep them guessing about whether we are going to run the ball. This sometimes opens up the field.

MADDEN FRANCHISE MODE

Contents

Thirty-two franchises want it

Franchise mode was made for the *Madden NFL* player who simply can't get enough football just playing online or Play Now games. This mode puts you totally in the driver's seat, allowing you to make every decision on and off the field. On the weekdays, you decide if you are going to build the new suites overlooking the 50-yard line to bring in higher revenue tickets, or if you are going to re-sign your quarterback to a huge multi-year contract. When Sunday rolls around you will lead your team to victory on the field. Franchise mode is a very complex mode that goes well past just playing *Madden NFL*, and this section covers some keys to running a successful franchise.

Let's get started on making a franchise that will dominate for many years to come. There are two ways to play Franchise mode: The first option is to simulate a Fantasy Draft and select your entire team one player at a time. The other option is to choose a team and play with its current roster and salary cap. Both of these are great ways to play Franchise mode, and they lend themselves to completely different styles of play.

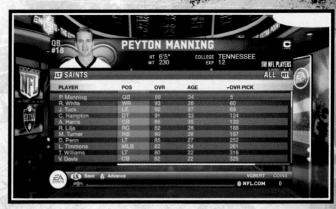

Now Peyton can wear his dad's jersey

FANTASY DRAFT

Ever wish that you could start your own NFL franchise from scratch? Well, now you can with Fantasy Draft. Fantasy Draft allows you to simulate a draft with every NFL player available for you to choose from. This gives you the chance to build your franchise any way you want to. You can build your team around one of today's elite quarterbacks or see if you can make a legend out of a rookie QB. Have fun with the draft; it's probably the only time in your life that you are going to get to spend $155,000,000. Let's dive into the workings of Fantasy Draft and see if we can prepare you to build a great team.

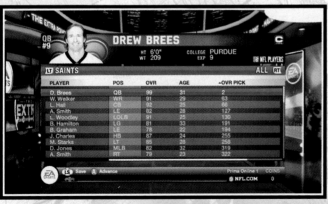

Can Brees lead this team to the Super Bowl again?

You can pick any player who is still on the board at any time, but remember that you need to fill all of the required roster spots to field a team. Don't get too carried away with picking a specific position round after round. The "Position Requirements" chart shows how many spots at each position need to be filled.

POSITION REQUIREMENTS	
Position	Number
Quarterback (QB)	3
Halfback (HB)	3
Fullback (FB)	1
Wide Receiver (WR)	4
Tight End (TE)	2
Offensive Tackle (LT, RT)	4
Offensive Guard (LG, RG)	4
Center (C)	2
Defensive End (LE, RE)	4

POSITION REQUIREMENTS	
Position	Number
Defensive Tackle (DT)	3
Outside Linebacker (LOLB, ROLB)	4
Middle Linebacker (MLB)	2
Cornerback (CB)	4
Free Safety (FS)	2
Strong Safety (SS)	2
Kicker (K)	1
Punter (P)	1

Rodgers is a great QB for the price

Now that we know how many positions we have to fill, we can start to think about putting these positions into a priority list. Each player's priority will vary based on how he or she plays. Make sure that you draft based on how you play. If you are a ground-and-pound player, focus more on landing good halfbacks and offensive linemen. If you like to put the ball in the air more, then go after a quarterback first and focus on wide receivers. The "Draft Priority Example" table offers some guidelines.

DRAFT PRIORITY EXAMPLE

Round	Position	Notes
1	Quarterback	The QB is the captain on the field. Look for a QB who has good arm strength and is accurate with at least short and medium passes.
2	Defensive End	A dominating DE with a lot of speed can kill an offense in the backfield all game long.
3	Cornerback	A lock-down CB can make getting pressure on the QB a lot easier, and you can also double-team other receivers on the field.
4	Halfback	Having a good back who can rack up yards on the ground and catch balls out of the backfield can make a QB's job a lot easier.
5	Wide Receiver	A WR who has good hands and speed can stretch the field. Look for a mixture of speed WRs and possession WRs.
6	Offensive Tackle	With a high-rated OT guarding your QB's backside, you can sit in the pocket much longer and find open receivers down the field.
7	Offensive Guard	With the improved run-blocking in this year's game, a great OG can make huge holes in the D-line and can flatten safeties on pulling plays.
8	Defensive Tackle	A big, powerful DT can plug the middle of the line and stop an opponent's running game.
9	Defensive End	Seal the other side of your defensive line with another DE.
10	Offensive Tackle	The better your line is, the easier it is to run the ball.
11	Middle Linebacker	The leader of the defense is usually the MLB. They can plug gaps to stop running backs as well as drop back in coverage.

DRAFT PRIORITY EXAMPLE

Round	Position	Notes
12	Center	The core of every offensive line is the center. Look to find a good one.
13	Offensive Guard	Secure a strong, big offensive line with this pick.
14	Wide Receiver	The better your number two option is in the passing game, the easier it is to move the ball down the field.
15	Tight End	The most versatile players on the field, TEs are asked to do many things, so look for a well-rounded TE for your team.
16	Free Safety	Look for a speedy FS to cover as much of the field as possible.
17	Cornerback	Another solid CB can help against three- and four-wide sets.
18	Halfback	Two-headed running attacks can keep a drive alive all game long.
19	Strong Safety	A hard-hitting SS can bring the pain if your opponents try to go long.
20	Outside Linebacker	Look for fast OLBs to run down HBs out of the backfield and cover the flats.

These are just a few ideas to think about when drafting your team. The biggest key is to draft to the strengths of your personal game first. After the first 20 rounds, you only have 30 left! Your goals should be to fill the needed slots in your roster and try to save some money. The more cap room you have, the easier it will be to pick up a player from another team. If you drain your salary cap on the draft, it's going to be hard to keep everyone around at the end of the year.

Finding Hidden Gems in a Draft

Sometimes, the difference between a team that doesn't make the playoffs and a team that wins the Super Bowl is the depth of the team. Every year there are breakout players who take their team to the next level. Here are a few tips to help you find a great player in the middle of the draft.

- Rule #1—Don't be afraid to draft a rookie. They may have lower attributes, but you can count on them for many years to come.

- Rule #2—Look deep into rosters to find players with speed. They can be used in different positions and still be effective.

- Rule #3—Sometimes you can find a player who was hurt in the previous year. This lowers his overall rating due to a lack of games, but he may still be a great player.

- Rule #4—Tight ends are a great place to kill two birds with one stone. A good TE can block well and give your QB a quality target.

PLAYING WITH A CURRENT TEAM

A great player to lead a team

If you don't feel like going through the process of drafting an entire team, you can always start off with a current franchise. You will be controlling the exact team that you see on the field on Sundays. Hit the field with the Super Bowl champion New Orleans Saints, or see if you can get the Vikings back to the top of the league.

There are two ways of playing this mode out. You can pick a team like the Vikings that is well established in the league and has a great group of players. This team is ready right now to go back to the playoffs, without any changes to the roster. This is a team that has a great ground game with Peterson and a legendary quarterback in Favre on the offensive side of the field. Their defense, led by Jared Allen, is also one of the best in the league.

Looking for two more wins this year

When you take on a franchise like this, you have to work hard to keep the team intact and try to bring the Lombardi trophy home. You have fewer than four million dollars in salary cap to work with, so you will have to be very smart with your cap to keep this team going for years to come. Teams like the Vikings that are on top of their divisions year after year are fun to play with but hard to keep up. Here are a few rules to follow when playing with one of these powerhouse franchises.

- Rule #1—Make sure that you have a younger player on your roster who can fill a key player's spot if he is getting close to retiring.
- Rule #2—Make sure that you are not spending too much money on non-starters. This can lead to you not being able to re-sign starters.
- Rule #3—Don't be afraid to give up your draft picks to acquire the specific positions that need to be filled.

If you are looking for more of a challenge in Franchise mode, try picking a team that is lower on the list of big market teams. Look at a team like the Panthers—they are a young team that has a lot of question marks on their roster. The Panthers have two things going for them: a good rookie QB and a lot of salary cap room to bring players into the system. It may take a few seasons,

Can this team recover this year?

but with young players and a boatload of cash, a team like this can be a team to fear after a few seasons. Here are a few rules that will help you turn a franchise like this around.

- Rule #1—Find your team's strengths and build directly around them.
- Rule #2—Make sure that you use all of your draft picks to bring in needed players.
- Rule #3—Go after a big-time player who will give your team a huge boost.

Key Free Agents

There's talent here

This year's free agency class is one of the best that we have seen in a few years. There are no superstars on this list that you are going to build a franchise around, but there are a few good players who can come in and be very productive. Free agents can help you get through a year while you are waiting for a rookie to mature. You always have to be careful when picking up a free agent; there is usually a reason why they were not signed by their former team. Players like Brian Westbrook and Terrell Owens are highly rated *Madden NFL* players who could be very productive for your team. On the other side of the ball, a player like Keith Bulluck can still plug the gaps and keep teams from putting points up on you. Let's look at a few rules to follow through free agency.

- Rule #1—Rarely sign a free agent to a multi-year contract. If they are productive in their first season, you can re-sign them.

- Rule #2—Try to sign younger players. This will take away the chance of the player retiring after one season on your team.

- Rule #3—Always start out with a low offer; if the player turns your offer down go a little higher.

- Rule #4—Only sign players where you have a hole in your roster, unless you are in great need of a player.

Added talent to the wide receivers

TEAM INCOME

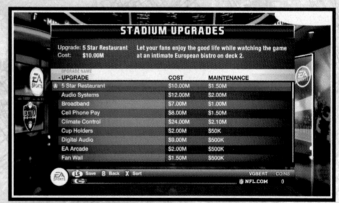

Money coming and going

Now we have to take time off the field and get back behind the desk to do some paperwork. At the end of the day, to be a successful franchise you have to bring in revenue. This can be done many different ways.

First you can look to raise or lower prices on tickets, food, and merchandise at your stadium. If your team just came off of a great season, raise prices a little. There is no doubt that fans will want to come to games the following year, and you will be there to take their tickets at the gate. If you didn't end up with a good record and you missed the playoffs, you may want to lower your prices, hoping to draw more fans to your stadium next year.

Upgrades can bring the money in

Player salaries are another place where you can save some money. Sometimes players just don't develop the way we thought they would, and they need to be cut from the team or traded. Look at your team contracts to see where most of your salary is being spent, then look at a player's stats and determine if cuts need to be made. Just watch out for cutting players that count against your salary cap.

The money men

How the money spreads out

Needing sponsorship

Making the big deal

Sponsorships and TV contracts are the best way to bring money into your organization. Large companies will pay a lot of money to sponsor your team's stadium. This is a great way to keep your numbers in the black at the end of the season. If you are building a young up-and-coming team, you may not want to sign a multi-year sponsorship. You don't want to be tied into a contract at the end of the upcoming year, when an even bigger company would be willing to give you more sponsorship money. TV contracts, on the other hand, are a great way to get your team in the public eye more. This will lead to more sponsorship opportunities. These are all great ways to help you run a successful franchise.

COACHING SCHEME

Those who love the workings of Franchise mode but do not intend to play any games are going to want to go into Coaching Schemes and move a few sliders. This will help the CPU control your team better and produce more wins. There are two sections in the coaching scheme: The first is philosophy and the second is strategy. Move the sliders to best match your player personnel. If you have a great QB and receiving corps think about passing more. If your team has a two-headed monster in the backfield with two great running backs you may want to share their carries. This will keep both of them fresh throughout the season and keep them from being injured. The other side of the coach's scheme is strategy. Break down each position on your roster and move the sliders to best reflect those positions. Changing these sliders to best mirror your roster will give your team the best chance of winning simmed games.

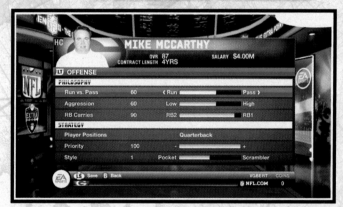

Sim your way to the Super Bowl

All of the hard work pays off

ROSTER ATTRIBUTES

Offensive Player List

CENTERS (C)

OVR	First Name	Last Name	Run Block Strength	Run Block Footwork	Pass Block Strength	Pass Block Footwork
97	Nick	Mangold	96	92	93	93
92	Andre	Gurode	96	87	92	77
92	Jeff	Saturday	85	89	91	96
91	Sean	O'Hara	92	88	93	92
91	Matt	Birk	89	95	83	90
90	Ryan	Kalil	88	97	82	89
89	Jason	Brown	95	89	87	80
88	Dan	Koppen	82	88	86	96
87	Alex	Mack	93	89	87	81
87	Jake	Grove	94	92	81	83
87	Tood	McClure	82	95	78	88
86	Nick	Hardwick	86	88	86	87
86	Jeff	Faine	84	85	84	90
86	Olin	Kreutz	83	81	89	85
85	Casey	Weigmann	85	91	82	89
84	Kevin	Mawae	88	85	85	74
84	Eric	Heitmann	93	89	88	75
83	Dominic	Raiola	82	87	80	85
81	Justin	Hartwig	86	82	85	84
81	Jonathan	Goodwin	85	81	89	91
80	Eugene	Amano	88	86	83	72
79	Samson	Satele	85	81	83	76
79	Chris	Spencer	85	88	76	88
79	Jamaal	Jackson	88	75	84	72
78	Uche	Nwaneri	92	85	86	74
78	Hank	Fraley	88	75	82	71
78	Brad	Meester	87	79	79	70
77	Kyle	Cook	89	88	83	81
77	John	Sullivan	83	85	79	82
76	Scott	Wells	76	79	72	82
76	Maurkice	Pouncey	76	79	72	82
75	Nick	Cole	92	69	83	60
74	Joe	Berger	87	79	80	72
74	Chris	Meyers	75	85	76	80
74	Geoff	Hangartner	85	80	82	78
74	Sean	Mahan	83	81	76	72
74	Melvin	Fowler	82	77	77	74
74	Casey	Rabach	75	77	79	83
73	Steve	Vallos	85	78	82	74
73	Scott	Mruczkowski	77	75	85	86
73	Brett	Romberg	77	82	78	83
72	Lyle	Sendlein	78	74	80	84
71	Kory	Lichtensteiger	85	80	79	70
71	Andy	Alleman	72	78	77	80
71	Rudy	Niswanger	84	83	69	76
71	Chris	Morris	83	85	74	78
70	David	Hale	82	82	81	80
70	Cody	Wallace	82	74	79	70
70	Steve	Justice	74	79	74	85

Fullbacks (FB)

OVR	First Name	Last Name	Speed	Run Block	Pass Block	Catching
94	Tony	Richardson	75	67	55	75
91	Lousaka	Polite	75	85	60	64
90	Leonard	Weaver	79	62	55	82
90	Le'Ron	McClain	79	70	50	70
88	Lawrence	Vickers	73	72	50	66
88	Ovie	Mughelli	71	74	48	66
86	Madison	Hedgecock	67	76	60	63
85	Mike	Karney	74	67	51	74
84	Ahmard	Hall	76	72	60	67
84	Greg	Jones	78	62	50	65
84	Mike	Sellers	70	67	62	79
82	Heath	Evans	77	59	60	72
80	Sammy	Morris	82	51	53	75
78	Jerome	Felton	73	67	55	75
78	Jason	McKie	67	65	55	59
78	Earnest	Graham	79	60	55	72
78	B.J.	Askew	75	67	55	72
77	Peyton	Hillis	84	57	61	70
77	Owen	Schmitt	73	62	44	55
77	Vonta	Leach	62	66	52	75
77	Dan	Kreider	63	74	50	55
77	Moran	Norris	65	74	48	64
77	Terrelle	Smith	64	78	58	52
76	Naufahu	Tahi	78	70	59	62
76	Deon	Anderson	73	66	47	72
75	Justin	Griffith	74	58	50	75
75	Carey	Davis	77	58	44	76
74	Mike	Tolbert	81	64	50	78
74	Jacob	Hester	79	60	50	78
74	Oren	O'Neal	70	73	40	56
73	John	Kuhn	71	60	52	69
73	Jeremi	Johnson	66	68	52	56
72	Korey	Hall	74	68	48	66
70	Gijon	Robinson	72	65	55	68
70	Jason	Davis	84	52	46	80
70	Corey	McIntyre	75	65	52	68
70	Mike	Cox	70	68	52	60
70	Verron	Haynes	81	54	50	66
68	Fui	Vakapuna	73	58	50	64
68	Montell	Owens	80	58	55	65
68	Jacob	Tamme	79	52	54	84
68	Kyle	Eckel	73	57	52	64
68	Gary	Russell	84	40	50	68
67	John	Conner	72	66	59	53
66	Quinn	Johnson	70	72	55	46
66	Tony	Fiammetta	82	64	62	55
65	Justin	Green	72	62	56	70
63	Chris	Pressley	70	64	54	61
63	Billy	Latsko	70	66	48	68
61	Byron	Storer	78	60	50	70

HALFBACKS (HB)

OVR	First Name	Last Name	Speed	Agility	Trucking	Elusiveness
99	Chris	Johnson	99	97	77	97
98	Adrian	Peterson	97	98	97	98
96	Maurice	Jones-Drew	94	96	88	93
95	Steven	Jackson	87	87	95	80
93	Frank	Gore	93	92	86	90
92	DeAngelo	Williams	94	97	70	96
90	Ray	Rice	89	96	74	92
90	Michael	Turner	87	82	97	69
89	Ronnie	Brown	92	92	76	85
89	Cedric	Benson	89	86	94	76
88	Jonathan	Stewart	90	86	94	77
88	Ryan	Grant	88	83	94	72
88	Thomas	Jones	87	87	87	78
87	Jamaal	Charles	97	96	64	97
87	Rashard	Mendenhall	89	84	93	75
87	Ricky	Williams	87	86	90	70
86	Matt	Forte	89	87	77	82
86	Joseph	Addai	90	96	64	88
85	Clinton	Portis	87	88	76	84
84	Pierre	Thomas	86	85	88	72
84	Brandon	Jacobs	85	82	96	62
84	Marion	Barber	84	83	88	69
83	Felix	Jones	96	93	64	93
83	Fred	Jackson	88	87	86	72
83	Regie	Bush	97	99	65	93
83	Jerome	Harrison	92	95	52	97
83	Willis	McGahee	86	84	88	62
83	Brian	Westbrook	91	90	55	85
83	LaDanian	Tomlinson	87	87	78	74
82	Knowshon	Moreno	88	97	76	87
82	Beanie	Wells	89	85	92	74
81	Marshawn	Lynch	87	83	88	70
81	Darren	Sproles	95	98	52	95
81	Larry	Johnson	85	79	90	64
80	Kevin	Smith	86	83	85	68
80	Leon	Washington	93	94	53	93
80	Shonn	Greene	86	85	91	65
79	Tim	Hightower	84	76	87	66
79	Lesean	McCoy	93	96	58	91
79	Chester	Taylor	86	89	65	87
79	C.J.	Spiller	95	95	59	92
78	Steve	Slaton	93	95	57	92
78	Ahmad	Bradshaw	93	95	65	87
78	Laurence	Maroney	86	78	87	63
78	Donald	Brown	89	88	77	74
78	Correll	Buckhalter	87	82	79	68
77	Tashard	Choice	87	89	65	85
77	Darren	McFadden	94	87	81	75
77	Michael	Bush	84	82	85	64
77	Mike	Bell	85	78	88	64

LEFT GUARDS (LG)

OVR	First Name	Last Name	Run Block Strength	Run Block Footwork	Pass Block Strength	Pass Block Footwork
97	Steve	Hutchinson	98	94	90	82
95	Logan	Mankins	97	90	87	82
94	Ben	Grubbs	96	93	89	87
93	Kris	Dielman	95	87	91	83
91	Carl	Nicks	90	88	93	87
91	Eric	Steinbach	94	89	89	82
91	Alan	Faneca	94	87	85	72
89	Todd	Herremans	90	85	92	88
85	Justin	Blalock	95	87	86	75
85	Jacob	Bell	87	89	79	82
85	Brian	Waters	94	80	85	69
83	Justin	Smiley	80	84	84	86
83	Travelle	Wharton	84	88	83	90
83	Mike	Iupati	94	85	85	65
82	Rob	Sims	87	75	91	82
82	Robert	Gallery	92	85	80	64
81	Ben	Hamilton	82	90	75	79
80	Derrick	Dockery	94	82	83	65
80	Kyle	Kosier	85	83	82	75
80	Rich	Seubert	89	80	84	74
80	Jason	Spitz	84	87	78	85
80	Chester	Pitts	82	86	79	82
79	Chris	Kemoeatu	96	77	87	67
79	Andy	Levitre	84	86	85	87
78	Kasey	Studdard	87	79	85	74
78	Leroy	Harris	89	84	85	75
78	David	Baas	87	89	80	69
78	Russ	Hochstein	86	83	82	78
77	Nate	Livings	90	85	85	75
77	Jeremy	Zuttah	85	79	81	69
77	Arron	Sears	88	78	84	73
77	Frank	Omiyale	80	67	91	80
77	Langston	Walker	89	73	85	65
77	Kynan	Forney	83	77	81	69
77	Maurice	Williams	90	84	81	62
76	Mike	Pollak	75	82	82	86
75	Evan	Mathis	75	85	74	85
75	T.J.	Lang	88	86	79	74
75	Jamar	Nesbit	79	78	81	78
75	Vladimir	Ducasse	91	74	92	69
75	Jon	Asamoah	83	86	77	82
73	Mark	Setterstorm	73	88	73	86
72	Josh	Beekman	84	80	82	72
72	Cory	Procter	84	75	79	69
72	Rex	Hadnot	84	74	78	67
72	Wade	Smith	79	75	76	69
71	Jamey	Richard	82	75	80	71
71	Seth	McKinney	80	69	80	73
70	Kevin	Boothe	87	69	77	65
70	Daryn	Colledge	68	84	73	82

LEFT TACKLES (LT)

OVR	First Name	Last Name	Run Block Strength	Run Block Footwork	Pass Block Strength	Pass Block Footwork
98	Ryan	Clady	88	97	99	99
96	Jake	Long	97	94	96	92
95	Joe	Thomas	86	93	95	98
95	Michael	Roos	94	96	93	93
95	Jordan	Gross	90	95	92	96
91	D'Brickashaw	Ferguson	89	96	88	94
91	Jammal	Brown	92	86	96	92
90	Bryant	McKinnie	98	96	93	73
89	Marcus	McNeil	84	87	93	97
89	Michael	Oher	98	95	95	84
89	Matt	Light	88	90	90	86
88	Andrew	Whitworth	97	96	91	82
88	Jason	Peters	97	90	90	74
87	Sam	Baker	89	86	94	92
87	Joe	Staley	86	93	87	91
85	Donald	Penn	92	88	88	86
85	Max	Starks	96	88	90	74
84	David	Diehl	91	86	87	77
84	Chad	Clifton	83	76	92	87
83	Charlie	Johnson	86	76	91	85
83	Jason	Smith	86	89	88	90
83	Tra	Thomas	89	78	90	80
82	Chris	Williams	82	85	86	89
82	Russell	Okung	82	88	86	95
81	Eugene	Monroe	81	86	87	93
81	Mike	Gandy	85	79	88	82
80	Doug	Free	80	84	83	91
80	Jeff	Backus	88	78	89	79
80	Flozell	Adams	96	82	85	64
80	Trent	Williams	91	85	89	79
80	Orlando	Pace	83	74	90	80
79	Duane	Brown	84	79	91	83
79	Anthony	Collins	89	86	85	79
79	Mario	Henderson	78	85	84	90
79	Levi	Brown	87	80	89	78
79	Sebastian	Vollmer	79	84	88	91
78	Branden	Albert	82	88	78	82
78	Bryant	Bulaga	80	88	84	90
77	Alex	Barron	81	83	86	84
76	Barry	Sims	84	79	84	74
76	William	Beatty	77	86	85	92
76	Levi	Jones	85	87	85	72
75	Jermon	Bushrod	76	83	84	87
75	Kwame	Harris	81	84	85	80
74	Demetrius	Bell	79	84	80	86
74	Charles	Brown	83	87	84	88
74	Ephraim	Salaam	80	80	81	85
72	Tony	Ugoh	83	78	81	72
72	Bruce	Campbell	85	78	85	90
71	Herb	Taylor	73	85	79	85

QUARTERBACKS (QB)

OVR	First Name	Last Name	Throwing Power	Short Throw Accuracy	Med. Throw Accuracy	Deep Throw Accuracy
99	Drew	Brees	88	99	98	92
99	Peyton	Manning	95	98	98	88
95	Tom	Brady	94	93	91	89
94	Aaron	Rodgers	94	93	89	86
94	Philip	Rivers	88	96	95	91
92	Brett	Favre	95	88	87	84
90	Tony	Romo	88	92	89	83
89	Matt	Schaub	88	94	92	81
89	Eli	Manning	89	89	87	85
89	Donovan	McNabb	96	72	83	87
88	Ben	Roethlisberger	93	85	82	76
87	Joe	Flacco	96	87	85	80
87	Carson	Palmer	94	89	85	82
86	Matt	Ryan	88	89	84	82
83	Jay	Cutler	97	82	79	77
83	Jason	Campbell	92	85	78	79
82	Mark	Sanchez	89	87	85	75
80	Kyle	Orton	80	88	84	77
80	Matthew	Stafford	97	81	76	80
80	Sam	Bradford	87	95	87	72
79	Chad	Henne	94	81	78	78
79	Vince	Young	89	81	76	72
79	David	Garrard	88	82	78	72
79	Matt	Hasselbeck	85	85	75	62
78	Matt	Cassel	85	93	73	58
78	Chad	Pennington	69	96	83	64
77	Alex	Smith	85	81	79	76
77	Josh	Freeman	96	79	80	76
76	Matt	Moore	87	81	75	82
75	Kevin	Kolb	86	82	79	79
75	Matt	Leinart	86	85	87	68
74	Marc	Bulger	82	87	76	68
74	Jimmy	Clausen	90	91	78	79
74	Jake	Delhomme	83	76	73	75
73	Michael	Vick	92	72	64	67
72	Seneca	Wallace	78	79	70	71
72	Kerry	Collins	88	80	72	71
71	Robert	You	94	87	77	72
71	Brady	Quinn	86	77	72	67
71	Tavaris	Jackson	94	69	66	69
71	Charlie	Whitehurst	88	78	80	64
71	Colt	McCoy	79	88	84	65
71	Daunte	Culpepper	90	70	67	66
70	Trent	Edwards	81	87	72	54
70	Kellen	Clemens	88	80	74	64
70	Ryan	Fitzpatrick	76	84	74	56
70	Luke	McCown	85	78	73	67
70	Shaun	Hill	75	87	77	60
70	Tim	Tebow	88	74	70	79
69	Byron	Leftwich	93	77	72	67

QUARTERBACKS (QB)

OVR	First Name	Last Name	Throwing Power	Short Throw Accuracy	Med. Throw Accuracy	Deep Throw Accuracy
69	Josh	McCown	78	75	79	66
69	Sage	Rosenfels	85	86	83	62
69	Chris	Redman	77	86	78	55
68	Jon	Kitna	85	76	68	66
68	Josh	Johnson	89	70	72	65
68	Chris	Simms	87	76	70	69
67	Troy	Smith	86	68	67	66
67	Bruce	Gradowski	77	86	77	46
67	Derek	Anderson	95	72	69	70
67	Billy	Volek	81	77	65	84
67	Charlie	Batch	80	79	74	55
66	Pat	White	85	79	72	62
66	J.P.	Losman	93	65	66	73
66	Kyle	Boller	90	71	64	69
66	A.J.	Feeley	85	75	72	68
66	Dan	Lefevour	86	81	75	58
65	Brian	Brohm	84	79	75	63
65	Brodie	Croyle	88	73	67	71
65	Charlie	Frye	77	80	74	55
65	Nate	Davis	93	83	77	69
65	Rex	Grossman	90	76	64	67
65	David	Carr	87	66	70	72
65	Mike	Kafka	79	87	77	55
65	Tony	Pike	89	85	74	64
64	Caleb	Hanie	83	74	72	62
64	Dennis	Dixon	84	69	68	67
64	Tyler	Thigpen	80	70	68	65
64	Jonathan	Crompton	94	76	73	71
64	Sean	Canfield	82	88	74	52
63	Dan	Orlovsky	78	77	71	64
63	Brian	Hoyer	87	76	68	56
63	Levi	Brown	87	83	81	64
62	Jamarcus	Russell	97	64	61	62
62	Stephen	McGee	82	74	68	61
62	Chase	Daniel	83	76	74	59
62	John	Skelton	96	74	72	70
61	Mike	Teel	79	79	76	62
61	Drew	Stanton	83	73	68	70
61	Rhett	Bomar	90	75	72	69
61	Curtis	Painter	87	83	77	67
60	Keith	Null	89	75	68	72
60	John	Parker Wilson	80	84	56	47
60	Tom	Brandstater	82	80	74	62
60	J.T.	O'Sullivan	79	77	68	48
59	Colt	Brennan	78	86	73	60
59	Jim	Sorgi	68	82	70	40
59	Zac	Robinson	82	82	66	54
58	Kevin	O'Connell	85	75	64	49
58	Matt	Gutierrez	83	74	76	49
58	John	Beck	78	79	70	49

RIGHT GUARDS (RG)

OVR	First Name	Last Name	Run Block Strength	Run Block Footwork	Pass Block Strength	Pass Block Footwork
98	Jhari	Evans	95	94	97	94
96	Chris	Snee	95	92	93	91
89	Leonard	Davis	99	86	88	67
88	Davin	Joseph	92	86	87	82
88	Brandon	Moore	95	91	87	81
88	Bobbie	Williams	97	88	86	74
87	Harvey	Dahl	95	90	87	82
85	Jake	Scott	79	85	85	86
83	Louis	Vasquez	97	85	92	78
83	Stephen	Neal	85	82	84	79
83	Randy	Thomas	84	86	84	82
82	Chris	Kuper	80	88	83	87
82	Ryan	Lilja	78	83	84	89
81	Adam	Snyder	92	87	82	76
81	Eric	Wood	86	83	82	77
80	Marshal	Yanda	83	85	79	80
80	Stacy	Andrews	95	75	83	61
80	Reggie	Wells	81	84	84	76
80	Mike	Williams	97	77	85	62
79	Chilo	Rachal	91	85	82	66
79	Max	Unger	89	82	82	76
79	Roberto	Garza	78	80	87	89
78	Josh	Sitton	85	84	83	74
78	Stephen	Peterman	89	75	80	70
78	Cooper	Carlisle	75	84	77	85
77	Mike	Goff	83	78	80	74
77	Trai	Essex	82	73	88	87
76	Mackenzy	Bernadeau	93	80	88	66
76	Nate	Garner	90	78	77	64
76	Chris	Chester	81	87	74	80
76	Deuce	Lutui	86	86	80	80
76	Richie	Incognito	89	81	78	63
76	Adam	Goldberg	82	72	84	73
76	Vince	Manuwai	91	78	83	57
76	Kendall	Simmons	87	79	80	66
76	Floyd	Womack	96	70	86	62
75	John	Greco	84	78	81	76
75	Donald	Thomas	88	72	77	62
74	Shawn	Murphy	84	80	78	65
74	Keydrick	Vincent	90	80	79	60
73	Antoine	Caldwell	88	81	77	66
72	Kyle	Devan	88	83	81	65
72	Chad	Rinehart	86	81	79	75
72	Max	Jean-Gilles	94	75	87	57
72	Adrian	Jones	79	75	80	70
71	Mike	Brisiel	79	82	79	78
71	Montrae	Holland	86	65	80	62
70	Drew	Miller	82	78	80	80
70	Paul	McQuistan	90	67	82	61
70	Junius	Coston	85	73	78	67

RIGHT TACKLES (RT)

OVR	First Name	Last Name	Run Block Strength	Run Block Footwork	Pass Block Strength	Pass Block Footwork
90	Jon	Stitchcomb	92	85	94	92
89	David	Stewart	97	95	90	80
89	Damien	Woody	94	91	89	82
86	Jeff	Otah	97	92	90	78
86	Jared	Gaither	90	81	95	92
86	Vernon	Carey	89	85	92	85
85	Ryan	Harris	86	84	92	88
85	Eric	Winston	83	89	85	93
85	Ryan	Diem	84	76	95	88
83	Eben	Britton	91	86	89	85
83	Tyson	Clabo	92	94	84	76
83	Mark	Tauscher	93	75	89	83
82	Willie	Colon	92	86	88	77
82	Kareem	McKenzie	95	86	87	69
79	Phil	Loadholt	97	90	88	74
79	Andre	Smith	97	92	88	76
78	Sean	Locklear	83	87	83	79
78	Marc	Colombo	95	83	85	64
78	Nick	Kaczur	84	78	88	79
77	Winston	Justice	86	81	87	82
77	Shawn	Andrews	97	82	88	65
76	Dennis	Roland	91	85	87	71
76	Ryan	O'Callaghan	97	85	87	64
76	Khalif	Barnes	90	80	83	68
76	Shane	Olivea	85	85	81	78
76	Jon	Runyan	93	79	84	63
75	Kevin	Shaffer	82	75	76	82
75	Anthony	Davis	91	84	88	75
74	Brandon	Keith	77	82	85	81
74	Gosder	Cherilus	88	82	84	70
74	Jeremy	Trueblood	93	77	86	62
74	Jon	Jansen	90	74	83	59
73	Jeromey	Clary	90	82	82	69
73	Guy	Whimper	82	84	78	82
73	Cornell	Green	84	77	82	72
72	Adam	Terry	81	74	87	73
72	Tony	Pashos	88	79	81	67
71	Jeremy	Bridges	85	74	84	69
71	Rodger	Saffold	75	82	84	91
71	John	St. Clair	91	70	80	60
70	Erik	Pears	82	85	76	71
69	Geoff	Schwartz	87	75	81	65
69	James	Marten	84	78	79	67
69	Pat	McQuistan	81	78	82	74
69	Jonathan	Scott	82	74	79	78
69	Troy	Kropog	74	82	77	83
68	Oniel	Cousins	87	80	82	70
68	Ikechuku	Ndukwe	81	83	74	65
68	Brandon	Gorin	80	75	77	73
68	Zane	Beadles	78	88	80	68

TIGHT ENDS (TE)

OVR	First Name	Last Name	Speed	Catching	Run Block	Pass Block
98	Tony	Gonzalez	72	95	55	50
97	Jason	Witten	73	88	57	50
96	Vernon	Davis	84	84	74	50
96	Antonio	Gates	77	92	58	48
96	Dallas	Clark	67	97	53	54
90	Heath	Miller	75	88	59	54
89	Chris	Cooley	69	89	54	54
89	Kellen	Winslow	70	84	58	53
88	Brent	Celek	78	89	57	50
87	Owen	Daniels	83	90	56	54
86	Jermichael	Finley	85	85	60	52
86	Zach	Miller	78	87	50	48
86	Visanthe	Shiancoe	78	84	52	48
86	Jeremy	Shockey	78	87	55	50
84	Jon	Carlson	74	86	61	55
84	Greg	Olson	87	86	56	55
83	Todd	Heap	82	88	54	48
82	Dustin	Keller	86	82	55	46
82	Marcedes	Lewis	72	78	65	55
82	Brandon	Pettigrew	72	76	70	58
81	Kevin	Boss	73	82	62	56
81	Bo	Scaife	79	85	56	52
81	Daniel	Graham	70	64	72	51
79	Anthony	Fasano	67	76	60	52
78	David	Thomas	74	79	57	54
78	Benjamin	Watson	85	76	53	49
78	Jermaine	Gresham	83	86	55	45
77	Donald	Lee	74	75	58	50
77	Chris	Baker	70	75	60	58
77	Rob	Gronkowski	74	80	66	62
76	Tom	Santi	70	76	58	60
76	Fred	Davis	79	80	52	49
76	Brandon	Manumaleuna	64	73	68	62
76	Jerramy	Stevens	77	73	58	58
76	Desmond	Clark	69	76	60	50
76	Anthony	Becht	60	65	70	62
75	Dan	Campbell	59	72	64	60
75	Steve	Heiden	64	78	59	55
75	Leonard	Pope	75	74	59	57
74	Martellus	Bennett	78	76	55	53
74	Tony	Scheffler	82	84	52	51
74	Randy	McMichael	73	72	57	52
74	Alge	Crumpler	68	74	60	50
74	Jim	Kleinsasser	65	65	70	50
74	Reggie	Kelly	65	71	60	57
73	Jeff	King	66	72	62	58
73	Alex	Smith	74	75	56	54
73	John	Phillips	72	74	64	60
73	Kris	Wilson	72	76	50	53
73	L.J.	Smith	72	72	53	58

OVR	First Name	Last Name	Speed	Catching	Catch in Traffic	Route Running
98	Andre	Johnson	94	95	96	95
97	Larry	Fitzgerald	88	98	94	98
96	Brandon	Marshall	88	97	99	93
96	Reggie	Wayne	88	98	95	99
95	Randy	Moss	96	95	82	95
93	Roddy	White	94	89	91	92
92	Steve	Smith	97	90	85	88
91	DeSean	Jackson	99	92	78	92
91	Calvin	Johnson Jr.	95	90	88	86
91	Wes	Welker	86	95	96	97
91	Anquan	Boldin	87	93	98	89
91	Chad	Ochocinco	92	92	82	98
90	Sidney	Rice	89	90	93	89
90	Greg	Jennings	93	89	88	90
90	Vincent	Jackson	88	91	90	88
89	Marques	Colston	84	94	97	90
89	Hines	Ward	85	90	95	95
89	Donald	Driver	87	92	97	92
88	Steve	Smith	87	92	90	94
88	Miles	Austin	94	89	88	87
87	Santonio	Holmes	94	90	72	88
87	T.J.	Houshmandzadeh	84	92	98	91
85	Mike	Sims-Walker	91	86	85	87
85	Braylon	Edwards	91	77	84	87
85	Jerricho	Cotchery	83	89	97	88
85	Derek	Mason	85	91	85	97
84	Dwayne	Bowe	86	81	95	86
84	Percy	Harvin	96	85	84	77
84	Lee	Evans	96	87	74	86
84	Antonio	Bryant	86	86	83	84
83	Michael	Crabtree	88	88	87	82
83	Santana	Moss	96	85	72	88
83	Terrell	Owens	88	76	88	89
82	Robert	Meachem	94	82	79	82
82	Kenny	Britt	87	85	94	78
82	Devery	Henderson	98	84	69	85
82	Roy	Williams	89	86	79	80
82	Chris	Chambers	88	84	72	84
81	Jeremy	Maclin	95	87	80	73
81	Hakeem	Nicks	87	85	88	75
80	Pierre	Garcon	93	85	78	77
80	Steve	Breaston	91	83	76	78
80	Dez	Bryant	91	89	88	70
79	Torry	Holt	85	88	77	88
78	Early	Doucet	86	84	84	79
78	Devin	Hester	98	80	72	77
78	Josh	Cribbs	92	79	75	74
78	Mike	Wallace	96	79	76	78
78	Michael	Jenkins	87	82	79	82
78	Nate	Burleson	93	83	68	79

OVR	First Name	Last Name	Speed	Catching	Catch in Traffic	Route Running
77	Kevin	Walter	82	86	87	86
77	Justin	Gage	80	85	77	78
76	Julian	Edelman	86	85	83	82
76	Eddie	Royal	94	84	74	78
76	Mario	Manningham	92	78	74	76
76	Jason	Avant	82	82	87	79
76	Nate	Washington	93	79	77	75
76	Malcom	Floyd	86	81	76	77
76	Mark	Clayton	86	80	74	82
76	Austin	Collie	87	87	82	84
76	Josh	Reed	78	87	85	85
76	Muhsin	Muhammad	76	85	85	86
76	Laveranues	Coles	89	82	80	82
75	Donnie	Avery	96	78	72	78
75	Andre	Caldwell	89	80	82	78
75	Anthony	Gonzalez	88	84	68	83
75	Lance	Moore	87	84	76	84
75	Patrick	Crayton	85	85	74	79
75	Johnny	Knox	97	80	69	77
75	Louis	Murphy	93	78	83	73
75	Mohamed	Massaquoi	84	82	84	72
75	Bernard	Berrian	96	80	63	79
75	Jabar	Gaffney	83	86	75	86
75	Golden	Tate	93	86	87	69
74	Davone	Bess	85	87	78	87
74	Josh	Morgan	87	80	78	67
74	Earl	Bennett	85	83	84	84
74	Devin	Thomas	91	75	75	70
74	Mike	Thomas	95	75	82	73
74	Brandon	Stokley	84	83	84	83
74	Demaryius	Thomas	96	84	77	54
73	Arrelious	Benn	90	79	91	65
73	Joey	Galloway	91	84	60	81
73	Chaz	Schilens	92	79	71	73
73	James	Jones	86	82	83	72
73	Greg	Camarillo	82	83	82	83
73	Sam	Aiken	86	79	85	75
73	Anttwaan	Randle El	87	76	64	79
72	Domenik	Hixon	91	77	65	77
72	Arnaz	Battle	80	81	83	75
72	Kelley	Washington	84	76	72	74
72	Isaac	Bruce	85	86	70	86
71	Maurice	Stovall	80	78	79	73
71	Brandon	Jones	91	77	68	78
71	Brian	Hartline	85	82	77	83
71	Brandon	Gibson	87	78	81	74
71	Damian	Williams	88	84	83	73
71	Brandon	LaFell	86	76	88	74
70	Jordy	Nelson	87	78	72	76
70	Malcolm	Kelly	85	81	78	68

Defensive Player List

CORNERBACKS (CB)

OVR	First Name	Last Name	Speed	Man Cover	Zone Cover	Press
99	Darrelle	Revis	93	98	95	92
98	Nnamdi	Asomugha	93	98	92	97
97	Charles	Woodson	89	88	98	95
95	Champ	Bailey	95	94	90	82
94	Asante	Samuel	90	94	98	80
93	Johnathan	Joseph	95	95	90	84
92	Leon	Hall	88	88	94	96
92	Cortland	Finnegan	91	90	92	90
92	Rahsean	Mathis	91	88	96	86
91	Chris	Gamble	92	95	89	88
90	Dominique	Rodgers-Cromartie	98	96	87	61
89	Corey	Webster	97	87	94	91
88	Antoine	Winfield	85	77	93	94
87	Aqib	Talib	88	89	87	88
87	Jabari	Greer	88	89	92	82
87	Marcus	Trufant	88	93	86	76
87	Terence	Newman	97	93	85	60
87	Sheldon	Brown	88	87	91	81
87	Quentin	Jammer	89	92	87	96
86	Eric	Wright	89	88	90	83
85	Tracy	Porter	92	89	84	71
85	Brandon	Flowers	86	87	88	84
85	Mike	Jenkins	93	92	79	93
85	Kelvin	Hayden	87	78	89	84
85	Dunta	Robinson	93	90	80	82
85	DeAngelo	Hall	97	90	84	70
85	Charles	Tillman	85	85	83	92
85	Al	Harris	84	93	77	97
84	Nate	Clements	86	85	83	87
84	Ronde	Barber	82	65	90	94
83	Antonio	Cromartie	95	88	84	79
83	Terrence	McGee	92	87	91	55
83	Ike	Taylor	96	84	84	88
82	Josh	Wilson	95	87	83	74
82	Richard	Marshall	93	89	78	73
82	Cedric	Griffin	85	85	88	78
82	Domonique	Foxworth	93	84	89	57
82	Derek	Cox	92	81	86	80
82	Vontae	Davis	92	85	82	95
82	Leigh	Bodden	86	78	85	83
82	Andre'	Goodman	92	89	86	68
81	Leodis	McKelvin	93	88	82	70
81	Ronald	Bartell	87	83	86	80
81	Shawntae	Spencer	88	88	87	64
81	Jerraud	Powers	87	85	88	71
81	Will	Allen	91	88	80	79
80	Ellis	Hobbs	90	85	81	79
80	Shawn	Springs	87	82	86	86
79	Bryant	McFadden	85	74	86	92

CORNERBACKS (CB)

OVR	First Name	Last Name	Speed	Man Cover	Zone Cover	Press
79	Carlos	Rogers	89	80	83	91
79	Sean	Smith	89	86	74	90
79	Joe	Haden	89	90	85	88
78	Antoine	Cason	88	87	84	55
78	Aaron	Ross	88	85	82	76
77	Terrell	Thomas	85	74	86	80
77	Brian	Williams	80	72	80	86
77	Lito	Sheppard	88	83	86	56
77	Ken	Lucas	88	79	81	85
76	Glover	Quin Jr.	86	71	82	88
76	Darius	Butler	91	84	75	75
76	Malcom	Jenkins	85	80	85	83
76	Chris	Johnson	97	85	72	67
76	Walt	Harris	76	79	86	79
76	Kyle	Wilson	69	88	80	90
75	Bruce	Johnson	93	82	76	67
75	Orlando	Scandrick	92	79	84	64
75	Brent	Grimes	85	84	74	64
75	Tramon	Williams	90	78	84	58
75	Randall	Gay	83	79	83	78
75	Gregory	Toler	93	82	74	65
75	Patrick	Robinson	92	89	75	87
75	DeShea	Townsend	80	76	83	83
75	Mike	McKenzie	83	71	85	88
74	Devin	McCourty	93	81	88	58
74	Zackary	Bowman	91	85	72	70
74	Dwight	Lowery	85	69	86	64
74	Pacman	Jones	93	83	76	56
74	Joselio	Hanson	86	79	84	66
74	Lardarius	Webb	93	82	76	87
74	Phillip	Buchanon	96	74	84	60
73	Tarell	Brown	87	80	79	64
73	Anthony	Henry	76	73	80	87
73	Fred	Smoot	87	82	85	40
73	Kareem	Jackson	90	90	81	83
72	Brandon	Carr	86	80	77	57
72	Justin	Tryon	92	80	76	75
72	Kelly	Jennings	90	82	78	62
72	Fabian	Washington	98	70	73	53
72	Chris	Owens	88	82	76	53
72	Captain	Munnerlyn	89	77	80	82
72	Macho	Harris	85	69	78	84
72	William	James	86	80	77	42
71	Jacob	Lacey	87	74	80	62
71	Chris	Houston	93	78	72	88
71	Nick	Harper	80	67	77	75
71	Javier	Arenas	86	72	85	64
70	Tye	Hill	97	77	68	55
70	Danieal	Manning	94	72	76	55
70	Rod	Hood	86	69	77	70

CORNERBACKS (CB)

OVR	First Name	Last Name	Speed	Man Cover	Zone Cover	Press
70	Chris	Cook	89	75	83	88
70	Jerome	Murphy	87	85	76	88
69	William	Gay	85	65	78	68
69	Benny	Sapp	86	81	69	70
69	Alphonso	Smith	90	85	75	54
69	Nathan	Vasher	85	68	79	60
68	Jason	McCourty	89	74	77	69
68	Brice	McCain	95	78	74	59
68	Elbert	Mack	87	71	76	69
68	Jonathan	Wilhite	92	75	72	63
68	Chevis	Jackson	83	67	79	75
68	Brandon	McDonald	85	77	76	68
68	Tim	Jennings	94	77	75	51
68	Eric	King	83	69	78	60
68	Jacques	Reeves	86	72	76	54
68	Bradley	Fletcher	86	71	75	69
68	Asher	Allen	89	72	85	70
68	Keiwan	Ratliff	86	73	75	55

DEFENSIVE TACKLES (DT)

OVR	First Name	Last Name	Speed	Strength	Power Moves	Finesse Moves
97	Kevin	Williams	70	91	88	88
95	Vince	Wilfork	55	97	92	70
94	Jay	Ratliff	70	87	81	91
94	Kris	Jenkins	61	97	94	69
93	Shaun	Rogers	49	98	97	68
91	Casey	Hampton	47	98	93	52
90	Aubrayo	Franklin	54	97	88	53
89	Randy	Starks	66	94	87	55
88	Sedrick	Ellis	66	94	90	73
88	Brodrick	Bunkley	62	96	88	72
88	Pat	Williams	48	98	87	45
87	Tommie	Harris	74	85	80	87
87	John	Henderson	55	95	90	47
87	Jamal	Williams	44	98	90	42
86	Brandon	Mebane	64	91	87	74
86	Domata	Peko	62	90	90	61
86	Jonathan	Babineaux	66	87	80	85
85	Ndamukong	Suh	71	95	85	50
84	Gerald	McCoy	72	89	94	68
84	Kelly	Gregg	46	91	83	47
83	Mike	Patterson	58	89	67	79
83	Tony	Brown	62	88	78	77
83	Terrance	Knighton	63	90	81	54
82	Jason	Ferguson	42	94	85	45
81	Barry	Cofield	64	89	82	61
81	Cornelius	Griffin	59	85	83	56
80	Fred	Robbins	54	92	84	45
79	Kyle	Williams	56	83	75	57
79	B.J.	Raji	62	93	88	69

DEFENSIVE TACKLES (DT)

OVR	First Name	Last Name	Speed	Strength	Power Moves	Finesse Moves
78	Jovan	Haye	67	89	77	63
78	Antonio	Johnson	67	84	82	67
78	Tommy	Kelly	63	88	83	58
78	Corey	Williams	64	86	83	64
78	Peria	Jerry	68	85	85	79
77	Jason	Jones	73	83	85	65
77	Pat	Sims	66	91	85	45
77	Cliff	Ryan	62	86	80	63
77	Chris	Canty	66	81	77	67
77	Tank	Johnson	70	82	69	80
77	Tyson	Alualu	69	90	79	44
77	Grady	Jackson	39	96	92	58
76	Remi	Ayodele	62	86	79	60
76	Paul	Soliai	55	96	84	65
76	Jay	Alford	60	85	81	70
76	Jonathan	Fanene	73	78	81	64
76	Colin	Cole	59	88	77	64
76	Ronald	Fields	49	88	82	58
76	Ma'ake	Kemoeatu	37	97	82	54
76	Dan	Williams	60	96	81	37
75	Brian	Price	63	84	84	88
75	Chris	Hovan	64	84	62	77
75	Daniel	Muir	60	85	82	57
75	Sammie	Hill	60	90	83	58
75	Rocky	Bernard	59	87	66	79
74	Ahtyba	Rubin	53	94	87	44
74	Amobi	Okoye	66	84	75	70
74	Tony	Hargrove	76	78	70	82
74	Dewayne	Robertson	58	87	80	69
74	Chris	Hoke	50	88	78	47
74	Ron	Edwards	55	90	71	50
73	Kedric	Golston	61	84	72	46
73	Shaun	Cody	59	84	60	71
73	Jimmy	Kennedy	52	90	79	49
72	Atiyyah	Ellison	61	86	80	55
72	Sione	Pouha	56	92	75	42
72	Shaun	Smith	57	92	80	54
72	Chuck	Darby	63	82	67	76
72	Ryan	Sims	58	89	71	64
72	Terrence	Cody	42	97	89	33
72	Kendrick	Clancy	45	92	86	42
72	Bryan	Robinson	50	82	80	74
71	Eric	Foster	70	79	80	70
71	Thomas	Johnson	58	88	72	50
71	Roy	Miller	60	90	79	43
71	Ian	Scott	59	83	75	65
71	Anthony	Adams	58	87	68	50
71	Kenny	Smith	64	81	77	62
70	Tank	Tyler	61	90	75	62
70	LaMarr	Houston	72	77	84	72

FREE SAFETIES (FS)

OVR	First Name	Last Name	Speed	Man Cover	Zone Cover	Hit Power
97	Ed	Reed	93	80	95	75
95	Antoine	Bethea	89	66	93	84
94	Darren	Sharper	86	72	99	64
93	Nick	Collins	89	73	87	81
92	O.J.	Atogwe	89	66	94	71
90	Brian	Dawkins	85	65	83	88
88	Tanard	Jackson	86	73	92	82
88	Kerry	Rhodes	83	58	89	82
87	Jairus	Byrd	87	64	92	60
86	Michael	Griffin	87	74	85	70
85	Louis	Delmas	87	74	84	85
84	Eric	Weddle	83	59	71	74
84	Eric	Berry	92	84	88	90
83	Antrel	Rolle	86	75	85	50
81	Jordan	Babineaux	85	68	82	70
81	Earl	Thomas	93	87	86	72
80	Dashon	Goldson	85	65	82	85
80	James	Sanders	78	55	75	85
80	Marlin	Jackson	83	71	84	69
79	Ryan	Clark	81	55	77	93
79	Eugene	Wilson	85	76	82	72
78	Michael	Huff	93	82	84	59
78	Chris	Crocker	83	55	78	80
77	Thomas	DeCoud	87	52	79	80
77	Reggie	Nelson	93	74	80	73
77	Eric	Smith	79	65	74	80
77	Brandon	McGowan	82	65	79	87
77	Mike	Adams	87	72	78	68
76	Tom	Zbikowski	88	53	72	84
76	Ken	Hamlin	84	62	79	84
75	Sherrod	Martin	88	77	80	74
75	Nate	Allen	87	64	84	60
74	Darcel	McBath	85	72	78	66
74	Madieu	Williams	82	65	81	69
73	Gibril	Wilson	82	58	75	72
73	Brian	Russell	75	60	78	84
73	Michael	Johnson	85	65	74	82
73	Daniel	Bullocks	79	63	74	74
73	Ko	Simpson	80	74	84	55
73	Al	Afalava	80	49	77	84
72	George	Wilson	82	60	71	69
72	Hiram	Eugene	83	52	71	70
72	Abram	Elam	82	59	69	75
72	Vincent	Fuller	80	70	75	68
72	Brodney	Pool	87	60	70	74
71	Kevin	Payne	85	55	70	83
70	Will	Allen	79	68	80	50
69	Alan	Ball	87	68	77	44
69	Reed	Doughty	78	47	65	75

LEFT DEFENSIVE ENDS (LE)

OVR	First Name	Last Name	Speed	Strength	Power Moves	Finesse Moves
95	Robert	Mathis	86	76	71	98
92	Justin	Tuck	84	84	85	94
92	Richard	Seymour	68	91	95	70
88	Luis	Castillo	65	97	90	65
87	Aaron	Smith	66	90	87	65
86	Calais	Campbell	76	82	76	85
86	Shaun	Ellis	66	91	93	69
85	Ray	Edwards	76	83	88	72
84	Ty	Warren	64	91	87	63
82	Antonio	Smith	72	80	83	74
82	Adewale	Ogunleye	78	73	59	89
82	Marcus	Stroud	54	95	87	65
82	Trevor	Pryce	64	93	88	58
81	Robert	Geathers	78	77	54	86
80	Alex	Brown	78	76	65	85
80	Juqua	Parker	74	80	62	84
79	Kendall	Langford	69	87	86	64
79	Lawrence	Jackson	77	80	84	70
78	Brandon	Graham	80	77	91	67
77	Justin	Bannan	63	92	84	67
77	Charles	Grant	69	80	79	67
77	Ryan	Picket	62	94	83	59
77	Leonard	Little	78	74	52	86
76	Jason	Pierre-Paul	84	65	75	90
76	Jimmy	Wilkerson	72	85	84	62
76	Cory	Redding	67	85	78	63
75	Phillip	Merling	72	82	79	67
75	Vernon	Gholston	85	87	65	76
75	Johnny	Jolly	66	92	78	52
75	Tyson	Jackson	69	87	79	61
75	Kenyon	Coleman	67	83	77	63
75	Reggie	Hayward	71	78	67	82
74	Adam	Carriker	73	86	80	60
74	Mark	Anderson	80	72	61	83
74	Chauncey	David	72	70	68	79
74	Tyler	Brayton	70	83	70	59
74	Carlos	Dunlap	84	77	75	83
73	Keyunta	Dawson	74	77	69	79
73	Ryan	McBean	65	86	78	58
73	Victor	Abiamiri	69	80	70	70
73	Marcus	Spears	64	88	79	57
73	Paul	Spicer	64	85	81	64
73	Phillip	Daniels	63	93	70	56
72	Ziggy	Hood	64	83	70	80
72	Corey	Wootton	73	84	87	55
71	William	Hayes	80	74	74	66
71	Jay	Richardson	74	82	68	55
71	Isaac	Sopoaga	52	95	74	50
71	Jared	Devries	67	80	67	67

LEFT OUTSIDE LINEBACKERS (LOLB)

OVR	First Name	Last Name	Speed	Tackling	Pursuit	Play Recognition
91	Lamarr	Woodley	83	88	94	84
91	Shaun	Phillips	84	87	95	85
89	Daryl	Smith	78	94	95	92
87	Thomas	Davis	88	90	91	75
87	Brian	Cushing	84	91	94	87
86	Julian	Peterson	84	84	96	88
85	Brian	Orakpo	84	86	93	73
85	Rey	Maualuga	80	90	94	83
84	Anthony	Spencer	80	85	90	78
84	Michael	Boley	83	89	94	87
83	Aaron	Curry	86	87	91	80
82	Jarret	Johnson	72	85	91	85
82	Mike	Peterson	77	89	87	94
82	Jason	Taylor	83	75	94	92
80	Ben	Leber	74	88	84	93
79	Geno	Hayes	84	84	92	73
79	Manny	Lawson	89	75	93	77
79	David	Thorton	73	89	94	84
78	Thomas	Howard	88	85	92	76
78	Sergio	Kindle	82	84	92	77
77	Mike	Vrabel	71	82	84	92
77	Adalius	Thomas	81	79	87	74
77	Trevor	Scott	79	79	85	75
77	Bryan	Thomas	76	80	90	70
75	Rashad	Jeanty	77	85	86	80
75	Clark	Haggans	72	84	79	85
75	Danny	Clark	74	87	87	88
74	Matt	Roth	72	85	83	84
73	Brad	Jones	82	84	89	76
73	Clint	Ingram	79	76	87	73
72	Antwan	Barnes	86	75	88	68
72	Robert	Ayers	78	82	80	83
72	Hunter	Hillenmeyer	71	84	84	83
71	Zac	Diles	75	83	87	70
71	Robert	Ninkovich	72	80	76	82
71	Derrick	Burgess	82	72	89	80
70	Nick	Roach	83	74	85	74
70	Moise	Fokou	70	82	86	78
70	Philip	Wheeler	78	84	86	67
70	Bobby	Carpenter	79	77	86	78
70	Thaddeus	Gibson	84	80	78	49
69	Andy	Studebaker	77	79	77	75
68	Tyjuan	Hagler	81	76	2	73
68	David	Veikune	75	73	81	67
67	Pierre	Woods	7	73	79	68
67	Chris	Kelsey	69	85	79	70
66	Jo-Lonn	Dunbar	77	77	81	66
66	Antwan	Applewhite	82	74	79	59
66	Jamar	Williams	74	82	82	72

MIDDLE LINEBACKERS (MLB)

OVR	First Name	Last Name	Speed	Tackling	Pursuit	Play Recognition
99	Patrick	Willis	90	99	98	92
96	Jon	Beason	85	97	99	98
94	Ray	Lewis	82	95	97	99
91	David	Harris	79	97	95	93
91	Barrett	Ruud	79	97	94	94
91	London	Fletcher	79	99	99	98
90	Demeco	Ryans	76	97	95	96
90	Jonathan	Vilma	84	93	97	96
90	Karlos	Dansby	79	94	93	89
90	Brian	Urlacher	84	92	95	92
89	Bart	Scott	77	92	92	90
88	Curtis	Lofton	79	96	94	89
88	Lofa	Tatupu	79	95	96	93
88	D.J.	Williams	83	94	93	85
88	James	Farrior	75	95	88	95
87	Gary	Brackett	77	92	93	97
87	Nick	Barnett	77	90	93	88
86	Jerod	Mayo	85	89	97	83
86	Paul	Posluszny	76	93	93	95
85	D'Qwell	Jackson	75	97	95	90
85	James	Laurinatis	76	94	95	96
85	Stephen	Cooper	76	93	92	87
85	Bradie	James	76	94	94	85
85	Gerald	Hayes	72	92	94	90
85	E.J.	Henderson	74	95	93	94
84	Keith	Brooking	74	91	87	95
84	Takeo	Spikes	74	87	88	96
82	Lawrence	Timmons	85	84	94	77
82	Kirk	Morrison	75	91	93	87
82	DeMorrio	Williams	80	95	94	90
82	Antonio	Pierce	77	85	88	93
82	Dhani	Jones	76	90	88	96
80	David	Hawthorne	79	91	87	82
79	Stewart	Bradley	74	86	89	84
79	A.J.	Hawk	82	84	89	77
79	Rocky	McIntosh	82	87	1	79
79	Channing	Crowder	77	88	87	74
79	Kawika	Mitchell	78	85	89	82
79	Larry	Foote	73	87	88	81
79	Rolando	McClain	81	88	88	88
79	Eric	Barton	71	87	87	91
78	Andra	Davis	72	87	90	88
77	Stephen	Tulloch	76	90	93	84
76	David	Bowens	75	84	86	82
76	Brandon	Siler	77	84	90	77
76	Kevin	Burnett	78	83	91	77
76	Derrick	Johnson	84	82	86	80
75	Gary	Guyton	85	85	90	73
75	DeAndre	Levy	83	87	86	81

KICKERS (K)

OVR	First Name	Last Name	Awareness	Kick Power	Kick Accuracy	Tackling
95	Robbie	Gould	89	92	96	23
95	Nate	Kadeing	88	92	97	16
93	Rob	Bironas	87	96	92	13
92	Ryan	Longwell	96	91	93	13
91	Stephen	Gostkowski	81	90	97	13
90	Sebastian	Janikowski	84	98	88	44
89	Jason	Hanson	96	88	93	23
89	David	Akers	95	90	92	13
87	Josh	Brown	83	97	87	15
87	John	Kasay	90	91	91	12
86	Jay	Feely	86	90	92	40
83	Shayne	Graham	87	87	92	15
82	Dan	Carpenter	62	92	94	20
82	Olindo	Mare	86	92	87	15
82	Phil	Dawson	91	86	91	20
82	Joe	Nedney	87	90	89	18
82	Adam	Vinatieri	91	88	89	32
81	Matt	Stover	95	80	95	21
80	Rian	Lindell	86	88	89	19
80	Jason	Elam	93	87	88	21
79	Ryan	Succop	67	92	90	29
77	Neil	Rackers	76	94	84	12
76	Garrett	Hartley	63	93	88	20
75	Jeff	Reed	77	87	89	26

PUNTERS (P)

OVR	First Name	Last Name	Awareness	Kick Power	Kick Accuracy	Tackling
98	Shane	Lechler	93	96	94	18
94	Andy	Lee	80	96	94	35
94	Donnie	Jones	77	98	93	23
93	Mike	Scifres	74	96	95	22
92	Mat	McBriar	79	97	92	10
91	Dustin	Colquitt	80	90	98	29
90	Brian	Moorman	88	92	93	19
86	Sam	Koch	75	88	98	33
84	Michael	Koenen	80	95	87	14
83	Ben	Graham	72	94	90	39
82	Brad	Maynard	96	84	92	12
80	Jon	Ryan	67	95	88	31
80	Josh	Bidwell	94	85	90	23
79	Hunter	Smith	88	85	91	14
79	Daniel	Sepulveda	66	88	95	55
78	Craig	Hentrich	97	87	85	12
77	Pat	McAfee	68	94	86	14
77	Dave	Zastudil	77	90	87	12
76	Kevin	Huber	65	89	91	22
76	Jason	Baker	82	86	89	14
75	Chris	Kluwe	68	93	85	20
75	Thomas	Morstead	66	95	84	14
73	Nick	Harris	75	87	88	13

RIGHT DEFENSIVE ENDS (RE)

OVR	First Name	Last Name	Speed	Strength	Power Moves	Finesse Moves
99	Jared	Allen	80	85	97	89
97	Dwight	Freeney	87	83	74	97
95	Mario	Williams	84	85	88	95
95	Trent	Cole	84	79	70	98
95	Julius	Peppers	85	80	86	95
94	Haloti	Ngata	67	98	97	65
94	Darnell	Dockett	73	91	95	84
90	Will	Smith	76	85	90	74
89	Justin	Smith	73	87	86	64
89	John	Abraham	81	83	89	71
87	Cullen	Jenkins	68	88	88	70
87	Aaron	Kampman	76	85	92	73
86	Albert	Haynesworth	65	98	97	55
85	Antwan	Odom	74	87	88	68
83	Mathias	Kiwanuka	73	78	76	86
83	Osi	Umenyiora	84	72	65	88
82	Brett	Keisel	73	87	80	56
80	Kyle	Vanden Bosch	69	83	85	60
80	Igor	Olshansky	60	93	85	60
79	Jacob	Ford	77	75	74	85
79	Dwan	Edwards	64	90	86	60
79	Derrick	Morgan	74	82	85	75
78	Glenn	Dorsey	69	85	73	78
78	Raheem	Brock	73	79	59	82
78	Jarvis	Green	63	83	78	83
77	Darryl	Tapp	78	74	68	82
77	Darren	Howard	66	79	82	80
76	Cliff	Avril	80	69	51	83
76	Bobby	McCray	77	74	65	84
76	Dewayne	White	73	75	64	82
76	James	Hall	74	77	64	85
75	Chris	Long	75	84	80	75
75	Jacques	Cesaire	73	75	75	79
75	Everette	Brown	83	69	76	88
74	Jerry	Hughes	85	64	64	78
74	Robaire	Smith	59	86	80	62
73	Stylez	White	77	72	63	83
73	Marques	Douglas	64	85	75	60
72	Chris	Clemons	77	66	50	78
72	Matt	Shaughnessy	73	82	82	57
72	Michael	Johnson	86	71	72	80
72	Kenny	Peterson	66	80	80	67
72	Damione	Lewis	64	86	74	73
71	Ray	McDonald	66	83	84	80
71	Mike	Wright	56	87	75	67
71	Josh	Thomas	69	78	62	82
71	Connor	Barwin	84	72	83	71
71	Jared	Odrick	67	87	82	54
70	Kroy	Biermann	73	80	81	55
69	Jeremy	Jarmon	75	74	76	65

RIGHT OUTSIDE LINEBACKERS (ROLB)

OVR	First Name	Last Name	Speed	Tackling	Pursuit	Play Recognition
97	Demarcus	Ware	86	88	99	88
97	James	Harrison	85	92	95	89
93	Elvis	Dumervil	86	87	99	94
92	Lance	Briggs	78	95	90	95
90	Terrell	Suggs	84	81	97	84
88	Chad	Greenway	79	93	95	93
86	Keith	Rivers	87	89	95	83
86	Clay	Matthews	84	88	95	80
86	Joey	Porter	78	85	92	84
85	Justin	Durant	85	93	97	88
85	Calvin	Pace	79	84	92	78
85	Keith	Bulluck	84	88	93	90
84	Shawne	Merriman	83	82	97	74
83	Ernie	Sims	88	86	90	55
82	Kamerion	Wimbley	79	83	92	68
82	Will	Witherspoon	84	86	93	86
81	Leroy	Hill	77	88	90	80
80	Clint	Session	84	87	92	78
80	Tamba	Hali	76	85	87	82
79	Akeem	Jordan	84	83	93	77
79	Tully	Banta-Cain	76	77	90	83
79	Scott	Fujita	77	86	92	88
78	Parys	Haralson	79	77	91	77
77	Larry	English	79	78	94	75
77	Scott	Shanle	78	88	88	87
76	Cameron	Wake	83	79	91	59
76	Andre	Carter	77	80	90	78
76	Aaron	Schobel	76	81	85	87
75	Stephen	Nicholas	77	85	89	83
75	Ahmad	Brooks	74	85	88	69
75	Angelo	Crowell	76	85	88	84
75	Sean	Weatherspoon	83	90	75	50
74	Na'il	Diggs	73	82	86	94
73	Jason	Trusnik	75	71	85	74
73	Gerald	McRath	81	85	88	83
73	Pisa	Tinoisamoa	85	84	89	87
72	Jyles	Tucker	77	76	87	67
72	Brandon	Johnson	82	75	84	69
72	Paul	Kruger	74	79	75	85
71	Xavier	Adibi	77	77	86	62
71	Chris	Gocong	69	82	88	70
71	Clint	Sintim	83	81	78	71
70	Zak	DeOssie	75	76	87	69
70	Quincy	Black	86	78	89	73
69	James	Anderson	76	76	80	66
69	Leon	Williams	75	85	95	78
69	Landon	Johnson	72	79	87	80
69	Daryl	Washington	85	84	85	75
68	David	Vobora	77	80	82	75
68	Heath	Farwell	76	80	88	75

STRONG SAFTIES (SS)

OVR	First Name	Last Name	Speed	Man Cover	Zone Cover	Hit Power
97	Troy	Polamalu	92	61	85	88
96	Adrian	Wilson	85	60	80	94
89	Bob	Sanders	92	64	85	95
88	Brandon	Meriweather	91	78	90	81
87	Laron	Landry	92	55	73	97
86	Tyvon	Branch	93	73	81	78
85	Jim	Leonhard	84	65	85	70
84	Bernard	Pollard	79	54	68	92
84	Erik	Coleman	81	57	75	74
84	Chris	Hope	78	54	71	85
83	Donte	Whitmer	88	70	85	83
83	Quintin	Mikell	88	64	77	76
82	Roman	Harper	81	56	73	86
82	Dawan	Landry	82	63	76	82
82	Yeremiah	Bell	85	54	64	88
81	Chris	Harris	79	47	62	96
80	Gerald	Sensabaugh	84	55	75	83
80	James	Butler	80	64	76	69
80	Bryan	Scott	80	50	74	86
80	Michael	Lewis	75	40	62	89
80	Deon	Grant	84	65	85	65
79	Melvin	Bullitt	87	57	73	83
79	Atari	Bigby	82	52	69	91
78	Kenny	Phillips	90	68	82	86
78	Jarrad	Page	79	62	86	86
77	Chinedum	Ndukwe	85	55	72	75
77	Sean	Jones	86	60	76	78
77	Roy	Williams	75	39	54	97
77	Lawyer	Milloy	75	49	70	76
76	Pat	Chung	85	54	67	92
76	Kevin	Ellison	79	46	63	91
76	Mike	Brown	78	60	83	63
75	Charles	Godfrey	90	65	78	75
75	Tyrell	Johnson	89	65	75	74
75	William	Moore	85	62	75	75
74	Sabby	Piscitelli	87	55	59	86
74	Gerald	Alexander	86	69	75	72
74	Renaldo	Hill	83	68	76	57
72	Chris	Horton	84	52	68	77
72	Marquand	Manuel	76	50	60	70
71	Taylor	Mays	95	55	80	91
71	Jamarca	Sanford	84	55	72	89
70	Sean	Considine	80	44	65	69
70	Nick	Ferguson	73	40	59	88
70	Tyrone	Carter	82	48	65	80
70	Morgan	Burnett	87	57	79	65
69	Josh	Bullocks	85	61	76	65
69	T.J.	Ward	84	45	81	85
68	Dominique	Barber	80	55	62	77
68	Steve	Gregory	84	68	64	65

XBOX 360 ACHIEVEMENTS

Icon	Name	Description
	Comeback Kids	Win after being behind in the last 2 min of a game (no OTP, min qtr. Len. 3 min)
	Old Spice Swagger Pick 6	Intercept a pass and return it for a td (no OTP)
	Man Dozer	Rush for 50 yards after the first hit in one game (no OTP)
	Laces Out	Kick a 60+ yard Field Goal (no OTP)
	Very Special Teams	Return 2 kicks for tds in one game with one player (no OTP)
	Butterfingers	Force 3 fumbles in a game (no OTP)
	He's Got All Day	Stay in the pocket for 10 seconds (no OTP)
	Did I Break It?	Win a game by at least 59 points (max. qtr. Len. 7 min, no OTP)
	Perfect Game	Have a perfect passer rating in a game (no OTP)
	Thanks for Coming	Play the Pro Bowl in Franchise
	The Elusive Man	Break 5 tackles in a game with one player (no OTP)
	Winning Isn't Everything	Catch 21 passes in a game with one player (no OTP)
	Old Spice Swagger Return	Return a punt for a touchdown (no OTP)
	No Offense	Intercept 5 passes in a game (no OTP)
	Fantasy Freak	Rush for over 200 yards in a game with one player (no OTP)
	Home Run	Break an 80+ yard touchdown run (no OTP)
	YACtastic	Have over 100 YAC in one game (no OTP)
	Pick Up 6	Win a Fight for the Fumble in the end zone for a TD (no OTP)
	Deadly Accurate	Have a 92% or higher completion percentage in a game (min 20 att., no OTP)
	Madden Moments	Complete the Super Bowl Sunday Madden Moment
	Defensive Dominance	Hold your opponent to under 100 yards of offense (min qtr len 5 min, no OTP)
	Sack Master	Record 5 sacks in a game with one player (no OTP)
	Master Strategist	Create a custom Gameplan
	Nano	Tackle the QB before he can hand the ball off (no OTP)

Icon	Name	Description
	Comeback Kids	Win after being behind in the last 2 min of a game (no OTP, min qtr. Len. 3 min)
	Old Spice Swagger Pick 6	Intercept a pass and return it for a td (no OTP)
	Man Dozer	Rush for 50 yards after the first hit in one game (no OTP)
	Laces Out	Kick a 60+ yard Field Goal (no OTP)
	Very Special Teams	Return 2 kicks for tds in one game with one player (no OTP)
	Butterfingers	Force 3 fumbles in a game (no OTP)
	He's Got All Day	Stay in the pocket for 10 seconds (no OTP)
	Did I Break It?	Win a game by at least 59 points (max. qtr. Len. 7 min, no OTP)
	Perfect Game	Have a perfect passer rating in a game (no OTP)
	Thanks for Coming	Play the Pro Bowl in Franchise
	The Elusive Man	Break 5 tackles in a game with one player (no OTP)
	Winning Isn't Everything	Catch 21 passes in a game with one player (no OTP)
	Old Spice Swagger Return	Return a punt for a touchdown (no OTP)
	No Offense	Intercept 5 passes in a game (no OTP)
	Fantasy Freak	Rush for over 200 yards in a game with one player (no OTP)
	Home Run	Break an 80+ yard touchdown run (no OTP)
	YACtastic	Have over 100 YAC in one game (no OTP)
	Pick Up 6	Win a Fight for the Fumble in the end zone for a TD (no OTP)
	Deadly Accurate	Have a 92% or higher completion percentage in a game (min 20 att., no OTP)
	Madden Moments	Complete the Super Bowl Sunday Madden Moment
	Defensive Dominance	Hold your opponent to under 100 yards of offense (min qtr len 5 min, no OTP)
	Sack Master	Record 5 sacks in a game with one player (no OTP)
	Master Strategist	Create a custom Gameplan
	Nano	Tackle the QB before he can hand the ball off (no OTP)

ACCELERATORS

Accelerators	MSFT Points	Description
One More Year	160	Using this, you will be able to keep one player out of retirement for one more year; usable twice per season, per franchise.
Not Done Yet	80	Downloading this allows you to keep one player out of retirement for one more year; usable once per season, per franchise. This is used in Franchise Mode only.
Hometown Hero	40	Downloading this content will allow you to keep one player out of retirement for one more year; usable once ever per franchise. This is used in Franchise Mode only.
Star Player	80	Downloading and using this allows you to pick a single player on a single team to get maximum progression for one season; usable once per season, per player, per franchise. This is used in Franchise Mode only.
World Class Training Staff	80	Downloading and using this allows for maximum progression for all players on a single team; permanent upgrade. This is used in Franchise Mode only.
Skilled Medical Staff	40	Using this content allows for a 10% bonus chance to avoid injury & 10% bonus to recovery time for all players on a team. Use this with the Expert Medical Staff accelerator for a 35% total bonus! This is usable during Franchise Mode only.
Expert Medical Staff	80	Using this content allows for a 25% bonus chance to avoid injury & 25% bonus to recovery time for all players on a team. Use this with the Skilled Medical Staff accelerator for a 35% total bonus! This is usable during Franchise Mode only.
Play Through The Pain	80	Using this allows for one player to recover from any injury no matter what the severity; usable once per season, per franchise.
QB Scout	40	Download this to use a special scout who will reveal all true stats for Quarterback prospects in the upcoming offseason. This is usable in Franchise only.
RB Scout	40	Download this to use a special scout who will reveal all true stats for Running Back prospects in the upcoming offseason. This is usable in Franchise only.
WR Scout	40	Download this to use a special scout who will reveal all true stats for Wide Receiver and Tight End prospects in the upcoming offseason. This is usable in Franchise only.
LB Scout	40	Download this to use a special scout who will reveal all true stats for Linebacker prospects in the upcoming offseason. This is usable in Franchise only.
DB Scout	40	Download this to use a special scout who will reveal all true stats for Defensive Back prospects in the upcoming offseason. This is usable in Franchise only.
OL Scout	40	Download this to use a special scout who will reveal all true stats for Offensive Line prospects in the upcoming offseason. This is usable in Franchise only.
DL Scout	40	Download this to use a special scout who will reveal all true stats for Defensive Line prospects in the upcoming offseason. This is usable in Franchise only.
PK Scout	40	Download this to use a special scout who will reveal all true stats for Punter and Kicker prospects in the upcoming offseason. This is usable in Franchise only.
Game Day Instincts	40	For one game, your coaching staff is in the zone. All players receive a 5% boost to all stats; can be used once per year, per franchise.
Dig Deep	40	For one play, your players respond to the challenges of the moment. All players receive a 10% boost to all stats. This is usable in Franchise only.
Super Superstar	160	Downloading this will enable your Superstar get maximum progression for the length of his career.
Franchise Player Pack	240	Downloading this pack gives you all of the Franchise Player packs available. Get One More Year and Star Player together.
Great Staff Pack	160	Downloading this pack gives you all of the Staff packs available. Get World Class Staff, Skilled Medical Staff, and Expert Medical Staff packs at a discounted price.
Expert Scout Pack	240	Dowloading this pack gives you all of the Scout packs available. Get all 8 position scout packs at a discounted price.
Max Franchise Pack	560	Downloading this pack gives you all of the Franchise packs available. Get all player, staff, and scout packs for one discounted price.
Madden Max Pack	800	Downloading this pack gives you all of the Madden packs available. Get all of your madden game accelerator content for one low price!